The Art of the Game

Understanding American Public Policy Making

STELLA Z. THEODOULOU
California State University, Northridge

CHRIS KOFINIS
California State University, Northridge

D0207934

THOMSON

WADSWORTH

Australia • Canada • Mexico • Singapore • Spain
United Kingdom • United States

THOMSON
— ✳ —
™
WADSWORTH

Publisher: Clark Baxter
Executive Editor: David Tatom
Development Editor: Drake Bush
Assistant Editor: Heather Hogan
Editorial Assistant: Reena Thomas
Technology Project Manager: Melinda
  Newfarmer
Marketing Manager: Janise Fry
Marketing Assistant: Mary Ho
Advertising Project Manager: Nathaniel
  Bergson-Michelson

Project Manager, Editorial Production: Paula
  Berman
Print/Media Buyer: Doreen Suruki
Permissions Editor: Sommy Ko
Production Service: Carlisle Communications
Copy Editor: Sharon O'Donnell
Illustrator: Carlisle Communications
Cover Designer: Laurie Anderson
Text and Cover Printer: Webcom
Compositor: Carlisle Communications

For more information about our products,
contact us at:
Thomson Learning Academic Resource Center
1-800-423-0563

For permission to use material from this text,
contact us by:
Phone: 1-800-730-2214 **Fax:** 1-800-730-2215
Web: http://www.thomsonrights.com

Library of Congress Control Number: 2003108549

ISBN 0-534-52904-6

Wadsworth/Thomson Learning
10 Davis Drive
Belmont, CA 94002-3098
USA

Asia
Thomson Learning
5 Shenton Way #01-01
UIC Building
Singapore 068808

Australia/New Zealand
Thomson Learning
102 Dodds Street
Southbank, Victoria 3006
Australia

Canada
Nelson
1120 Birchmount Road
Toronto, Ontario M1K 5G4
Canada

Europe/Middle East/Africa
Thomson Learning
High Holborn House
50/51 Bedford Row
London WC1R 4LR
United Kingdom

Latin America
Thomson Learning
Seneca, 53
Colonia Polanco
11560 Mexico D.F.
Mexico

Spain/Portugal
Paraninfo
Calle/Magallanes, 25
28015 Madrid, Spain

To Marti, Alex, and Peg
For your patience and understanding,
with love

Contents

III   POLICY ARENAS: EXPLORING THE POLICY PROCESS

13   ENVIRONMENTAL POLICY: DEFINING AND IDENTIFYING A PROBLEM   226

14   EDUCATION POLICY: SETTING AND BUILDING AN AGENDA   237

List of Boxes, Figures, and Tables

Preface

Public policy today represents not only a growing area within the study of political science, but also a field with cross-disciplinary significance. Clearly, all subjects within the discipline of political science garner significance through the design and implementation of public policies. With respect to the field of Public Policy, the intimate interconnection between politics, government, and policy represents an area of study not only necessary for scholars and students, but also a bourgeoning area of interest for professional consultants, public administrators, and citizens. Yet, for many within and out of the halls of academia, the field of public policy remains a confusing game of players, dynamics, processes and stages. Thus, the overriding purpose of **The Art of the Game** is but a *simple one*—to teach students and laypersons alike the art and process of American policy making.

Understanding the complexity of American Public Policy demands a dynamic method of explanation. The objective of this text is to define the dynamics of public policy, to elucidate the complexity intrinsic to each stage of the policy process, and to delve into the implications that public policy has for American politics and society. **The Art of the Game** utilizes illustrations of concepts and theories relevant to the policy process. The text also incorporates contemporary examples of policy and a variety of creative exercises with which to develop a theoretical and practical understanding of public policy.

Underscoring this approach is a desire to merge both the academic and applied perspectives. This approach allows readers to comprehend the significance of each stage and the dynamics of the policy process. In other words, rather than offer mere description or a standard explanation of the subject matter, **The Art of Game** merges an applied policy approach to the theoretical discussion.

The Art of the Game emerges from both courses we have developed and taught and from our consulting experiences within the policy arena. Based on our academic and professional experience, we strongly contend there is a significant need for a text that blends a rigorous and detailed introduction to public policy with a set of innovative exercises that allow students to develop both analytical and applied policy tools. This text transcends a standard introduction to public policy with a more innovative and challenging approach. The objective is to complement a thorough introductory discussion of public policy and the relevant theories with an array of exercises that will develop and hone analytical and consultative skills for the reader.

Finally, we would like to express our thanks and appreciation to our editors for their patience, our publisher's representative Marcy Pearlman for encouraging us to pursue the project, and to Janice Olsen for helping us to deliver the manuscript at each stage of the publication process. Finally, to our families, thank you for being there no matter what.

Stella Z. Theodoulou

Chris Kofinis

About the Authors

Stella Z. Theodoulou is currently interim dean of the College of Social and Behavioral Sciences at California State University as well as a professor of political science.

She received her Ph.D. from Tulane University in 1984. Dr. Theodoulou has authored and coauthored several publications in the areas of public policy and political science, including *Public Policy: The Essential Readings; AIDS: The Politics and Policy of Disease,* and *Methods for Political Inquiry: The Discipline, Philosophy, and Analysis of Politics.* Her most recent book is *Policy and Politics in Six Nations: A Comparative Perspective on Policy Making* (Prentice Hall, 2002).

Chris Kofinis was a lecturer in political science at California State University, Northridge. He received his Ph.D. in Public Policy and International Affairs/National Security from Claremont Graduate University in 2000. Dr. Kofinis works in Washington, DC as a political consultant and political strategist. His most recent consulting work involves policy research, polling analysis, and message development for a variety of political clients.

PART I

The Foundation of Public Policy

The Language, The What, The Where, and The Who of Policy Making

1

The Language of Public Policy

Critical Concepts

No army can withstand the strength
of an idea whose time has come.

VICTOR HUGO

Every day the intended and unintended consequences of public policy inti-mately touch the lives of everyone within the United States. From social poli-cies dealing with immigration, crime, health care, social security, and abortion, to policies dealing with national security, foreign aid, international affairs, and trade, it is an inescapable reality that an array of public policies will affect how each in-dividual will live and interact within our complex society. Ironically, we may come to fear, love, respect, or admonish the political and policy process and the often-profound policy actions of the government—sometimes all in the same day.

However, to fairly evaluate or critique the government, the policy process, and the policy actions that result, it is essential to first become aware of the diverse set of conceptual influences and tensions that mark the field of American public pol-icy. The challenge is to understand how the nature of American politics and pub-lic policy is borne out of a series of contestable concepts whose significance is not only considerable but also allows us to understand why we still struggle with what is the ultimate nature and purpose of politics and policy within our society.

A SERIES OF CRITICAL CONCEPTS

The field of public policy emerges out of and within a series of theoretical concepts that help provide a beginning foundation for our understanding of public policy. These concepts offer an important basis for developing the necessary appreciation of the factors, dynamics, and tensions that affect American public policy and the policy-making process. By exploring each concept individually, one can begin to appreciate the complex foundation upon which the political and policy process is founded. Of course, whereas the following concepts discussed are by no means exhaustive, they arguably represent the dominant concepts found within the field of public policy (see Box 1.1).

POWER

No concept is as central to an analysis of politics, political science, and public policy as is the notion of power. Simply defined, power represents the ability to alter or influence a course of action. Power also helps define the significance of public policy, because it is the power of the state that is communicated through legislative acts and policy positions. As a concept, however, power remains essentially contested in light of its many elements and dimensions. Although the concept of power can be defined in multiple ways, it is arguably best to focus on three facets essential to understanding its relevance for public

policy.[1] Specifically, power can be understood in terms of (a) the influence on decision making, (b) the ability to set the agenda, and (c) the ability to persuade and alter perceptions.[2]

With respect to decision making, power is most often described in terms of the direct influence on behavior that one actor may have on another. Power is conceptualized as the ability to influence a course of action in one's favor. Put differently, power is made synonymous with influence, or the ability to influence actors to do what they otherwise might not want to do. Yet, power is more than the strict ability to influence a particular action or decision. What is more telling, arguably, is how power influences those actions and decisions that are not made. In other words, power can also reflect the ability of actors to define the agenda of options that will be considered and the actions that will be taken.

The second face of power relates to the more complex realization that the consequence of power manifests an agenda for both action and nonaction. E. E. Schattschneider, for instance, captures this duality by realizing that "some issues are organized into politics, while others are organized out; power, quite simply, is the ability to set the agenda."[3] Traditionally, such an explanation of power falls along elitist and pluralist divisions, with disagreements emerging as to whether the vested interests of the elite overcome popular pressures, or whether popular pressures have the opportunity to overcome the many advantages of the elite. In other words, who in the society has or controls the political power to define the agenda within the policy-making realm.

Robert Dahl, in both "A Critique of the Ruling Elite Model" and "Who Governs?", suggests that popular whims can and do intervene to check the power of the elite to define the agenda.[4] In contrast, other perspectives, such as those held by Bachrach and Baratz, assert that power manifests as the result of the ability to delimit the policy arena, and that such power is utilized by, and benefits, the elite.[5] In general, each perspective helps identify that the concept of power should not be measured as solely an explicit consequence, but as a much more complex interrelationship between the ability of certain actors to influence what actions are taken. The final dimension understands the concept of power as the ability to persuade and alter perceptions.

In theory, power manifests not only as an influence on actions but also through its influence on ideas, thoughts, and the opinions of individuals. The persuasion of the public—the ability to shape thoughts, ideas, and perceptions—is a significant dimension of power. Consider, for instance, that the adherence of the public, even in the absence of direct force, does not necessarily imply the absence of power. Rather, even without threat or physical force, the power of beliefs, whether religious, ideological, or political, can shape, mold, and define the thoughts, ideas, perceptions, and actions of individuals. Thus, the power to shape ideas underscores the conceptual complexity that power cannot always be readily assessed, easily measured, or effectively evaluated.[6]

What, then, is the concept of power? This is a question that continues to blur our understanding of politics and government. At a minimum, it may be easier to consider that the concept of power should not be oversimplified. Power should not be thought of as mere capability or simple brute force. Power is a multidimensional concept. Although power can and will be derived by some degree of material or technological capability, method of governing, political position, or support offered by the elite or mass public, the degree to which all of these elements may substantially influence decision making, the agenda, or perceptions remains relative to time, place, and issue.

One could argue that power varies based on the time in which power is applied. During a period of domestic economic decline or political unrest, for instance, political decision makers may lose credibility, authority, and legitimacy to utilize the power of their office. Similarly, depending on the issue, whether it is of great national significance and importance for the parties involved, the degree of power that may be required to compel or coerce various policy actors involved may rise substantially. Again, it may be most beneficial to think of power not as some specific entity or capability that is absolute in every condition, but as relative to the circumstances in which power is applied. This distinction between relative and absolute power allows one to understand that military, economic, or technological power, although clearly significant, does not always overcome the power of a belief, an idea, or a conviction. Conversely, the power of a belief, an idea, or a conviction does not always overcome the brutal realities of tangible power derived from military, economic, or technological means.

AUTHORITY AND LEGITIMACY

Authority and legitimacy underpin the significance of the concept of power. Authority reflects the disparity in the power relationship between the actor who is attempting to influence the actions of others and the target of this influence. In other words, authority helps identify one's position of power. An actor with authority can and does enjoy more power over another actor lacking such authority. Additionally, authority refers to a rightful disposition to wield power.

In the context of public policy, authority represents the notion that those with the power to legislate possess the rightful basis to compel obedience upon those who are the targets of their influence. Moreover, the concept of authority implies that the ruled will obey those who govern them. In contrast, in the absence of authority, it is assumed that a higher degree of brute force is necessary to ensure the obedience of those who are being governed.

The path from rightful authority to sheer brute force is determined by the presence or absence of legitimacy. Legitimacy captures the quality that those who possess the power to make policy decisions do so under some public ascension of right. That is, legitimacy refers to the added assumption that the public willingly grants to others the right to influence and govern them. Legitimacy provides the essential justification by which authority and power become rightful authority and just use of power. Overall, effective and just governing requires not only the necessary power but also the rightful authority and the granting of legitimacy to wield such policy power.

REPRESENTATION

The evolution of democracy from the direct democracy of Ancient Greece to the modern versions of representative democracy reflects a value assumption and a preference for the inclusion of the people within the policy process. The value of democratically elected representation is often taken without critical question. However, to what extent the public should be directly involved in policy making has long been debated. An enduring question remains: Should the people govern themselves directly or should elected officials be chosen to govern for them?

With direct democracy the power of representation remains explicitly with the people themselves. Although the most legitimate and democratic form of representa-

tion, such a method of governing has long raised concerns over the brutish power of the majority to impose their will over the minority. James Madison, in *Federalist Paper 10* raised the concern that citizens united and stoked by passion may very well endanger the rights of the few and many, as well as risk the stability of the state itself.[7] Representative democracy, in contrast, sought to temper the explicit power of the majority by delegating governing to a select set of chosen representatives.

Representative democracy is based on the premise that officials will be elected by the people to serve their interests and the interests of the state. The basis by which the people govern is indirect. Through voting and political pressure the citizenry can guide or compel elected officials, but it is still not the people that explicitly determine the outcome of policy debates. Under such a method of elected representation, public officials must decide whether and when they are to balance the needs and demands of their constituents with the necessity for policy actions that may be undesired by these same constituents. Put differently, should elected representatives defer to the public's demands, acting as delegates of the public, or must the officials act as trustees guided by their own convictions of what is best for their constituents and the society?

The true or ideal nature of elected representatives, whether they should act as trustees or delegates, is a heated issue of discussion. Are elected representatives only interested in reelection or does conviction for what is best for the society override concerns for reelection? Do the convictions of elected representatives supercede the policy demands of their constituents or do the preferences of the public that may be blinded or misguided by their own whims and passions overrule the convictions of the representatives? Of course, debate continues as to which method and type of representation best serve the interests of government, society, and the field of public policy.[8]

In actuality, neither vision of representation predominates over the other. Rather, the two faces of the representative, whether delegate or trustee, can emerge at varying points. Depending on the policy issue, elected officials confront the realities of the political process in which they must trade off between personal conviction and the necessity to serve the policy demands of their constituents. Certain issues, such as those that affect constituents from other districts or states, may encourage elected representatives to act more like trustees. In comparison, issues of great political importance to their own constituents can compel representatives to act more like classic delegates. Ironically, given the vast array of policy issues that must be considered within a given session of Congress, it is unlikely that any public officials will act exclusively as either delegates or trustees.

The delegate concept of representation, as it interplays within the American policy process, is one that seems to evolve in light of the political reality that elected representatives confront. Assuming the policy issue has great importance, and, out of political necessity, elected officials may have to defer to the demands of their constituents. For delegates, public officials must defer to the demands and preferences of their constituents or rightly bear the political consequences during the next election cycle.

Good governing and good policies, however, are not necessarily the byproducts of elected officials acting as delegates. Within the increasing complexity of many social, economic, and foreign policy issues, it is unclear to what extent the policy positions of the public are based on sound evidence, analysis, and judgment. Moreover, the demands of the public, their changing passions, and their fleeting support for difficult courses of action, raise questions as to whether delegate representatives may produce policies that are pleasing to a select segment of the public, but are deleterious to the greater society. Still, given the role of elections, no representatives can deny that they must act as delegates for the interests of their constituents.

Aside from the delegate, the notion of elected representatives as trustees underscores the notion that elected officials must and should be guided by their belief that they know what is best for their constituents. Trustee-minded representatives seek to utilize knowledge, conscience, belief, and good judgment to determine positions that disregard the potentially narrow motivations of the public or their constituents. Trustee-type representatives serve their citizens by overcoming or disregarding the reigns of the public that may sacrifice good government for the sake of selfish or narrow interest. Within the realm of politics, the trustee method of representation suggests that those who are elected can better serve if they indeed disregard or diminish the influence of the public within the policy process.

Although a trustee representative suggests an ideal for representative democracy, such a role can also threaten the democratic nature of the state. Taken to an extreme, public officials may disregard the rightful needs and interests of their constituents. Moreover, the notion of the trustee hints at elitist notions that a certain segment of the society is better suited than others to govern. What is unclear, however, is what qualifies one to be a successful trustee? Does a trustee better serve the interests of the society if the interests of the people are disregarded?

Again, whether a trustee or a delegate is the preferred method of representation remains unclear. Realistically, each perspective captures the inescapable duality of representation. Specifically, elected representatives, rather than being a single type, are both trustee and delegate in nature.

Ironically, neither form of representation may ensure that government is either effective or representative. Rather, both representative roles serve critical functions at given times and help ensure that the elected leaders embrace the notion that they are chosen to lead, as well as to best represent and decide for the people they govern.

PUBLIC INTEREST

What is the public interest? Essentially, the concept of public interest can be defined as what is in the best interests of the nation. Representative democracy is based on a premise that elected officials can both define and determine the public interest. Yet, determining the public interest endures as a question that inspires debate. The notion of public interest is a concept whose importance is central to the very core of politics and public policy.

To understand the concept of public interest, one must clarify what are public interests. At the most extreme, in periods of public crisis such as war, it is clear what the public interest is: defense of the nation. However, other crises, those that lack a similar degree of threat, do not inspire such clarity as to how to distinguish private from public interests.

In general, one might say that the public interest includes the critical concerns of all or most members of the civic community. Public consensus may emerge over those issues that affect the many, but what of those issues that affect the few? Are issues of concern that affect a small number of individuals in the public interest? Arguably, as the intensity and consequence of certain interests increase, a consensus may emerge within the polity as to what the public interests are or should be. For example, there is little debate, especially in the post-September 11 world, that defending against a terrorist threat is in the public interest. A terrorist threat is easily defined as a national threat to the entire community. Determining which other issues are in the public interest, however, is not as easy a task.

A *clear* public interest may fail to emerge because individuals do not always agree— even with equal analysis, a wealth of information, and motivation—what is in their own or the public's best interest. Individuals will, at times, fail to accurately calculate the negative consequences of their own actions on society. Not surprisingly, individuals may fail to see what issues are of public concern for the community. It is rare, for example, that there is either unanimity or consensus on what is the public interest. As such, in many circumstances, government may have to define and impose a specific public interest on its citizenry through governmental actions.

Public policy is basically an imposed definition of the public interest on society. It is rare that all citizens will see a policy problem or action as in the public interest. The failures and the victories of public policy depend on how clearly public interest is defined. Yet, the dilemma that persists is that those who define the public interest may be doing so in a manner that serves their own private interests and not the common good.

POLITICS

Politics is derived from the term *polis* which means city-state. By extension, politics emerges as reference to the affairs of the state or what concerns the state. Traditionally, politics is defined in the context of governmental decisions and the institutional processes by which the state determines the direction for the community and society. Such an understanding of politics refers not only to the decision-making process but also to the art of debate and consensus that underscores the institutional process. Politics also raises an important awareness of the seemingly gossamer division between the public affairs relevant to the state and the private lives of individuals. Overall, each critical dimension of politics, both institutional and public affairs, reflects the richness of the concept and how it interplays throughout the policy process.

Institutionally, the notion of politics describes the overall defining quality of the governmental and decision-making process. More often than not, the legislative and policy process, the bureaucracy, the varied interactions among the members of the executive, legislative, and judicial branches, and the relations between the state and federal government are all described within the simple rubric of politics. In other words, politics encompasses the dynamics and exchanges that interweave the institutional manner by which a state determines its strategic plan of public policies. David Easton, for example, defined this notion of politics as the "authoritative allocation of values."[9] Still, an institutional definition of politics does not simply refer to the strict governmental process, but helps describe the manner and path by which such decisions are made.

Politics, at its essence, captures the competitive communication, exchange, discussion, and debate that emerge between competing ideas and groups within the state. According to Bernard Crick, politics is the "solution to the problem of order which chooses conciliation rather than violence and coercion."[10] Crick's interpretation of politics reflects the importance that discussion, negotiation, and consensus have in minimizing the consequences of social differences. Without politics, it could be argued, society would lack the discussion of issues and policy solutions that helps lubricate the institutional process, and helps stymie the escalation to societal conflict and violence. Ironically, although politics is often marked with a negative connotation,

used as a term to describe the failings of the process, it may well be that it is the art of politics that gives strength and weakness to the legislative process. Arguably, Harold Lasswell may have best summed up the concept of politics as an exploration of "who gets what, when, and how."[11]

PLURALISM AND ELITISM

Who governs within a democratic state? This enduring question raises many an issue as to the political forces and dynamics that intermingle within a democratic state and the policy process. Do circles of political power, the legislative process, and policy direction of a state remain open or closed even within the democratic state? Clearly, any state that is not governed as a direct democracy ensures that circles of power, politics, and policy will be potentially limited to those elected to represent the people, as well as those attempting to influence the elected representatives. Still, debate endures as to how accessible and how representative elected officials are, as does the question of whether all people from all classes enjoy similar access or influence in the policy process. The theoretical answers to this debate of who governs can be derived from either a pluralist or elitist approach.

Elite theory perceives the political and policy process as dominated by the few rather than the many. In general, elite theory proposes that society is divisible along class lines, in which the power of the masses, derived simply by their multitude, confronts the power of the elite, derived by wealth and status within the polity. Alexander Hamilton summarizes this view of society and the necessity for some elite direction for the sake of the state:

All communities divide themselves into the few and the many. The first are the rich and the wellborn, the other the masses of the people. . . . The people are turbulent and changing; they seldom judge or determine right. Give therefore to the first class a distinct, permanent share in the government. They will check the unsteadiness of the second, and as they cannot receive any advantage by a change, they therefore will ever maintain good government.[12]

According to elite theory, the preeminence of class, wealth, and education are the basis by which a select number of individuals possess a disproportionate political influence over the governing institutions and policy process. Specific political decisions are influenced and determined by a "small, cohesive elite class" of individuals.[13] Consequently, the government remains an unadulterated prisoner to the driving interests of the few over the many.

In contrast, pluralism takes an entirely different view of governing and the policy process. Pluralism assumes that a democratic governing system can operate even in light of an unquestionable inequality of resources between classes. Pluralism suggests that politics and policy are the consequence of the interaction and conflict among groups. Underscoring pluralism is an assumption that all individuals possess the opportunity and ability to organize and collectively influence the political and policy process. Moreover, pluralism contends that the political competition and conflict among such groups, coupled with the divided nature of the American political system, the degree of political access assumed available to all constituents, as well as the critical nature of political representation, ensure a path by which consensus, compromise, and negotiation can permit a variety of constituent groups to check the influence of other groups.

Within pluralism theory, the power of the elite is counterbalanced with the realization that organized and impassioned groups possess the power to overcome elitist interests and actions. As a result, the ruling elite cannot entirely divorce themselves from the considerable power of a mobilized and active public. Robert Dahl summarizes the ambiguity that seems to underscore the concept of pluralism and the critical question of who governs:

> Viewed from one position, leaders are enormously influential—so influential that if they are seen only in this perspective they may be considered a kind of ruling elite. Viewed from another position, however, many influential leaders seem to be captive of their constituents. . . . To some a pluralistic democracy is all head and no body; to others it is all body and no head.[14]

Both pluralism and elitism capture a critical dimension and seemingly powerful contradiction within American democracy and politics. Even though a ruling and political elite may be evident within the political and policy process, it is also apparent that such an elite can be constrained by a variety of constituent groups that may not be elitist. Of course, debate persists as to whether the promise of pluralism effectively counters the power of the elite. Overall, it may be best to recognize that the political process is marked by the interplay of pluralistic and elitist dynamics.

PUBLIC VS. PRIVATE

When should government intervene in private affairs? This is a fundamental question that deserves consideration. Answers to this critical question emerge along a theoretical discussion of what is a private and public concern. Understandably, the difference between "what is public" and "what is private" demands a rationale for framing why and when government should or should not intervene in the private affairs of individuals within the civic community.

One contentious rationale that provides a basis for understanding the difference between public and private emerges from the idealized notions of economics and the concepts of market failures.[15] According to this theoretical approach, public policy should be thought of as a governmental decision to intervene in the private dealings and interactions of groups, individuals, or other actors within the state. Public policies, in part, represent government's attempt to encourage, discourage, prohibit, or prescribe certain optimal behavior within the public that is or is not occurring privately.[16] Accordingly, a rationale for explaining government action can be understood in terms of the economic principle of market failures.

For David Weiner and Aiden Vining, the notion of market failure helps explain the critical conditions under which government should and should not intervene in the development of the society: The market failure approach to understanding the public and private dichotomy assumes that government actions should be limited to specific attempts to correct the failings of the *idealized* market.[17] Essentially, the idealized market represents the hypothesized efficient allocation of socioeconomic resources within a given state that emerges from the interactions of private individuals. In other words, public policy is a response by the state to correct an inefficient allocation, or a market failure,

that without government intervention will continue to pervert an assumed idealized efficiency. Implicit within the market failure method of understanding the public versus private character of public policy is a powerful assumption that government action should be limited to attempting to remedy private failures with consequences that are great for the society.

The market failure rationale highlights one of the more enduring conceptual difficulties within the field of public policy—understanding the difference between public and private realms. In other words, what is a policy issue that is of primary concern and interest to the government versus those issues that are of primary concern and interest to the individual? At a minimum, the analytical value of a market failure approach to understanding public policy is that it provides context by which one can begin to conceptualize the range between a public and private affair. Graphically, one could conceive the public and private realms along a public policy continuum (see Figure 1.1).

The graphic illustration of public and private affairs provides a visual basis for conceptualizing the different directions that government and public policy can undertake. Both extremes of the continuum help illustrate the graphic difference between a policy that is entirely public versus a policy that is entirely private in character. A policy position that falls at the private extreme of the continuum is viewed, either in terms of actual policy or ideologically, as an issue that

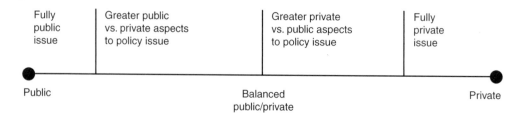

FIGURE 1.1 Theoretical Continuum of Policy Solutions

the individual is solely responsible for addressing. Such a position justifies or explains why government, either in terms of regulation, programs, or services, should have no role. Issues that fall exclusively in this zone reflect a belief that government has no responsibility or role in addressing certain issues of *private* concern.

The issues that fall exclusively in the private zone of personal responsibility, with no role to be played by the government, are not as obvious as one might assume. A somewhat classic example of a private issue is that of the practice of religious beliefs and the position that favors separation of church and state. However, whereas it may be argued and popularly accepted that the state should not have an active role in advocating or regulating a particular religion, it is not as clear to what extent religious behavior should be regulated so that it does not intermingle with the state. Recent federal court cases, for instance, have explored the meaning of separation of church and state in terms of religious practices that occur at public school sporting events, at extracurricular school activities, as well as during official proceedings at local and state courtrooms.[18] Again, what is seemingly a private issue can be also seen as a public issue if it is decided that certain behavior or practices, like religious beliefs, should not

be supported or sanctioned by the government and must then be effectively regulated. The point is that the notion of what is clearly a public or private issue depends on how one perceives or is affected by the issue.

Another example of this dichotomy between public or private issues is the interesting case of cigarette smoking. Until the last few decades, most levels of government had perceived this issue as, at best, a personal vice that did not warrant specific regulation by the state. However, fueled by increasing evidence that has shown strong correlations between various serious health ailments and cigarette smoking, as well as the increased public costs in treating such ailments, the government's position on this issue has changed considerably. Aside from merely regulating the selling and packaging of cigarettes, some states, such as California, have taken the dramatic step of regulating where people smoke in public forums by preventing smoking in all restaurants and bars—irrespective of the wishes of the smoking customer.

One of the most dramatic examples of the tension between public and private solutions is that of social security and personal retirement (see Figure 1.2). Social security and the issue of saving for retirement represent a public policy that currently falls to

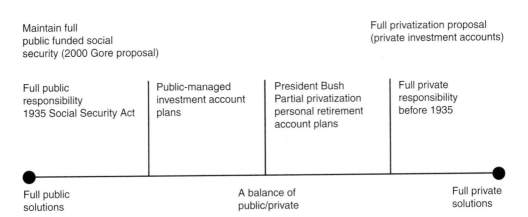

FIGURE 1.2 Public vs. Private Policy Solutions—Issue of Savings and Retirement

the extreme left of the continuum—a purely public solution. Social security was a public policy originally designed to regulate the savings behavior of all individuals. Irrespective of one's private preference, social security allocations from one's paycheck cannot be avoided and is not voluntary. This particular program was not initially seen in the United States as a public issue but given the economic conditions of the Great Depression, it became an issue that was no longer easily framed in terms of personal or private responsibility.

Prior to the enactment of the 1935 Social Security Act, savings and retirement were considered to be a private concern and not a government or a public responsibility. The logic was, of course, that individuals should be responsible for managing their financial means to ensure their future livelihood. Clearly, it was not the state's responsibility to provide individuals with savings if the individuals were not responsible—or was it? With any private issue, such as savings and retirement, the concern is whether a public role is justified or necessary. With the onset of the depression in the 1930s, the political acceptance of a public role in this issue increased because of a dramatic and dire change in the economic conditions facing the entire state and most individuals. The depression showed that individuals were not saving sufficiently. Hence, the passage of the 1935 Social Security Act reflected a dramatic reversal from what was previously seen as a purely private issue. The social security issue helps highlight that the preference for more or less government intervention is by no means fixed, but can and does change dramatically over time.

Recently, the debate over the fate of social security has again become a heated discussion over the responsibility and role that government and individuals have in ensuring savings and retirement. Effectively, social security is again becoming a debate between basic public and private perspectives surrounding the issue of savings and retirement. Arguably, this debate may not hit its nadir until 2016 when the federal retirement system will pay out more than it receives, or by 2038 when the social security fund will be completely depleted.[19] Consequently, according to the 2001 Moynihan-Parsons Commission on Social Security, difficult choices will have to be made as to whether to maintain social security as it is through increased taxation, or to cut social security benefits, or institute some kind of privatization.[20]

The current and future debate concerning social security will increasingly hinge on whether political decision makers, the public, and various interest groups view this as either a public or a private issue. In the future, an eventual position will reflect some compromise along this public or private continuum. What is inevitable, however, is that the nation and the policy actors involved will have to make the difficult decision of what public position, if any, is preferred, acceptable, or even fiscally and politically possible with respect to the issue of social security.

In comparison to social security, the issue of national defense represents the quintessential public issue. With respect to national security, the public role of the government is justified and well accepted because an attack on the state is seen as an attack on all. Although debate may exist as to the size of the defense budget, the means necessary to achieve national security, and the performance of the military in combat, there is no general discussion as to whether or not the state should play the role in providing national defense. In contrast, other issues, even those that had been traditionally seen as public issues, are increasingly being redefined as private issues.

Aside from social security, proposals to privatize public services dealing with education, prisons, health care, and transportation have become increasingly debated across all levels of government. A school voucher proposal, for instance, is an attempt to address failings in education through privatization. Numerous state prisons are now being managed not by the state government or state employees, but by private companies. Although public health care is available in emergency situations, versions of universal health care, as in Canada, are rare in the United States, and a large number of Americans continue to go without coverage. In transportation, for example, certain highways are now under private management. Again, few policy issues seem to fall exclusively and absolutely within the public or private realm.

Determining the desired role of government in a particular policy issue area highlights some fascinating ideological contradictions within American politics. The classic perception is that liberals will seek to use public power to actively address social ills and economic inequalities through dramatic and intrusive policy actions. For example, in addressing the issue of poverty or education, the "liberal" prefers public-funded and managed government programs. In contrast, "conservatives" would generally be described as favoring a limited role for the state, and preference for private actions and responsibility. In terms of the issues of education and poverty, the conservative favors private responsibility and personal initiative over government funding and management. Yet, if the policy issue being debated deals with abortion, the conservative would favor intrusive government actions and a more dramatic use of public power, whereas the liberal would argue that such an issue is one of private concern. The point is that there is no set map as to what type of policy actions best serve the problem in question.

The policy action preferred by interest groups, the public at large, or the political decision makers represents, at its core, an ideological belief as to the role government should have in one's life. The purpose of describing policy action along a private and public continuum is to emphasize that on any given issue that a society confronts, it is open to often-heated debate as to the extent and role the government should play.

The choice for more or less government is seldom as clear or as obvious as it is sometimes made to seem within the political arena. Although one may suggest that the state has the responsibility for national security, is it any less obvious that the state has the added responsibility for personal health, education, and community security—be it in the form of policing, welfare, education, or health care? Simply put, the extent and nature of the role of government within a society is not predetermined. The scope of policy action is a reflection of the array of political, policy, and ideological interests involved in the policy process, the period of time in which a problem manifests, and the pervasive belief that a certain course of action—whether public or private—is best given the nature of the problem. In the end, it may be best to avoid simplistic notions that more or less government is the solution to the problem. Rather, an array of public or private solutions should be considered and evaluated as to their merits in positively addressing the issue in question. Clearly, the goal of public policy is to achieve not a smaller or larger government but a better government through policy actions designed and focused to solve the problem at hand.

NEEDS AND RIGHTS

What are the needs and rights of individuals within a complex polity? Clearly, the political debate over the allocation of resources to meet society's needs pervades the policy process. Similarly, the notion of rights and the role of government in protecting those rights are fundamental, though they remain in dispute. For public policy, the dilemma is discerning between what is a need and what should be protected as rights under the law.

Needs, whether for an individual or group, are qualitatively different than notions of want. A need can be thought of as fundamental to human survival, essential to one's existence, and critical to the sustenance of life. In stark contrast, a want is to be thought of as an extravagance and as superficial to one's being or survival. Wants exist as products of personal choice and social influence that result out of a desire to add to one's being, qualitatively or quantitatively, rather than to ensure one's human existence. Needs, however, are shared by all human beings, irrespective of culture or politics.

Food, water, air, clothing, and shelter may suffice to meet a conception of the needs essential to human survival. Yet, this simple conception leaves out the factors of health, security, and education, and disregards any aspect of the real qualitative nature that underscores a debate of needs. For example, what type of water, food, clothing, and shelter will suffice to satisfy the needs of individuals? Moreover, are health, education, and security not a need given their critical importance to survival and the persistence of life in a complex society? Once this debate about need is placed within the forum of domestic politics, it becomes quite unclear where the definitive line can be drawn that differentiates need from want.

The line between need and want remains open to political debate because it is only at the extremes that clarity seems to emerge as to the appropriate role for government. If members of a community are hungry, lack water, or require shelter, it may appear obvious what role government should have in addressing such societal woes. Yet, individuals still remain homeless,

whereas others may lack sufficiently healthy foods or clean water. There is no universal list of needs a government must provide and ensure for its citizenry. Rather, through the political process and policy actions, government defines and redefines what is a need, the extent to which society's resources will be reallocated to meet these needs, and the role government agencies will play in delivering and ensuring these needs for the betterment of individuals and society.

In comparison, an individual's rights is a concept that captures the moral entitlement that one expects to be treated by others and the state in a certain manner. The idea of rights seeks to delimit the extent to which government, or other actors in a society, can intrude upon the individual behavior and one's chosen method of existence. American politics is unique in that the Bill of Rights has codified the broad areas within which each individual is ensured constitutional protection. Yet, even though a set of rights was defined within the first ten amendments of the Constitution, these rights and freedoms still exist as essentially contestable concepts whose definitions emerge within a broader political and legal context.

The debate within American public policy concerns not only what rights individuals have but also how such rights will be defined or redefined within a given polity. Those in positions of legal or policy power traditionally define the very notion of what are the rights of individuals. Still, such definitions of rights will react to the pressures of the public or elite and basically evolve as a society progresses. For public policy, the significance of defining one's rights proves substantial. Once defined by law, the rights of individuals represent a check against the enormous power of the state. Rights also provide a legal basis for deterring or punishing the actions of individuals, and establish a moral frame within which to view the behavior of all individuals and the state. For example, a legal right to sufficient food, water, and shelter would obligate the state to provide a minimum level of care to satisfy the basic needs of its populace. Such a unique right, if ever granted, would redefine what quality of needs is necessary for survival.

EQUALITY AND JUSTICE

Can a political society be unequal and just or does justice demand equality for all? Is social justice essential for the betterment of a society, and does such a goal demand a certain degree and type of equality? Although such questions of social justice and equality raise an array of prickly dilemmas for the policy maker, they remain integral to the puzzle that often frames the debate over what policy responses should be taken to address profound societal failings. The challenge, however, is in defining what is social justice and what form of equality can best assist in its end.

Social justice remains a term that escapes a clean and simple definition. Arguably, social justice would seem to suggest a degree of equality across a society that both alleviates obstacles that delimit one's future possibilities and removes those forces which cause or sustain undue suffering. As a concept, social justice raises awareness of the societal pains of inequality, discrimination, racism, sexism, ageism, segregation, homophobia, and economic suffering that hinder the achievement of a more complete and egalitarian society. Some would argue that social justice extends further to suggest the moral necessity and a responsibility to define and determine "a morally defensible distribution of rewards in society, evaluated in terms of wages, profits, housing, medical care, welfare benefits, and so forth."[21] In terms of equality, such an understanding of social justice carries with it the expectation that the government will redress inequali-

ties so that those who lack certain means or are in greatest need obtain assistance. Yet, this still begs the question, what form of equality is truly socially just?

When is a society equal? If equality is deemed necessary for a society, then the obligations of the state and expectations of public policy may extend far beyond a reallocation of resources, the deliverance of programs, or even in the protection of individual rights and freedoms. The stark absence of equality within the society, for instance, carries staggering pejorative images of unfairness, cruelty, brutality, and individual suffering. Yet, actions taken to ensuring equality, although defined as a positive outcome for the society, may also come at the expense of individuals who enjoy the benefits of inequality.

One method of grasping the complexity of equality is to distinguish between the various notions of equality. For instance, foundational equality addresses the belief that all individuals share a similar natural imperative by which all are recognized as equal to one another in terms of moral worth. Foundational equality demands that all individuals be seen as equal to one another and that no one individual or member of a group garners special benefit or persecution under the law or in the treatment by the state. Legally, and in terms of public policy, foundational equality helps us to grasp the notion of equal protection before the law.

Whereas foundational equality may address issues of stark societal unfairness, and can help rectify conditions of discrimination before the law, it does not offer a basis with which to eradicate the greater sociocultural and political conditions that may prohibit greater individual equality. Equality of opportunity, in comparison, represents a basis by which individuals are provided with a roughly equal footing when competing within the greater society. For example, providing suffrage to African Americans and women, removing poll taxes, and expanding the right to vote to eighteen-year-olds offered an increased equality in the right to vote, but this opportunity did not ensure that individuals would vote. Essentially, equality of opportunity represents an attempt to ensure that individual effort and ability determine the outcome of societal interactions, rather than other obstacles beyond the capacity of the individual. In other words, if segments of the population are restricted from voting, then that society is by definition unequal. However, if one chooses not to vote even though granted the opportunity to do so, such a society is not necessarily unequal.

The existence of inequality of opportunity can help justify, even demand, an array of policy roles for the government. To ensure equality of opportunity, the state may have to address those conditions that hinder personal development and growth deemed essential for maximizing one's potential. Profound differences in educational opportunities could be seen as a striking example of an inequality in opportunity given the importance education has in maximizing one's future potential.

Ironically, although such conceptualizations of equality may suggest a dramatic and expansive degree of intervention by the government, it does not remove the resulting condition of inequality. Individual and societal inequality can and will exist because of variances in individual choice, desire, and capability. However, inequality should not exist because of societal obstacles, whether in terms of social or legal, that makes it impossible for individuals to choose their own destiny. Of course, equal opportunity can lead to an even more dramatic understanding of equality—equality of outcome.

Rather than focusing on the initial opportunities by which equality is judged, the most radical conceptualization of equality focuses on the resulting equality of outcomes.

Equality of outcome is defined by the existence of a societal similarity in the quality and quantity of the critical needs and rights within the polity. Minimally, such notions may simply justify such government initiatives as a progressive income tax, a minimum wage, or government-sponsored public health care and education. Taken to the extreme, equality of outcome can justify a wide role for public policy and the redistribution of all societal resources to achieve this material equality for all individuals. Put differently, a just society will exist once inequality, whether material or not, is eradicated.

Overall, each vision of equality focuses on different paths toward a more just society. Each vision, however, can still be taken to such radical extremes that the very notion of equality is threatened by its pursuit. For instance, how aggressive should the government be in defining when and where the practical conditions of inequality exist? Moreover, to what extent should public policies be developed and implemented to ensure against various aspects of inequality? In the end, fundamental notions of equality remain open to definition, as do the very public policies that seek to address the causes and conditions that lead to greater equality. Thus, although social justice may seem an obvious pursuit of the state, defining the path of equality that best serves such a goal is a political and policy question that continues to escape clarity. Such a question remains laden with concern over how such equality and social justice will indeed be practically achieved through the specific design and implementation of public policies.

EFFICIENCY AND EFFECTIVENESS

The entire range of public policies and government programs are judged in terms of their efficiency and effectiveness. Efficiency, for example, can be understood in terms of whether a government program or service is operating at the most optimal level in terms of resources—such as time, dollars, or human resources. Put differently, efficiency highlights the importance of whether programs and services are wasting resources. In contrast, effectiveness helps define whether a specific program or service is achieving the intended effect and degree of change in behavior sought by the public policy. Effectiveness emphasizes the importance of achieving the desired positive or negative impacts of a public policy on the desired group of actors.

Efficiency is a term often utilized in understanding the motivations and constraints of the business world. A waste of resources, whether people, time, dollars, or other capital resources, is indicative of an unnecessary cost that comes at the expense of greater profitability. For the business community, efficiency is an essential end because capital resources are limited, not infinite, and the competitive nature of the marketplace will extract a high price from companies that are inefficient. Government, however, operates in a noncompetitive market environment, where no semblance of market competition exists to compel efficient practices.

In the context of public policy, the concept of efficiency remains open to significant interpretation, even political manipulation, over what is deemed an acceptable or unacceptable inefficiency. In the absence of a private market that punishes broad inefficiencies, public policy and programs bear the political consequences that may arise from the perception that programs or services are too costly for the state to fulfill. Consequently, some semblance of a competitive environment does emerge given that government is limited by the finite fiscal resources that it is able to extract from the public in terms of taxes or fees. Hence, pressure exists, albeit political rather than market, whereby government programs are pushed to be as efficient as possible to minimize the needless waste of limited taxpayer resources.

What is deemed efficient and what is politically acceptable inefficiency depends on the political and policy preferences of the actors involved, as well as changing societal realities. Political competition, rather than the market, determines the standard that is used to evaluate both efficiency and inefficiency. Various programs administered by the government, from national missile defense research and space exploration to the postal service, have at times been described or criticized as fiscally inefficient. The public and political preference for such programs, however, can redefine the very meaning of what inefficiency is. Consequently, depending on the socioeconomic and political context, an inefficient welfare program may garner more criticism than an inefficient defense program. More important, aside from the skewing effect of political realities, an even more powerful observation is that the goal of efficiency may prove difficult given that government programs and services are designed to redress complex policy problems. As such, any notion of efficiency may be sacrificed given the political priorities that emphasize effectiveness over efficiency.

Effectiveness is a criterion with which to gauge whether a specific policy action is achieving the desired effects on the specific target population. Effectiveness reflects the conclusion that a program or service is having the intended positive or negative effect. For example, a policy that seeks to create a program that addresses recidivism through rehabilitation and retraining can be deemed substantively effective only if it achieves the goals set down by the program. Clearly, a program that fails to be effective perpetuates the effects that follow from such severe socioeconomic problems, like recidivism.

However, as with efficiency, the very notion of effectiveness operates not in a political vacuum, but is defined and redefined by the political and policy preferences of the actors involved throughout the policy process.

Effectiveness is both an objective and subjective evaluation of the impact a government program or service may be having within and for the polity. Objectively, a government program is ineffective if it fails to alter the behavior of a target population in the manner specified or sought by the policy. As such, if the behavior persists unchanged, it should seem clear that the policy is ineffective. In actuality, notions of objective effectiveness remain open to subjective definition.

Subjectively, because the evaluation of effectiveness develops within the political arena, determining what is a programmatic failure is not as clear as one would assume. Because of the political preferences, poor analytical skills, or lack of proper evaluation, a policy may be deemed effective even though it is actually ineffective. In particular, programs that garner great political support may persist even in the absence of any evidence of tangible benefit. For instance, Drug Awareness Resistance Education (DARE) programs have long achieved wide support among a variety of political and public actors. Critical evaluations of DARE programs have questioned the program's impact on drug use among schoolchildren because no discernable change in patterns of drug use can be credited to the exposure to DARE programs.[22] Nevertheless, public and political support continues for these programs because the same political actors that designed and adopted the policy are also critical to evaluating its effectiveness. In sum, although effectiveness may be the ideal end of public policy, it often confronts the complexity of a problem, and the political vagaries that serve to redefine when a program fails and succeeds.

HUMAN NATURE

Whereas power is often discussed as being almost synonymous with politics, one could consider the concept of human nature as implicitly synonymous with policy. Human nature, which refers to that "essential and immutable character of all human beings," is a constant thread that permeates our discussions and analysis of the political society in which we all live.[23] How often is it said in everyday conversation that this or that problem exists because it is human nature? How often has human nature been used to explain that certain behavior cannot be changed through public policy because it is fixed? Conversely, it is sometimes said with beaming optimism that individuals have the capacity to learn, change, and improve. The answer is not merely of great theoretical importance, but helps justify the types of policies we may come to believe are necessary to address the many social problems we confront.

The concept of human nature enables us to generalize the expected behavior of all individuals (see Figure 1.3). Are individuals born good or bad, are individuals socialized to become bad, and can individuals be conditioned to be good? Such generalizations justify the logic, the design, and the necessity

		NATURE	
		GOOD	BAD
NURTURE	GOOD	Individuals are "good," optimistic, limited policy role by government	Regulation of "bad" innate behavior
	BAD	Reform individual, positive role for government	Individuals are "bad," pessimistic, expanded role for government, significant regulation, laws on all behavior

FIGURE 1.3 Policy Implications of Nature vs. Nurture

of the public policies that seek to govern and regulate individual behavior and actions. Again, public policies are rarely tailored to the realities of each individual nature, but represent sweeping policy statements as to what we believe about human nature. Politically, invoking this concept carries with it a powerful connotation of what one believes individuals are, what they can be, and what they cannot be. Yet, the concept remains so frustratingly intriguing because the answer to the question of what human nature is remains elusive and contestable.

Central to the debate about human nature is whether it is nature versus nurture. Are individuals fixed to the nature of genetic programming or can we be nurtured by the environment, and by changes in the environment? Based on a Hobbesian vision, for instance, atavistic tendencies—the basic selfishness, aggressiveness, and weaknesses of individuals—cannot be reformed, but only constrained by a state.[24] The opinions of such classic theorists as Aristotle, Plato, and Polybius offer a severe critique of what is the weak and self-destructive nature of individuals and justify a system of government that separates and minimizes the political power afforded to the individual because of their nature.[25] Conversely, other theorists, such as Thomas Aquinas, seem to offer a more optimistic vision of human nature that holds to the potential goodness of individuals.[26] Is human nature good or bad? The answer remains elusive.

In light of the issue of human nature, to what extent can this nature be nurtured? Can the environment, whether it is family, or peers, or the community, or the state, nurture the behavior of the individual? As with the debate surrounding nature, nurture can similarly be seen in both a positive and negative light. Obviously, if the notion of nurture affects how we develop as individuals, then an environment that is either negative or positive can nurture or condition one

to be either more good or more bad. Individuals are not fixed from a nurture perspective, but are products of the respective "nature" of their environment. Change the character of the environment, for good or bad, and the individual is nurtured to reflect the character of that environment. Based on this perspective, if appropriate public policies can be developed to alter the weaknesses or failings of the environment, then all individuals can be nurtured to change, improve, and excel beyond their initial condition. In contrast, a negative environment left unchanged will simply fuel a cycle of nurturing character weaknesses and failings.

At some level, the very notion of human nature permeates all discussions of politics and policy. Seemingly every facet of politics and public policy—whether it is the nature of political representation, the institutional structure of government, the rights and freedoms given to individuals or to policies dealing with nuclear deterrence, speed limits, education training programs, or programs that attempt to rehabilitate convicted criminals—involve some decision on what is the evident state of human nature. Public policy, in particular, will inevitably make reference to whether certain behavior can be deterred or changed, whether the actors involved can be changed, or whether behavior is fixed and can only be restrained and punished.

The beliefs held about human nature carry with it cross-cultural and national significance for what all individuals are capable of, what the role of government should be, the purpose and nature of public policy, as well as the state of the society we live in. The challenge with such a complex concept, however, is in practically defining and understanding what human nature and nurture are and are not. Taken to an extreme, the nurture argument can be used to justify radical policies of social engineering that seek to remake the individual through programmatic conditioning. State-sponsored reeducation programs, such as those in the Soviet Union, Maoist China, and Nazi Germany, sought to indoctrinate complete ideological and political loyalty to the state. Similarly, extreme notions of the "nature" argument can manifest into arguments of the natural superiority of one group over another, and have long justified ethnic, racial, and religious genocide. Clearly, either extreme can produce horrific policy and political outcomes.

SUMMARY

This chapter presented a variety of concepts that provide insight into the conceptual foundation to the field of public policy. The concepts discussed are instrumental to appreciating the wide conceptual context that is indicative of the field of public policy. The significance of each of these concepts captures the many dimensions and complexities that underscore many areas critical to public policy. Of course, this list of concepts is by no means complete; rather, it offers an insight into the array of complex concepts that help shape our understanding of public policy and the policy process.

DISCUSSION QUESTIONS

1. What role does power have in changing the behavior and ideas of others? In your opinion, what is the basis for such power in American politics?

2. Is legitimacy critical to effective authority or can an authority govern effectively without legitimacy? On what basis is such legitimacy achieved? Also, when do democratic governments and their officials lose legitimacy? In your opinion, at any time over the last twenty years,

have American authorities lost legitimacy? Discuss.

3. Can the public interest be objectively defined? If so, on what basis should it be defined? In your opinion, what issues are in the public interest? Discuss.

4. At what point does an issue—whether economic, political, or social—become a public policy issue? Are there some issues that are always private? Discuss.

5. Should the needs of the individual—those critical for life—be protected as rights under the law? In other words, do individuals have the right to certain needs critical to life? If so, determine what is necessary for an individual to have in order to live (e.g., food, housing, health, education).

SUGGESTED READINGS

Berry, C. *Human Nature*. New Jersey: Humanities Press, 1986.

Crick, B. *In Defense of Politics*. New York: Harmondworth, 1983.

Ebenstein, W. and A. Ebenstein. *Great Political Thinkers*. 6th ed. New York: Harcourt, 2000.

Heywood, A. *Political Ideas and Concepts: An Introduction*. New York: St Martin's Press, 1994.

Lasswell, H. D. *Politics: Who Gets What, When, and How?* New York: McGraw-Hill, 1936.

Reich, R. B., ed. *Power of Public Ideas*. Cambridge, MA: Ballinger, 1986.

Robert, D. *Who Governs: Democracy and Power in an American City*. New Haven, CT: Yale University Press, 1963.

Schattschneider, E. E. *The Semisovereign People*. New York: Holt, Rinehart and Winston, 1960.

Schumpeter, J. *Capitalism, Socialism and Democracy*. London: Allen & Unwin, 1976.

Stone, D. A. *Policy Paradox: The Art of Political Decisionmaking*. 2nd ed. New York: Scott Foresman, 1997.

ENDNOTES

1. The concept of power remains one of the most contested of concepts with political science. A variety of definitions and theoretical interpretations exist. For more discussion, see S. Lukes, *Power: A Radical View* (Basingstoke, England: Macmillan, 1974); Andrew Heywood, *Political Ideas and Concepts: An Introduction* (New York: St. Martin's Press, 1994).

2. This approach reflects Heywood's approach to discussing the three faces of the concept of power.

3. E. E. Schattschneider, *The Semisovereign People* (New York: Holt, Rinehart and Winston, 1969).

4. R. F. Dahl, "A Critique of the Ruling Elite Model," *American Political Science Review* 52 (1958): 463–469 and *Who Governs* (New Haven: Yale University Press, 1990).

5. P. Bachrach and M. Baratz, "The Two Faces of Power," in F. G. Castles, D. J. Murray, and D. C. Potter, eds., *Decisions, Organizations and Society* (Harmondsworth: Penguin, 1981).

6. This dimension of power conforms to the radical notions of power. See Lukes, *Power*, 9–12.

7. Federalist paper. In P. Nivola & D. Rosenbloom, *Classic Readings in American Politics* (New York: St. Martens, 1990), 29–34.

8. The debate about the value or curse of democracy centers to a great extent on the necessary role of the public and necessity and type of representation best for governing. Among the classics to explore are Plato, "The Republic," Aristotle, "The Republic," and Polybius, "The Histories," in W. Ebenstein and A. Ebenstein, *Great Political Thinkers*, 6th ed. (New York: Harcourt, 2000).

9. D. Easton, *The Political System*, 3rd ed. (Chicago: Chicago University Press, 1981). See also David Easton, *A Systems Analysis of Political Life* (New York: Wiley, 1965).

10. B. Crick, *In Defense of Politics* (Harmondworth and New York: Penguin, 1962), 30.

11. H. D. Lasswell, *Politics: Who Gets What, When, and How?* (New York: McGraw-Hill. 1936).

12. A. Hamilton, "The Federalist No. 15," in Ann G. Serow, ed., *The Polity Reader* (New York: Lanahar, 2000), 45.

13. M. Parenti, *Democracy for the Few*, 7th ed. (New York: St. Martin's Press, 1995).

14. R. F. Dahl, "The Ambiguity of Leadership," in Ann G. Serow et al., *The Polity Reader* (New York: Lanahan, 2000), 100.

15. There are very vocal critics and proponents as to the significance of and insight derived from the concept of efficiency, as well as a more rational methodological approach to public policy. For an opponent's perspective, see: D. A. Stone, *Policy Paradox: The Art of Political Decisionmaking*, 2nd ed. (New York: Scott Foresman, 1997). For a proponent's perspective on the applications of the efficiency concept, see David L. Weiner and Aiden R. Vining, *Policy Analysis: Concepts and Practice* (Englewood Cliffs, NJ: Prentice Hall, 1989).

16. Weiner and Vining, *Policy Analysis*, 29.

17. Ibid., 29.

18. K. Axtman, "Praying in Public Schools," *Christian Science Monitor*, October 25, 2001. See also "Delay Urges More Religion in Texas Schools," AP Wire, April 18, 2002.

19. Major Garret, "Report: Social Security Needs Reform to Remain Solvent," CNN Web site, July 19, 2001.

20. The various policy positions were derived from a recent government study. The positions on the continuum are a rough approximation. See *Presidential Commission to Strengthen Social Security, Final Report*, December 11, 2001, and *Revised Version* on March 19, 2002, http://www.csss.gov.

21. Heywood, *Political Ideas and Concepts*, 235.

22. P. Waldron, "St. Charles Schools Question Value of DARE," *Daily Herald*, April 24, 2002; J. Levoy, "Police Resistance to Gutting DARE Program Angers Panel," *Los Angeles Times*, April 30, 2002.

23. Heywood, *Political Ideas and Concepts*, 316.

24. Thomas Hobbes, "Leviathan," in Alan Ebenstein, *Introduction to Political Thinkers*, 2nd ed. (New York: Harcourt, 2000).

25. Ebenstein, *Political Thinkers*.

26. Ibid.

2

The What

Policy Typologies, Policy Tools, and the Policy-Making Process

WHAT IS PUBLIC POLICY?

The answer to this question is deceivingly difficult. Not surprisingly, a number of definitions and answers have been offered to help us better understand the concept of public policy. The term *public policy,* most simply defined, refers to an action of government designed to serve a politically defined purpose. Yet, the term *public policy* encompasses a variety of conceptual elements that extend beyond any single simple definition.[1]

In general, the concept of public policy is surprisingly complex with many insights as to the nature and scope of politics, policy, and government. Many conceptual definitions of public policy will invariably refer to various aspects related to the purpose, place, and type of policies. Furthermore, many definitions will also reference the political realm in which policy develops and operates, the institutional constraints, the array of actors involved, and the supposed process by which policy may develop. From an analytical perspective, a definition of public policy assists in our understanding of what policy is and the significance and complexity of the process of making policy.

A number of scholars have provided useful and important definitions of public policy. These competing definitions provide a useful foundation that begins to expand on what public policy is. At first glance, these definitions may seem redundant. Although the term *public policy* suggests simplicity, this simplicity has yet to manifest in a single universal definition. This may be seen as the failing of policy scholars and the like to come to some universal agreement. However, these competing definitions offer a useful basis to emphasize the very complexity of public policy.

PUBLIC POLICY DEFINITIONS—COMPETING PERSPECTIVES

For Thomas R. Dye, "public policy is whatever government chooses to do or not to do."[2] The value of Dye's deceivingly simple definition is to emphasize the role of government in society through public policy, and the impacts that government can have through public policy. Yet, for Dye, policy inaction, or what governments choose not to do, is as important as policy action. Dye's subtle distinction between action and inaction is a powerful point that helps emphasize the significance of government decisions not to pursue policy action and to prefer noninvolvement.

In comparison, for Clarke E. Cochran, Lawrence C. Mayer, T. R. Carr, and N. Joseph Cayer, public policy "always refers to the actions of government and the intentions that determine those actions."[3] More specifically, public policy should not be thought of as an accidental action or result. Policy does not arise out of happenstance even though it may be described, in retrospect, as poorly thought out or bad policy. Rather, "making policy requires choosing among goals, and alternatives, and choice always involves intention."[4] In sum, public policy may be defined as "an intentional course of action followed by a government institution or official for resolving an issue of public concern."[5] Hence, from this definition, an understanding of what public policy is would include a reference to an intentional government decision that emerges out of a set of competing alternatives, that results in some kind of action "manifested in laws, public statements, official regulations, or widely accepted and public visible patterns of behavior."[6]

In contrast, according to B. Guy Peters, a definition of public policy should reference its overarching significance and implications. A basic definition, for Peters, suggests that public policy "is the sum of the government activities, whether pursued directly or through agents . . . which have an influence on the lives of citizens."[7] Peters expands on his definition to include three separate levels of policy that include choices, outputs, and impacts. The choices level captures the distinction that policy is a decision made by a particular government actor "granted authority and directed toward using the public power to affect the lives of citizens."[8] The outputs level emphasizes that the result of these choices leads to some kind of government action that has the effect of redefining the society in some manner. Finally, the impacts level of policy captures the distinction that policy choices and actions are not impact-free, but directly and indirectly affect the citizenry. The notion of impacts is of particular significance because it helps to underscore that once decided on, policy affects and leads to effects within the society, and provides a basis with which to determine the success or failure of policies.

James E. Anderson, in comparison, suggests that public policy is "a relatively stable, purposive course of action followed by an actor or set of actors in dealing with a problem or matter of concern."[9] Of significance, for Anderson, is the importance of differentiating between policy alternatives, the decision, and the eventual action that represents the policy. Moreover, it is the government actors who develop public policies, whereas nongovernmental actors can be thought of as attempting to influence this behavior. Still, it is Anderson's reference to a "purposive action . . . in dealing with a problem" that provides some clarity that policy seeks to redress and address problems confronted within the society.

In summary, each of these definitions highlights the many dimensions to an understanding of public policy. No one definition, however, should be thought of as complete because public policy remains the quintessential contestable concept. Arguably, a more encompassing explanation of public policy requires a discussion of the "composite of ideas and elements" that comprise an understanding of public policy.[10] Even though no definition is likely to prove complete, a broad discussion of the ideas and elements essential to what is understood by the concept of public policy can be represented by six critical components (see Box 2.1).

The six components should be understood in terms of their specific contribution to the concept of public policy. Each element captures a different, but integral, dimension of what public policy means and represents. Hence, each of the six elements will be explored to better appreciate and understand what public policy is.

Box 2.1   Essential Components of a Public Policy Definition

1. Represents both action and inaction
2. Involves an array of formal and informal players within and outside the arenas of government
3. Includes a variety of types of public policy actions
4. Is focused on achieving an intentional course of action with a specific or sometimes vague goal as its objective
5. Is an action that leads to intentional and unintentional consequences
6. Follows a definable, yet fluid evolutionary course of stages, represented by a predecision, decision, and post-decision phase, to the policy-making process

SOURCE: S. Theodoulou, "The Nature of Public Policy," in S. Theodoulou and M. Cahn, *Public Policy—The Essential Readings* (Englewood Cliffs NJ: Prentice Hall, 1995), 1.

ESSENTIAL COMPONENTS OF A PUBLIC POLICY DEFINITION

Action and Inaction

It is somewhat perplexing to think of public policy in light of the actions government or decision makers may choose to take or not take. How is it possible for public policy to encompass both action and inaction? The most obvious form of public policy is an explicit policy action, a legislative, judicial, or executive decision, that is readily perceived and understood by all as the stark action taken by the respective governing authority. Understanding this distinction between action and inaction is critical to appreciating that public policy involves a decision over what issues and problems the state will or will not become involved in.

The decisions to bomb another nation–state, to establish the social security program, to build a new highway infrastructure, to execute a judicial order, are all diverse examples of explicit actions undertaken by a governing political body to address a specific issue or problem. Such policy actions cannot be ignored or disregarded. The decision to act, made by the appropriate authorities, will result in some degree of substantive policy action. The policy actions taken by the state are often significant, tangible, and readily visible statements of what the government or authorities intend. The decision to act matters because it formally introduces the state within the public area in some dramatic and substantial fashion.

Conversely, choosing not to bomb another state, preferring not to establish a social security program, deciding never to build a new highway, or preferring not to hear a case before the court are all representations of inactions with comparable significance for the greater society. The decision not to go to war, for instance, is a powerful decision with potentially dramatic repercussions. The decision by President George Bush not to invade Iraq in 1991 and battle the regime of Saddam Hussein during the Persian Gulf War represents a classic decision of inaction with longstanding implications for American national interests. The decision by the Clinton administration not to become directly involved in Rwanda, during the bloody civil war in that nation, represents another example of inaction. Yet, to fairly criticize the actions of these presidents, or any decision maker, one must appreciate the basic calculation between whether to choose to act or accept the present circumstances.

The preference for inaction or action can be understood in light of *a simple calculation* as to whether the present social, economic, or political status quo should be altered in some manner. This is not as simple a calculation as it is often suggested in the media, by pundits, or armchair political experts. Once action is taken, irrespective of the form or kind, the current status quo will be changed.

The status quo represents a realization that if absolutely no action is taken by a decision maker, the present state of affairs with respect to the issue will remain the same. However, once some action is taken, the status quo will be changed. It is this change in the status quo that results in a significant dilemma and constraint on all decisions and actions. Why? Because it is unclear exactly what the outcome and consequences will be from any specific policy action taken by a decision maker.

Clearly, there must be a motivation, even a justification, for why government should or should not intervene in a given situation. For instance, justification depends on what government seeks to redress or address in light of the current status quo. In addition, government must consider the potential consequences of action versus inaction. In-

ACTION = Seek change
Political/Policy consequences of status quo unacceptable—
problem solved or new problem emerges STATUS QUO

INACTION = Seek no change
Political/Policy consequences of status quo acceptable—
problem or issue persists

FIGURE 2.1 Policy Action vs. Inaction

evitably, the key question as to whether action must be taken is whether the status quo is politically acceptable or demands a transformation through public policy.

In the abstract, every decision by the government to alter the status quo is a binary decision between either action or inaction (see Figure 2.1). Such decisions, however, are not the result of mere fiscal calculations of costs and benefits. Rather, governmental decisions involve the many aspects of "messy real world politics" where calculations of cost and benefit, evaluations of consequences from action or inaction, are often made subjective by the political realities of the policy process. Put differently, as the political preference for the current status quo begins to wane, and if the status quo is deemed unacceptable, so will the preference for action versus inaction.

The point to appreciate is that the preference for policy action and inaction is the product of a union of political motivations unique to each policy issue. Many factors as diverse as ideological, partisan affiliation, constituent interest, or national interest may affect the decision for action. To understand why government may prefer to act or not, one must understand the array of motivations that influence the decision to act or not. In sum, public policy represents both the action and inaction of government in light of the motivations and preference for or against the current status quo as defined and decided by the set of decision makers.

Formal and Informal Players

The scope of actors critical to the legislative process includes an array of formal and informal players from inside and outside the institutions within which policy is made. The formal players represent the set of institutional actors with policy authority as defined by the United States Constitution, as well as those actors who assist these authorities in the design, adoption, implementation, and evaluation of public policy. Across all levels of government, from local to federal, elected officials, appointed officials, members of the judiciary, professional staff, and the bureaucracy represent the many sources of formal power that influence and shape the policy process from within the institutional arenas of government. Additionally, an eclectic array of informal actors, from interest groups, lobbyists, citizen activists, to the media, represent a particularly interesting and powerful force that seeks to influence and shape the policy process from outside the institutional arena.

Formal Players. At the federal level, the formal players relevant to the policy process represent an assortment of actors that operate with constitutional and extraconstitutional legitimacy within the institutional arenas of government. Most obvious to the policy process are the so-called "magic 537" formally elected federal officials critical to the legislative process.[11] Among the magic 537 are the 435 members of the House of Representatives, 100 senators, and the president and vice president. These 537 officials represent the core of formal players who, without question, are the foci of attention when exploring the significance and role of government within the policy process.

The magic 537 encapsulate two branches of the federal government—the legislative and the executive branch. With respect to the legislative branch, both the House of Representatives and the Senate represent uniquely different chambers in terms of procedures, politics, and stature. The Senate, for example, represents an institution in which each formal official enjoys considerable influence over the formulation and adoption of public policy. Senators, in particular, garner unique legislative influence through their limited numbers and the significant length of the six-year term in office. In contrast, members of the House of Representatives operate within a realm in which legislative specialization comes with the constraints that follow from greater party influence and a two-year elected term. As for the executive branch, the president and vice president not only lead this branch but also are often seen as the initiators of public policy. With respect to policy, the president and vice president provide policy direction and help define the set of policy and budget priorities to be debated within the legislature in a given fiscal year. Nevertheless, it is a unique set of extraconstitutional formal players that deserve specific attention in light of their profound impact on the public policy process.

Aside from the magic 537 that comprise the legislative and executive players, there are the untold thousands of additional formal players. Among the most important players are judicial officials, as well as the array of government officials and elected representatives from state and local governments. At the federal level, such players include appointed cabinet members, members of the civil service, hired professional committee staff, as well as House, Senate, and executive personal staff. Appointed cabinet members, for example, extend far beyond the actual cabinet officials, and include the many appointed undersecretaries, deputy undersecretaries, and advisors that permeate the top echelon of each of the respective federal bureaucracies. At the state and local levels, an array of appointed government officials and staff possess influence and power even though, in some cases, their power is based not on their office but on their ability to persuade the elected or appointed decision maker.

Overall, each of these formal players, whether elected or appointed, professional staff or temporary political appointee, enjoy various and sometimes considerable influence over the policy process. From beginning to end, this wide swath of formal players affects the evolution of public policy.

Informal Players. The informal players influencing the legislative process represent an array of actors that operate outside the institutional arenas of policy, but garner influence through their relationships, role, and access to the formal players. The panoply of these informal actors includes experts and academics, lobbyists, citizen activists, political consultants, interest groups, and the media. Experts and academics are often called on by presidents, cabinet officials, and members of Congress for their perspective, expertise, and analysis of issues and potential policy solutions. Lobbyists are employed to further or stymie the legislative interests of their clients. Political consultants, whether members of a specific political party or "hired guns," advise various officials in Congress or the executive branch on the prospective political costs or benefits from certain legislative and policy positions. Additionally, interest groups represent and attempt to further the legislative ends of their members throughout the institutional arena across an array of policy issues. Finally, the media provides information to the public, acts as a watchdog over government, and also represents the vehicle whereby formal and informal players attempt to make their case for or against public policy.

Although public policy is often thought of as the product of decisions made by government officials with the requisite author-

ity, the reality is that public policy is also sparked, influenced, designed, adopted, executed, and evaluated by an array of policy-making players of a formal and informal nature. Some actors may garner greater influence at certain periods of time, or at specific stages of the policy-making process; however, it is unquestionable that public policy results from the contribution of a vast array of players. Public policy, therefore, should be thought of as the actions and decisions taken as the result of formal and informal players operating within institutional and noninstitutional settings.

Types of Public Policies

Public policy is a label applied liberally to help describe the basic categories of government actions, legislation, or decision making. As reflected by the sheer scope and number of decisions, legislation, and actions taken by policy makers, it is evident that each type of policy can reflect a different purpose intended by the government entity. To assist in classifying these various public policies, a number of typologies can be found within the public policy literature (see Box 2.2).[12] The typologies discussed here are by no means exhaustive, but they do offer a foundation with which to begin to understand the varying types of public policies.

Substantive and Procedural Policies. A substantive policy is a tangible action undertaken by the government to deal with a particular policy problem. Substantive policies may assign benefits or costs, and can focus advantages or disadvantages toward specific target populations.[17] For example, constructing a new school, developing a new military aircraft, or lowering the state's blood–alcohol level for legal intoxication represent the potential variety of substantive policies.

Box 2.2   Policy Typologies

POLICY TYPE	DESCRIPTION	EXAMPLE OF POLICY	LITERATURE
Substantive	Specific actions, with costs and benefits, advantages and disadvantages	War, bombing	J. E. Anderson[13]
Procedural	Directions as to how substantive actions will be taken, specification of actor responsibility	Rules of war	
Redistributive	Reallocation of rights, monies, property to assist a specific individual/group segment of population	Social security program	T. J. Lowi[14]
Distributive	Allocation of goods, services for specific individual/group or segment of population	Farm subsidies	
Regulatory	Application of rules of behavior on industry, individuals, or groups	Airline safety regulations	
Self-regulatory[15]	Self-monitoring by individual/group		
Material	Provision of tangible costs or benefits, imposition of real disadvantages or advantages on a select actor or population	Food stamps program	M. Edelman[16]
Symbolic	Declaration or action without tangible disadvantages or advantages	Speech calling for "world peace"	

Procedural policies, in comparison, can establish a set of legislative criteria that prescribe the conditions and actors responsible for a policy action. Such procedural policies help determine which institutional or bureaucratic actors are responsible for particular policy areas, as well as outline the rules and regulations available to the administrative agency.

Aside from classifying public policy as substantive or procedural, another insightful typology defines public policy based on the social and economic effects on society, as well as the relationship between government and the target of the public policy.[18] Such a classification includes four categories: distributive, redistributive, regulatory, and self-regulatory.

Distributive Policies. Distributive public policies involve the assignment of goods and services to target populations specified by the government. The array of goods and services can vary greatly to include public monies, research grants, or tax deductions. With respect to target populations, benefits and services can serve specific groups or individuals. Politically, such distributive policies tend to be portrayed as "win-win" policies because benefits are targeted, whereas the various costs of such policies are sufficiently distributed to minimize or temper the potential for political opposition. Distributive programs and policies are likely to thrive within the legislative process because it is often difficult for opposition to emerge unless clear costs are associated with a specific policy. Not surprisingly, distributive policies reflect the power of traditional so-called "pork-barrel" projects.

Redistributive Policies. The most highly contentious of public policies fall within the rubric of redistributive policy. The explicit goal of redistributive policies is to shift resources, material benefits, rights, and privileges among the various population segments of the state. Traditionally, redistributive policies involve the reallocation of public or private resources from one particular class to another. In general, such redistributive policies are viewed along class lines, and reflect a desire for a more equitable allocation of resources with the polity. As a result, because specific target populations garner benefits at the expense of other target populations, redistributive policies are often the most politically charged of policies with segments of the population being proverbial "winners" and "losers."

Classic examples of redistributive policy include the Social Security Act, Medicare, Medicaid, as well as civil rights legislation. Each of these well-known areas of public policy reflect the government's position to prescribe a reallocation of state resources or specific rights to benefit sizeable segments of the population. Nonetheless, redistributive policies can also result in a reallocation of benefits that are specifically focused on a select few. For example, the bail-out of the Chrysler Corporation is an example of a redistributive policy that can benefit a select company.

Regulatory Policies. Regulatory policies represent governmentally mandated rules on the actions of specific target populations. The objective of regulatory policies is to either alter or restrict behaviors and practices that are deemed to have a negative effect on a given aspect of the society. For example, criminal statutes, gun control measures, and environmental protection reflect the various nature of regulatory measures. Overall, the political significance of such public policies emerges in light of the specific costs and distributed benefits that characterize regulatory policy.

Depending on the type of regulatory policy, and the costs imposed on specific target populations, the likelihood of political conflict can increase to counter or alter the type of regulations imposed. For instance, regulation of corporate practices or industrial development results in significant political reactions by such actors given the fiscal costs associated with increased regulation. In contrast, regulation of individual behavior, as evidenced by criminal statutes, may result in varied political reactions in light of the public's acceptance of costs imposed on types of behavior deemed unacceptable. Nevertheless, attempts to regulate certain personal behavior, such as the decision to terminate a pregnancy or the use of illegal drugs, can result in a more complex political dynamic as the actors involved may contest the policy value and moral righteousness of such regulation.

Self-Regulatory Policies. Self-regulatory policies represent an attempt to self-manage rules that restrict or control behavior by the actual target population. Various professions, from attorneys to medical doctors, will support public policies that impart licenses or other professional standards in order to regulate who, how, and when individuals become such professionals. Such self-regulation seeks to impose a level of costs deemed reasonable by the governing members of the professions. Self-regulation tends to benefit the regulated group because it often preempts the degree of regulation that might otherwise be imposed by the government.

Material and Symbolic Policies. Public policies may also be categorized as either material or symbolic. Such a classification highlights policies that contain either substantive effects or those with no allocation or assignment of costs or benefits. Material policies "provide tangible benefits or substantive power to their beneficiaries, or impose real disadvantages on those adversely affected."[19] A new regulation restricting car emissions is an example of a material policy. Such policies represent significant actions taken by government officials to address or redress a specific issue of concern.

In comparison, symbolic policies are principally rhetorical and seek to inform or persuade the population, often by presenting a particular point of view. Such policies can include a speech made commemorating an event or a statement of concern made by a president or adopted in a resolution by Congress. Such symbolic policies may attempt to appeal to the emotional or patriotic nature of the population. Recent examples of symbolic policies include resolutions and declarations made by senior policy makers calling on all Americans to stand united after the terrorist events of September 11, 2001. Additional statements after the attacks referred to the need for national unity, support of American troops, condemnation of the terrorist actions, as well as those public statements made to persuade Americans to venture out, travel, and help the nation's economy avoid recession.

The distinctions between material and symbolic policies are often one of degree. Many policies may be perceived as providing little benefit, resulting in no effects, and may appear to have little consequence on the various issues confronting the public. A material policy may become symbolic if it fails to be implemented after it is adopted. New administrations, for instance, will often rescind executive actions by the previous president, effectively making substantive changes to certain rules or regulations a symbolic statement. Additionally, symbolic policies can be translated into material policies if the issues

of concern require more substantial policy redress. For example, an initial condemnation of Iraq's invasion of Kuwait in 1990 was followed by more material policies and actions taken in the following months that led to the Persian Gulf War in 1991.

The previous descriptions of types of public policy might suggest an array of diverse policies. In actuality, each of these classifications offers a different perspective with which to understand the purpose and intent of public policy. Interestingly, each of the types, rather than competing with another, should be thought of as complementary to one another. Rather than consider the types of public policies as fitting a single classification, it may better serve the realities of the policy process to appreciate that many policies will reflect a number of types within a given policy action. In sum, public policies cannot be classified as one type exclusively, but reflect an array of descriptions befitting the complex and multipurpose nature of public policies within the political world. Thus, a policy could be classified as material in one situation and classified as something else in another situation.

Intended Course of Action

Each type of public policy, regardless of type or character, seeks to accomplish some end in relation to an identified problem. Of course, based on one's own perspective, certain policies may have seemingly significant or insignificant goals. Certain policy goals, and the actions taken to achieve them, are by definition dramatic public policies. The decisions to go to war in light of the attack on Pearl Harbor, to desegregate schools in the South, to establish Great Society programs in the 1960s, or to deregulate certain industries are dramatic policy actions. Explicit or implicit within these policy actions is the desire to achieve a prescribed goal through an intentional course of action. In other words, public policy actions do not simply materialize without thought nor are they accidents, but are reflective of the decisions taken by the various authorities to address a recognized issue or problem in a specified manner.

Every public policy, regardless of type or scope, will have a basic intent of achieving a specified outcome or stated goal in relation to a recognized policy problem. This policy goal is accomplished through the use of various policy instruments, such as laws, services, taxes, and monies. The art of creating public policy is that no scientific blueprint exists as to which instruments best address a policy problem. There is no roadmap that helps delineate which policy instruments to utilize, or how such instruments should be designed to solve a problem, or how to best achieve a desired policy goal. Still, which instruments are selected reflects an intentional course of action by the respective authorities, and provides insight into the logic and method by which certain policy goals might be achieved.

The evolution of policy action, in addressing a social, economic, or political issue, begins first with an identification of the problem, a statement of the policy change and goal desired, and specification of the instruments with which to achieve this change. The description of the goal, however, can range from the exact to the vague. For instance, reducing crime represents an often-stated policy and political goal. Stated as such, however, the goal remains vague. A more specific goal would seek to reduce the number of particular crimes, such as murder or rape, and by some specific percentage.

If a policy goal evolves from general to specific, the selection of instruments and the basis with which to evaluate success or failure becomes much clearer. Essentially, one can better gauge the success or failure of a policy goal when it is stated definitively. In terms of the selection of instruments, a clear policy goal provides added focus for which instruments may best serve the desired ends.

B. Guy Peters describes an array of policy instruments available to the policy maker, including laws, services, monies, taxes, and suasion.[20] **Laws** are legislative decrees backed by the enforcement power of the state. Still, laws, even backed by sufficient enforcement, may not address the quandary of civil disobedience or the possibility that individuals willingly choose to break the law in light of minimal consequences. **Services** can be thought of as instruments whereby the state attempts to provide a service that cannot be readily delivered by the private sector, or which is seen as being more equally delivered by the state than the private sector, such as utilities. The provision of **monies** may seek to further certain goals by transferring or reallocating public funds to private individuals in pursuit of policy goals. The reallocation of public funds, whether in terms of federal programs like social security or block and categorical grants provided to states for various programs, is usually an attempt to improve a social and economic condition that affects some segment of society.

Taxes can and do alter behavior of individuals by encouraging certain desired behaviors through deductions or penalties. Also, taxes provide the means by which the state garners the essential monies necessary to support each and every other policy instrument. **Suasion** refers to the attempt to achieve certain goals by promoting or encouraging behavior through appeals to patriotism or other emotional sources for action. There are additional policy tools that we will discuss in Chapter 8 on policy design and formulation.

Although the policy instrument represents the means by which policy makers achieve their desired policy ends, it is still the specificity of the expected goal that provides the basis for judging success and failure. Vague goals cloud the measure of success or failure. A vague policy goal adds to the confusion as to which instruments offer the best means to address the policy problem. Specific goals, even though advantageous from one perspective, do not fully address the political consequences that may come if success and failure of a policy can be easily determined. Thus, an inevitable tension exists in the policy process between the policy value of clear goals versus the political value of vague goals.

In a perfect policy world, instruments would be perfectly interlocked with the understanding of the problem in order to achieve a stated goal. In the reality of the political world within which the policy process operates, instruments are often mismatched with a poorly misunderstood problem designed to achieve a vague goal. The consequence of this dynamic mismatch between problems, instruments, and goals is to impede the ability of the policy to achieve the desired action. In other words, poor public policy is not simply an accident, but a byproduct of the political failings that exist within the policy-making process.

Intentional and Unintentional Consequences

Once a policy decision is made, and the set of instruments are selected, some consequence will result from the policy action. No policy action, once executed, fails to have any impact whatsoever. Every public policy, once decided on and executed, can alter the administrative environment, alter the political interest of certain stakeholders within and outside government, deplete or redirect limited resources away from other areas, or heighten the interest of the public or media in a specific issue. Realistically, government policies will have some consequence, and the question becomes whether the action resulted in intentional consequences as desired by the decision maker, unintentional consequences unforeseen by the decision maker, or whether some degree of both types of consequences arose from the introduction of the policy.

With respect to intentional consequences, a policy seeks to achieve some stated goal. If the policy issue deals with the poor, and the program is food stamps, the intentional consequence desired is a reduction in the number of poor adults, children, and families who are hungry. Sometimes a public policy does not achieve the intended consequences because the nature of legislation, the structure of the program created, the rules and regulations governing the program, as well as the success in implementing and evaluating the program, may lead to a set of unintended consequences. For example, if a food stamp program disallows legal immigrants, then a class of individuals that may be poor and hungry will not qualify for assistance. Additionally, if abuse or waste, either by the administrative agency or the user of food stamps, leads to a misdirection of monies away from the purchasing of necessary food stuffs, then not only will a problem not be solved but it may also result in additional unforeseen, sometimes costly, unintended consequences.

Although unintended by the initial designers and decision makers of this policy, an unintentional consequence of the food stamps program was the creation of a secondary black market in which food stamps were used to trade and purchase goods other than foods. As a result, already limited resources were wasted, criminal behavior and abuse related to the food stamps program arose, the positive perception of the program was damaged, and the success of the program was diminished. Yet, aside from the example of the food stamps program, it is unlikely that any program or policy action can sidestep some degree of unintended consequences.

A public policy is an attempt to solve a problem that may be intrinsically complex and difficult to fully understand. As such, the design of solutions, driven by politics, the legislative process, and administrative realities, may not effectively address the nature of the problem and its actual causes. Quite simply, certain public policies are just bad policy solutions. The ripple effects of the policy may result in new problems. Although the policy may have been designed and intended as a solution, the reality is that no effects of a policy solution can be perfectly foreseen until the policy is introduced. Past experience, policy research, expertise among the actors, and simple logic may all suggest that the policy action is indeed the right solution, with the intended consequences fully understood and realized; however, it still may prove to be a failure once implemented.

Seldom will policy problems, as complex as child poverty, adult illiteracy, youth unemployment, urban pollution, gun-related violence, or traffic congestion, remain static and unchanged. Moreover, it is unclear beforehand how administrative difficulties, regional socioeconomic differences, and the nature of the problem may impact the policy solution. As a result, even the supposed best solution, well designed and politically supported, may result in some negative consequences that are fully appreciated only once the policy is put into action. This realization, that policies will likely have both intended and unintended consequences, helps emphasize the obstacles and difficulties in addressing any specific policy problem.

Policy Making as a Process

Effectively describing policy making as a process captures its proverbial method and madness, and has inspired a series of theoretical approaches to understanding the process. These theoretical approaches represent a series of abstract phases on stages for how public policy develops within the American political system. Many of these approaches, which will be discussed in later chapters, provide a pattern or framework within which the student can understand the evolution of public policy. In reality, seldom does the process work in the exact manner described by any one theory. Nevertheless, for the student of policy, such theoretical models prove invaluable. Although no one theory may prove to be perfectly reflective of the policy and political realities, each theory can offer insights and a perspective that is essential to learning the many dimensions that are intrinsic to the field of public policy.

To observers of the policy-making world, the policy process appears as a jumbled maze and a process almost absent any pattern.[21] Clearly, the evolution of policy is not simple, nor is there any single standard evolutionary path. Each respective public policy, whether falling under the broad rubrics of foreign, social, or economic policy, is virtually unique in the manner in which it can develop. Nevertheless, politics and perceptions aside, it is of value to explore the process as if it developed along a series of fluid policy stages. This text, although acknowledging and discussing a multitude of theories of the policy process, utilizes a **policy cycle,** or **stages–heuristic,** approach to understanding American policy making (see Figure 2.2).

Briefly, the policy cycle approach identifies the public policy process as an evolutionary cycle. Under the policy cycle approach, the policy process is assessed along

---

A. Predecision Phase
1. Problem definition
2. Agenda setting
3. Policy formulation
B. Decision Phase
4. Policy adoption
C. Postdecision Phase
5. Policy implementation
6. Policy evaluation
7. Policy change or policy termination

FIGURE 2.2 Policy Cycle (Stages-Heuristic) Approach

a series of abstract phases and stages by which policy emerges, develops, and changes within the given polity. As a methodological approach, the policy cycle deconstructs the policy process in a manner most conducive to understanding how private issues evolve into public and political concerns, how the legislative process structures political concerns into legislative proposals and law, how such laws are formulated and put into effect, as well as how such policies are evaluated and may eventually change or end.

The policy cycle can also be broadly characterized by a series of phases labeled as predecision, decision, and postdecision. Each of these respective phases includes policy stages. Specifically, within the predecision phase, analytical attention focuses on the identification of a policy problem, the agenda setting of issues, and the formulation and design of policy solutions. At the decision phase, policy adoption explores the legislative actions that government actors undertake to address specific policy problems. Finally, during the postdecision phase, we see the necessity of policy implementation, the role of policy evaluation, and the decision to change or terminate a policy.

By focusing on each of these phases, and the various additional stages, students may come to understand how policies originate, develop, and grow in a step-by-step process. Although no method is perfect, the policy cycle approach offers students a solid, practical tool with which to understand the dynamics and structure of American policy making.

SUMMARY

Public policy is a multifaceted and theoretically complex concept. Public policy raises attention to the many facets and dimensions underscoring the seeming simplicity of policy decisions, the array of actors involved, the set of instruments available, and the goal for what the policy is intended to accomplish within the polity. This entire process is captured within a series of policy stages in which societal issues evolve from an awareness of a problem to the formulation of solutions, to the adoption of a certain course of action, to implementation and evaluation of policy programs, to the eventual change or termination in public policy. In short, public policy is a sequential pattern of activity that hinges upon the interplay of actors, the environment, and the realities of politics that interjects at all times throughout this evolutionary process of policy making.

DISCUSSION QUESTIONS

1. Is policy simply the passing of legislation? What does public policy represent and imply within the political system?

2. Is public policy only what government has chosen to do, or does the decision not to act represent an even more profound action?

3. When looking at who makes and influences public policy, who are the most influential set of players? Is it more important to look at the role played by informal actors or formal actors?

4. In spite of the different ways to classify policy, in the end the most important classification scheme is the effect and purpose of a specific policy. Discuss this statement.

5. List and describe the public policies that you believe have had an intentional and unintentional effect on your life. What tangible effect have these policies had on you and your interests? Discuss.

SUGGESTED READINGS

Anderson, J. E. *Public Policymaking.* 3rd ed. Boston: Houghton Mifflin, 1997.

Dye, T. R. *Top-Down Policymaking.* New York: Chatham House, 2001.

Dye, T. R. *Understanding Public Policy.* 7th ed. Englewood Cliffs, NJ: Prentice Hall, 1992.

Lester, James P. and Joseph Stewart, Jr. *Public Policy: An Evolutionary Approach.* Minneapolis: West
Publishing, 1995.

Lester, James P., and Martin A. Levin, eds. *The New Politics of Public Policy.* Baltimore: Johns Hopkins University Press, 1995.

McCool, D. C. *Public Policy Theories, Models, and Concepts.* Englewood Cliffs, NJ: Prentice Hall, 1995.

Peters, B. G. *American Public Policy.* 4th ed. Chatham, NJ: Chatham House, 1996.

Theodoulou, S. Z., and Mathew A. Cahn. *Public Policy: The Essential Readings.* Englewood Cliffs, NJ: Prentice Hall, 1995.

ENDNOTES

1. D. C. McCool, *Public Policy Theories, Models, and Concepts* (Englewood Cliffs, NJ: Prentice Hall, 1995), 8–15.

2. T. R. Dye, *Understanding Public Policy* (Englewood Cliffs, NJ: Prentice Hall, 1987), 2–3.

3. C. E. Cochran et al., *American Public Policy—An Introduction* (New York: St. Martin's Press, 1999), 1.

4. Ibid., 1.

5. Ibid., 1.

6. Ibid., 1.

7. B. G. Peters, *American Public Policy—Promise and Performance,* 5th ed. (Chatham, NJ: Chatham House, 1999), 4.

8. Ibid., 4.

9. J. E. Anderson, *Public Policymaking* (New York: Houghton Mifflin, 1997), 9.

10. S. Theodoulou, "The Nature of Public Policy," in S. Theodoulou and M. Cahn, *Public Policy—The Essential Readings* (Englewood Cliffs, NJ: Prentice Hall, 1995), 1.

11. In conversations with staffers, this was the term used to describe the 537 elected officials in the executive and legislative branches of government.

12. A number of typologies are referenced in the literature. See B. G. Peters, *American Public Policy,* 4th ed. (Chatham, NJ: Chatham House, 1996); J. E. Anderson, *Public Policymaking,* T. R. Dye, *Understanding Public Policy,* 7th ed. (Englewood Cliffs, NJ: Prentice Hall, 1992); A. L. Schneider and H. Ingram, *Policy Design for Democracy* (Lawrence: University Press of Kansas, 1997).

13. Anderson, *Public Policymaking,* 12–25.

14. T. J. Lowi, "American Business, Public Policy Case Studies, and Political Theory," *World Politics* XVI (July 1964): 677–715.

15. R. H. Salisbury, "The Analysis of Public Policy: A Search for Theories and Models," in S. Theodoulou and M. Cahn, eds., *Public Policy,* 34–38.

16. Murray Edelman, "Symbols and Political Quiescence," in S. Theodoulou and M. Cahn, eds., *Public Policy,* 26–33.

17. Anderson, *Public Policymaking,* 12–25.

18. Peters, *American Public Policy.*

19. Anderson, *Public Policymaking,* 18.

20. Peters, *American Public Policy.*

21. Insight derived by Dr. Chris Kofinis from interviews with members of Congress, former members of Congress, congressional staffers, and professional lobbyists between spring 1997 and spring 2001. Research was conducted in Washington, DC, in relation to this book, and papers being developed on legislative strategy and the public policy process.

3

The Where

Institutional Structure, Legislative Centers, and Policy Arenas

We the People of the United States, in Order to form a more
perfect Union, establish Justice, insure domestic Tranquility,
provide for the common defense, promote the general Welfare,
and secure the Blessings of Liberty to ourselves and our
Posterity, do ordain and establish this Constitution for the
United States of America.

PREAMBLE TO THE U.S. CONSTITUTION

With its ratification in 1789, the U.S. Constitution established the enduring duality of a fixed structure and a fluid framework for American politics and policy. The fixed nature of American politics was institutionalized through a specific governmental structure and legislative process defined by a written constitution. In comparison, the fluid nature of American politics and policy making was established through a political process that extends beyond the confines of governing institutions and structural boundaries and includes the public and interest groups.[1] Hence, the answer to the question of *where does American policy making occur* is not as simple as referring to the language of the Constitution, or as obvious as identifying the three branches of the federal government.

To better understand where public policy occurs, one must recognize that modern American politics and policy making operates beyond and within the institutional structure established by the Constitution. The critical elements that can help us better understand where policy making occurs include the role of the public, the system of checks and balances, the separation of powers, federalism, and policy arenas—also referred to as subgovernments or issue networks.[2] The interplay between institutional power and politics, the dynamics between various policy actors and the legislative process, as well as the basic institutional structure of American government can help explain *where* public policy is made. Overall, the language of the Constitution not only provides the basic institutional framework for where policy making occurs but has further ensured that the policy process extends beyond the formal constitutional structure of American government.

UNDERSTANDING THE WHERE OF AMERICAN POLICY MAKING

American policy making is based on a specific structure and process outlined by the Constitution. The Constitution can be described as both a basic blueprint and a living document of the policy process. As a blueprint, the Constitution has helped define the basic legislative process, as well as the power and roles of various policy actors and institutions. However, the Constitution is also a living document that has evolved over time to address fundamental changes in society and in governing. Since 1787, diverse amendments have sought to revise the nature of the Constitution and the society it governs. Similarly, political parties and committees have emerged as powerful forces within American politics and policy making even though they remain unmentioned in the formal language of the Constitution.

Still, this remarkably "simple document" which provided a constitutional framework for governing, and that continues to evolve to reflect new sociopolitical realities, remains institutionally identical in its basic structure.[3] Although subsequent amendments have addressed issues such as slavery, voting, presidential succession, representation, and the rights and freedoms of the American people, not a single amendment has altered the basic structural framework initially outlined by the framers. In fact, what is unique about the U.S. Constitution is that it is largely unaltered since its adoption in 1787.

In terms of its character, the Constitution is a written mixture of specific and equivocal sections that includes both direct and indirect elected representation, demands different and conflicting roles from each branch of government, separates power between state and federal levels, and provides a forum for the evolution of various policy arenas. Ironically, it is a constitution that seems to have created a set of policy-making contradictions. These constitutional contradictions have all but ensured a policy-making process that seems almost self-defeating: No matter where policy making may occur, no actor or branch of government will have or hold exclusive policy-making power over all others. In the end, neither governing nor policy making is entirely effective or efficient under the system of government established by the Constitution.

The Constitution established an entire political system that is essentially in conflict with itself. In general, the legislative structure of American government is designed to be inefficient to promote governmental stability over the threats posed by more dramatic and immediate policy actions. Policy making, and the influences on policy making, seems to occur almost everywhere with little ability to hinder the influence or effects of competing branches of government or policy actors. Thus, great changes in public policy are rare unless extenuating political circumstances

---

> ### Box 3.1   Structural Elements to American Government
>
> - Public arena—direct and indirect elected representation
> - Separation of powers and checks and balances
> - Federalism
> - Policy arenas and subgovernments

---

emerge. Ironically, under certain political conditions, such as crisis, the structure of American government can respond quickly and can prove to be an efficient policy-making system. The point is, policy making operates within an expansive circle, and defining the *where* is a task that requires attention to a series of structural elements.

Structurally, the Constitution designed a national government where representation and the electoral role played by the public would vary, where powers were separated among governments and institutions, where institutional power was checked and balanced, and where the relationships to government and policy making included policy arenas that extended beyond the set structure of American government. Hence, to better understand the *where* of American policy making, we will discuss the following structural elements (see Box 3.1).

PUBLIC ARENA—DIRECT AND INDIRECT ELECTED REPRESENTATION

A central tenet of the legitimacy of American policy making rests on the public granting the rightful authority to elected representatives to govern them. The election of governing representatives, their role

and purpose, has long been an issue of theoretical and practical debate.[4] Theorists such as Plato, Aristotle, and Polybius have long debated the value versus the danger posed by democratic governance.[5] The framers debated these same concerns.

For American politics, the democratic method by which citizens are able to check the power of elected representatives is critical to understanding where policy making begins and where it ends. Moreover, elected representation proves central to explaining how policy develops and can be characterized. However, contrary to many perceptions, American policy making is not founded on clearly democratic terms. Rather, the founders designed a national government in which the public did not necessarily elect all of the representatives that would govern over them.[6]

The election of representatives by the citizenry and the differentiation between how the various levels of national government would be elected reflect the enduring duality to American government: It is founded on both direct and indirect elected representation. Through such representation, American policy making exists as a pluralistic endeavor in which direct and indirect political pressure by the public would constrain the actions of policy makers. Yet, because of the varied structure of representation adopted by the Constitution, policy decisions would not escape political constraints, but would also not be a prisoner to them. The resulting structure, in other words, balanced the degree of elected representation perceived essential for legitimacy against the degree of elected representation that would make government too responsive to the demands of the public. American government, as such, is not a direct democracy of the people, but is a republic in which semblances of democratic governance exist (see Box 3.2).

To balance the necessities of democracy and liberty, the framers designed a national

---

Box 3.2   Republicanism vs. Democracy

Republicanism	Democracy
Government by popular consent	Government by popular consent
Indirect rule by representatives	Rule by people—direct or indirect
Eligible electorate is strictly defined	Eligible electorate is broadly defined
Elected representatives act as trustees	Elected representatives act as delegates
Minority and majority rule	Majority rule supercedes minority rule
Limited government	Responsive government
Safeguards rights and freedoms	Safeguards rights and freedoms

SOURCE: Adapted from Edward S. Greenberg and Benjamin Pape, *The Struggle for Democracy*, 4th ed. (New York: Longman, 1999), 36.

Box 3.3   Elected Representation and the Influence on Policy Makers

BRANCH OF GOVERNMENT	METHOD OF ELECTION	PUBLIC'S INFLUENCE	TERM OF OFFICE
Senate	Indirect*	Indirect*	6 years
House of Representatives	Direct	Direct	2 years
Judiciary	Nonelected	Indirect	Lifetime
Presidency	Indirect	Direct	4–8 years
Executive branch (bureaucracy)	Nonelected	Indirect	? years

*Direct elections of senators was instituted under the Seventeenth Amendment adopted in 1913.

---

government in which the direct policy power of the public was checked through elected representation (see Box 3.3). The resulting formula for governing reflected a balance between the fears of an unbridled direct democracy, or a tyranny of the majority, with the necessity that a legitimate government must grant the public a means to check those who govern them. As Robert Dahl stated, "To achieve their goal of preserving a set of inalienable rights superior to the majority principle . . . the framers deliberately created a framework of government that was carefully designed to impede and even prevent the operation of majority rule."[7] As a consequence, the resulting national government included both direct and indirect representation ensuring that the public would possess varying degrees of influence over institutions and decision makers.[8]

The indirect and direct nature of representation emerged out of a desire of the framers to ensure the legitimacy of the national government while mitigating the power of the masses that could threaten stability of the government. Indirect representation means that the power of the public to directly influence policy making would be limited in specific branches of the government. Because an electoral role for the public was provided in American government, it has ensured that the citizenry can still hold responsible many of the critical policy actors who govern them. Although the constitution purposely limits a more dominant role by the public, the necessity of popular support has ensured that policy makers—such as members of Congress and the president—can seldom escape the electoral constraints of the people.

Because popular support is the bedrock to U.S. republic democracy, it is difficult to avoid the influence, or potential influence, of the people in policy making when it manifests. The Congress and the president are often greatly affected by the manner in which the public can hold them accountable for policy decisions. Public opinion, as indicated by polling results, public protests, letter campaigns, or organized marches, can provide powerful constraints on the policy process. Whereas the judicial and executive branches may be exposed to less direct pressure than the legislative branch, the foundation of shared governance ensures that each action taken by a branch of the national government is, or can become, an electoral issue. No bureaucratic agency or federal court can ignore the political pressure from elected officials that can and does emerge in light of public pressures. As a consequence, *where* policy making occurs, in part, is within an inescapable public realm.

Although the Constitution ensures a role for the public in the policy-making process, the potential for influence does not always manifest. Given the lack of voting among registered voters, as well as the low rates of general political participation, it is debatable whether and to what extent the public influences the policy process. Nevertheless, one should not confuse what is the ideal level of public participation in the political process, with the realization that at any given moment some segment of the public—large or small—can actively attempt to define or alter the course of the policy process. Again, one cannot ignore that policy making does indeed occur within a public arena, even though many members of the public may choose not to include themselves. Policy making, therefore, is not simply an institutional or procedural exercise. Rather, policy making develops within a greater political arena in which the public proves critical to the manner and content of public policy. In short, American policy making is as much about the institutions that make policy as it is about the role of the public in making policy.

SEPARATION OF POWERS AND CHECKS AND BALANCES

Underscoring the concerns with popular sovereignty, and the role of the public in governing, the Constitution further seeks to counter any concentration of policy-making power. The separation of powers, and the systematic series of checks and balances, created the context for the development of an offsetting institutional structure in which national policy making involves a series of institutional partners. At the federal level, each of the three branches, the executive, judicial, and legislative, possesses significant power to make policy although it is checked and balanced by the other branches of the government.

The separation of powers is an organizational method for government that ensures that no one institution possesses absolute policy-making power.[9] Rather, at the federal level, policy-making power is diffused among the three branches. The resulting compromise creates a republic that is effective and efficient to a degree, but which lacks a concentration of power that allows the federal government to be too efficient and effective in policy making. Interestingly, designing a more efficient government would require a greater concentration of policy-making power within one of three branches of government.

An efficient government system cannot diffuse political or policy-making power among too many parties, institutions, or branches of government. In particular, the greater the role played by the public, as in direct democracy, the more inefficient the governing system becomes. However, too much power in a few hands can lead to brutish, albeit efficient, policy-making regimes. Again, the trade-off is between ensuring legitimacy through an active role by the public in policy making and risking stability if the public is intimately involved in all facets of the policy process. Perplexingly, the most oppressive and undemocratic of regimes can also be considered some of the most efficient policy-making systems (see Figure 3.1).

Dictatorships or totalitarian regimes, for example, are far more efficient policy-making systems, but are the least democratic (see Figures 3.1 and 3.2). Parliamentary systems, in which majority power is held by a single party, also tend to be more efficient because of the fusion of the executive and legislative policy-making power in one branch of government.[10] A parliamentary system in which the government is based on multiparty coalition governments can prove to be either efficient or inefficient depending on the unity of the coalition. In contrast, American government is a system of government that was purposely designed to be structurally inefficient, but does not preclude the potential for efficient policy making.

Because of the separation of powers and checks and balances, American government can generally be described as an inefficient system of governance. Ironically, by adopting

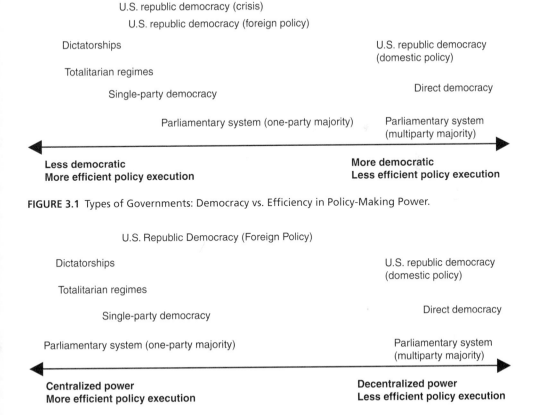

FIGURE 3.1 Types of Governments: Democracy vs. Efficiency in Policy-Making Power.

FIGURE 3.2 Types of Governments: Concentration of Institutional Policy Making.

a republic democracy the framers all but in-stitutionalized an inefficient system of federal policy making. Nevertheless, what is inter-esting about the American policy process is that depending on the policy issue and the politics involved, American government can transform itself into a quite efficient govern-ing system (see Figures 3.1 and 3.2).

Depending on the issue, whether it is a matter of foreign policy or crisis of some kind, American government can be an effi-cient policy-making system. Although checks and balances may guard against the legislative tyranny of one institution over an-other, and even though it comes with a price on the usual capacity of the government to govern more efficiently, the American sys-tem of government does not prevent effi-cient policy making (see Figure 3.2).

Within American government, efficient policy making can emerge depending on the issue and politics. For example, the president is primarily responsible for addressing for-eign policy and national security matters. Within this policy area, more efficient pol-icy making exists because the president has the constitutional power to identify prob-lems, set the foreign policy agenda, formu-late options, adopt courses of action, as well as order the implementation of specific pol-icy actions. Although the role of the presi-dent in national security matters has evolved over the last two hundred years, there are few explicit constitutional checks on the president's power to manage matters of for-eign policy and national security. This is not to suggest that a president can operate free of oversight by the other branches of govern-ment or can ignore the will and influence of the public. Public pressure, congressional oversight, and judicial review can temper and constrain the president's management of foreign policy. In particular, the degree of public support, or the lack of it, can repre-sent one of the greatest checks on the presi-dent's policy-making power in matters of foreign policy or national security.[11]

Domestic Policy Arenas

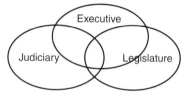

National Security or "Crisis" Policy Arena

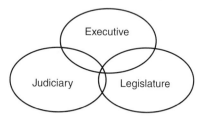

FIGURE 3.3 Government Structure and Circles of Policy Making.

The structure of American government also allows the executive branch to garner considerable policy-making influence at particular times—for example, during crisis or war (see Figure 3.3). Again, depending on the circumstances, American govern-ment can be either an efficient or inefficient system of governance.

The apparent inefficiency of American policy making can be overcome by the emergence of (a) coalitions of broad politi-cal support within the legislative and the ex-ecutive branch, or (b) a unifying national crisis that compels each branch to cooperate with one another. Each of these circum-stances helps us understand how American government can—when compelled—work beyond structural obstacles, like a separation of powers, that otherwise complicate effi-cient governing.

Coalitions of Broad Political Support

Because of institutional divisions in Ameri-can government, efficient policy making of-ten requires a coalition of broad political support across the two branches most critical to the legislative process—the executive and the legislative. In other words, unless one political party enjoys supermajorities in both the Senate and the House, the same party controls the presidency, and both institutions agree on the policy in question, efficient policy making will require a broad coalition of political support across all actors and institutions.

What is a broad coalition of political support? A simplistic picture of the legislative process presupposes that a majority in the Senate, a majority in the House, and the president's signature represents the essential winning political coalition. In the case of a presidential veto, a supermajority of two thirds would seem to represent the winning political coalition. The realities of modern American politics, however, make it clear that developing a winning political coalition demands compromise across and within institutions to foster consensus among the political parties, party leadership, senior committee members, the president, and the various public constituencies that are active in the policy process.

The leadership of the political parties, for instance, cannot impose its policy preferences on fellow party members. Individual senators, whether members of the majority or not, possess considerable power over how the legislative process proceeds within the Senate. A single senator, for example, by filibustering legislation or placing riders can greatly complicate the efficiency of the policy process. Committee members, especially senior members, possess considerable power over the language of legislation considered for adoption. By setting the legislative calendar, party leadership in both chambers can influence the order and timing in which policy issues are considered for action. In the House of Representatives, although party line votes are common and party leadership is generally more successful in whipping up support, there are no procedural rules or institutional customs that prevent House members from opposing the policy proposals of their own party.

A president, in comparison, often requires the support of members from both parties and the support from senior members to successfully achieve a policy agenda. Finally, because of the direct influence of various constituencies over elected members, all members of Congress and the president must consider the role and influence of various interests groups, associations, and individual citizens that have a stake in the policy process. Therefore, dramatic actions in current policies demand that a substantial degree of cooperation manifests among all the relevant policy actors across party affiliation.

Successfully weathering the structural obstacles of the legislative process demands the close cooperation and a broad coalition among a number of political actors. Essentially, the stronger the political coalition, the greater the consensus, and the more likely the system will operate efficiently. However, such cooperation across all branches of government is the exception rather than the rule as the average policy issue does not foster such unifying cooperation and consensus among otherwise conflicted political actors. Ironically, the most efficient policy making may best emerge under the worst of circumstances—a national crisis.

The Unifying Political Force of National Crisis

National crisis represents that rare occurrence that compels the critical legislative actors to favor action versus inaction, and to favor change versus the status quo. The national events that can inspire dramatic and immediate policy consensus and political cooperation include such diverse incidents as natural disasters, ecological disasters, health epidemics, economic depression, civil unrest, terrorist attacks, war, or threat of war

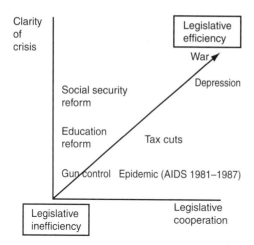

FIGURE 3.4 National Crisis and Efficient vs. Inefficient Policy Making.

(see Figure 3.4). Such issues represent clear incidents that demand action and expose the actors involved to the political consequences from perceived inaction. In other words, even if they choose, elected actors cannot easily ignore an event or issue that is of grave significance for the state.

A national crisis serves as an accelerant that leads to more efficient policy making by raising the legislative role of the presidency, while also compelling the competing political parties and members of Congress to cooperate with the initiatives proposed. Essentially, a crisis overcomes the constitutional separation of powers that, in its absence, ensures a more methodical, contemplative, incremental, often frustrating and debate-filled policy process. Moreover, a truly severe crisis, such as September 11, weakens the checks and balances that were constitutionally intended to impede such efficient policy making. Such a crisis, highlighted by the exigency of the event, compels the institutions and the various actors to cooperate—even among competing factions—and reach consensus within a shortened time frame.

Essential to this crisis dynamic is that a semblance of clarity emerges among the critical policy actors and institutions involved as to the seriousness of the specific event or issue for the nation. Most policy issues, although arguably significant for the specific groups or populations affected, are not often seen as representing a national crisis of such consequence that immediate action is essential. In reality, few policy issues garner such a stature. Ironically, whereas many advocates, within and out of the government, may strive to frame an issue of concern as a "national crisis," few issues seem to garner the clarity or consensus that emerges with a *true* crisis.

The power of a crisis, if and when it occurs, is that it brings overwhelming clarity to the policy debate, compels action regardless of the perfectibility of the proposed solution, and reduces the inevitable politicking and institutional trade-offs that are endemic to the normal legislative process. A "true" national crisis fuels cooperation and tends to ensure that immediate policy actions are taken to redress the consequences of the event.

Although the legislative significance of crises should not be discounted, their rarity in occurrence, coupled with the intrinsic subjectivity of such events, suggests that their effect on the legislative process is rare and fleeting.[12] The cooperation and clarity, which can aid legislative efficiency, occurs for as long as the crisis exists—whether in terms of perception or reality. Once the consequences and severity of the crisis are diminished, some decline in legislative cooperation is inevitable. Moreover, as the crisis declines in significance, the method of policy making snaps back to its more methodical and incremental nature.

The structural reality of the American legislative process is that most public policies must weather the considerable trials and tribulations of a constitutional structure that is designed and inclined to hinder legislative initiatives and dramatic policy actions. Not surprisingly, the statistical reality is that only a small percentage of the bills introduced within Congress become law, and the historical trend is that a smaller percentage of bills introduced are in fact becoming law.[13] Arguably, what the separation of powers has wrought is a system of governance that all but ensures inefficient policy making, except under rare circumstances where broad coalitions or crises can inspire more efficient cooperation. Interestingly, it is this very policy-making reality, in which no branch or actor has ultimate control or power, even if it is at the expense of more efficient governing, that the framers sought and established. Again, in light of where policy making occurs, given the separation of powers, and the rarity of crisis and coalitions of support, it is clear that the policy process extends throughout and across a federal structure that all but ensures a slow and incremental policy process.

FEDERALISM

The separation of powers within the federal government across three branches of government is complemented by a separation of powers between the federal and state governments. The division of policy-making power between states and the federal government helps to further explain the considerable structural complexity to American policy making. The American federal system can be compared to two other forms of government and sovereign power sharing: a confederation and a unitary government (see Figure 3.5).

Confederations represent a type of government in which the balance of sovereign and policy-making power is skewed toward local or state units. Under a confederation, for instance, the central government exists as a creature of the states or local entities, and

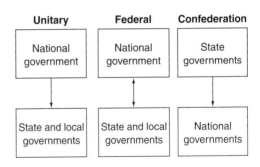

FIGURE 3.5 National Governing Arrangements.

tends to perform perfunctory roles deemed and defined by the states. The United States, under the Articles of Confederation, was an example of a confederation.

Within a confederation, the implications for policy making are that each of the states can pursue an independent course of action that complicates the development of a national or comprehensive policy that serves the whole nation. As under the 1781 Articles of Confederation, emerging divisions in policies, rules, and regulations weakened the collective ties and endangered the bind between states and the national government. In terms of efficiency or effectiveness in national policy making, such a system of government appears to severely weaken, or at least greatly complicate, the goal of national cohesion. In contrast, the unitary form of government is designed to focus sovereign power of the government under a central body, while supplanting the role of states under this central government.

Under a unitary system of government, a central government possesses ultimate sovereign power over all other government entities within the state. Under a unitary government, directions in policy making are made by the central government. Whereas consideration may be given to local preferences or perspectives, the central government remains the primary arbiter of the direction that policy making will undertake.

The United Kingdom is a classic example of a unitary system of government.

The implications for policy making from a unitary system of government are quite distinct. Centralization of policy-making power within one level of government, with the authority to impose its policies, rules, and regulations on lower units, provides the opportunity for more efficient and comprehensive policy actions. In the absence of the countervailing power of other sovereign actors, the central government can pursue clear courses of actions with little concern about the preferences of lesser bodies. The trade-off for the opportunity for such efficient governing, however, is that with greater national power to govern more freely at the national level comes the concern over how such policy power will be utilized. The imposition of national policy can come at the expense of the preferences of states or lesser governments. Such imposition raises concerns that the liberty of states and individuals will and can be disregarded.

The American system of government is a federal system of government. Theoretically, a federal system is based on a sharing of sovereign power between states and lower units of government and the central government. This system of government is designed to divide responsibilities between the central and state governments, while maintaining an effective balance that will serve both the liberty of states and the stability of the nation. Division is based on constitutional power, with each level of government possessing sovereign responsibility within roughly defined circles of public policy, while also enjoying concurrent and exclusive sovereign power in other policy areas.

An accurate description of American federalism would emphasize that policy power, although divided to some explicit degree between states and the federal level, is a far more fluid division of power. As it has been suggested by others, federalism "resembles a marble cake, where functions and financing are shared between national, state, and local governments."[14] In actuality, it may be best to describe modern American federalism as an explosion of governing centers, all of which can and do play an intricate role in the policy process.

Over 80,000 Legislative Centers and Counting

American policy making extends beyond a central government and fifty states to include thousands of local governments. Over the last two hundred years, the growth of American government has occurred not in the federal bureaucracy, but in the bureaucracies of the states and cities.[15] Moreover, the legislative centers of American public policy are by no means simply fixed within the central government, nor are they neatly defined to each level of government—federal, state, or local. Rather, the U.S. Constitution ensures that the role of states, as with the role of the central government, remain fluid, more ambiguous than definitive, adapting to changing circumstances both within the nation and across the political spectrum.[16] Thus, a more accurate modern image of American federalism identifies the substantial number of local governments that are critical to American governance and the policy-making process (see Figure 3.6).

What is intriguing about American federalism is the degree to which the Constitution defines, and leaves open to interpretation, the complex relationship between federal and state governments. The powers of the central government are derived from a fusion of expressed and inherent powers. Article 1, Section 8 of the Constitution specifies the enumerated powers given to the national government. These expressed powers include the sovereign responsibility over, for example, the coinage of money, the declaration of war, regulation of interstate com-

Classic image of American federalism

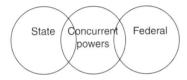

Reality of American federalism

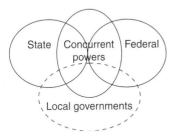

FIGURE 3.6 Theoretical and Policy Reality of Federalism.

merce, and the levy and collection of taxes. Underscoring these expressed powers is the flexibility provided by the implied powers of the national government that fall under Article 1, Section 8, Clause 18, and is commonly referred to as the "necessary and proper clause" or "elastic clause":

> To make all Laws which shall be necessary and proper for carrying into Execution the foregoing powers, and all other Powers vested by this Constitution in the Government of the United States, or in any Department or Officer thereof.

The implication of the elastic clause for American federalism is distinct. Although open to continuing debate over the last two hundred years, the constitutional interpretation of the elastic clause has helped define the expansion of the power of the national government. Specifically, the elastic clause may be interpreted to mean that Congress shall be given those powers that can be reasonably inferred. Such interpretations have

expanded the power and scope of the national government at the expense of state governments. Further underscoring the role and power of the national government are the implications proffered by the "supremacy clause," found in Article 6, Clause 2:

> This constitution, and the Laws of the United States which shall be made in Pursuance thereof; and all Treaties made, or which shall be made, under the Authority of the United States, shall be the supreme law of the Land; and the Judges in every state shall be bound thereby, any Thing in the Constitution or Laws of any State to the contrary notwithstanding.

The resulting effect of the supremacy clause is to ensure the relative omnipotence of the national government over states and local governments. More important, the supremacy clause serves as an instrument with which the national government can, if it chooses, ensure national cohesion and solidarity in policy actions within fundamental areas of concern. Yet, the power of the central government, although substantial, is far from absolute.

Based on the Tenth Amendment, the hallmark constitutional amendment that defines the scope of state power, all powers not effectively delegated to the national government, nor prohibited by the Constitution, are essentially reserved and assumed to fall under the purview of the states. However, the so-called reserved powers of the state, because they are not clearly listed within the Constitution, remain open to considerable debate.

The accepted ambiguity of the Tenth Amendment raises important questions as to which level of government has responsibility over specific issues and policy areas. State powers have been held to include, for example, the right to regulate intrastate commerce, to conduct elections, to establish local governments, as well as to provide for public health, safety, and morals. In particular, the power to provide public health, safety, and morals, or the so-called police powers, have provided states with the sovereign responsibility to legislate and govern policy areas dealing with such areas as crime and punishment, marriage and divorce, education, pornography, traffic laws, and the use of lands. In terms of public policy, and the manner in which we live our day-to-day lives, the power to create local governments may represent one of the most profound, and often overlooked, powers of the states.

Classic images aside, American federalism has evolved and grown far beyond the constitutionally recognized two levels of government. Local governments, from cities to counties, have exploded in number, and possess substantial policy-making power to affect the direction in such critical areas as education, policing, welfare, and taxation. The growing role of local government is quite clear. In terms of the size of government, based on employees, local governments employ a far greater number than both the state and federal governments combined—a statistical reality that questions the presumption of where "big government" really exists.[17]

Overall, even though local governments may be creatures of state governments, the scope of their policy responsibilities and the total size of their bureaucracy is considerable. Again, on a day-to-day basis it is difficult to suggest that local governments do not have a significant legislative effect on the citizenry. From property taxes to surcharges, from waste pickup to city beautification programs, from fire prevention to community policing, local governments are for many citizens the most visible and active form of all the levels of American government. Local government, simply put, is now a defining element to American federalism and helps explain that the policy-making

process cannot be confined to just the federal and state government. Still, the realities of American federalism must also consider that although the policy roles of local governments have expanded, the fiscal realities of federalism suggest that much power still lies with the national and state governments.

Fiscal Federalism

The fiscal reality of federalism suggests that the national government plays a critical role in subsidizing a variety of areas of public policy that develop and are administered at the state and local levels. The fiscal dependency of state government on federal aid has remained relatively stable over the last three decades. From 1970 to 1995, states have relied on federal assistance for an average of one fifth of their total revenues. Surprisingly, local governments have been receiving an increasingly diminishing percentage of monies from the federal government.[18] Fiscal assistance from the federal government to local governments has declined from a high of 9 percent in 1978, to an average of about 3 percent through the late eighties and early nineties.[19] Local governments are still dependent on state government assistance for roughly one third of total revenues.[20] In sum, the image of federalism derived from this fiscal reality is that of the significant role played by the federal and state government in subsidizing policies and programs for lower levels of government (see Figure 3.7).

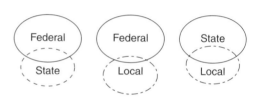

FIGURE 3.7 Fiscal Federalism Means Fiscal Dependence.

Among the means the federal government has used to fund and support policies and programs are **categorical grants-in-aid** and **block grants.** The rules or mandates associated with such grants provide the federal government the ability to influence the method by which programs and services are administered at the state and local levels across the nation.

Categorical grants are federal grants that are provided to states and local governments to serve specific policy programs. Based on the particular categorical grant, associated rules can require matching funds that require state or local governments to match a percentage of the funds provided by the federal government. The Medicare program of 1965 is an example of a categorical grant that provided federal monies with instructions on how to use and implement the program. As with the Medicare program, such categorical grants have sought to establish a clear standard for how programs and services are administered.

In terms of the nature of federalism, categorical grants reflect the intent of the federal government to establish some national uniformity in the implementation of policies in state and local governments. However, because of increasing rules and regulations associated with the proper implementation of programs funded by categorical grants, there is an increasing preference among states, local governments, and many citizens to provide fewer rules and more discretion in how programs are administered.

Block grants provide federal monies with fewer rules and restrictions and intend to serve general policy areas, rather than specific policy programs or objectives. The objective of block grants is to reduce the role played by the national government and increase the role played by the state governments. The "New Federalism" under the Nixon administration ushered in an era for the preference for block grants, and

the belief that administrative control would better serve policy if it were shifted to state and local governments. Aside from block grants, **general revenue sharing (GRS) grants** provided federal aid to states without any conditions related as to how the monies could be spent. Such GRS grants, however, ended in 1987, whereas block grants continue.

Interestingly, the recent history of American federalism suggests a fiscal struggle during the last four decades over the delineation of where the legislative centers of American politics will be defined—state or federal.[21] During the Johnson administration, a preference for more nationally directed policies, with fiscal and management directives, was deemed essential to the goal of establishing a more comprehensive vision for such policy areas as health and poverty. President Nixon, in contrast, sought to reform the nature of federalism by redefining the fiscal foundation of national policy. By utilizing block grants and general revenue sharing, Nixon sought to lessen restrictions that were believed to impede the effective and efficient allocation of national policies. Above all, Nixon's initiatives sought to shift policy responsibilities back to the states.

Reagan favored a reduction in the size of government and a shifting of legislative responsibilities back to state and local governments. Nevertheless, confronted with a Congress that held a different vision than Reagan, the result was a federal government that grew in size and expenditures, even though the notion of a smaller government seemed to gain public popularity.[22]

Under the Clinton administration, an initial attempt to expand the power of the federal government by establishing a national health care program was quickly stymied. President Clinton's health care initiative of 1993 was a classic example of a federal policy that sought to establish uniformity and a comprehensive health system throughout the nation. Although bold in scope, the policy failed under a political avalanche of critiques as to the bureaucratic implications, the cost, and the rules that many believed would be imposed on states and individuals. The ambitious experiment to shift the center of health care away from states, and firmly within the national government, failed and may have marked a defining moment in how far the balance of American federalism can be redefined.

Critical Insights

The reality of American federalism is that substantial policy power lies within all levels of government—federal, state, and local. Even though management and oversight may have somewhat shifted to state and local governments, a dominant role for the federal government is firmly established because of the fiscal dependence of state governments on federal monies. Similarly, local governments remain dependent, to a great degree, on the fiscal support of the state and federal government. In sum, whereas the legislative centers of American policy making may exist within an increasing array of government entities, it is indisputable that the fiscal role of the federal government represents a powerful force in ensuring that the legislative center remains somewhat skewed toward the national level.

POLICY ARENAS AND SUBGOVERNMENTS

The fragmentation of American politics creates a fertile ground for what are commonly referred to as policy arenas or subgovernments. Subgovernments reflect legislative centers of policy development that extend beyond specific institutions or levels of government outlined by the Constitution. Rather than focus simply on the formal insti-

tutions, the phenomena of subgovernments identifies the dynamic legislative centers or arenas that highlight the political and policy ties that bind actors together. These subgovernments can be considered fluid alliances, built on close relationships between various institutional and noninstitutional actors, which develop along a particular policy issue or issues.[23]

Subgovernments, as conceptualized by E. S. Griffith, describe policy making as extending beyond the halls of Congress and the White House, and include those actors whose similar policy interests fostered close relationships:

> Looking at our government from another angle, one can see it to be composed of a number of dispersive and virtually uncoordinated units, each whirling in its own orbit. . . . the relationship among these . . . legislators, administrators, lobbyists, scholars . . . interested in a common problem is a much more real relationship than the relationships between congressmen generally or between administrators generally.[24]

For Griffith, greater understanding could be gained about the nature of politics and policy if specific attention were paid to "these whirlpools" of special interest.[25] These so-called whirlpools have since been described and relabeled as iron triangles, issue networks, and policy subsystems.[26] The classic image of these subgovernments is that of a series of policy interconnections among three parties—public, institutional, and bureaucratic. More specifically, these subgovernments consist of interest groups, congressional committees, and administrative agencies (see Figure 3.8).

Interest groups influence the policy process by advocating specific issue positions. Such influence includes not only classic lobbying of issue positions but also the

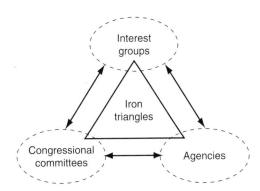

FIGURE 3.8 Classic Iron Triangle Image.

active role interest groups play in providing information and analysis about proposed legislation to members of Congress, their staff, and officials within administrative agencies. Furthermore, government officials and staff come to depend on interest groups to provide expertise and critical information on legislative proposals and prospective legislative language, as well as serve as a critical bridge with which to build political support across the legislative process.

Congressional committees and subcommittees represent the second part of the classic iron triangle. With the increase in complexity and number of legislative proposals, committees have become powerful legislative centers. The power of the committee is the result of its members' influence over the shape of legislative proposals. Committees and subcommittees are responsible for the analysis, evaluation, and markup of various policy proposals and initiatives. The members of these committees garner critical control over legislative language and the structure of prospective legislation. Strikingly, a significantly small number of members of a congressional committee possess substantial influence over the manner in which a given policy problem is addressed in terms of formal legislation.

The final actor within the classic iron triangle is the administrative agency. The agency represents the bureaucratic actors responsible for executing the legislative proposals adopted. Because legislation may lack explicit detail with which to structure and manage the implementation of a policy, the agency has considerable influence over the method and manner in which a given government action may affect the public. As a consequence, agencies operate in a public environment in which political forces and actors can and do seek to manipulate the nature by which they execute government decisions. Each agency, for instance, remains concerned with yearly budget allocations, public and political opposition to agency oversight, and the perceptions held by the public, political officials, interest groups, or other actors that question and critique the purpose of agencies. The politics that surround each agency is further affected by the administrative rule-making process that is open to public comment, and the routine year-to-year nature of the federal budget cycle which ensures that agencies will remain closely connected with congressional committees and interest groups.

The greatest thread of bond within these iron triangles may arise from the social relationships that develop between these three groups of actors.[27] Socially, the ties of the iron triangle grow greater as interest groups pursue members of Congress for director positions, seek senior staffers as lobbyists and analysts, and recruit agency officials for senior management positions. Additionally, members of Congress and senior staff are often tapped for senior appointments within the various governmental agencies. Moreover, the concentration of interest groups, committees, and agency officials within the confines of the policy-making community fosters a striking social dynamic. As a result, a powerful social fabric of personal ties and friendships is woven daily during the practical aspects of the

policy process. These ties strengthen relationships and help build an even more powerful
iron triangle.

SUMMARY

The structural realities of American government reflect a dynamic union between the
diffusion and concentration of policy-
making power. Structurally, each branch of
the federal government, as well as all levels
of government, garner significant power to
influence and shape the policy process.
Most interesting is the realization that the
structure of American politics does not necessarily serve the goal of effective and efficient government. At certain periods, such
as national crisis, or in dealing with certain
issues, such as foreign policy and war, American government can act in an especially efficient manner. However, in the absence of
crisis, American politics and policy making
operates within a structural realm seemingly
more conducive to inaction and frustration
than policy action.

The student of public policy must recognize that the failures of government and the
policy process are not simply because of the
fickle demands of the public, the politics of the
parties, the agendas of special interests, the
machinations of bureaucratic agencies, or the
failings of individual political leaders. Rather,
the failures are the very byproduct of the structure unique to American government. Again,
American government is a political system
where policy making is neither designed nor
intended to be efficient or productive except
under rare circumstances. It is a system that by
dividing power across branches and levels of
government, and by ensuring a role for the
public, creates an inefficient and ineffective
policy-making process. Yet, it is also a system
of government *where,* at unique times, dramatic policy actions are possible and do occur.

DISCUSSION QUESTIONS

1. Is indirect representation a threat to
democracy or is it compatible with the
idea of democracy? If it is compatible,
should the U.S. Senate be changed back
to an indirect branch of government?

2. Is a national crisis necessary for
immediate policy action within such a
divided structural government? Absent
war or threat of war, what qualifies as a
national crisis in your opinion?

3. Should state and local governments be
given more power to govern? Why or
why not?

4. What level of government—local, state,
or federal—has the most significant
impact on your life on a day-to-day basis?
Which level of government has the most
significant impact on the quality of your
life?

5. Do iron triangles and subgovernments
have a positive or negative effect on
policy making? Are these triangles
compatible with the idea of democracy?
Why or why not?

SUGGESTED READINGS

Canon, D. T., ed. *The Enduring Debate: Classic
Contemporary Readings in American Politics.*
New York: Norton, 2000.

Corwin, E. S. *The Constitution and What It Means
Today.* Princeton, NJ: Princeton University
Press, 1978.

Elazar, D. *American Federalism: A View from the
States.* 3rd ed. New York: Harper & Row,
1984.

Greenberg, E. S., and Benjamin Pape. *The Struggle
for Democracy.* 4th ed. New York: Longman,
1999.

Heclo, H. "Issue Networks and the Executive
Government." In Anthony King, (ed.), *The
New American Political System.* Washington,
DC: Enterprise Institute, 1978, 87–124.

Rossiter, C., ed. *The Federalist Papers.* New York:
New American Library, 1961.

Storin, H. J. *What the Anti-Federalists Were For.* Chicago: University of Chicago Press, 1981.

Theodoulou, S. *Politics and Policy in Six Nations: A Comparative Perspective on Policymaking.* Englewood Cliffs, NJ: Prentice Hall, 2002.

ENDNOTES

1. A central theoretical debate exists concerning the constitutional intent of the framers. Charles Beard, for example, argues that the framers sought to protect their elite interests rather than pursue democracy. Robert Brown suggests that, all failings aside, the Constitution was written with a clear democratic intent. See Charles A. Beard, "An Economic Interpretation of the Constitution of the United States," and Robert E. Brown, "A Critical Analysis of an Economic Interpretation of the Constitution," in David Canon, ed., *The Enduring Debate* (New York: Norton, 2000).

2. Subgovernments also refer to the notion of iron triangles. For an additional discussion of this phenomena and the role of issue networks, see H. Heclo, "Issue Networks and the Executive Government," in Anthony King, ed., *The New American Political System* (Washington, DC: Enterprise Institute, 1978), 87–124.

3. Michael Kammen, "The Origins of the American Constitution," in Ann G. Serow, ed., *The American Polity Reader* (New York: Norton, 1993).

4. Among some of the Classic Greek philosophers (e.g., Plato, Aristotle, Polybius) a love for democracy seems at best tempered, if not outright suspect. See W. Ebenstein and A. Ebenstein, *Great Political Thinkers,* 6th ed. (New York: Harcourt, 2000).

5. Ibid.

6. The classic anecdotal test is to suggest to individuals whether America is a democracy. Once answered in the affirmative to deconstruct the answer by showing the direct and indirect nature of elected representation. Such a test proves challenging to many who have never sought to question what democracy is and where it begins and ends. Again, for a review of the concept and theories, see W. Ebenstein and A. Ebenstein,

Great Political Thinkers; A. Heywood, *Political Ideas and Concepts: An Introduction* (New York: St Martin's Press, 1994).

7. Robert Dahl, "On Removing the Impediments to Democracy in the United States," *Political Science Quarterly* 92 (Spring 1977), 5.

8. Initially, of the three branches of the federal government, only members of the House of Representatives were elected by direct vote of the people. Senate members and the president were elected by indirect means—Electoral College for the president and state legislatures for the Senate. Additionally, neither the judiciary, nor the emerging power of the bureaucracy under the executive branch, are elected or open to the direct constraints of popular consent. Not until the passage of the Seventeenth Amendment in 1913 would the entire Congress be elected by popular consent.

9. Review J. Madison, "The Federalists, Nos. 51 & 46," in D. T. Canon, ed., *The Enduring Debate: Classic Contemporary Readings in American Politics* (New York: Norton, 2000).

10. A multiparty parliamentary system that requires coalitions of two or more parties can, however, prove to be an inefficient governing system.

11. As evidenced in numerous cases where military force is applied and leads to American casualties, modern presidents remain vulnerable to the changes in public opinion. See Ole R. Holsti, *Public Opinion and American Foreign Policy* (Ann Arbor: University of Michigan Press, 1996).

12. To our knowledge, there has been no systematic and specific research on the extent to which national crises, in the post-World War II era, have diminished or redefined the constitutional constraints imposed by separation of powers or balance of powers.

13. H. W. Stanley and R. G. Niemi, *Vital Statistics on American Politics 1999–2000* (Washington, DC: CQ Press, 2000), 195–238.

14. S. Theodoulou, *Politics and Policy in Six Nations: A Comparative Perspective on Policymaking* (Englewood Cliffs, NJ: Prentice Hall, 2002), 94.

15. Stanley and Niemi, *Vital Statistics,* 211.

16. For additional information on federalism, American politics, and policy making, see

Robert F. Nagel, *The Implosion of American Federalism* (Oxford, England: Oxford University Press, 2001); J. F. Zimmerman, *Contemporary American Federalism: The Growth of National Power* (Denver: Greenwood Publishing Group, 1998); T. J. Anton, *American Federalism and Public Policy: How the System Works* (Philadelphia, PA: Temple University Press, 1988).

17. Stanley and Niemi, *Vital Statistics,* 288–324.

18. Ibid, 290.

19. Ibid, 301.

20. Ibid, 324.

21. See D. Elazar, *American Federalism: A View from the States,* 3rd ed. (New York: Harper & Row, 1984).

22. The statistical reality is that the size of government and government expenditures increased under President Ronald Reagan. The often-cited misperception is that the Reagan administration initiated a true revolution in federalism in which power was returned to the states and the size of the federal government declined substantially. Rather, fiscal dependency by state governments on the federal government declined from 22.3 percent to only 18.5 percent, and federal expenditures increased significantly. For statistical data, see Stanley and Niemi, *Vital Statistics.* For a review of the Reagan tenure, see Richard Neustadt, *Presidential Power and the Modern Presidents: The Politics of Leadership from Roosevelt to Reagan* (New York: Simon & Schuster, 1997).

23. The phenomenon of subgovernments has been theoretically redefined by other scholars into notions of issue networks and policy subsystems. For a review of various pieces on subgovernments and issue networks, see D. C. McCool, *Public Policy Theories, Models, and Concepts* (Englewood Cliffs, NJ: Prentice Hall, 1995).

24. E. S. Griffith, *The Impasse of Democracy* (New York: Harrison-Hilton Books, 1939), 182–183.

25. Ibid, 182–183.

26. McCool, *Public Policy,* 73–75.

27. Ibid.

4

The Who

The Policy-Making Actors

The policy game involves a number of actors whose importance and influence extends and varies throughout the stages of the policy process. Some policy actors, for instance, possess influence on specific issues and at specific points in the policy process. Certain institutional actors, like Congress or the President, may have a cross section of influence across many stages of the policy process. Other institutional actors may play critical roles at certain phases, such as the predecision stages of problem identification, agenda setting, and policy formulation, but their influence and importance begins to wane during the latter stages that lead to adoption and execution of the policy. In contrast, noninstitutional actors, such as the public, lobbyists, interest groups, media, and think tanks, will lack institutional means of power, but remain quite important in shaping the evolution of public policy. Overall, both institutional and noninstitutional actors play various important roles throughout the policy-making process in determining the content, execution, and impact of public policy.

The importance of respective policy actors throughout the policy process is based on the extent of influence they possess over public policy. Such influence reflects the actors' explicit power to impact policy and the policy process. In other words, the most powerful actors are those that possess the power to directly shape, define, and execute policy. In general, the most powerful policy actors are the institutional actors. Still, noninstitutional actors without direct power over the policy process, can and do influence elected officials and the policy decisions they make. Overall, although no one actor possesses omnipotent influence across every

---

Box 4.1 Policy Stages and Importance of Policy Actors

STAGES OF POLICY PROCESS	INSTITUTIONAL					NONINSTITUTIONAL				
	MC	President	Courts	Staff	Bureaucracy	Public	IGs	Lobbyists	Media	Think Tank
Problem identification	□	□	△	○	○	□	□	△	□	○
Agenda setting	□	□	□	△	△	□	□	△	□	○
Policy formulation	□	□	△	□	△	△	□	□	△	△
Policy adoption	□	□	□	○	△	△	□	□	△	○
Policy implementation	△	□	△	○	□	○	△	△	△	○
Policy evaluation	□	△	△	○	□	○	△	△	□	○
Policy change/ termination	□	□	□	○	△	□	□	□	□	○

□ Very influential policy actor
△ Influential policy actor
○ Less influential policy actor

---

stage of the policy process, one can generalize that certain institutional or noninstitutional actors do have more or less influence within particular policy stages (see Box 4.1).

Box 4.1 helps one visualize the influence of particular policy actors across the policy process, as well as compare the influence an actor enjoys relative to other policy players. The significance of a given actor within a specific stage, and across the policy process, can be roughly described along a continuum of very influential to less influential. The term *influential* is used to identify the general degree of policy-making power an actor can enjoy. Even though it remains difficult to determine the exact degree of influence of any given actor, we believe it is fair to suggest and recognize that certain actors do have greater influence at specific policy stages. A more focused discussion of the role of certain policy actors within a given stage of the policy process will occur in subsequent chapters. The following discussion will describe the basic character, role, and influence of these institutional and noninstitutional actors.

THE POLICY PLAYERS— INSTITUTIONAL ACTORS

The array of institutional actors includes players that operate within and throughout the institutional setting of the policy process. They include the familiar in name and the constitutionally powerful, as well as the unfamiliar and the constitutionally weak but institutionally powerful. These actors fall under the three branches of the government and include members of Congress, personal and professional staff, the president, the president's inner circle, the Executive Office of the President, the cabinet, Supreme Court justices, federal judges, and the bureaucracy. Their influence can be roughly determined by understanding the nature of the power and position they enjoy within American government and the policy process.

Members of Congress

The central legislative and policy role of members of Congress is well established within American government. The power of individual members is founded on the strong influence they enjoy within the legislative branch over the policy process. As a member of the legislative branch, members can define problems, set the agenda, formulate policy solutions, and assist in the adoption of a specific course of action. Additionally, through their oversight function, members of Congress are able to evaluate the bureaucracy and help ensure that agencies effectively implement federal policies and programs. Overall, each member of Congress must balance an array of professional functions throughout the policy process.

The Constitution established the **legislative** or **lawmaking** function within the confines of the legislative branch or Congress. Although other policy actors can and do influence the legislative process, only a member can formally introduce, discuss, and negotiate legislative proposals. Through the introduction of bills, legislative debate, compromise, logrolling, and deal making, each member can prove significant in shaping the eventual direction of the policy process. Underscoring this lawmaking function is the service or broker function that each congressional member performs to satisfy the demands and concerns of constituents.

Traditionally, members of Congress are seen as brokers for the concerns of their constituents. Varied issues such as displeasure over a particular piece of legislation, difficulty with a government agency, or desire for an internship or tickets to the White House tour become the responsibility of the member to broker. In terms of the policy process, ideas for policy solutions will often emerge from constituents who are displeased with the manner in which a public or private actor has treated them. Closely related to the broker function is the critical function of representation.

Representation is not only a matter of service but is also a political necessity for each and every member of Congress. Every member must balance the political and policy demands placed upon him or her. At a minimum, members must effectively represent their constituents' ideological or policy interests if they are to remain in these elected positions. The choice for congressional members is whether to act as the so-called trustee or the delegate. More accurately, the representative function may be portrayed as one where the member chooses to take either a trustee or a delegate role. What determines such a choice? The policy issue itself, what the representative perceives the constituents' interests are, the effectiveness of the policy proposal, and the inevitable political calculation that must underscore most legislative decisions. It is arguably even more accurate to suggest that each member of Congress is indeed a trustee until he or she is politically compelled to act as a delegate.

Aside from addressing specific legislative proposals, members of Congress are also responsible for governmental oversight. **Oversight** is basically the formal power granted to members to evaluate various federal agencies. Oversight ensures that Congress can, when deemed necessary, evaluate whether laws are being enforced correctly, whether programs and services are being appropriately administered, and whether waste or abuse is occurring within specific federal agencies. Across the federal government, from the Internal Revenue Service (IRS) to the Bureau of Citizenship and Immigration Services (BCIS), from the Federal Bureau of Investigation (FBI) to the Central Intelligence Agency

(CIA), Congress and its members are given the authority to evaluate failures, errors, and abuses that may occur across the wide spectrum of government and society.

Finally, the public education function reflects the role that members play in informing the public of policy issues and solutions being debated within Congress. Through traditional legislative actions, such as hearings, speeches, and floor debates, members will strive to spark attention, raise awareness, as well as educate their constituents about a given problem and their preferred policy solution. More recently, nontraditional actions, such as participating in debates and discussions on an array of media outlets, including the Internet, allow members to pursue an aggressive media campaign on behalf of the issues they wish to educate the public on. Given the need to satisfy constituent requests or questions, the public education function is as much about providing help to the voters as it is about furthering members' careers.

Congressional Staff

[Committee and personal] Staffers are an ubiquitous presence, riding elevators and congressional subways besides Senators and House members rushing to a vote; at their elbows, giving advice; behind them at hearings, whispering questions; preparing their bosses for press interviews or shoving speeches into their hands; giving them political and substantive guidance; handling constituents; screening lobbyists; setting the agenda for committees; briefing members on the budget or haggling over its provisions; formulating proposals; making decisions; mastering procedures; managing hearings; cross-examining generals; probing the Central Intelligence Agency; negotiating with the White House.[1]

Staffers—men and women of differing ideologies, from the congressional staff intern to the chief of staff, from the staff assistant to the committee staff member—play an especially critical, but often overlooked policy role. Each congressional office in Washington, DC, each congressional committee, is comprised of a small army of staff. Depending on their assigned role and seniority, as well their degree of access to the senator or representative, congressional staff can be quite influential during various stages of the policy process.

Organizationally, staff positions are defined along a familiar pattern within both House and Senate offices (see Figure 4.1). Potential influence on the policy process tends to be greater among the senior legislative staff. Depending on their position, these staffers play a critical role in researching policy issues, they communicate back to the member the legislative concerns of interest groups and lobbyists, they provide political and policy analysis of legislative issues, and they help orchestrate backroom negotiations between their member and interest groups, lobbyists, the White House, agency officials, and other congressional offices.

The primary leadership and management of the congressional office is provided by the chief of staff and the deputy chief of staff. These senior staffers traditionally have the most policy influence and access to the member of Congress. In comparison, the legislative director offers policy advice, helps direct the legislative agenda, and is instrumental in managing the lower legislative staff. The counsel provides legal advice to the staff and member. The press secretary develops the media message in support of certain policy positions, as well as acting as a liaison with the media when necessary. Underpinning the senior staff is an array of legislative assistants.

The legislative assistants are responsible for researching and overseeing legislative developments over assigned policy areas,

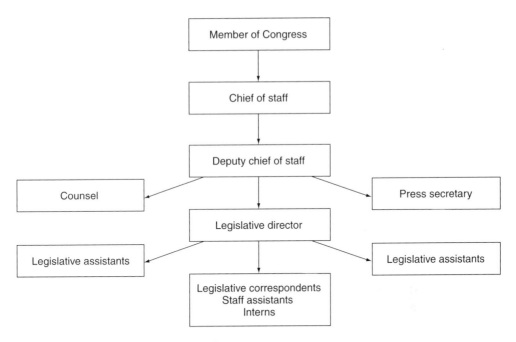

FIGURE 4.1 Congressional Office and Staff Roles

and provide political and policy analysis for senior staff and the member. Additionally, these staffers are often the front line through which interest groups, lobbyists, and concerned constituents gain access to advocate their policy positions. In comparison, legislative correspondents, staff assistants, and interns will conduct critical research for senior staff, provide administrative assistance, and respond to mail and telephone correspondence from constituents. Overall, given the sheer size and complexity of legislation that flows through Congress, each senator and representative can become highly dependent on the skills, analyses, and ideas provided by their personal staff.

Aside from the personal staff, members of Congress also employ or have access to a series of professional committee staff. The actual number of committee staff is determined through agreement between the majority and minority parties, and larger committee staffs are usually accorded to the majority party in each congressional chamber. Regardless of the size, committee staffers not only help develop and prepare a committee's legislative agenda but also supplement the majority party's power over the legislative and policy process, while also attempting to further the minority party's influence on proposed legislation. Overall, given the large number of congressional committees and subcommittees, committee staff prove instrumental and quite influential to the very management of the legislative process.

Each and every majority and minority committee chair depends on the professional committee staff to formulate and synthesize the disparate details to any piece of proposed legislation. The structure of the committee's agenda, the language of legislation, and the fiscal allocations to projects can be shaped and defined by the explicit influence certain committee staffers have in the formulation of policy solutions. Within the House of Representatives, in particular, majority committee staff can wield considerable power because the size of the chamber, coupled with the greater prominence of the majority party's committee leadership, only enhances the legislative role and influence of the committee staff. As Hedrick Smith aptly points out, the size of such staff becomes a de facto indicator of political and policy power:

> [Committee] staff became not only an instrument of power but a measure of power. The larger a senator's or a House committee chairman's staff, the more power it was assumed he had. Small staff was a sign of weakness. Large and able staffs gravitated to the powerful legislators. The political syllogism moved through phases—from staff buttresses power, to staff follows power, to staff symbolizes power.[2]

The policy influence of the committee staff depends, to a large degree, on their responsibility in translating the array of policy proposals, amendments, and fiscal allocations into specific legislative language that will comprise the final legislation to be considered for adoption. Additionally, because many pieces of national legislation, such as appropriations bills, are in the hundreds of pages, the mere writing of legislation provides committee staff with enormous political power over the final legislative product.

President

The policy power of the president emerges from a unique mixture of constitutional and perceptual power. Formal presidential powers are, ironically, often overstated and misunderstood. The explicit power of these titular figures in American politics stems from the seemingly limited explicit powers given to them under the Constitution. Still, the president does derive implicit political power from being the only national representative. In other words, presidential power and influence over the policy process extends beyond constitutional powers, and is relative to whether the issue deals with domestic or foreign policy (see Box 4.2).

In terms of domestic policy, the president's power is constrained by constitutional realities. Legislatively, a president's formal power is limited to veto and signature. Although presidential power remains limited, the reality of American politics establishes the president's broad significance in domestic political affairs. From the introduction of policy initiatives, to the ability to focus the nation on a specific issue, to the formulation

---

Box 4.2   Presidential Power and the Policy Process

EXPLICIT CONSTITUTIONAL POWERS	POLICY STAGE	POLICY REALM
Veto and sign	Problem definition, agenda setting, policy formulation, adoption	Domestic
Commander and chief of the military	Problem definition, agenda setting, policy formulation, adoption, evaluation, policy change/termination	Foreign
Grant reprieves and pardons	Problem definition, agenda setting, policy adoption, implementation	Domestic
Negotiate treaties	Policy formulation, adoption	Foreign
Appoint ambassadors	Policy formulation, adoption	Foreign
Appoint Supreme Court nominees	Policy formulation, adoption	Domestic

of policy proposals, the president emerges as a central figure within each and every significant policy debate. Still, a president's legislative power over domestic policy remains essentially constrained by the countervailing powers of Congress. These checks and balances ensure that negotiation, even compromise, will likely mark most discussions of domestic policy that involve the president and Congress.

Presidential powers in foreign policy, even though minimal in number, are significant in scope and effect on the direction of the nation's foreign and national security affairs. Specifically, the powers as commander and chief, receiving ambassadors, and negotiating treaties have established the president as the predominant actor within foreign and national security affairs. The power of commander and chief, for instance, ensures that the president acts as the definitive leader of the nation's armed forces, as well the leader for national security and defense-related public policies. The negotiation of foreign treaties and the receiving of ambassadors further underscore the president's foreign policy power. These explicit powers have helped establish the president's ability to identify national security and foreign policy problems, shape the foreign policy agenda, formulate policy solutions, as well as implement, evaluate, and change the direction of policy within foreign affairs. Yet, the *real* power of a president may not lie with the position's explicit powers, but with the perceived power associated with the position as the only national representative within American politics.

For every president, the public's perception of leadership is a basis of power or weakness. A popular president, for instance, can use favor with the public to persuade members of Congress to rally in support of a legislative agenda. An unpopular president is effectively weakened throughout the policy process and congressional members are often embold-

ened to challenge the policy agenda of a weak president from beginning to end. As such, every president, even more than any other legislative actor, must seek popular support for policy initiatives. Furthermore, across both policy realms, domestic and foreign, policy successes and failures will have substantial effect on the perception of the president. A policy failure, whether it is because of a national economic crisis that continues unabated or a foreign policy debacle, can effectively poison a president's popularity. In comparison, a policy success, whether it is because of a growing economy or successful war, can greatly boost the public's opinion of the president. Perception, however, is a fickle commodity in politics, and a president's popularity is often victim to the changing whims of the national public. The most dramatic example of a president's reversal of fortune is that of President George H. Bush, who enjoyed remarkably high approval ratings following the 1991 Persian Gulf War only to lose the next president election. In terms of the policy process, it is the successful exploitation of these implicit powers that can often lead a president to become truly powerful and influential across all segments of the policy process.

Presidential Inner Circle

Successful presidents depend greatly on a small, yet politically powerful, contingent of inner circle staff. Such staff members serve at the pleasure of the president. For the members of the inner circle, influence and power is derived from their access and proximity to the president. This level of access to the president can lead to an "imperial advisor" whose power and prominence in affecting presidential policy making can be quite substantial.[3] For example, Karl Rove, a political advisor to President George W. Bush, is regarded by many political pundits as one of the most influential of advisors in the recent history of the presidency.[4]

In general, access and prominence does come at some price. For this inner circle, professional misfortunes—whether demotions, tensions, or conflicts with the president or other staff—can be well publicized in the media. Certain staff can quickly lose favor and prominence if the president's agenda falters. Still, the power to influence and make policy represents an often-acceptable trade-off to the inevitable public and professional scrutiny surrounding the position.

Politically, given the effects that arise from how a president is perceived by the public and other political actors, it falls to the inner advisory circle to ensure that a president is perceived as politically powerful, achieves the legislative agenda desired, and is viewed positively by the American public. It is the abilities of these political advisors—from the speechwriters to the press secretary, from the communications director to the chief of staff—that determine how the White House is managed and how well the staff aids a president's policy and political agenda (see Box 4.3).

The chief of staff represents the heart of the inner circle by helping direct and sched-

ule the president's political or policy agenda, and represents the critical gatekeeper to the office of the president:

> The chief of staff's post is arguably the most testing job in any administration—next to the president's. . . . The agenda of the chief of staff, like the president's stretches from wall to wall. He must deal with every faction, consider every major issue, and most important scan the horizon for trouble.[5]

Underscoring the power of the chief of staff are a series of political advisors whose titles may vary but whose purpose is to analyze the political consequences of presidential proposals or decisions. These advisors strive to determine the political effects of specific actions taken by the president in both foreign and domestic policy realms. The communications director and press secretary, in comparison, are responsible for developing, directing, and presenting the media message and images that will be associated with a given president.

The chief speechwriters, although they may be unfamiliar names, gain significant prominence through their chosen words and phrases. These speeches, highlighted by the state of the union address or other dramatic pronouncements, garner a significance that can greatly enhance the stature of a president, not to mention furthering the popular and political support invaluable to the president's agenda.

Among the policy advisors, responsibilities are divided along broad policy areas. Intergovernmental affairs staff, for example, are responsible for the serious negotiations that occur with members of Congress. Such staff members are effectively institutional lobbyists for a president, and they assist in developing the winning political coalitions that are necessary to further the president's agenda. Additionally, intergovernmental affairs provides intelligence about potential

---

Box 4.3   President's Inner Advisory Circle

Chief of staff

Political staff
Communications director
Press secretary
Political advisors
Chief speechwriters
Pollsters

Domestic policy
Intergovernmental affairs
Budget director
Domestic policy advisors

Foreign policy
National security advisor

obstacles to the president's policy agenda that may arise, as well as indicating what form of compromises may be necessary to increase legislative success. Finally, the budget director is given the responsibility for preparing the executive budget and providing fiscal clarity to the budget requests that will emerge from the policy priorities of the president, the cabinet, Congress, and various domestic interests groups with influence or access to the White House.

With respect to foreign affairs, the national security advisor heads the president's National Security Council, provides critical analysis of issues, and assists in the formulation and adoption of policy actions within the broad confines of national security. Because these advisors are often the closest aides for the president in foreign affairs, providing briefings of key developments in national security, their power and influence over the course of foreign policy can be substantial.

Executive Office of the President

The Executive Office of the President (EOP) is comprised of groups and councils associated with critical policy issues (see Box 4.4). The EOP is organized around policy areas, and its members assist the president in the analysis, formulation, implementation, and evaluation of public policies. The structure of the EOP is not static, however. The EOP of President George W. Bush, for example, includes the newly formed Office of Faith-Based and Community Initiatives reflecting the president's goal of exploring the appropriate role and value of faith-based programs within the realm of public policy.

Presidential Cabinet

The president's cabinet, which includes the formal cabinet officials of each of fifteen federal departments and the extracabinet officials, such as the head of the CIA, the vice

---

Box 4.4 Executive Office of the President

- Council of Economic Advisers
- Council on Environmental Quality
- Domestic Policy Council
- National Economic Council
- National Security Council
- Office of Administration
- Office of Faith-Based and Community Initiatives
- Office of Homeland Security
- President's Critical Infrastructure Protection Board
- Office of Management and Budget
- Office of National AIDS Policy
- Office of National Drug Control Policy
- Office of Science & Technology Policy
- President's Foreign Intelligence Advisory Board
- Office of the United States Trade Representative
- White House Military Office
- USA Freedom Corps

---

president, and the chief of staff, represent the elite leaders who are responsible for executing the president's major programs and overseeing the bureaucratic arm of the federal government (see Box 4.5).

Traditional cabinet positions head a federal agency and are nominated by the president and confirmed by the U.S. Senate. The political significance of such appointments reflects the dramatic impact that changes in presidential administration can have on all facets of the bureaucracy. Each cabinet official is responsible for executing current policies, undertaking the new initiatives that have just become law, and ensuring that the administrative vision held by the president is implemented. For the president, the cabinet and extended cabinet represent the administrative arm through which decisions evolve

Box 4.5   President's Extended Cabinet

Executive Cabinet
- Secretary of Agriculture
- Secretary of Interior
- Secretary of Commerce
- Attorney General
- Secretary of Defense
- Secretary of Labor
- Secretary of Education
- Secretary of State
- Secretary of Energy
- Secretary of Transportation
- Secretary of Homeland Security
- Secretary of Health & Human Services
- Secretary of Treasury
- Secretary of Housing & Urban Development
- Secretary of Veterans Affairs
- The Vice President
- President's Chief of Staff
- Environmental Protection Agency
- Head of Central Intelligence Agency
- National Security Council

SOURCE: From the White House Web site, retrieved April 24, 2002, from http://www.Whitehouse.gov.

into actual policy actions, programs are managed effectively and efficiently, and specific impacts result on the designated target population(s).

As of 2002, the largest reorganization of the federal government is under way with the establishment of the Department of Homeland Security (DHS). The DHS will bring together a variety of security- and enforcement-related agencies and departments across the federal government under one agency. This agency's primary function will be in deterring, preparing for, and responding to any terrorist threat or attack against the United States. The DHS represents one the most ambitious reorganiza-

tions of the federal government in the history of American politics.

Federal Courts

Although the role for the federal courts is now accepted as constitutional tradition, it continues to be debated what the appropriate role of the courts should be within the political and policy process. Before discussing this more substantive issue, a brief description of the structure of the federal courts follows (see Figure 4.2).

The structure of the federal court system involves three basic elements: the U.S. Supreme Court, the U.S. courts of appeals, and the U.S. district courts. The U.S. district courts represent the trial courts of the federal government, and have the power to review federal cases of a civil or criminal matter. In total, there are ninety-four such courts. District courts are courts of original jurisdiction and do not hear appeals. U.S. courts of appeals, of which there are thirteen, review appeals and render decisions related to the district courts that fall within their circuit. The Supreme Court currently consists of nine justices, and serves as an appellate court and a court of original jurisdiction. The jurisdiction of all federal courts to review cases is based on their discretion, and on certain guidelines established by Congress.

The federal courts' influence on the policy process comes through the court's power of judicial review, which allows the courts to renew the constitutionality of policy actions taken by the other branches and levels of American government. According to David Horowitz, a policy-making role for the courts was not intended by the Constitution.[6] In part, the substantial policy role played by the federal courts emerged as a byproduct of the intrinsic ambiguity in the language of the Constitution. Quite simply, the Constitution did not establish the scope and meaning of the concept of judicial power as it related to the

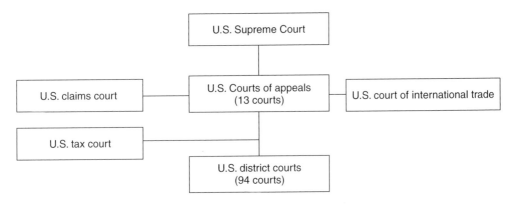

FIGURE 4.2 Structure of the U.S. Federal Courts

role of the judiciary in the policy process. Article 3, Section 2, for example, defines the broad scope of the judiciary's jurisdiction, but provides no definition of judicial power or reference to judicial review:

> The judicial power shall extend to all Cases, in Law and Equity, arising under the Constitution, the Laws of the United States, and Treaties made, or which shall be made, under their Authority;—to all Cases affecting Ambassadors, other public Ministers and Consuls;—to all Cases of admiralty and maritime Jurisdiction;—to Controversies to which the United States shall be a party;—to Controversies between two or more States;—between a State and Citizens of another State;—between Citizens of different States;—between Citizens of the same State claiming lands under Grants of different States

Whereas the scope of judicial power arguably may have been unclear at the writing of the Constitution, over the last 215 years the courts have established a wide and firm foothold in the legislative, policy, and political process. What continues to be debated is the role the courts should have within the polity. For Alexander Hamilton, the federal courts were essential to American governance and there could be no liberty if the judiciary was not separated from the powers of the legislative and executive branches.[7] What is unclear, however, is how the judiciary should utilize its constitutional powers of judicial review.

Judicial review refers explicitly to the power to declare laws and government actions "null and void on the ground that they conflict with the law of the Constitution."[8] Judicial review allows the courts to review cases, determine the constitutionality of a specific case, and decide the appropriate remedies that must be undertaken by the appropriate actors to rectify the issue. Basically, two perspectives on judicial review, either strict constructionism or activism, have emerged to describe the appropriate role for the judiciary in the policy-making process.

From the perspective of strict constructionism, judicial review and the interpretation of constitution should remain consistent with the intentions and meaning of the framers. Justices, based on this perspective, must refrain from affirming positions at variance with the purportedly clear meaning of the Constitution. For Robert Bork, a former Supreme Court nominee, to disregard such a strict constructionist perspective threatens the very legitimacy of the court's role within this system of government.[9] The judiciary, in other words, should not make policy when it renders legal decisions.

In contrast, the activist perspective embraces the position that true intent of the Constitution is not clearly established. Because the Constitution is an intrinsically ambiguous document, and society today is increasingly complex, proponents of activism contend that the judiciary is justified in a more aggressive interpretation. In order to deal with issues and problems not evident during the writing of the Constitution, it is essential to view the Constitution not as a static object, but a living document that must change and react to the changing realities of a complex and modern society. Yet, whichever perspective is adopted, the Court continues to have significant implications for the field of public policy. Whether activist or strict constructionist in philosophy, the power of judicial review has led the Supreme Court to rule and impose remedies in issues dealing with some of the most contentious and divisive so-cioeconomic problems and policy issues confronted by the United States (see Box 4.6).

Still, as significant as some of the judicial decisions have been, the courts remain a comparatively weak and potentially constrained branch of the federal government. The judiciary's power to effect change, similar in degree and consequence to that of legislation passed by Congress or an executive order signed by the president, depends on the degree of respect and deference enjoyed by the Court. To have an explicit effect on society or public policy, the judiciary depends wholeheartedly on the deference and cooperation of other institutional and noninstitutional actors. Based on the judicial decision, and the remedies it may impose, the federal courts will require varying cooperation and support of Congress, the president, the bureaucracy, the fifty states, and especially the public. This places the judiciary at some disadvantage, as it must recognize the possibility that if the Court is not

---

Box 4.6 Important Judicial Cases and the Policy Issues

CASE	POLICY ISSUE
McCulloch v. Maryland (1819)	Federalism
Gibbons v. Ogden (1824)	Regulate interstate commerce
Dred Scott v. Sanford (1857)	Slavery
Plessy v. Ferguson (1896)	Minority rights
Schenck v. United States (1919)	Free speech
Powell v. Alabama (1932)	Right to counsel
Brown v. Board of Education of Topeka (1954)	Desegregation of schools
NAACP v. Alabama (1958)	Freedom of association
Abington School District v. Schempp (1963)	Separation of church and state
Gideon v. Wainright (1963)	Right to legal counsel
Miranda v. Arizona (1966)	Rights of the accused
Roe v. Wade (1973)	Woman's right to an abortion
United States v. Nixon (1974)	Executive privilege
Regents of U of Cal v. Bakke (1978)	Affirmative action
Gregg v. Georgia (1976)	Capital punishment
Bush v. Gore (2000)	Voting rights

> ### Box 4.7   Constraints on Judicial Policy-Making Power
>
> - Amending the U.S. Constitution to nullify a court ruling
> - Congressional power over size and scope of federal courts
> - Legislating to overrule the judicial interpretation of federal law
> - Presidential control over appointment
> - Lack of administrative enforcement
> - Public opinion
>
> SOURCE: From D. McKay, *Essentials of American Government* (New York: Westview Press, 2000). Reprinted by permission.

---

respected any remedy imposed may fail to be implemented. As David O'Brien states, "denied the power of the sword or the purse, the Court must cultivate its institutional prestige."[10] Essentially, constraints over the judiciary can help shape and temper their legal decisions and their resulting impact on policy (see Box 4.7).

Overall, whereas the courts can be deemed weak or constrained, it is difficult to disregard the power of the judiciary to render decisions that have significant implications for the policy-making process. Because the judiciary has enjoyed consistently high public favor, even sometimes higher than the other elected branches of the federal government, the power of the court to review and render decisions that have and will have substantial effects on the polity remains intact. Although the appropriate role for the federal courts may be debated, and the ideological content of their decisions may inspire substantial question and disagreement, it is the present respect and deference to the courts that ensures they are presently influential throughout the policy process. However, if the prestige or status of the court becomes in question, or if various institutional and non-institutional actors begin to doubt the legiti-

macy of the courts' decisions, the influence of this actor on the policy process could decline substantially. In the future, to what extent the courts remain powerful policy actors may depend on whether or not their decisions are more radical in implication than is or will be politically acceptable by the vast number of other policy actors.

Bureaucracy

The bureaucracy represents the administrative means by which the policy decisions and actions of the various branches of the government are executed. The power and impact of the bureaucracy resides within this critical stage of policy implementation. Although the Constitution does not mention the bureaucracy, it is often referred to as the "fourth branch" of the federal government because of the power such agencies and departments have in implementing public policy. Given the increasing scope and prominence the bureaucracy has within a modern society, it does indeed seem that "it is getting to be harder to run a constitution than to frame one."[11] Because it is easy and politically expedient to criticize the bureaucracy, the importance of this actor's role within the policy process is often discounted or debased. Woodrow Wilson, in "The Study of Administration," summarized quite well the tendency to ignore how essential the bureaucracy is for society:

> Who shall make law, and what shall that law be? The other question, how shall law be administered with enlightenment, equity, with speed, and without friction was put aside as a practical matter.[12]

The influence of the bureaucracy is most substantial during the implementation stage. Because the language of many adopted policy actions is ambiguous, the bureaucracy is responsible for actively defining the intent of

---

Box 4.8 Administrative Power and Policy-Making Implications

BASIS OF ADMINISTRATIVE POWER	POLICY IMPLICATION
Rule making	Rules and procedures for implementation
Adjudication	Discretion to decide program scope of implementation
Information	Collection and publication of information
Programmatic history	Development of policy expertise
Clientism	Relationship with other policy actors
Political appointments	Political support for administrative goals
Leadership of agency	Quality of public management
Organizational capacity	Resources and capability for implementation

---

the government decision. The bureaucracy will also develop rules and regulations related to a piece of legislation or government program, as well as provide critical information and expertise to other institutional and noninstitutional actors. Overall, the basis of the administrative power of the bureaucracy resides in many areas. Box 4.8 outlines the various policy-making implications of administrative power:

An additional role of the bureaucracy is as a political instrument that provides leadership and the organizational capacity for how government is managed. In theory, the ideal purpose of the bureaucracy is to provide efficient and effective execution of policy decisions. In reality, the bureaucracy operates as a clash of two cultures both within and outside the agency. Outside the agency, "politicians and bureaucrats represent two different personality types, playing two different games."[13] Inside the agency, the clash continues, as an elite set of political appointees and staff may often clash with members of the professional civil service. As such, the constancy of politics cannot be completely removed from the method and manner in which the bureaucracy implements policy decisions. In total, roughly 6,000 appointees and staff positions will help fill the executive management team that sits atop the various

federal agencies.[14] As a result, although politics may damage the ideal goal of an impartial bureaucracy, each bureaucratic actor is expected to perform at the highest levels.

The performance expectations placed on the modern bureaucracy can be summed by three words: *accountability, efficiency,* and *effectiveness* (AEE). Each government agency, within the sometimes diffuse or strict area defined politically, must strive to achieve optimal AEE. In terms of accountability, each agency must ensure that it is accountable to the public it serves and the political leaders who are its administrative masters. Clearly, the bureaucracy does not operate in a vacuum of public or political influence, but within an arena of constant influence. In practice, an agency is pushed and pulled by the various institutional and noninstitutional actors that prefer the agency to perform its mission in a manner that best serves their interests. As such, because an agency remains de facto accountable through its dependence on political leaders and the public for its mandate, mission, and resources, the "smart" agency must remain aware of how its administrative actions may impact and serve this difficult goal of accountability.

In contrast, efficiency and effectiveness represent two long-standing goals within the field of public management as it relates to government bureaucracies. Efficiency represents the achievement of administrative goals at the lowest possible cost with the highest level of productivity. Efficiency, however, does not always ensure effectiveness. The goal of effectiveness is to ensure that the administrative program, whatever its purpose, achieves its mandated goals as was specified by the policy makers. Ironically, given the complex policy and political areas within which such bureaucratic goals develop and operate, the end of effectiveness may jeopardize or come at the expense of efficiency.

The failure of the bureaucracy to achieve optimal AEE does not simply threaten the agency, but can lead to the failure of an essential policy or program. At the extreme, a failure of the bureaucracy is a failure of the federal government to perform its public functions and responsibilities. Basically, the optimal influence of the agency throughout the policy process depends on to what extent it can achieve and maintain an optimal level of AEE. Yet, achieving these ends within bureaucratic realm of government, within a world in which politics redefines failure and success, is far easier stated than achieved.

THE POLICY PLAYERS—
NONINSTITUTIONAL ACTORS

Noninstitutional actors, such as interest groups, the media, members of think tanks, and the general public, are those with varying degrees of influence on making policy but no formal institutional credentials. Such actors can and do play critical roles in influencing the direction of the policy process. Interestingly, it often seems that such actors attain an even greater prominence than many institutional actors. To a certain extent, the level of influence many noninstitutional actors enjoy depends on

how actively involved they are or become within the many stages of the policy process.

Interest Groups

The power and influence of interest groups is of long-standing historical and political importance in American public policy. Alexis De Tocqueville observed that "better use has been made of association and this powerful instrument of action has been applied to more varied aims in America than anywhere else in the world."[15] Historically, the structure of American government designed by the framers ensured the place and opportunity for influence by the private actor and the organized group. One could argue that the very history of American politics is derived from a constant battle among interests and groups. As pluralists would suggest, segments of the citizenry develop an interest and passion for a particular issue of concern, and the ability to associate and organize leads to an ability to influence the opinions and perceptions of others:

> In America the citizens who form the minority associate in the first place to show their numbers and to lessen the moral authority of the majority, and secondly by stimulating competition, to discover the arguments most likely to make an impression on the majority, for they always hope to draw a majority over to their side and then to exercise power in its name.[16]

The basis for the power of interest groups, in politics and public policy, is the result of the emphasis within the U.S. Constitution for "a concern for liberty and freedom of political expression."[17] Structurally, American government represents a system in which both majorities and minorities, groups and individuals, are able to influence the direction and nature of public policy as it develops. In designing a government of checks and balances, differentiated degree of direct elected representation, as well as instituting a bill of rights ensuring certain rights and freedoms, the framers ensured the influence of interest groups. John Wright sums up this observation in discussing the intent of the framers and the rise of interest groups:

> Madison and his contemporaries succeeded brilliantly in designing a constitutional system to attenuate the power of majority factions, but in doing so, they created unanticipated opportunities for minority factions to be influential.[18]

The term *interest group* is used to describe a diverse set of political groups. Basically, interest groups fall into three categories: economic, professional, and promotional.[19] Economic groups represent the class of corporate interests, trade unions, and farmers. Professional groups represent the interests of a distinct profession, such as the American Bar Association (ABA), American Association of Retired Persons (AARP), and the American Political Science Association (APSA). Finally, promotional groups define those groups that are organized around a singular cause or interest, such as the environment, prochoice or prolife, gun control or gun rights, and senior citizens. Additionally, one may also include intergovernmental groups, such as the National League of Cities or the National Governors Association, and nonprofits, charitable or religious groups, such as the YMCA, the Red Cross, and the Salvation Army.

Overall, the influence of an interest group is based on its ability to effectively mobilize, organize, utilize fiscal and political resources, and focus its attention to a given issue within the political arena. Such groups will attempt to influence the formulation and implementation of legislation to benefit their interests. Depending on their political influence and prominence, interest groups can and do effectively push their issues to the forefront of the agenda, altering the language of legislation, adding amendments that favor their group, improving their fiscal or regulatory interests, and blocking or revising bills before they are voted on or adopted. The extent to which such groups have influence varies with time and the significance of the policy issue.

Lobbyists

If lobbying groups were judged like figure skaters, the alcohol wholesalers' recent performance on Capitol Hill would rate a perfect 10.[20]

The lobbyist is a political actor whose role in the political process is often criticized by the public while praised by private interests. The perspective one takes depends on where one stands. What cannot be denied is that these actors play significant roles in the policy process at varying times. Overall, a lobbyist's influence is derived from a mixture of elements (see Box 4.9).

Experience refers to the years a lobbyist has committed to the profession of government and political advocacy. In general, an influential lobbyist will have years of previous experience in one or more branches of the federal government. With years of experience in government, a lobbyist will have built close professional or personal relationships with key individuals of power. Such relationships allow a lobbyist to gain access to an array of decision makers that are often critical to agenda setting, formulation of

---

Box 4.9   The Lobbyist—Elements of Influence

- Experience
- Access
- Expertise
- Resources
- Character

Box 4.10 Top Ten Lobbying Firms	
LOBBYING FIRM	**FEES UNDER THE LOBBYING DISCLOSURE ACT**
1. Patton Boggs	$18,100,000
2. Verner, Lipfert, Bernhard, McPherson and Hand	$16,100,000
3. Akin Gump	$13,100,000
4. Cassidy & Associates	$12,600,000
5. Preston Gates	$11,700,000
6. PricewaterhouseCoopers	$10,300,000
7. Washington Counsel	$9,700,000
8. William & Jensen	$8,900,000
9. Hogan & Hartson	$8,400,000
10. BKSH & Associates	$4,100,000

SOURCE: Data adapted from K. Ackley, "The K Street Divide: Big 4 Lead the Way," *Influence: The Business of Lobbying,* September 20, 2000, 5.

policies, as well as policy adoption. Interestingly, the size of a lobbyist's rolodex is often a good indicator of the degree of access, and potential influence, he or she enjoys within the halls of government. Expertise, in comparison, represents the level of knowledge and skill a lobbyist may have in understanding the legislative process, as well as in developing a winning legislative strategy.

The importance of resources refers to the monies and capabilities available to the lobbyist.[21] Because of the array of corporate and special interests that require lobbyists, the profession of lobbying can be a very lucrative affair (see Box 4.10). Many multinational corporations, from Microsoft to Boeing, have an army of corporate lobbyists, as well as a series of lobbyists and firms on retainer. Finally, a lobbyist's character describes that elusive commodity from which much power and influence is derived.[22] A lobbyist whose character is open to question will seldom develop close relationships or gain the level of influence sought. Moreover, questions surrounding integrity result in a ripple of consequences in which future access is denied by the various decision makers and their staff.

Media

The importance of the media, especially in modern American public policy, is derived from the realization that information is power. How citizens are exposed to and absorb information is an increasingly potent political and policy weapon. Clearly, information and the media is a constant and effusive force that permeates America's culture. The growing presence of the media in our daily lives has led to considerable and valid attention being paid to the influence the media has on the nature of politics and the policy process.

In general, the media's influence is derived from two interrelated elements: access and interpretation. The media's access to individual citizens is constant and ever growing given the media's prevalent role in today's society. In addition, access applies to the close relationship between the media and institutional actors. Institutional actors, such as presidents, members of Congress, cabinet officials, bureaucratic officials, and personal staff, feed the media's demand for insider information and perspective. These institutional actors use the media to reach various noninstitutional actors, to push certain issues or proposals, to undercut certain policy and political agendas, as well as to foster a relationship and image that it is hoped will bias the media toward its perspective on political and policy issues. As such, the media's role as a conduit between the public and the political establishment, and between various political or institutional factions, has led to an increasing degree of access for the media across a wide swath of governmental arenas.

The constant demand for news and stories in a twenty-four-hour news cycle, in which television news and the Internet are a constant, is fostering a mutual dependence between the media and the political and policy actors. The dependence of the media on the government for news has led some critics to proclaim the diminution of the media's stature in light of the seeming decline in hard analysis and investigation of government and policy issues. In short, rather than provide the public critical information for making decisions, many media sources are increasingly described

as being too superficial in their coverage of public affairs. Additional criticisms have focused on the supposed ideological biases of various media outlets and the perception that news and analysis is used to serve a greater political agenda (see Figure 4.3). Nevertheless, the media's power within society and the policy process remains substantial given the reliance average citizens have on the attention, information, analysis, and perspective of the many news outlets presently available.

The weight of the analytical evidence suggests that the media's power to shape, define, and redefine does indeed affect the policy process.[23] Past research, for instance, indicates that the media does influence the public's salience for certain policy issues, their perceptions of social reality, and how the public defines and frames the problems considered to be important.[24] As Iyenger and Kinder suggest, "Americans' view of their society and nation are powerfully shaped by the stories that appear on the evening news."[25] As a result, if it is accepted that the media has such a critical role in framing our understanding, skewing our attention, iden-

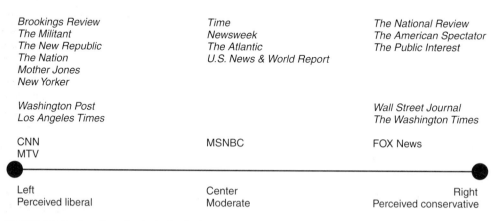

FIGURE 4.3 Real vs. Perceived Ideological Biases in the Media

SOURCE: From C. F. Bosner, E. B. McGregor, and C. V. Oster, Jr., *Policy Choices and Public Action* (Upper Saddle River, NJ: Prentice Hall, 1996), 11.

Note: The data were adapted and extended with additional media choices. The position of the national news networks reflects a general perception of the liberal and conservative bias in the news. At best, the data represent a rough estimation.

tifying problems, and setting the agenda, it is reasonable to raise concerns and doubts about the ideological bias in the media and its impact on policy.

The array of media sources has seemingly exploded in number. As stated, news and media is a twenty-four-hour enterprise and provides a constant prism from which to gain information. With the onset of the digital media age, no longer is television or television news the central outlet for images and information. With the explosion of Web pages, Internet news, e-mail, online chat, online polls, discussion groups, online video, and real-time simulcast, the reach of the media now extends far beyond traditional TV news channels. Whereas it has been suggested that "news matters," it may be far more appropriate to suggest that "digital news matters." With digital media, the sheer wealth of information, the coupling of images and stories, the interaction between the consumer and media, the real-time coverage, and the twenty-four-hour access and rapid e-mail updates suggest an emerging age in which the media's power on the policy process will not dissipate, but could greatly increase. The role of the Internet, and of digital media—once it effectively couples or replaces traditional media sources such as the TV, and once its access and usage reaches levels of those seen with television—may very well alter how policy issues evolve within the public policy arena.[26]

In terms of the policy process, the power of delivering and framing constant information to the public leads the media to have a significant role in identifying problems, setting the public and political agendas, influencing the understanding policy issues, providing particular analysis of policy proposals, and affecting how programs and policies are perceived and evaluated within the public and by the government. The rising concern with the media, especially in light of the increased prominence of the Internet and the twenty-four-hour news networks, is whether balanced and fair reporting is being presented to the public. What is unclear, for instance, is whether the constant demands for information to fill this twenty-four-hour news cycle jeopardizes more thoughtful and critical analysis of the many important domestic and foreign policy issues that affect society. Nevertheless, given the growing role of the media within society, a role that may simply explode in the coming years of the digital revolution, the real power and influence of the media within the political and policy process may have yet to reach its full potential.

Think Tanks

Think tanks represent an institute, academic or nonacademic affiliated, in which resident scholars, researchers, and fellows assigned from government, universities, the corporate world, or the media conduct original policy research analysis, and programmatic evaluation. The policy role of such groups can vary considerably depending on whether such organizations are ideologically driven or research driven with a preference against any partisan bias. In general, the influence of think tanks is derived from the ideological compatibility with respective legislators and decision makers, as well as the analytical value of their research and the insight of their expertise.

As for policy issues, depending on the think tank, an array of social, economic, domestic, and international issues may be analyzed. Think tanks may also focus on a specific policy area, such as foreign or immigration policy. The level of expertise, garnered from such research and analysis, has permitted the various researchers and scholars to sometimes play an integral role in the policy process. Experts will often be called

> **Box 4.11   Prominent Think Tanks within the United States**
>
> - The Brookings Institution
> - The Urban Institute
> - Center on Budget and Policy Priorities
> - Rand Corporation
> - The Heritage Foundation
> - American Enterprise Institute
> - Council on Foreign Relations
> - The CATO Institute
> - Tomás Rivera Policy Institute
> - Hoover Institution

on to provide testimony on proposed policy solutions or on the design of policy solutions best suited for a particular problem. Additionally, a number of institutional actors depend on think tank expertise when developing policy proposals or when deciding the consequences that may follow from a particular course of action. Aside from the specific value of their expertise, think tanks identify new policy concerns through their research, provide evaluation of the effects of past policies and programs, and help emphasize the possible consequences from specific policy actions. Finally, think tanks offer a useful forum where academics, scholars, former government officials, and other experts can collaborate and pursue research, with potentially dramatic policy implications, by focusing attention toward new and possibly better directions in public policy. Box 4.11 lists some of the most prominent think tanks.

THE PUBLIC—A MASS
OF INDIVIDUAL CITIZENS

In theory, the most significant influence on the policy process is the public. Within the context of the policy process, the public can prove vital, when attention is given and action is taken, to identifying and classifying the issues that should be identified as problems, as well as in pushing certain issues onto the agenda. Additionally, the public support for certain solutions and the demands for government action can lead to sometimes-dramatic instances of political and policy actions. For decision makers, because the citizenry is critical to the election and re-election, and indirectly influences those policy actors that are appointed by elected leaders, the public can clearly affect each and every stage of the policy process. In reality, however, the potential political power of the public often fails to materialize.

In part, ideology may offer an explanation for why the majority of the American public may be less involved in the policy process. The public, in general, is not heavily divided along ideological lines. Ideologically, based on public opinion data between 1973 and 1998, the opinions of Americans are neither extremely liberal (2 percent) nor extremely conservative (3 percent).[27] Public opinion data also suggest that the largest percentage of voters identify themselves as moderates (34 percent). Hence, there is no impassioned ideological debate within American politics. Rather, American politics tends to reflect the influence of moderates who constrain dramatic changes in policy direction. The lack of ideological fervor within American politics may also explain the public's lack of political participation.

With respect to electoral participation, no more than 51 percent of voting-age Americans voted in the 1996 and 2000 presidential elections.[28] Public opinion data also portray an American electorate that is distrusting of its government, which tolerates apathy, and fails to vote at a high percentage across all levels of government.[29] Moreover, the data suggest a public of individuals whose opinions are fickle, and whose attention of certain problems is fleeting. Issues perceived as problems at one moment will often have to compete with other issues of much less significance. In short, the image of the public derived from the data suggests, as one democratic theorist stated, an electorate whose actions and deeds question the very foundation of democratic theory.[30]

The lack of participation within American politics has especially profound implications for the policy process. At a minimum, those who do not participate in the political process delegate their power over decision makers to those interest groups, political parties, government officials, and citizens who do actively participate. More troubling, lack of political involvement may fuel even greater apathy in the future. For decision makers, because so many citizens fail to become active in the policy process, it is simply smart politics to focus more on the interests of individuals and groups that are active factors in their political future. Arguably, the apathetic may become active and mobilized only if a particular issue of concern materializes with some personal significance. Still, whether the public participates or not, the citizenry will continue to have a dominant role in the policy process.

The public's role, and its potential political influence if members become active, is cemented in the Constitution through the basis of the vote, elected representation, and a republic system of government that operates with a pluralistic character. Although it is not entirely evident that citizens can rise to the demands of the modern polity in which policy-making develops, the public can, when mobilized, shift the policy agenda toward issues and positions that favor its interests. Of course, to what extent segments of the public can impact the policy process is directly dependent on whether they choose to expend the time and energy required.

Because decisions as to the course of policy action will be made, irrespective of who does or does not participate, it becomes inevitable that certain individuals and groups will gather a disproportionate influence on the policy process because of their willingness to participate. Interestingly, an analysis of recent national, state, and local voting results, coupled with a realization that even fewer individuals choose to actively participate after an election, suggests that an increasingly small percentage of individuals influences politics and policy. Essentially, those who remove themselves from the policy process feed a costly spiral of apathy that can have significant consequences on whether their problems are identified or ignored, whether the design of policy solutions is appropriate to their concerns, and, whether certain policies are adopted or defeated by the more active interests within the political society. In the end, the impact of the public seems to begin and end with a decision by many citizens who choose less influence over potentially more influence through the various stages of the policy process.

SUMMARY

The focus of this chapter was to provide a brief overview of many of the most important actors or players in the policy process. These actors were classified as institutional and noninstitutional actors. The institutional actors represent the set of actors central to the governmental role in the policy-making process. The noninstitutional actors include those actors that seek to influence, directly and indirectly, the actions and decisions of the institutional actors. Overall, each of these actors does enjoy varying degrees of influence at various stages of the policy process. Subsequent chapters will attempt to expand on those actors that are especially influential at a given stage of the policy process.

DISCUSSION QUESTIONS

1. In your opinion, which actor proves most influential to the overall policy-making process?

2. Do you believe that the policies that matter most to members of Congress are the ones that help get them reelected?

3. Which actor(s) should have the primary responsibility for making foreign policy? Should the same actor(s) have the primary responsibility for making domestic policy? Discuss.

4. To what extent are the policy role and influence of the media understood?

   a. Does the bias of the media shape the direction of public policy?

   b. Discuss the bias and impact of the major news networks.

5. Should academics or think tanks have more or less of a role in the policy process? Does expert opinion pose a threat to pluralism and the policy process?

SUGGESTED READINGS

Altschull, J. H. *Agents of Power: The Media and Public Policy*. 2nd ed. White Plains, NY: Longman, 1995.

McKay, D. *Essentials of American Government*. Boulder, CO: Westview Press, 2000.

Sherrill, R. T. *Why They Call It Politics*. 6th ed. Fort Worth, TX: Harcourt, 2000.

Smith, H. *The Power Game: How Washington Works*. New York: Ballantine Books, 1988.

Van Horn, C. E., D. C. Baumer, and W. T. Gormley, *Politics and Public Policy*. Washington, DC: *Congressional Quarterly*, 1992.

Wilson, J. Q. *Bureaucracy: What Governments Do and Why They Do It*. New York: Basic Books, 1989.

Wright, J. R. *Interest Groups and Congress: Lobbying, Contributions, and Influence*. Needham Heights, MA: Allyn & Bacon, 1996.

ENDNOTES

1. H. Smith, *The Power Game: How Washington Works* (New York: Ballantine Books, 1988), 280.

2. Ibid, 281.

3. Ken O'Donnell, aide to President John F. Kennedy, is a famous example.

4. J. Moore and W. Slater, *Bush's Brain: How Karl Rove Made George W. Bush Presidential* (New York: Public Affairs, 2003).

5. Smith, *The Power Game*, 311.

6. D. L. Horowitz, *The Courts and Social Policy* (New York: Brookings University Press, 1977), 19.

7. A. Hamilton, "The Federalist, No. 78," in D. T. Canon, ed., *The Enduring Debate: Classic Contemporary Readings in American Politics* (New York: Norton, 2000), 236.

8. T. C. Pocklington, *Liberal Democracy* (Toronto: Holt Reinhart, 1985), 141.

9. R. Bork, "Neutral Principles and Some First Amendment Problems," in John H. Garvey and T. Alexander Aleinkoff, eds., *Modern Constitutionalist Theory* (St Paul, MN: West, 1989), 42.

10. David O'Brien, "The Court in American Life," in D. T. Canon, ed., *The Enduring Debate: Classic Contemporary Readings in American Politics* (New York: Norton, 2000), 242–248.

11. W. Wilson, "The Study of Administration," in J. M. Shafritz and A. C. Hyde, *Classics of Public Administration* (Fort Worth, TX: Harcourt, 1997), 14–26.

12. Ibid, 15.

13. Smith, *The Power Game*, 573.

14. The rough number of executive and staff-related appointments is about 6,000 positions. These positions include those that require Senate confirmation, as well as advisors for the president and senior executive officials, and support staff.

15. A. De Tocqueville, "Political Association in the United States," in Ann G. Serow, W. Wayne Shannon, and Everett Carll Ladd, eds., *The American Polity Reader* (New York: Norton, 1990), 420–421.

16. Ibid, 420.

17. J. R. Wright, *Interest Groups and Congress: Lobbying, Contributions, and Influence* (Needham Heights, MA: Allyn & Bacon, 1996), 12.

18. Ibid, 14.

19. D. McKay, *Essentials of American Government* (New York: Westview Press, 2000).

20. John Moore, "The Grapes of Wrath," in D. T. Canon, ed., *The Enduring Debate: Classic Contemporary Readings in American Politics* (New York: Norton, 2000), 422.

21. K. Ackley, "The K Street Divide: Big 4 Lead the Way," *Influence: The Business of Lobbying,* September 20, 2000.

22. In the course of interviews for researching this book, and additional work on legislative strategy and lobbying, the term *character* was repeatedly mentioned by those interviewed. The notion of character was emphasized as if it were a commodity that staffers, members of Congress, and other government professionals used to gauge whether or not they could trust the individual who was lobbying them. Once lost, this commodity was difficult, if not impossible, to replace. Ironically, many noted that this is far more important than financial contributions that a lobbyist could provide.

23. See J. H. Altschull, *Agents of Power: The Media and Public Policy,* 2nd ed. (White Plains, NY: Longman, 1995): S. Iyenger, The Media Game: American Politics in the Television Age (Boston: Allyn & Bacon, 1993)

24. M. E. McCombs and D. L. Shaw, *The Emergence of American Political Issues—The Agenda Setting Function of the Press* (St. Paul, MN: West, 1977).

25. S. Iyenger and D. Kinder, "News That Matters," in S. Theodoulou and M. Cahn, *Public Policy: The Essential Readings* (Upper Saddle River, NJ: Prentice Hall, 1995), 296.

26. It is our opinion, based on the growing role of the Internet, that once these two mediums— TV and Internet—are coupled together effectively for the layperson, the power of the media may take an exponential jump. In other words, if and when an average person has ready access to the Internet and broadband capability, the media, in general, may become an even greater agenda-setting force. For a recent book on this possibility, and the growing role of the Internet on politics, see: G. Browning, *Electronic Democracy: Using the Internet to Transform American Politics,* 2nd ed. (Information Today, Inc., 2002).

27. H. W. Stanley and R. G. Niemi, *Vital Statistics on American Politics 1999–2000* (Washington, DC: CQ Press, 2000), 116.

28. Thomas R. Dye, *Politics in America* (Upper Saddle River, NJ: Prentice Hall, 2002), 105.

29. Stanley and Niemi, *Vital Statistics,* 108–162.

30. Bernard Berelson, "Democratic Theory and Public Opinion," *Public Opinion Quarterly* 16 (1952): 313–330.

PART II

Understanding How Policy Is Made

5

The Policy Process

Diverse Models
and Theories

Understanding the policy process, the method by which policy develops, changes, and is executed, requires a theoretical framework. Within the field of public policy there are a number of theoretical perspectives, models, and schools of thought, but there is no one universally accepted theoretical approach. To the contrary, a diverse set of theories and models compete with one another in providing uniquely different perspectives on the policy process.[1]

For the student of public policy, the theory one selects in order to understand the evolution of the policy process has lasting analytical consequences. The manner in which policy makers, scholars, and leaders within government come to understand the many complex policy issues depends on theoretical framework. In short, the role of theory proves critical to how we understand areas of public policy and the policy process as a whole.[2]

THE ROLE OF THEORY

The ultimate role of theory is to help us better understand the complexity of social, economic, and political phenomena. What theory strives to offer is a parsimonious path of understanding that illuminates the elements and dynamics intrinsic to any given policy issue. Through simplification and abstraction, theory helps clarify the complexity of the policy process before us. Additionally, theory provides an explanation of how phenomena may develop and offers a basis with which to evaluate these explanations through empirical validation.[3] Theory also helps guide and focus our analysis of policy problems and issues. Yet, no theory is a perfect illustration of any phenomenon or of reality.

Most theories, if not all, are intrinsically weak in how well they describe and explain the dynamics of the political and policy process. Each theoretical framework is based on a set of assumptions that seek to explain the phenomena in question. Every theory has its respective strengths and weaknesses. Differing theoretical perspectives, however, should not be seen in polemic arguments of right and wrong. Rather, there is analytical value gained from applying differing theories to the same phenomena in question. The challenge is in deriving valid insights from the variety of theoretical perspectives. In the end, although some policy practitioners discount the explicit value of theory and theorizing, suggesting it is more of an academic than practical exercise, it is clear that both theory and theorizing are critical to improving our understanding of the policy process and to improving the content, purpose, and impact of public policy.[4]

DOMINANT THEORIES
OF THE POLICY PROCESS

The primary theoretical approach taken by this text in explaining the policy process is that of the stages-heuristic or policy cycle approach. To many scholars this represents the theoretical paradigm with which to *best* understand the policy process. Yet, for others, this approach is less than dominant in its explanatory value.[5] Overall, a variety of competing theories have been developed to explain the dynamics and evolution of the policy process. Among the dominant schools of thought within the field of public policy, the following will be discussed:

- Stages-heuristic (policy cycle) approach
- Rational choice approaches
- Advocacy coalition framework approach
- Incrementalism
- Multiple streams model
- Punctuated equilibrium model

Stages-Heuristic (Policy Cycle) Approach

As discussed in Chapter 2, the stages-heuristic or policy cycle approach conceptualizes the policy process as an interrelated series of stages. This theoretical perspective was borne from the works of Harold Lasswell, who sought to provide a conceptual map with which to describe the evolution of policy as a "decision process."[6] Since Lasswell's work, the stages-heuristic approach has evolved into a cycle of recognized policy stages that include the emergence of a problem through enactment of the policy solution to evaluation and possible policy change. The commonly agreed-on stages of the policy process are noted in Box 5.1.

The stages-heuristic or policy cycle approach is the framework adopted for this text and many others.[7] The analytical value of this approach is derived from dividing the policy process along a series of fluid stages so one can better dissect the dynamics, actors, and institutions that impact a specific stage or the policy process as a whole.[8] The theoretical strength of the approach is that it helps to simplify the imposing complexities of the overall policy process.

What Lasswell sought to initially provide, and what other scholars have sought to build on, is a theoretical generalization that allows one to better understand the policy process as a whole, at specific phases, or at a specific stage. As discussed in Chapter 2,

---

Box 5.1   Stages-Heuristic (Policy Cycle) Approach

- Problem identification
- Agenda setting
- Policy formulation or design
- Policy adoption
- Policy implementation
- Policy evaluation
- Policy termination or change

SOURCES: Adapted from Charles Jones, *An Introduction to the Study of Public Policy* (Belmont, CA: Wadsworth, 1984); James E. Anderson, *Public Policymaking* (New York: Holt, Rinehart & Winston, 1975).

Note: There are variants on the stages-heuristic (policy cycle) approach, with some authors collapsing the stages and others adding to or deemphasizing them. Charles Jones and James E. Anderson were the first to use this approach.

---

these policy stages can be further grouped into three phases—predecision, decision, and postdecision.[9] Such a division allows one to focus on the predecision dynamics of problem identification, agenda setting, and policy formulation, the decision dynamics of adoption, or the factors that shape the postdecision stages of implementation, evaluation, and termination or change.

Essentially, it is assumed that each stage of the policy process has "a distinctive characteristic and mannerism and process that give the individual stage a life and presence of its own."[10] The strength of the framework is that it provides a basis within which to gain an overall understanding of the policy process as a fluid cycle of stages involving a variety of dynamics, institutions, and actors. Each stage represents an integral part of an interlocking and ongoing policy process whereby issues evolve into problems, problems enter the agenda, and solutions are formulated, adopted, and implemented. Finally, evaluation of policy can lead to political or administrative consideration for maintaining, changing, or

terminating the policy. Nevertheless, the stages-heuristic approach has gathered its share of scholarly criticism for what some argue is a lack of theoretical specificity, an absence of empirical validation, and its descriptive inaccuracy of the "actual" policy process.[11]

For critics, the main weakness of the theory is that the public policy process does not operate in the step-by-step manner as described. The essence of the critiques highlights that Lasswell's initial identification of a series of policy stages does not mirror actual stages identifiable within the American public policy process. Moreover, it is quite rare to even hear policy makers discuss the policy process in such a clearly defined manner. More severe criticisms suggest that stages-heuristic is not a theory at all because no causal assumptions exist that can be verified empirically. Still, whereas the actual policy process may not operate in a perfect set of step-by-step stages, the stages-heuristic approach provides the necessary direction, clarity, and structure to better understand what otherwise would be a jumbled maze by which policy evolves.

The stages-heuristic approach, by dividing the process into a series of interrelated and fluid series of phases and stages, proves a useful framework to explore the evolution of public policy. Although the practical policy process may not exactly mirror each stage, the theory does capture the dynamics of an evolutionary policy process that begins with an identification of the problem and the setting of the agenda, then continues on to adoption, implementation, evaluation, and termination or policy change. Even though weaknesses do exist within the stages-heuristic theory, it is clear that this theoretical approach has proved valuable to improving our understanding of the policy process.[12] Some of the key theoretical insights derived from this approach are summarized in Box 5.2.

- Helps deconstruct what is a complex abstract policy-making process
- Provides a conceptual framework for the policy process based on different stages
- Assumes policy making is the product of a dynamic political and policy process
- Assumes an evolutionary character to public policy making (i.e., there is a beginning and identifiable end to the stages of policy making, but the policy process continues on)
- Emphasizes the significance of a series of interrelated policy stages:
  - Problem identification
  - Agenda setting
  - Policy formulation or design
  - Policy adoption
  - Policy implementation
  - Policy evaluation
  - Policy termination or change
- These stages can be divided into three additional phases:
  - Predecision
  - Decision,
  - Postdecision
- Serves to focus attention and understanding on dynamics relevant within a specific policy stage (e.g., theories of agenda setting)
- Highlights the unique impact of differing stages or phases on the entire policy process (e.g., importance of policy implementation for effective policy making)

SOURCE: From P. Sabatier, ed., *Theories of the Policy Process* (Boulder, CO: Westview Press, 1999), 3–18. Reprinted by permission.

Stages-Heuristic (Policy Cycle) Approach—A Summary

The stages–heuristic theory adds to our collective theoretical insights and base of knowledge by allowing us to explore each policy stage, phase, and the policy process in a variety of manners and directions.[13] The significance of this approach is evident from research into how an issue is identified as a policy problem, to the dynamics that explain which problems enter the political agenda, from the analysis of the forces that shape policy design and policy formulations, to the actors and elements that affect policy implementation and evaluation.[14] As such, greater knowledge, differing perspectives, and additional insights have been and continue to be gained from this theoretical approach.

Rational Choice Approaches

Rational choice models provide analysis of the policy process based on models and theories focused on assumptions of rationality, the impact of context on rationality, and the consequences that result from the rational pursuits undertaken by groups or individuals. The analytical utility of rational choice is based on the assumption of how individuals or groups will act and decide within a given decision context. Although some authors rebuke rational choice as an approach to understanding politics and policy, there is theoretical value to it because the approach allows analysts to understand how rational actions often dictate decision making in the policy process.[15] In order to better understand this expansive school of thought, a variety of rational choice models, including institutional, public choice, game theory, and expected utility, will be briefly discussed.

Institutional Rational Choice. This broad school of thought is theoretically focused on actor-centered institutionalism and on how the policy process can be understood as an interaction between the rational actions of individuals and groups. Three main elements are associated with the institutional rational choice approach:[16]

1. Humans are rational

2. Behavior is strongly influenced by institutional rules

3. Institutional rules alter rational behavior

The institutional analysis and development (IAD) framework highlights the promise of such institutional rational choice. The IAD framework identifies three tiers of decision making—constitutional, collective choice, and operational decisions—that are seen as valuable elements for analysis and evaluation of government decisions and policy outcomes.[17] The value of the IAD approach is that it offers a rational basis with which to explore the policy process and decision making both theoretically and practically. This approach, for example, has been used in the analysis of policing services, in understanding how local governments are organized, in analyzing common resource problems, in exploring the effect of institutions on forest usage, and in the analysis of constitutional issues related to American and Canadian governments.[18]

Public Choice. The public choice theory is "the study of collective decisions made by groups of individuals through the political process to maximize their own self-interest."[19] This approach applies the assumptions of rationality, self-interest, and maximization to understand the policy and political arenas. The public choice approach assumes that individuals have preferences, and that they pursue a course of action that seeks to maximize the benefits of their optimal preferences. However, public choice theory, and the assumption of rationality, does not assume that individuals make the best decisions or are incapable of making moral or immoral decisions. Rather, it assumes that decisions by policy actors are often made based on limited information and that actions taken will be based on the maximization of benefits as calculated by the decision maker.

The central premise of public choice theory suggests that individuals will act in a predictable manner given certain incentives or disincentives. In particular, it is assumed that individuals will not "knowingly choose a higher-cost means of achieving a given end when a lower cost alternative is available."[20] The implication of this assumption for public policy is far-reaching and provides the means with which to predict or forecast the effect that policies, programs, and governmental structure may have on individual behavior:

> The notion that people will respond to incentives in predictable ways is central to rational choice and to public policy. If the cost of health care rises in real terms (adjusted for changes in inflation), less will be demanded. Drivers will buckle their seat belts if the perceived benefits (reduced risk of injury) outweigh the cost (time spent buckling and the discomfort of the restraint). But, if the cost of their use is viewed as exceeding the benefit, seat belts will remain unbuckled. People will try to reduce costs and increase benefits to themselves.[21]

Aside from highlighting the expected behavior of individuals, public choice provides further insight into the collective consequences that arise from individual decisions. Given that public policy operates in a political forum where individual and group decisions interact, it is invaluable to understand that individuals' decisions, when taken collectively, can have negative consequences for the individual, group, and society. These collective negative consequences resulting from individual rational actions are highlighted by the notion of the "tragedy of the commons."

The tragedy of the commons describes how individuals may pursue decisions that maximize their benefits, even exploiting others or overconsuming certain resources, because the direct costs are distributed within and across the society. Hence, the resulting consequences of individual rationality, if left unchecked or unregulated, may prove damaging to the individual and society. The implication of this assumption has profound consequences for understanding the purpose and role of public policy within a society. Public policy, for instance, can be assumed necessary to address failings arising from the natural interactions of individuals pursuing their self-interests. Government regulation and oversight, laws and policies governing individual behavior, can be assumed necessary to address certain decisions that do not rationally calculate the adverse effect that private actions have on the greater public interest.

Game Theory. Game theory can be defined as a "theory of interdependent decisions—when the decisions of two or more individuals jointly determine the outcome of a situation."[22] The aim of game theory is to study the strategic interactions and decisions of individuals, as well as predict the outcomes that arise from any specific decision. Game theory has also been utilized to explore many issues within foreign policy, national security, and economic policy. As an analytical tool, game theory provides focus, rigor, precision, and even clarity as to how policy makers make decisions within the policy process.[23]

As with other approaches under the broad rubric of rational choice, game theory assumes decision makers are rational and will pursue a course of action that seeks to optimize the ends desired. Again, the rationality assumption does not necessarily assume that decision makers will make "good" choices or that actors will make decisions that are truly best for them when judged by hindsight. Rather, the rationality assumption presumes that individuals will make the best decision for themselves based on the information available and given the goal that they prefer to obtain. In other words, one can indeed make "bad" decisions because of poor infor-

mation, limited information, or goals that may be poorly defined or poorly thought through. Thus, rational behavior should not be thought of as always achieving the best outcome, but as goal directed as actors are assumed to prefer "more desired outcomes rather than less desired outcomes."[24]

Game theory permits an understanding of political decision making that can be both simplistic and complex. There are many variants of games from the simple two-person game to the more complex games involving iterated steps and many actors. An example of a relatively simple game within the public policy process is the Prisoner's Dilemma (see Figure 5.1).

Prisoner's Dilemma highlights the collective negative consequences that can result if individuals pursue their self-interests. Basically, the game involves two partners arrested for a crime. The police are interrogating the two partners to determine which one is responsible for the crime. The situation confronting the two partners-in-crime is difficult in light of the potential dire consequences—a prison sentence of ten years if they are found individually guilty of the most serious of the charges.

The dilemma confronting the partners is whether they will choose to stay quiet or not. If each of them stays quiet, they will both receive a relatively light sentence of two years because the police lack the more substantial evidence required to charge them with a greater crime. If, however, a prisoner

	Prisoner B	
	Stay Silent	Talk to the Police
Prisoner A Stay Silent	2.2	10.0
Talk to the Police	0.10	5.5

FIGURE 5.1 Classic Prisoner's Dilemma

SOURCE: From James E. Dougherty and Robert F. Pfaltzgraff, Jr., *Contending Theories of International Relations* (New York: Pearson Education, 2001), 506–507. Reprinted by permission.

chooses to talk to the police while the other stays quiet, the partner who talks to the police will go free on probation. However, if both prisoners talk to the police and admit the guilt of the other they will receive a sentence of five years—a much harsher sentence than if they had stayed quiet. The strategic dilemma is whether each partner can trust the other to stay quiet, or will the "rational actor" prefer no jail time—as well as fear the potential consequences if the other partner talks first? In the end, if both partners do what is most rational for them individually, the interaction of these individual decisions will prove less than optimal for each of them, and far less optimal than if they had found some method of cooperating with each other before the game ended.

Overall, the Prisoner's Dilemma game illustrates the societal consequences of lack of cooperation. Individuals who focus only to maximize their own self-interests produce collective consequences that can prove costly. Interestingly, the outcome of this game is by no means fixed. Rather, as information and learning occur, it is inevitable that these partners, and other rational actors in similar situations, will develop strategies for avoiding the more negative outcome.

Prisoner's Dilemma provides a powerful example of the societal consequences that can follow decisions driven by only narrow self-interests. In terms of public policy, this particular game allows us to deduce the value and importance of certain policies that regulate individual behaviors that have a negative effect on society. Game theory also helps explain the potentially negative effects that arise if individuals make decisions based on poor information, poor analysis, and a poor understanding of future consequences. Moreover, such games also provide a basis with which to explore the theoretical conditions under which policy actors, even with diverse interests, could and would choose to cooperate. From improving our understanding of regulations, whether criminal or environ-

mental, to determining the stability of nuclear deterrence, game theory provides a powerful tool for exploring the process by which policy decisions are made.

Expected Utility. In this rational choice approach, the actions taken by individuals in a decision context are driven by a desire to maximize the "expected utility" of benefits versus the costs. What is unique about the expected utility model is the emphasis placed upon how individuals decide their actions based on the *expected* benefits they will recieve versus the *expected* costs they will confront.

Essentially, the "expected utility model is concerned with explaining how policy positions of competing interests evolve over time."[25] The value of this theoretical approach is that it can be used to explain—even predict—political decisions at any level of analysis and the outcomes of certain policy actions, the effect of various actors on the policy process, and the strategies that can help achieve desired policy goals.[26]

The profound insights derived from this model are based on understanding how the potential power of the actors involved, their respective policy positions, and their salience for the issue can lead to a dynamic outcome that can be roughly forecasted. This approach has already been used in government and by various consulting firms to address a range of economic, political, and social policy issues. As of yet, this model has not gained wide acceptance within the field of public policy.

Rational Choice Approaches— A Summary

The power of rational choice, whether discussed in terms of the IAD framework, public choice, game theory, or expected utility, is that it provides a logical basis with which to attempt to understand, analyze, and predict the decisions of individuals within a political and policy context. The approach garners specific criticism over the high level of abstraction, simplicity, and assumptions of rationality.[27] Clearly, this broad theoretical approach is by no means flawless as there are practical weaknesses given the significant abstraction involved. Nevertheless, rational models can prove an invaluable tool with which to better understand the effect of context, the impact of actor preferences, the rational calculations underscoring political decisions, and the resulting consequences that can follow from the pursuit of individual actions within a greater community or societal context.

Advocacy Coalition
Framework Approach

The advocacy coalition framework (ACF) approach to understanding the policy process emerged in light of questions and concerns with the validity of the stages-heuristic approach. The ACF approach was an attempt by Paul Sabatier to develop a theoretical model of the policy process that was more reflective of its complexity and reality. The initial premises of the ACF approach emphasized the following factors:

- The role of technical information on the understanding of the problem

- A time frame in which policy change occurred over a decade

- A focus on the policy subsystem as the analytical center for the policy process

- An expansion of the traditional notion of the iron triangle to include all levels of governmental actors and noninstitutional actors

- An understanding that programs reflect an implicit belief system

The ACF approach, based on these five broad premises, defines the policy process as a broad structure in which a specific policy subsystem is constrained and impacted by

the stability and dynamic nature of elements external to the subsystem. Sabatier identifies two classes of external elements—stable and dynamic. The stable class of external events includes elements determined to be difficult to change over time. Such elements are the constitutional structure of the state or political system, the sociocultural values within the polity, and the natural resources available to the state.[28] These factors represent the stable context in which a policy subsystem is framed.

In contrast, the dynamic factors reflect those elements that do change over time. For example, the election of a new presidential administration, and changes in the majority party within Congress can and do alter the political landscape. Additionally, socioeconomic changes, brought on by economic downturns or social cleavages, also redefine the greater context in which policy develops. Finally, policy decisions, once adopted and implemented, can alter the context by redefining both the problem and policies that are explored within a given policy subsystem.

The notion of a policy subsystem, according to the ACF approach, is the core with which to understand the policy process. Such subsystems develop around various policy issues and the policy actors involved coalesce and interact with set groups defined as "advocacy coalitions." Advocacy coalitions involve both traditional and nontraditional actors who share beliefs and engage in "a nontrivial degree of coordinated activity over time."[29] Within each advocacy coalition, the role of beliefs is used to explain the cohesiveness and the actions of the groups that operate in the policy subsystem.

According to the ACF model, three levels of beliefs are conceptualized: deep core, policy core, and secondary. Deep core beliefs represent the critical normative beliefs of the members. Policy core beliefs represent "a coalition's basic normative commitments and causal perceptions across an entire policy domain or subsystem."[30] Policy core beliefs are also the "fundamental glue of coalitions."[31] Secondary beliefs are narrower beliefs concerning the policy issue, and may not extend throughout the subsystem. Overall, deep core beliefs remain difficult to change, whereas policy core and secondary beliefs are open to change as new information and pressures alter the basis for such beliefs.

For each advocacy coalition, strategies are pursued to alter the outcomes and decisions of governing agencies. The goal for such coalitions is to alter policies so that they conform to their members' beliefs and preferences. As new information emerges, coalitions may rethink their strategies and preferences for certain policy goals. However, members are unlikely to change their views concerning deep core and policy core beliefs. For example, a coalition that holds a deep ideological belief about the Second Amendment, and whose policy core beliefs do not favor gun control, will prove difficult to change even if valid information exists that questions such policy positions. Hence, whereas secondary beliefs can be changed, revision of deep core and policy core beliefs may require extreme measures to shift the members' belief system.

As a theoretical approach, advocacy coalition framework has been utilized within a wide variety of policy arenas including the environment, education, nuclear waste, drug policy, forest policy, airline regulation, and gender discrimination. The research undertaken over the last decade, and the insights derived, has also led to subsequent modifications in the ACF model. An updated version of the ACF approach incorporates the role of public opinion as an external factor that shocks the policy subsystem, and the factor of political consensus, required for policy change, which differs depending on the institutional context. Still, concerns do exist with this promising school of thought as well.

The ACF approach strives to capture the complex context, dynamics, and structure of the policy process, but presents an image of the policy process that is arguably as abstract and unrealistic as any other model—if not more so. Are there, for example, groups and actors that recognize themselves as part of an "advocacy coalition framework?" Moreover, in the pursuit to address the various aspects of the policy process, it remains unclear whether the assumptions made by the ACF are indeed theoretically accurate. For example, can deep core, policy core, and secondary beliefs be readily distinguished? If so, how can such beliefs be clearly defined nonarbitrarily? Additionally, are stable factors, such as sociocultural values, really that stable or is the very judgment of stability subjective? Finally, what effects do dynamic or stable factors have on beliefs, strategy, and information? Clearly, when evaluating the ACF model many questions arise and persist.

Advocacy Coalition Framework Approach—A Summary

As a theoretical endeavor, the ACF is the most aggressive of recent attempts to develop a comprehensive theory of the entire policy process. Although certain concerns may persist, ACF still represents a promising approach and a valuable foil to the stages-heuristic approach. Specifically, ACF highlights the importance of information and beliefs in the policy process. In addition, it expands the traditional notions of the policy subsystem to include an array of noninstitutional and institutional actors. Arguably, the most significant insights lie in the assumption that certain beliefs held do not change readily and that dramatic or differing directions in policy require external shocks to such beliefs. For the future, this framework remains one of the most promising theoretical paradigms in the field of public policy and may, with additional refinements, offer the most cogent and persuasive theory of the policy process.

Incremental Approach

Charles Lindblom, the architect of incrementalism, sought to develop an alternative to the rational model of understanding the policy process. Lindblom questioned the very notion that public policies could ever be formulated in a rational and calculating process. For Lindblom, rational calculation, comprehensive understanding, and effective analysis were beyond the capacities of those in the policy process, and were at best possible only with the simplest problems.[32] Rather than a rational exercise, the incremental approach suggests that the policy process operates within an inefficient political and institutional environment where policy decisions naturally favor minimal over dramatic policy change.

According to Lindblom, the rational comprehensive approach suggests that policy decisions are made in a clear and logical manner. By extension, the rational approach suggests that the entire policy process can be described as rational exercise that logically leads to the best policy decisions in relation to the problems observed.

Incrementalism, in contrast, describes the process of policy development as that of a series of "successive limited comparisons." For Lindblom, successive limited comparisons was a better description of the policy process because it emphasized the practical nature of the policy and political process versus a rational ideal desired for the process. This contrast is striking, and is best evident in comparing the rational comprehensive approach with that of successive limited comparisons (see Box 5.3).

The rational approach suggests that values and objectives can be clearly specified. The incremental approach, however, assumes that the selection of values eludes clear articulation because a number of values may be put forth, and clarity of the goals of policy remains open to contention. As such, incremental adjustment to present policies is preferred in light of the lack of clarity over what is the better policy. In other words, the policy process will not result in dramatically better policy solutions

---

Box 5.3   Comparison of the Rational and Incremental Approaches

Rational Comprehensive Approach
1. Clarification of values and objectives.
2. Policy formulation is approached through means-ends analysis. First, ends and then the means to achieve them are sought.
3. Test of a good policy is that it is shown to be most appropriate means to the desired ends.
4. Analysis is comprehensive—every important factor is taken into account.
5. Theory is often heavily relied on.

Incremental Approach
1. Selection of values, goals, and empirical analyses are not distinct but closely intertwined.
2. Because means and ends are not distinct, means-ends analysis is often inappropriate or limited.
3. Test of a good policy is determined by the extent of agreement among analysts for a particular policy.
4. Analysis is drastically limited, resulting in the neglecting of possible outcomes, alternative policies, and values.
5. A succession of comparison greatly reduces the reliance on theory.

SOURCES: From C. E. Lindblom, "The Science of Muddling Through," in S. Z. Theodoulou and Mathew A. Cahn, *Public Policy: The Essential Readings* (Englewood Cliffs, NJ: Prentice Hall, 1995), 113–127; C. E. Lindblom, "The Science of Muddling Through," *Public Administration Review* 19 (1959): 117. Reprinted by permission.

because it is unclear within this policy process what *is* a better policy solution. For Lindblom, agreement and consensus among analysts will become the criteria for determining the "best" policy. Hence, in lieu of more information, marginal or incremental change is preferred to dramatic change.

For Lindblom, rather than an all-encompassing analysis demanded by the rational method, successive limited comparisons highlights the notion that only policies that differ marginally are considered, and only those policies that differ from the status quo. Finally, the succession of comparison assumes that rather than seek the best policy, policy makers confront the political and institutional reality that policy is an ongoing process and mistakes in policy action should be mitigated where possible. Thus, the proclivity for the analyst and policy maker, according to Lindblom, is to pursue limited policy change "through a succession of incremental changes."[33]

The Lindblom model of incrementalism offers a theoretical description of the policy process that is quite telling. Simply, the realities of the policy process lead to small changes to policy rather than bold changes. However, in striving to critique the rational comprehensive approach, the incremental approach raises some questions and doubts. For instance, how does one judge when or how means-ends analysis is limited in nature? Is the test of good policy really based on broad agreement among analysts or does it also require broader agreement among the critical institutional and noninstitutional policy actors? For example, even if all the economic analysts within the government were to suggest that the right course of policy action to redress an economic downturn was substantially increased taxation, would this be deemed a "good" policy? Is not whether the public approves a policy action a mitigating factor in how incremental the policy process may be? Moreover, how does

one judge what sufficient analysis is of a given issue?

In many policy cases, such as airline security before September 11, substantial government studies and analyses were conducted, understanding was gained, and options were proposed, but the changes were not deemed politically acceptable or possible at the time these reports were published. What was lacking, in the case of airline security, was the political will to pursue more dramatic actions which, based on the evidence, did rationally suggest that dramatic actions were necessary and warranted. Finally, it is clear that in some cases, such as with the New Deal programs and civil rights, dramatic policy changes can be made that are distinct from previous directions in policy. Arguably, incrementalism may best describe a process that leads to small changes, not because of inadequate rational calculations, poor analysis, or limited information, but because the underlying political conditions that can justify dramatic changes have yet to materialize.

Incremental Approach—A Summary

Overall, the incremental approach represents an attempt to describe the "true" nature of the policy process. Above all, it is a potent rebuke to the claims of rational decision making, and how decisions are the product of calculations of costs and benefits that result in the best policy action being adopted. Clearly, as an approach to understanding the entire policy process, incrementalism does offer analytical value. In terms of the predecision and decision stages, incrementalism may help explain why the policy process would seem to produce so few actual solutions to what are seemingly persistent and endemic public problems. Moreover, the theory offers an explanation of why dramatic policy actions are rare, even in circumstances when dramatic policy actions are warranted.[34]

Multiple Streams Model

Multiple streams, a theory developed by John Kingdon, is an attempt to explain both the dynamics of how issues enter the agenda, and how policy is made within American politics. As an approach to explaining the policy process, multiple streams may be best considered as a partial theory of the policy process. Kingdon's theory, for example, will be used in Chapter 7 as a specific explanation of the agenda-setting process. Nonetheless, a brief discussion of the theory is provided because it does offer a theoretical explanation of both the predecision and decision phases of the policy process.

The multiple streams paradigm emphasizes how issues and policy solutions emerge out of a complex context of three central dynamics or so-called streams—problems, policies, and politics. According to Kingdon's conceptualization, these streams highlight how certain issues and policy proposals gain greater attention over others within the broad political and policy environment. These broad streams operate constantly within the governmental and political system, but are seen merging at unique moments within the political system. Kingdon described these moments as "policy windows." The policy process, in other words, is marked by the opening and closing of policy windows that result from the evolving confluence between streams of problems, policies, and politics.

The "problem" stream refers to how a decision maker becomes aware of certain socioeconomic conditions or events and how these conditions or events are then viewed as a problem. The "policies" stream refers to the constant flow of policy solutions and proposals that interweave throughout the political system as a response to the presence of an identified problem. For Kingdon, policies are the byproduct of "a variety of ideas floating around in a policy primeval soup. . . [and] are generated by specialists in policy communities—networks that include bureaucrats, congressional staff members, academics, and researchers in think tanks who share a common concern in a single policy area, such as health or environmental policy."[35] The "politics" stream emphasizes the broad culture in which policy and solutions operate.[36] The significance of these three streams—problems, policies, and politics—emerges as policy windows open intermittently within American politics.

Policy windows, as conceptualized by Kingdon, occur and open at "critical moments in time."[37] Such windows are opened either by the nature of a problem or by politics. The windows provide an opening for policy actors to attempt to push through certain policy solutions over others. Hence, for policy actors and policy entrepreneurs involved, action and reaction to the emergence of such windows is critical because it is during these periods that policy solutions are selected. In a sense, for Kingdon, policy process and policy action revolve around the opening of these critical policy windows.

The theoretical value of multiple streams stems from an emphasis on the interrelationship between political and policy dynamics evident in the beginning phases of the policy-making process. Furthermore, the theory may explain why some problems and certain policy solutions are not recognized politically as important issues or relevant solutions. Evidently, for Kingdon, the character of the policy process reflects a seemingly constant competition. This competition manifests among policy actors who must struggle over who will define the nature of the problem, set the agenda, formulate solutions, and influence the adoption of policy actions. As a theoretical approach, although multiple streams offers valuable insights for improving our understanding of the beginning stages of the policy process, questions do arise over some of the assumptions.

The multiple streams paradigm does not effectively make distinctions among the three streams and whether they are independent or interdependent. Additionally, the notion of policy windows—why they result and whether they are fleeting—remains unclear. In practical terms, how does one ascertain when a policy window has or has not opened? It is also unclear what the exact impact is from actors and policy entrepreneurs on the resulting selection of certain solutions over others. Even more important are the issues as to how multiple streams aid our understanding of the entire policy process, including the implementation and evaluation of policy solutions. For instance, how do these streams strengthen or weaken policy solutions that have been adopted? Again, the specific role of implementation and evaluation within the multiple streams framework remains unclear.

Multiple Streams Model—A Summary

Overall, multiple streams offers a promising approach to understanding the seemingly chaotic nature of the policy process. Specifically, multiple streams may help explain why certain policy problems and solutions emerge and dominate our attention at a given time and not at other times. Multiple streams also explains that the understanding of problems and the emergence of certain policy solutions are not the product of clean rational analysis, but are the products of rational decisions and policy ideas borne out of the intrinsic ambiguity and seeming chaos of the policy and political process. In particular, the framework seems to provide a potent theoretical explanation for improving our understanding of the predecision and decision stages of the policy process.

Punctuated Equilibrium Model

Punctuated equilibrium is a theory that attempts to explain how dramatic changes in policy can occur, even though the policy process can also be characterized as incremental and relatively stable in nature. This seemingly contradictory nature in the policy process, between dynamic and stable policy change, coexists depending on the greater socioeconomic or political conditions that emerge. As with multiple streams, the theory of punctuated equilibrium may best explain the beginning stages and phases of the policy process.

According to Frank Baumgartner and Bryan Jones, the architects of the theory, the policy process is framed by political institutions and bounded rationality. In terms of the policy process, whereas the theory centers on the issue attention and agenda-setting stages, it does help understand both policy formulation and adoption. In general, the theory attempts to explain why the focus on certain policy issues changes over time, how certain policies reinforce the status quo, but also how certain periods emerge within the polity in which the issues, the status quo, and the policies once deemed acceptable can change dramatically.[38]

Punctuated equilibrium theory suggests that the diffuse governing nature of American politics—the divisions created by the unique institutional, constitutional, and subsystems evident within American politics—favors a general stability in the policy process, but still provides an opportunity for dramatic change to arise:

> [S]eparated institutions, overlapping jurisdictions, and relatively open access to mobilization in the United States combine to create a dynamic between the politics of a subsystem and the macro politics of Congress and presidency—a dynamic that usually works against any impetus for change but occasionally reinforces it.[39]

The diffuse nature of American politics, according to Baumgartner and Jones, promotes pronounced institutional stability. Still, this same institutional structure provides a path from which actors can and do mobilize to alter the status quo. In other words, although not necessarily the norm of the policy process, dramatic change is a possibility when cooperation or clarity emerge as to the immediacy of a particular policy issue. The tendency for both stability and dramatic change in the status quo can be explained by better understanding the agenda-setting process.

For Baumgartner and Jones, a series of policy subsystems continuously operate within and across the institutional and constitutional confines of American politics. These policy subsystems can surround single or multiple issues, can be dominated by specific interests, or could involve competition among a variety of special interests. As the issues confronted by the subsystem increase in number, the tendency is for policy solutions to be incremental rather than dramatic. However, this incremental nature can fuel dissatisfaction among groups and interests displeased with current policy proposals and solutions. As a result, an issue can be forced onto a macrolevel political agenda, within the institutional agenda of Congress or the executive branch, because of the mobilization of the disaffected. Fueling this mobilization, according to punctuated equilibrium theory, are changing policy images surrounding the issue that have been redefined by new information leading to increases in the number of disaffected.

The image of a policy, or how it is perceived within the policy process, is critical to explaining which subsystems remain stable. Policy images that foster consensus over how to understand or describe policy issues are more often associated with a stable agenda. In contrast, as a new image gains adherents, new opportunities exist to challenge the static nature of a policy subsystem—either

within the subsystem, or more dramatically at the macrolevel. Overall, the defining nature of American politics is that gridlock and general incrementalism coexist with the opportunities for punctuated change in the direction and content of public policy.

Punctuated change can occur not only because of the institutional context and agenda-setting dynamic but also because of the substantial effect that new information and new images have on political decision making. Baumgartner and Jones explain these "bursts of change and policy punctuations as arising from the interaction of images and institutions."[40] Essentially, dramatic change is possible because preferences of individuals for certain policies are not fixed indefinitely. As individual opinions change, so can the attention and understanding of a policy issue. Such dramatic change is possible because of a theoretical assumption of how individual and collective decisions can change.

Punctuated equilibrium assumes a bounded rationality in how individuals or groups come to decisions. Bounded rationality suggests that attention is paid only to an aspect of an issue rather than its totality. The consequence of this dynamic is that shifts in attention can lead to different understandings and preferences among policy actors. New information and new images can lead to schisms in how policy issues or problems were once viewed. This, in turn, can lead to new policy solutions and results in distinct changes in the direction of public policy. Thus, rather than classic incrementalism, punctuated equilibrium offers an explanation of the policy process that is both static and dramatic—the nature of change depending, in large part, on the degree of new information that can alter the image of the policy problem and mobilize the various interests within the policy process.

Overall, as a theory of policy change, punctuated equilibrium offers an innovative explanation of the policy process. One of the most fruitful areas of research using this approach has been an evaluation of the national budgeting process.[41] Because budgets are negotiated on a yearly basis, they provide a fertile empirical ground for observing dramatic changes in policy images that lead to changes in fiscal allocations.[42] Yet, even though the theory is intuitively appealing, and its theoretical explanation of policy change is an elegant extension of classic incrementalism, it remains somewhat limited in offering insight to all aspects and stages of the policy process.

Punctuated equilibrium can help us understand how problems are identified, issues develop, the agenda is set, as well as how certain issues may become the center focus for various policy actors; however, the theory does not address what happens after a policy is adopted. Yet, failures in implementation, as highlighted by consistently poor public administration of government programs, may be a critical cause for the perceptual changes in the images of an issue. For example, federal funding of welfare programs underwent a dramatic change with the 1996 passage of welfare reform. In part, what fueled this growing political desire to reexamine welfare policy was a perception that current government welfare programs and policies were inefficient and ineffective. As such, because of poor implementation, a negative image of public welfare programs became legitimized and helped fuel, to some extent, the dramatic changes in welfare policy that have recently occurred.

Punctuated Equilibrium Model— A Summary

Punctuated equilibrium offers an important extension of the incrementalist approach to understanding the policy process. Although by no means a complete theory of the policy process, punctuated equilibrium does provide theoretical insight into the predeci-sion and decision phases of the policy process. In particular, the theory offers a dramatic explanation of the reasons for sometimes-dramatic changes that can occur in the early phases of the policy process.

SUMMARY OF DOMINANT THEORIES OF THE POLICY PROCESS

A persistent quest within the field of public policy is conceptualizing the holy grail of public policy theory—or a theory that captures the *true* dynamic and nature of the entire public policy process. The value of such a theory, of course, is self-evident. With perfect understanding comes perfect analysis, and with perfect analyses come perfect policies to address the many socioeconomic problems that have seemingly endured for generations. Although such a goal is admirable, it will likely prove elusive. The goal should not be for a "perfect" theory, but a "better" theory, clearer understanding, and more insightful analysis. As the discussion of the previous frameworks, theories, and models has indicated, each perspective and approach offers valuable insights.

The choice between theories, models, and frameworks should not be seen as an either–or proposition. Rather, the challenge should be to utilize the approaches where warranted, derive analytical value from them where applicable, compare and contrast the insights gained from each, and utilize the best theory or theories with which to understand the intrinsic complexity of the policy process. Above all, one should not become so wedded to a single approach that it becomes the sole prism with which to understand public policy. Undoubtedly, each school of thought offers a variety of perspectives on the nature of the policy process that is useful to improving

Box 5.4   Understanding the Policy Process Use of Various Policy Theories & Models

Stages of Policy Process

Theories & Models	PRE DECISION PHASE			DECISION PHASE	POST DECISION PHASE		
	Problem Identification	*Agenda Setting*	*Policy Formation*	*Policy Adoption*	*Policy Implementation*	*Policy Evaluation*	*Termination or Change*
Stages-Heuristic	*	*	*	*	*	*	*
Rational Choice Approach		*	*	*			*
Multiple Streams Model	*	*	*	*			
Incremental Approach	*	*	*	*	*		*
Punctuated Equilibrium Model	*	*	*	*			
Advocacy Coalition Framework	*	*	*	*	*		*

our understanding of public policy. Although one may perceive an intrinsic need to find the best theory, we believe there is a value to each of theories when placed within the framework provided by the stages-heuristic model. In the end, how one should apply these differing schools of thought to better understand the public policy process is open to wide debate.

Determining which is the better theory of the policy process will remain an openly contentious and subjective exercise. Clearly, even though no one theory provides all of the answers, no one theory should be immediately discounted or ignored. Moreover, although many of these theories were not designed to explain all facets and stages of the policy process, it is still possible to derive theoretical knowledge and practical value from them.[43] In fact, subsequent extensions of these theories may offer even more promising explanations of the policy process. The goal for students, analysts, and policy makers should be to use each of the theories in order to build on their overall understanding of the policy process.

Our position is that each of us must first understand the overall policy process, and then begin to develop greater theoretical insight into the overall complexity and fluidity of the policy process. We believe that this difficult task is accomplished by first utilizing the stages-heuristic approach to establish the conceptual foundation and framework for understanding the basic policy process. Although other approaches have their utility, and may offer a more promising theoretical analysis of specific stages or phases of the policy process, we believe that the stages-heuristic approach continues to prove instrumental if one is to gain a better understanding of the overall policy process.

It may be suggested that better under-standing requires a structured and diverse path of thinking. To that end, we offer an ar-guably *better* manner with which to under-stand the place and purpose of the theories discussed in this chapter. Rather than adopt a single theory or model, each of the previ-ous theories can be seen as providing greater understanding of specific phases and stages outlined by the stage-heuristic framework. Rational models, for example, can provide an understanding of the dynamics of deci-sion making and strategic negotiations that pervade the policy formulation and adop-tion stages. The multiple streams and punc-tuated equilibrium theories can help focus our explanations of the dynamics to problem identification and agenda setting, as well as policy adoption. Similarly, incrementalism can offer a theoretical perspective on the limitations to dramatic policy formulation, adoption, and implementation. Finally, the ACF approach can be utilized, in part, to understand how the many stages of the pol-icy process are intimately interrelated and af-fected by so-called advocacy coalitions.

Box 5.4 compares the six theories de-scribed in this chapter and how each attempts to explain the dynamics and evolution of the policy process.

As stated, we believe that the dominant theory for understanding the overall struc-ture of the policy process remains the stages-heuristic approach. Other theories, such as ACF, the incremental approach, multiple streams, punctuated equilibrium, and ra-tional choice, can and should be used to im-prove the depth of our understanding of specific phases, stages, or dynamics of policy change. Over time, this theoretical exercise may indeed lead to a new theory that evolves from all or parts of the theories that have been discussed. At a minimum, it is im-perative that a student of public policy con-sider the value and insight that all of these

theories, as well as others not discussed, can offer in understanding what is a complex field and process.

The remaining chapters will provide a description of the policy process through a stages-heuristic process. Although this ap-proach is by no means perfect, it remains an essential part—a first step—in beginning to understand the process of how policies de-velop and change. As Professor Randall Ripley once suggested, the stages-heuristic theory is invaluable to the student who wishes to understand how policy develops and evolves:

> Such stage-oriented discussions . . . are rough chronological and logical guides for observers who want to see important activities in some ordered pattern or se-quence. Such organizational helpers are useful and, in fact, essential for anyone trying to plow through the complexities of policy making and policy analysis. At best, such maps—even with their rough spots and simplifications—lend some clarity to the observer/reader/student as he or she grapples with a complicated and sometimes murky set of interactions and processes.[44]

DISCUSSION QUESTIONS

1. Do you agree that the trouble with all of the theories put forward is that none of them are rooted in reality? Do such theories have any practical value for the real-world policy actor? Discuss.

2. In your opinion, which of the theories discussed "best" explains the policy process? Conversely, which theory offers the weakest explanation of the policy process?

3. All of the theories discussed never really answer Harold Lasswell's age-old question

of "who gets what, when, and how?" Are such political questions important for a theoretical discussion of the policy process?

4. The trouble with the theories explaining policy making is that they all more or less say the same thing. Do you agree or disagree? Discuss.

5. Select each theoretical approach, and discuss what dynamic or factor should be added to make the theory better and more complete.

SUGGESTED READINGS

Baumgartner, F., and B. D. Jones. *Agendas and Instability in American Politics.* Chicago: University of Chicago Press, 1993.

Bueno De Mesquita, B. "A Decision-Making Model: Its Structure and Form." *International Interactions* 23, no. 3–4 (1997): 236.

Kingdon, J. *Agendas, Alternatives, and Public Policies.* New York: Longman, 1995.

Kuhn, T. *The Structure of Scientific Revolutions.* 2nd ed. Chicago: University of Chicago Press, 1970.

McCool, D. *Public Policy Theories, Models, and Concepts: An Anthology.* Englewood Cliffs, NJ: Prentice Hall, 1995.

Morrow, J. *Game Theory for Political Scientists.* Princeton, NJ: Princeton University Press, 1994.

Sabatier, P., ed. *Theories of the Policy Process.* Boulder, CO: Westview Press, 1999.

Sabatier, P. A., and H. Jenkins-Smith. *Policy Change and Learning: An Advocacy Coalition Framework.* Boulder, CO: Westview Press, 1993.

ENDNOTES

1. For a review of select readings, see S. Z. Theodoulou and Mathew A. Cahn, *Public Policy: The Essential Readings* (Englewood Cliffs, NJ: Prentice Hall, 1995). For more in-depth review, see P. Sabatier, ed., *Theories of the Policy Process* (Boulder, CO: Westview Press, 1999); D. McCool, *Public Policy Theories, Models, and Concepts: An*

Anthology (Englewood Cliffs, NJ: Prentice Hall, 1995).

2. For an overview, see Sabatier, ed., *Theories;* K. Q. Hill, "In Search of Theory," *Policy Currents* 7 (April 1997); McCool, *Public Policy.*

3. C. F. Nachmias and D. Nachmias, *Research Methods in the Social Sciences* (New York: St Martin's Press, 1996), 38; Thomas Kuhn, *The Structure of Scientific Revolutions,* 2nd ed. (Chicago: University of Chicago Press, 1970).

4. Public policy, as with all of political science, exists within practical and theoretical realms. For those in the "game" of politics and policy, little time is spent on theory or theorizing, as they focus on the action. In contrast, the academic community remains concerned on better understanding the actual nature of this practical process. To what extent this divide can be merged will be critical to what extent public policy, the process of policy making, and, by extension, society can be improved.

5. Sabatier, *Theories.*

6. H. D. Lasswell, *The Decision Process* (College Park: University of Maryland Press, 1956), and H. D. Lasswell, *A Pre-View of Policy Sciences* (New York: American Elsevier, 1971).

7. Others who have applied this approach are B. G. Peters, *American Public Policy,* 4th ed. (Chatham, NJ: Chatham House, 1996); Theodoulou and Cahn, *Public Policy;* J. A. Anderson, *Public Policymaking,* 3rd ed. (Boston: Houghton Mifflin, 1997); T. R. Dye, *Understanding Public Policy,* 7th ed. (Englewood Cliffs, NJ: Prentice Hall, 1992); J. P. Lester and J. Stewart, Jr., *Public Policy: An Evolutionary Approach,* 2nd ed. (New York: West, 2000).

8. Among the works on various stages are J. Kingdon, *Agendas, Alternatives, and Public Policies* (New York: Longman, 1995); A. L. Schneider and H. Ingram, *Policy Design for Democracy.* (Lawrence: University Press of Kansas, 1997); D. Bobrow and J. Dyrzek, *Policy Analysis by Design* (Pittsburgh: University of Pittsburgh Press, 1987); G. C. Edwards III, *Public Policy Implementation* (Greenwich, CT: Jai Press, 1988).

9. This division reflects the basic actions that occur in the policy process.

10. P. Deleon, "The Stages Approach to the Policy Process: What Has It Done? Where Is It Going?" in Sabatier, 21.

11. This opinion is summarized well in Sabatier, *Theories,* 3–18.

12. Ibid., 21.

13. There is an intrinsic value to being able to deconstruct such a complex process into stages to better understand the overall method and madness to policy making.

14. For a review of various articles expanding on the stages of the policy process, see Theodoulou and Cahn, Public Policy.

15. See D. A Stone, *Policy Paradox: The Art of Political Decision Making,* 2nd ed. (New York: Norton, 1997).

16. E. Ostrom, "Institutional Rational Choice: An Assessment of the Institutional Analysis and Development Framework," in Sabatier, *Theories.*

17. Ibid., 26.

18. Ibid., 26.

19. C. E. Cochran et al., *American Public Policy— An Introduction* (New York: St. Martin's Press, 1999), 55.

20. Ibid., 59.

21. Ibid., 58.

22. J. Morrow, *Game Theory for Political Scientists* (Princeton, NJ: Princeton University Press, 1994), 1–2.

23. Scott Gates and Brian D. Humes, *Games, Information, and Politics* (Ann Arbor: University of Michigan Press, 1997), 1–23.

24. Ibid., 17.

25. Bruce Bueno De Mesquita, "A Decision-Making Model: Its Structure and Form," *International Interactions* 23, no. 3–4 (1997): 236.

26. Ibid., 236.

27. Stone, Policy Paradox.

28. P. A. Sabatier and H. C. Jenkins-Smith, "The Advocacy Coalition Framework," in Sabatier, ed., *Theories,* 120. For more detail, see P. A. Sabatier and H. Jenkins-Smith, *Policy Change and Learning: An Advocacy Coalition Framework* (Boulder, CO: Westview Press, 1993).

29. Ibid., 120.

30. Ibid., 121.

31. Ibid., 122.

32. C. E. Lindblom, "The Science of Muddling Through," in Theodoulou and Cahn, *Public Policy, The Essential Readings* (Englewood Cliffs: Prentice Hall, 1995) 113–127. For more detail, see C. E. Lindblom, "The Science of Muddling Through," *Public Administration Review* 19 (1959): 79–88, 114–115.

33. Ibid., 117.

34. Ibid., 124.

35. N. Zahariadis, "Ambiguity, Time, and Multiple Streams," in Sabatier, ed., *Theories.* Also, for more detail, see Kingdon, *Agendas.*

36. Ibid., 77.

37. Ibid., 77.

38. F. Baumgartner, B. D. Jones, and J. L. Jones, "Punctuated Equilibrium Theory: Explaining Stability and Change in American Policymaking," in Sabatier, ed., *Theories,* 97–98. Also, for a more detailed explanation, see F. Baumgartner and B. D. Jones, *Agendas and Instability in American Politics* (Chicago: University of Chicago Press, 1993).

39. Ibid., 99.

40. Ibid., 103.

41. Ibid., 103–105.

42. Baumgartner and Jones, *Agendas and Instability.*

43. As certain reviewers of the text correctly pointedout, many of the theories and approaches discussed were not intended to provide a theoretical explanation of the policy process. However, most theories have not been solely used to explain certain facets of the policy process, but have evolved to describe a policy process that incorrectly disregards the impact of certain policy stages.

44. Randall B. Ripley, "Stages of the Policy Process," in McCool, *Public Policy,* 157.

6

Problem Identification

Recognition of Problems and Issues

Problem identification is not a simple task, but it remains the initial spark to the entire policy process. Public policies are developed to address some identified issue, social ill, or problem of public importance. Public policies are not intended to address or rectify what is an issue, ill, or problem of private importance. However, identifying which issues demand or deserve recognition as public policy problems remains open to considerable debate within the political system. What remains unclear is, when does an issue of private concern manifest into a public policy problem?

Private individuals suffer countless difficulties on a daily basis that are not necessarily deemed to be the concern of any government actor. Yet, why does it seem that some problems are clearly public policy issues, while others are not? For example, little debate would ensue as to whether threats to national security are a public policy problem. In contrast, threats to national health care, education, or the environment do not result in the same degree of consensus as to whether they are or are not public policy problems. What must occur in order for a private issue to be redefined into a problem demanding attention and possible action by various policy actors? The answers to these questions depend greatly on how we come to identify and define issues as public problems.

IDENTIFYING AND DEFINING THE PUBLIC PROBLEM

The notion of what is a public policy problem is fundamental to understanding how the policy process begins—and if it begins at all. Proposals for policy actions do not simply materialize to address unidentifiable issues or unrecognized concerns. To the contrary, the setting of the agenda and formulation of a policy action, whatever its form may be, is in direct response to an issue that some policy actors have identified and defined as a problem.

At a minimum, a so-called problem, whether private or public, can be defined as an *issue of concern* that entails some degree of personal, social, or economic cost for the parties affected. Problems can also be conceptualized as stark anomalies from what is deemed either socially or individually acceptable. The number and type of issues that could be considered as actual problems is also by no means definitive. Put differently, there is not a single agreed-upon list of problems that individuals, society, or the state must focus on. Still, in terms of public policy, the issues that become the focus for policy action must first be identified and defined as issues of public concern. But what is the real difference between a public and private issue of concern?

An issue of public concern can be defined as an issue that entails some kind of social or individual obstacle or difficulty, with great consequence for the parties affected, that cannot be easily addressed or should not be ignored by individuals or society. Such issues can be defined as public problems. Public problems are perceived as representing an unacceptable social or individual anomaly that cannot be permitted to exist or persist. Public problems also result in degrees of individual or societal pain deemed unacceptable by the various policy actors

interested in or affected by such issues. An example of a seemingly obvious public problem is the issue of national security. A single individual cannot ignore, nor singularly address, a threat to national security. Issues, such as threats to national security, represent the classic public problem that is more readily identified and defined as a public problem.

In contrast, an issue of private concern, or private problems, can be defined as a class of problems that are seen as more sanguine. Private problems are perceived to be the responsibility of the parties affected. Although private problems may cause discomfort and difficulty, and in some cases may cause substantial suffering, it is perceived that the individuals or groups affected by such issues will have or should have the capacity to deal with the issue. Overall, private problems are more readily perceived by policy actors as those issues that fall in the purview of one's personal responsibility.

The distinction between private and public issues is important to the policy process. Before the 1930s New Deal programs, for example, issues such as poverty, failing to save for retirement, and unemployment were more readily considered as private problems. Similarly, before the Great Society initiatives of the 1960s, issues such as family hunger or unaffordable housing were not easily identified as public problems. Yet, since the 1990s, with the onset of welfare reform initiatives, issues such as the plight of the poor have become reshaped by a redefinition of the problem. Ironically, in less than four decades, poverty has been fundamentally redefined into an issue that is increasingly identified by many policy actors as more of a private problem.

The debate over what is a public problem is not simply one of semantics. How an issue is identified and defined, whether it is a private or public problem, raises important questions as to the scope of government action that may be necessary. If social security can be redefined as an issue of private responsibility, as some have suggested, the government will no longer have to gather and redistribute resources to provide retirement assistance for seniors. In other words, how one perceives any issue of concern has stark implications for the policy process.

The reason such debate exists is that identifying and defining issues of public concern remains an incredibly subjective enterprise. As beliefs and perceptions change, issues can be defined or redefined into either public or private issues. Again, that an issue is presently perceived to fall in the rubric of private responsibility does not mean that this issue will be forever identified as a private problem. Instead, how issues are evaluated and judged by various policy actors can change as beliefs change within the society. As Christopher Bosso suggests, identifying and defining what is a public problem remains an especially difficult challenge:

[P]erhaps we are in an indeterminate period where all definitions of public problems are up for grabs, a free-for-all of meaning that eventually settle into new cleavages. Perhaps it is because of macro-level social and economic

trends—the globalization of everything, it seems—have destroyed once stable policy and political alignments, or because the penetration of virtually instantaneous electronic mass media into every facet of policy formation makes rhetoric and symbolism all the more critical to framing policy debates and policy directions.[1]

Historically, whereas the plethora of issues that one could consider as public problems is almost innumerable, certain issues are seen as public problems and rank higher in importance during certain periods. As public opinion research helps illustrate, the general category of issues that the public may consider to be problems remains relatively static, but changes can and do occur over time as new information and pressing concerns emerge. Consider, for example, the changes and consistencies in the list of issues of concern between 1980 and 2002 (see Box 6.1).

As indicated in Box 6.1, the issues of concern identified by the public often represent broad categories of problems. Such general categorizations of problems, however, rarely capture the specific problem(s) impacting the individual, group, or society. Within

---

Box 6.1   Top Issues of Concern, 1980–2002

1980	Inflation, unemployment, and Iran
1984	Unemployment, government spending, fear of war, inflation
1988	Drugs, unemployment, budget deficit
1992	The economy, unemployment, poverty/homelessness
1995	Crime/violence, unemployment, the budget deficit
2000	Morals/family decline, crime/violence, education
2002	Terrorism, national security, economy, unemployment

SOURCE: Adapted from data in Thomas R. Dye, *Politics in America* (Upper Saddle River, NJ: Prentice Hall, 2002), 92.

Note: The data is based on public opinion polls conducted by the Gallup organization. The final issues of concern for 2002 are based on polls conducted over the year. For a review of a wide array of polls on various social or political issues, go to http://www.gallup.com.

such generalizations of problems, as with the issues described as "crime/violence" or "drugs," can exist a multitude of more specific problems. For example, homelessness, poor education, family breakdown, unemployment, and urban decay may all be part and parcel to the more general problems of crime/violence or drugs. In short, how issues are identified and defined, whether they are framed as private or public issues, is critical to how and whether various policy actors identify them as the most critical for policy action.

Defining an issue as a public problem is made increasingly difficult by the pervasive disagreements that can exist among policy actors over whether an issue is or is not a public policy problem. At the heart of many heated political and policy debates is a fundamental difference in beliefs and whether the issue is so serious as to demand some kind of policy action. Basically, depending on the ideological perspective one may have at a given time, an issue of concern can be defined by some policy actors as a severe problem demanding an array of intrusive public

actions, whereas others will suggest that this is an insignificant issue that is best associated with individual responsibility. In other words, because of differing beliefs, identifying and defining which issues are public problems remains an openly contentious exercise.

Disagreements among policy actors over what are public problems helps explain why the policy process does not immediately and dramatically react to address issues of seemingly obvious concern. As suggested, there are very few issues that inspire such widespread unanimity and consensus. Consequently, sometimes heated debate, discussion, and disagreement will emerge over what should or should not be identified as the public problem (see Box 6.2).

As Box 6.2 suggests, debate and disagreement are to be expected when discussing complex issues with many facets. Consider, for instance, the issue of unemployment. The general problem of unemployment can describe those out of work, those looking for work, as well as those who no longer look for work. Furthermore, unemployment can also

---

Box 6.2   General to Specific—The Debate over Problem Definition

General Problem Area	Specific Problem	Debate over Problem Definition
Economy	Minimum wage increase	Higher employer cost vs. living wages
Health care	Higher infant mortality	Poor health care system vs. careless parents
Unemployment	Long-term unemployment	Lack of education vs. individual laziness
Savings rate	Limited personal savings	Smart investing vs. fiscal irresponsibility
Poverty	Welfare dependence	Workfare vs. fiscal aid for the poor
Homelessness	Affordable housing	Poor work ethic vs. public assistance
War	Decline in public support	Questioning of war vs. patriotism
Terrorism	Homeland security	Increased national security vs. individual liberty
Moral decline	Amoral society	Consumerist culture vs. personal failings
Crime	Lack of rehabilitation	Criminal nature vs. nurture

be indicative of more specific problems such as long-term or high rates of unemployment in certain regions, industries, or among certain minorities. The even more interesting question, however, is when does such an issue become so serious as to warrant identification as a public problem?

For example, as of March 2002, the national unemployment rate was 5.7 percent, but in South Central Los Angeles, the rate was 25 percent.[2] As of May 2002, the unemployment rate stood at 6 percent or 8.9 million unemployed Americans out of a labor force of 142.6 million.[3] For minorities, the national unemployment rate stood at 7.9 percent for Latinos/Latinas, and 11.2 percent for African Americans.[4] Will unemployment become easily identified as a national policy problem if 8 or 10 percent of all Americans are unemployed? What if you are a minority—is it a national policy problem at 7.9 percent or 13.2 percent? Arguably, the answer depends on whether one is unemployed, concerned about becoming unemployed, or simply concerned about the unemployed. In other words, the answer depends on whether or not one chooses to identify an issue as a public problem.

No issue, even if it is serious to some policy actors, is by definition a public problem. Every public policy action is the result of a belief and judgment among policy actors that this respective issue should not defined as a private problem. Almost inevitably, because of differing beliefs, some group or individual will disagree with whether an issue is of public concern. Interestingly, aside from narrow issues related to threats to national security, it does remain unclear where and when the government should become involved in the affairs of individuals and groups.[5] Again, the exercise of problem identification may seem simple and obvious to some, but it is rare that an issue will be so clearly defined and identified by all policy actors as a public problem. As a consequence, only those issues that are *clearly* recognized—either in perception or in reality—as obvious public problems can hope to quickly enter the agenda of policy making.

Once an issue is identified as a public problem, the resulting policy process, the infusion of politics, and the array of actors involved will determine where this issue ranks in relation to the many other public problems the nation confronts. In contrast, a private issue that is perceived as insignificant may remain ignored. For instance, the issue of AIDS languished in obscurity in the early 1980s, in large part because it was perceived as a problem that inflicted only narrow segments of the public and was judged to be an issue of personal responsibility. However, as the beliefs of policy actors changed by the late 1980s, the issue of AIDS was more easily identified and defined as a public problem. Overall, the perceptual confusion over problem identification helps explain why many issues of concern, even serious issues like AIDS, seem to be needlessly defined as private problems.

THE CONFUSION OVER PROBLEM IDENTIFICATION

The basis of confusion over what is a public problem stems, in part, from the intrinsic differences in our social reality. *Social reality* refers to the "simple" realization that our reality is not the product of objective analysis or perfect understanding. Instead, our reality is a social construct, derived from perceptions and beliefs, of the reality we experience and are made aware of. Individual knowledge and analysis is bounded by the social realities that are experienced directly or indirectly within one's social environment. In addition, individual beliefs, which are learned and socialized, further define the world that we see and experience. Social reality, in other words, is a powerful perceptual frame derived from the incessant interactions between what we see, what we experience, what we learn, and

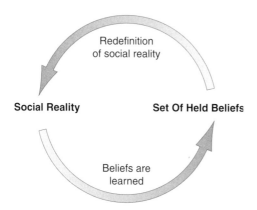

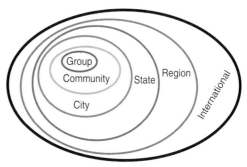

FIGURE 6.2 Levels of Social Reality

FIGURE 6.1 Dynamics of an Individual's Perceptual Frame

what we believe. As a result, our social reality, and the beliefs we develop and hold, serve as a constant perceptual frame that interprets the events that occur within our lives, as well as the issues that come to our attention (see Figure 6.1).

The notion of social reality refers to what individuals see, perceive, and experience on a day-to-day basis. An individual's social reality represents an intrinsically personal frame of reference. Each person possesses a unique social reality within which potential policy issues are evaluated and understood. Given disparate religious, ethnic, racial, gender, cultural, and regional backgrounds, it is more likely than not that one's social reality will differ to some degree, sometimes considerably, with the social realities of others within the society. Thus, because of sometimes marked differences in our social realities, and depending on our set of held beliefs, it is also quite likely that we will perceive both political and policy issues differently.

Further complicating the impact of social reality on problem identification is the realization that social reality does not manifest from personal experience alone. Over the course of the last six decades within the American polity, through an ever expanding exposure to an array of modern telecommunication technologies, such as computers,

televisions, telephones, and the Internet, every decade has led each individual to experience a social reality ever more expansive.[6] Furthermore, the constancy of this exposure to events outside one's strict circle of personal experiences ensures an almost endless flood of issues that an individual is exposed to. Today, social reality, for most Americans, truly extends from the group to the international level (see Figure 6.2).

The expansion in the levels of social reality has important consequences for problem identification. No longer are individuals limited to judgments on events or issues they experience firsthand. From the group to city level, and from the state to international level, individuals are exposed to a constant stream of stimuli, information, images, and events that they seldom experience firsthand. The global level, for example, allows many individuals to be exposed to an array of issues, events, and circumstances, such as war, famine, and terrorism, that extend far beyond the nation's borders or their own personal circle of experience. The question, of course, is which of the many issues arising from these multiple levels of social reality should we identify and define as public problems demanding policy action?

As the levels of social reality have expanded, so has the exposure to an array of issues of seemingly great importance. Modern media technologies, especially the Internet and television, have made it possible for a diverse set of domestic and international events—such as natural disasters, crime, famine, genocide, pollution, poverty, civil unrest, or terrorism—to be perceived as impacting us directly. This impact may not be based on actual experience, or even physical contact, but may be based solely on the perception that these issues somehow matter and have significance for the individual, the group, the community, the state, the region, or the international society. One could even argue that we are increasingly living in a faux world of perceptual experiences rather than a real world based on our actual experiences. Hence, given the array of issues that can materialize across our social reality, it is our respective belief systems that help focus and define which issues we become concerned with.

Essentially, individuals remain limited by their cognitive and informational capacities because they cannot truly be aware of, perceive, understand, and render a well-balanced opinion on the entire class of issues that they are exposed to almost daily. Our belief systems provide a path by which we redefine our social reality and the issues that we are concerned with. These beliefs not only provide the tool by which we winnow away the supposedly insignificant issues but also help guide and focus our attention on which issues we consider to be public problems. Even though "reality is always more complex, inchoate, contradictory, and inexplicable than our images and metaphors of it," we must come to some understanding of which issues are the greatest concern to us as individuals.[7]

THE PERCEPTUAL PROCESS OF PROBLEM IDENTIFICATION

Determining which problems gain our attention and inspire clarity requires an understanding that problem identification must first pass through a powerful filter or screen of beliefs that develops within and is affected by our social reality. These beliefs explicitly affect whether diverse individuals, even from varied backgrounds, can derive similar perceptions on what is or is not a problem. Depending on the nature of learned beliefs shared or individually held, the interpretation, significance, and analysis of events or actions can differ widely within a group, a community, a city, state, or a nation.

Individual and societal beliefs frame what we see and understand. For Rein and Schon, learned facts, values, theories, and interests frame and define one's social reality. Such a framing of beliefs essentially alters the understanding and implications of the various issues, actions, and events that emerge across our levels of social reality. More specifically, these frames, which emerge from a fusion of an array of cultural, political, ideological, religious, and moral beliefs, offer a "way of selecting, organizing, interpreting, and making sense of a complex reality."[8]

The impact of such differing sets of beliefs is that multiple levels of social realities emerge; multiple interpretations of similar issues, actions, and events can emerge as well. Individuals and the opinions they render, as to what is or is not a public problem, can vary widely depending on the beliefs held by the respective policy actors at particular periods. In the abstract, one can outline a perceptual process of how issues may come to be identified as policy problems (see Figure 6.3).

In the first stage, individuals learn a set of beliefs that evolve within their societal environment. Such beliefs develop and are shaped by all levels of social reality to which they are exposed. The strength of these beliefs can redefine one's social reality in terms of what they believe they experience, observe, and perceive. One's social reality not only further shapes the formation of one's beliefs but can also expose each individual to an increasing number of potential policy

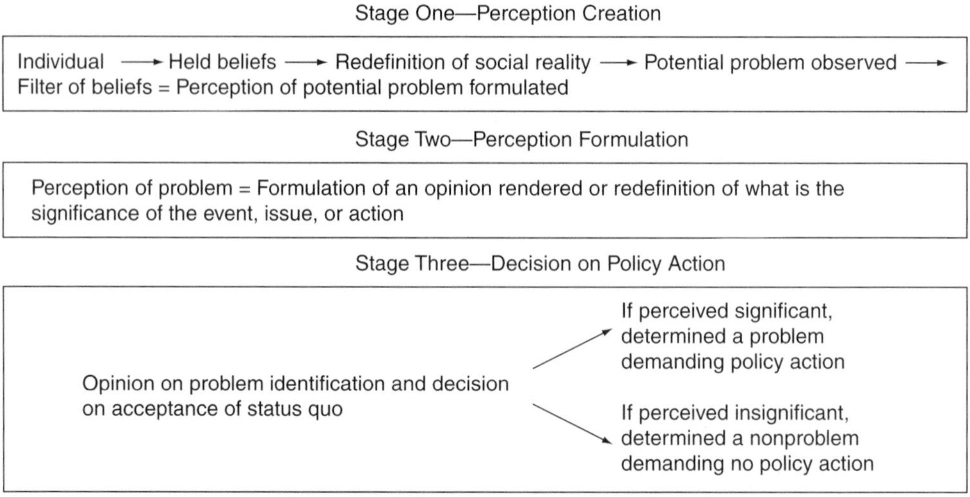

Stage One—Perception Creation

Individual ⟶ Held beliefs ⟶ Redefinition of social reality ⟶ Potential problem observed ⟶
Filter of beliefs = Perception of potential problem formulated

Stage Two—Perception Formulation

Perception of problem = Formulation of an opinion rendered or redefinition of what is the
significance of the event, issue, or action

Stage Three—Decision on Policy Action

Opinion on problem identification and decision
on acceptance of status quo

If perceived significant,
determined a problem
demanding policy action

If perceived insignificant,
determined a nonproblem
demanding no policy action

FIGURE 6.3 Perceptual Process of Problem Identification

problems. These beliefs manifest into a powerful and implicit filter through which potential problems are framed and perceived. It is from this filter of beliefs that opinions are formulated as to whether an issue is or is not a problem.

In the second stage, individual perceptions affect the evaluation of what is or is not an actual policy problem. These beliefs, learned over the course of a lifetime, influence the formulation of opinions, perspectives, and perceptions that emerge out of an individual's social reality. For the individual, these sets of beliefs, whether moral, ideological, political, or religious, are influenced and operate within a greater culture. These beliefs are further reinforced by facts and information learned. This learning helps to further define and refine one's evaluation of what is an issue of concern.

In the third stage, a decision on whether one perceives an issue as a public problem is rendered. If the actor believes an issue is a policy problem, then public policy action is justified or rationalized. If the decision is that the issue is not a problem, then the actor can easily justify or rationalize the lack of policy

action. In general, if differences in sets of beliefs emerge among individuals and policy actors, so does the likelihood that issues will be perceived in widely different manners. Overall, the perceptual process of problem identification highlights the importance of both social reality and power of beliefs to emphasize certain issues over others.

The effect of beliefs on problem identification can prove significant. For example, certain political beliefs characterized as liberal in nature may sensitize individuals and policy actors to the concerns of the working class, the plight of the poor, environmental threats, and civil rights. Conversely, learned political beliefs characterized as conservative may sensitize individuals and policy actors to concerns with excessive regulation, increased taxation, privacy issues, and the growth of the federal government. Similarly, other influences on one's belief system, such as ideological, ethnic, racial, religious, or cultural, may effectively heighten one's awareness toward particular issues, actions, and events. For example, an African American, having experienced discrimination within the respective social reality, and having developed certain beliefs as to the persistence of racism within society, will be understandably sensitive to whether issues of discrimination or racism are problems that require some kind of public policy action. In contrast, other individuals, who may have not experienced discrimination, or are unfamiliar with such events within their social reality, become directly dependent on the degree of learning and beliefs that they develop as to how they perceive issues such as discrimination. It is to be expected, unless social realities change or new beliefs are learned, that disagreements will persist among actors over which issues should be identified as public problems.

The dynamic nature of problem identification is that neither our social reality nor our beliefs are by any means fixed and innate. Although sets of beliefs and opinions may remain relatively stable, they can and do change over time.[9] New information, significant life experiences, and basic changes in and across one's social reality can change one's set of beliefs. Profound and striking new information, in particular, is a significant force in the perceptual process "that bears upon beliefs about policy alternatives," and which "can change people's policy preferences."[10]

Although the potential for redefinition of beliefs is possible as new information is learned, the influence of beliefs, and the power of these beliefs in shaping one's social reality, can prove a formidable obstacle. The power of information to reframe how individuals perceive certain policy issues depends on whether they learn new information. Long-held beliefs, quite simply, do not easily change unless new information or experiences compel a reevaluation of the meaning of such beliefs. Moreover, held beliefs can provide a powerful short-cut for both analysis and opinion on which issues are of concern. Beliefs, depending on their strength, can lead one to have perceptions and derive conclusions that disregard and discount the

importance of contradictory information. Amazingly, the extent and nature of beliefs an individual can develop within the American polity can even seem at odds with one another:

> The dualistic state of mind may be found in the domestic political values subscribed to by most Americans. We are comfortable believing in majority and minority rights, in both consensus and freedom, federalism and centralization. . . . Americans have managed to be both puritanical and hedonistic, idealistic and materialistic, peace-loving and war-mongering, isolationist and interventionist, conformist and individualist, consensus-minded and conflict-prone.[11]

The influence of beliefs on how we view specific policy issues does have real implications for the policy process. Consider, for instance, the issue of gun violence. Gun violence within America far exceeds every other Western industrialized nation.[12] In 2000, according to the Department of Justice, it was estimated that 66 percent of the 15,517 murders within the United States were committed with firearms.[13] Also, among all deaths from firearms in 2000, 57 percent were suicides and 3 percent were caused by unintentional use.[14] Yet, even with thousands of murders, suicides, and unintentional deaths, there is no semblance of clarity among the critical policy actors as to what is the issue of concern or what kind of policy action should be taken. Why?

In terms of the gun debate, it is the beliefs of certain policy actors that lead them toward or away from certain problem definitions. For groups like the National Rifle Association (NRA), the issue of gun ownership is seen as a matter of personal responsibility. The NRA subscribes to the belief that the government should not infringe on one's "right to bear arms." Although research and evidence does suggest that the extent of access and the number of guns within a society is associated with the rate of gun violence, the NRA disagrees with such positions.[15] For the NRA, notions that gun ownership contributes to the rate of gun violence represent a poor analysis of what is the problem. Hence, the NRA seeks, as it has, to refocus the debate on the need to ensure self-defense, the growing threat posed by crime, as well as the right to bear arms which the NRA believes is afforded under the Second Amendment. In stark comparison, the beliefs of other policy actors, such as the James Brady Foundation, consider gun violence to be an especially serious public problem that demands more aggressive regulatory policy actions to control the public's use and access to guns. The striking difference between these two policy actors, in terms of how they view the issue of guns, is not in whether one is objectively right and the other is wrong. In reality, such debates over problem identification are seldom academic discussions where validity of research and evidence is objectively weighed before opinions are rendered. Rather, the difference stems in the beliefs these policy actors hold. It is these beliefs that affect how such policy actors perceive and analyze the nature of issue. It is these very beliefs that help them determine whether they will judge an issue to be a public or private problem.

In sum, the power of beliefs within the problem identification stage can prove formidable in both identifying and defining which issues are of importance. This set of complex beliefs can prove so significant that political discourse surrounding important societal and political issues can essentially be changed or muted. As Christopher Bosso suggests, the strength of some beliefs can quickly nullify public debate:

> The national ideology of free-market capitalism is so potent that anyone who suggests real alternatives is labeled

quickly a radical or dreamer, an image that ultimately exiles advocates to the margins of mainstream discourse. So powerful is the ideology of the free and demonstrably impersonal market that even those most harmed—the workers playing their assigned roles as unfortunate victims—usually can only shake their heads and shrug their shoulders. What, after all, is to be done if "the market" takes away your job?[16]

FACTORS INFLUENCING PROBLEM IDENTIFICATION

As discussed, the perceptual process of problem identification can prove difficult and complicated. However, there are factors that can assist and improve perceptual clarity. D. A. Rochefort and R. W. Cobb identify a series of elements that can influence whether policy actors identify and define an issue as a public policy problem.[17] Among the critical factors that help focus problem identification are

- Causality
- Severity
- Incidence
- Proximity
- Crisis

Causality is an element intrinsic to any discussion of whether an issue is a potential policy problem. Identifying and understanding the factors or actors responsible for a certain problem is essential in determining whether an issue is perceived as a private or public problem. A problem that is clearly perceived as the product of institutional or societal failures may be more easily perceived as a public problem. Perceptions of problems believed to be caused by faults in personal character may suggest to some that this is a private problem. In contrast, if causality remains unclear, the potential problem may be diminished in significance and could confuse problem definition.

Establishing causality, however, is by no means a simple task. Most issues of concern confronting a complex society, whether poverty, health care, unemployment, education, crime, or social security, can be debated as being caused by an array of factors. Such issues can be framed as being caused by the failings of individuals, groups, institutions or society. Although analysis and research may support certain causal understandings, the debate rages because there is seldom agreement regarding the cause of any specific problem.

Severity represents the seriousness of a particular problem.[18] Arguably, this element highlights the crux of what can be clearly identified as a problem demanding government action. For many actors within the policy process, issues are described in stark terms that emphasize calamity, catastrophe, or disaster. Whether the discussion surrounds issues such as AIDS, unemployment, gun violence, environmental pollution, or terrorism, the notion of severity reflects a belief that the specific issue is of grave importance.

The difficulty is that an issue does not simply attain the status of severity. The issue in question must reflect a level of consequence that is rare and profound. Determining severity is itself a subjective exercise because the consequences of a potential problem are not often clear to all. Severity is made clearer at some extremes where great cost is borne on a large or specific segment of society. For example, wars and natural disasters are seldom defined as private problems because they adversely affect a large population. Still, because such clear examples of severe events are rare, severity can often be defined or redefined into issues that are not obvious policy problems.

Incidence, or the frequency of an event, is also a factor in identifying problems. Fre-

quency, real and perceived, characterizes the occurrence of an issue, event, or action. Occurrence, and the rate of such occurrence, affects the awareness of actors by emphasizing whether a potential problem is worsening, improving, or remaining static. Accordingly, "linear or even exponential projections are the most ominous, and when accepted as valid, tend to create the most pressure for quick public intervention."[19]

Incidence may also desensitize policy actors to the severity of the problem. Problems that are seen as frequent and inevitable may result in issues being diminished in significance. American murder rates, for instance, although significantly higher than other Western industrialized nations, do not elicit the same public reaction or alarm.[20] One could argue that murders, both real and within the popular culture, have desensitized those who are directly affected or concerned with such an issue.

Proximity represents how close an issue of concern affects an individual. In the context of social reality, a problem that develops closer to one's immediate level of social reality is more likely to be identified as a problem. Conversely, issues far removed from one's social reality are more likely not to be readily perceived as problems. The impact of proximity varies depending on how sensitive an individual is to potential problems across various levels of their social reality.

Except in circumstances in which a potential problem directly impacts the individual, the concern over proximity is again one of perception. Based on one's beliefs, an individual may be greatly concerned over issues such as Third World poverty, whereas others will rationalize such issues being beyond their scope of concern. In comparison, increasing unemployment, for example, may lead to little concern among the working population. However, once layoffs begin at one's own respective employer, it becomes clear that unemployment and a slowing economy is now a problem close to home.

Crisis, or a problem with unique quali- ties of severity, proximity, and incidence, represents the elusive point by which a new level of significance is attained. What differ- entiates a crisis from a noncrisis is a difficult and subjective matter to determine. The term *crisis,* for example, has significant "po- litical implications because it can be used by claim-makers to elevate a concern when facing an environment overloaded with competing claims."[21] Within the general rubric of a crisis are notions that a problem has crossed a threshold of severity and im- mediacy, and impacts the individual or na- tion with a clear proximity. A crisis, for instance, cannot be avoided or ignored, and represents a class of problems that demands action by the government. Yet, because the term is often used to spark heightened at- tention, the label itself does not necessarily mean that a crisis exists. Nevertheless, a *real* crisis, if it is perceived, represents the most serious of problems that can focus attention within and across social realities, and can limit debate among policy actors as to whether or not a problem exists. A classic example of a crisis is the terrorist attack of September 11, 2001.

Public Problem or Private Issue?

The debate over what should be identified as a public problem is not simply an academic exercise, but carries with it enormous polit- ical and social implications. Policy actions cannot be taken to solve all potential prob- lems a society may confront. Because of lim- itations on fiscal or budgetary resources, difficulties posed by agency implementation, the degree of political or public support for certain actions, and the sheer administrative time demanded to address certain issues through programs and services, it is essential to somehow accurately determine what is a public problem. Problem identification, however, remains a perceptual exercise, and not an exercise based on objective fact. Rea-

sonable people can disagree on whether an issue is a problem, because reasonable people can and do have differing social realities and sets of beliefs.

Differing social realities and the filter of our beliefs systems we develop as we become socialized will constantly skew problem identification. Thus, clarity in whether an is- sue is identified as a public problem may be considered an exception, rather than the norm. Still, as new information and under- standing emerges, so does the potential for redefining whether an issue should be a pub- lic or private problem. For instance, the issue of obesity and diet may appear to most as a private issue that falls far beyond the purview of the government regulation. At present, there are no initiatives to place warning la- bels on fast-food selections at restaurants that are high in fat content and over a lifetime can contribute to a number of long-term health ailments. Yet, the illnesses associated with obesity cost society billions of dollars and af- fect millions of lives. Therefore, is this an is- sue of private or public concern? Again, although many policy actors may easily per- ceive certain issues as *clearly* private, transfor- mations in perceptions can and do occur. Consider the dramatic changes in how a bad habit of private responsibility became radi- cally transformed into a behavior that is seen as a serious health issue and is significantly regulated by various levels of government— cigarette smoking.

Cigarette smoking was once seen in a harmless light, and the consequences of health ailments surrounding long-term use were discounted or ignored. Less than three decades ago, for instance, smoking was so- cially acceptable at home and at work. Basi- cally, cigarette smoking was seen as relatively harmless and as a matter of private choice that did not demand nor require any kind of government action. However, as new infor- mation emerged as to the harmful nature of smoking, our beliefs pertaining to the costs and impact of smoking changed. As beliefs and perceptions of cigarette smoking changed from a "bad habit" to a harmful and addictive carcinogen, so did positions among many policy actors as to whether public action was necessary to address this previously private issue. From regulating advertising, limiting how the product is sold and used, as well as applying significant taxations to decrease user demand, cigarette smoking represents an issue that is now considered much more a clear public problem than it was in the 1950s or 1960s.

The cigarette-smoking example highlights how an issue, as beliefs and perceptions change, can be transformed from a private to public problem. Essentially, the distinction between what is a private and public issue is not absolute or static. As new conditions emerge within one's social reality, as changes in beliefs occur, and as a new definition of an issue gains dominance among the critical policy actors, a private issue can become transformed into a public issue. However, as discussed earlier in the chapter, this process is by no means simple as it is rare that policy actors will agree on the change. To the contrary, throughout the policy process, policy actors will battle over how an issue is framed, the information that is used to describe it, as well as whether it should be considered a public or private problem.

Most issues of concern begin as a private issue of individual responsibility. In other words, aside from national defense, there is no ready-made list of issues that the government must address as falling under public responsibility. Rather, the case of why this issue matters must be made. Policy actors can and do debate whether or not an issue is a problem and whether government action is warranted. A private issue will transform into a public problem as it is redefined as being unacceptable for the society and as greater clarity emerges among policy actors as to the pejorative effects of the respective issue on society. Such private issues develop into potential public problems through this perceptual process by which beliefs and understanding redefine the issue as one of collective or public responsibility. What then is a public policy problem?

A *public policy problem* is an issue that can no longer remain within the private realm because of its perceived significance or consequence for all or part of the society. Such significance is, in part, determined by the extent of negative conditions associated with the issue. For example, most policy actors accept the state's role in providing national defense given the believed dire consequences that would follow without national security. Such rare clarity in perception of a public policy problem is aided if the issue in question involves an important human need necessary for survival or is central to the quality of life agreed to by the society or relevant policy actors. Above all, a clear public problem will prove to be an issue that cannot be resolved privately because of the substantial costs borne by the number of individuals affected, as well as the concomitant impact it may have on society. Put differently, it was not the single case of unemployment and poverty that led to the New Deal; it was the thousands and millions of individuals who were in similar plight, and the perceived consequences to the society if no public assistance was provided. The question, of course, is why does the state not become concerned earlier with this issue when it affects, even severely possibly, just a few individuals?

A clear public policy problem is an issue that bears significant costs and negatively affects a substantial percentage or segment of society. In particular, as the degree of cost and the scope of those affected increases to the extreme, greater clarity emerges among policy actors that it is a public problem and demands government involvement. Unfortunately, as the dynamics of cost and scope will help emphasize, few issues are easily identified or defined as classic public problems.

THE ROLE OF SCOPE AND COST IN PROBLEM IDENTIFICATION

Focusing on these two important dimensions—scope and cost—can greatly assist our understanding of the abstract manner by which an issue transforms from a private to public problem. In combination, both scope and cost help explain why problem identification remains a difficult perceptual exercise within the policy process. As seems to be the case, there is rarely consensus among policy actors as to which issues are problems, as well as which issues are the most pressing problems. The notions of scope and cost, we believe, are fundamental to explaining which issues will gain the attention of the public, as well as which issues will be defined as public problems.

Scope

The dimension of scope defines the percentage of the public affected by an issue of concern within the greater society. As an issue impacts a larger and definable percentage of the public, greater clarity can emerge that this is an issue of consequence for the polity. In contrast, if an issue affects a single individual or small group it is unlikely to be easily defined as a public problem. Individual problems, which may lack greater societal implication, do not easily manifest into clear public problems. With such issues, it is inevitable that contentious debate will emerge among policy actors who seek to change perceptions of whether the issue is of importance for the greater community.

In general, individual problems do not necessarily instigate concern among policy actors unless they have a dire effect on a larger segment or group within the polity. Individual issues or problems—whether it is individuals making bad investment decisions, losing their jobs, getting ill, losing their savings, or getting in a car accident—often remain secluded within the private realm of individual responsibility. Of course, exceptions may occur when a seemingly private issue is redefined into one that can threaten a greater number of individuals over time. For example, a single illness may not normally result in public alarm, but if the illness is due to the exposure to a contagious virus, such as Smallpox or Ebola, such an issue will be clearly seen as demanding policy action—even if a single case remains evident.

As suggested, the notion of scope is not simply a matter of calculating the exact number of those affected by an issue. The policy significance of scope is both a perceived and real calculation. In part, it is rare than an issue that affects only a single individual will become a policy problem. Of course, such problem identification depends on whether the issue affecting the individual is perceived as a substantial problem. Again, in the absence of indisputable severity, it is our beliefs and perceptions that help define whether the scope of individuals affected justify the issue being defined as a public problem. Such beliefs and perceptions become even more vital as the issue extends further beyond the immediate level of one's social reality—because only perception, and not direct experience, can be used to assess the adverse effects of the issue. Put differently, issues such as global famine or civil wars in foreign lands do not always manifest into issues that are clearly defined as public problems. Still, the scope or the perception of those affected by an issue is but one dimension with which to better understand the evolution from private to public problem.

Cost

Aside from scope, the dimension of cost reflects the degree of dire effects associated with an issue of concern. The notion of cost represents the sum of negative consequences that develop, are associated with, and persist because of the existence of the problem. In reality, the concept of cost may be seen in the starkest of terms. For example, the effects of economic decline, hunger, poverty, poor health care, unemployment, illiteracy, crime, or terrorism can have dramatic costs for individuals and society. The most dramatic example of cost is the loss or threat posed to the lives of the citizenry. Overall, as the severity of these costs increases, so does the likelihood of a previous private problem sparking attention and causing particular concern among political actors.

As with scope, objectively determining cost is a task replete with challenges because it is often a perceptual calculation. Even if based on personal experience, determining cost must be based on the information available because no individual can directly experience the negative effects of all those affected by an issue. Again, as with scope, assessing the impact of cost is affected by the belief system held by the individual. However, as the costs associated with an issue increase in consequence, both for the individual and society, it is also expected that such issues will be more easily perceived as a policy problem.

THE CLASSIC PUBLIC POLICY PROBLEM

Which issues are policy actors most likely to become concerned with? They are the issues that can be definitively identified as having the greatest negative effect on the greatest number of individuals. As costs increase, for instance, the social consequences become of concern to the various policy actors and focus attention on the issue. Costs, in particular, highlight the necessity of government action because the negative effects

of certain issues extend beyond the capability of private individuals. Extreme severity of cost ensures that the attentions and perceptions of policy actors will center on the necessity for government action to address what is now believed to be the most important policy issue. Still, the notion of cost does not completely explain why a certain issue may be identified as a public problem. Aside from the factor of cost, it is also the number of affected individuals that can help determine which issues will be identified as public problems.

The interrelationship between the dimensions of scope and cost can help define and identify the classic public problem. Specifically, if the negative effects of an issue increase considerably, and if this issue severely affects a significant number of individuals, it becomes more likely, as the impact of this issue grows, that various policy actors will identify and define this issue as a public problem necessitating some kind of policy action. In contrast, those issues that impact few, and have little severity, are more likely to be justified as private issues that do not require government action. The difficulty is that only at the extremes does real perceptual clarity emerge through the filter of the many belief systems and differing social realities that operate within the complex society (see Figure 6.4).

At the extremes, the costs associated with the issue are extremely high or low and an overwhelming and inescapable majority of the public is, or is not, affected. In terms of cost, the more severe and negative—whether in the form of deaths, sicknesses, unemployment, or homelessness—the clearer it will become to most policy actors that this is a public problem that demands policy action. In terms of scope, as an issue affects a substantially larger percentage of the public, it becomes almost impossible to ignore or avoid.

Why do issues at the extremes represent a classic policy problem? It is at the extremes

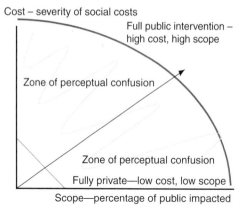

Cost – severity of social costs

Full public intervention – high cost, high scope

Zone of perceptual confusion

Zone of perceptual confusion

Fully private—low cost, low scope

Scope—percentage of public impacted

FIGURE 6.4 Path to Perceptual Clarity—The Role of Scope and Cost

of scope and cost that an issue transcends the skewing effect of countervailing beliefs. At the extremes, the perceptions of policy actors become increasingly redefined toward greater shared meaning and clarity—irrespective of their belief systems. Of course, this does not suggest that all policy actors will share in this clarity. The power of one's beliefs is that they can long outlast the realities of what they experience. In other words, even though one may be unemployed, and even if national unemployment were to reach a record high of 20 or 30 percent, there would inevitably remain individuals, groups, and policy makers—even some of them unemployed—who would oppose the perception that this was a public issue demanding *radical* policies such as a new version of the New Deal. Historically, it is this inevitable debate over perceptions that all but ensures that only a few issues will be clearly seen as a classic public problem.

More often, as it would seem, the majority of issues fall into the "zone of perceptual confusion," where debate, persuasion, ideology, organization, and sheer politics determine which issues are deemed public problems. Although at the extremes issues can be more clearly perceived, few issues fall

into such obvious extremes. Most potential policy issues develop within the so-called zone of perceptual confusion where constant political debate exists over whether or not the issue in question is even a public problem (see Figure 6.4). Within this zone of perceptual confusion, differing beliefs and social realities will continue to complicate how various actors perceive the issue in question. However, during a crisis, the sheer magnitude of the issue fosters much greater clarity in identifying the issue as a public problem.

Crises can be readily framed and identified as issues that demand immediate and substantial government action. Policy actors, when confronted by a severe crisis, cannot easily redefine the issue into one of nonsignificance for the society. In other words, an issue that has dire costs and affects a large scope of individuals within the polity will be considered a classic public problem.

National defense, because of the scope and costs of those affected, represents a classic public problem. This does not suggest that all policy actors will agree on how threats to national defense should be addressed. In fact, consensus among most policy actors that an issue is a public problem does not necessarily translate into consensus in how the issue should be addressed through actual policy. To the contrary, even with consensus in problem identification, wide disagreements can and do persist over how to best solve this problem.

SUMMARY

The significance of problem identification to the policy process cannot be overstated. This stage represents the very beginning for each and every policy issue. Although certain issues may appear to some as obvious public policy problems, an ongoing debate exists among the many policy actors over what is a public problem. Different social realities and sets of beliefs can effectively redefine how one perceives certain policy issues. Any issue can theoretically be defined as a public problem; however, only those rare issues that represent a clear crisis for the polity are likely to foster real consensus among policy actors. For those many issues that fall within this so-called zone of perceptual confusion, it is the dynamic process of agenda setting that can help explain how issues that are clearly not "classic public problems" still come to be identified as issues that demand policy action.

DISCUSSION QUESTIONS

1. Aside from the areas of national security, national defense, terrorism, or war, which other issues can be "clearly" identified and defined as public problems? Discuss.

2. Which level of social reality, as described in Figure 6.2, do you believe is the most and least important. Why?

3. Which beliefs are most influential in affecting how we as individuals and as a society perceive our reality?

4. Congratulations! You have just been hired as a political consultant specializing in the area of domestic policy for the upcoming presidential campaign. Your candidate, being a smart political animal, wants to be aware of the most important social problems and how the public perceives them. Using the following media sites on the Internet, your first task is to research how the issue of poverty has been presented to the public over the last twelve weeks:

   a. Your city's major local newspaper

   b. *Los Angeles Times* (http://www.latimes.com)

   c. *New York Times* (http://www.nytimes.com)

   d. *Washington Post* (http://washingtonpost.com)

   e. CNN (http://www.cnn.com)

   f. MSNBC (http://www.msnbc.com)

   g. *Time* magazine (http://www.time.com)

   h. *Newsweek* (http://newsweek.com)

   i. *U.S. News & World Report* (http://www.usnews.com)

   Once your research is completed, provide a written analysis for the client that includes the following:

   - Background: Offer a brief ideological and historical explanation as to how poverty, and related issues, is perceived within America.

   - Research and Analysis: Prior to your written analysis of the issue, document the following based on your research:

   - A numeric count of the number of stories within the various media outlets dealing with the issue of poverty.

   - A numeric count of the number of stories within the various media outlets dealing with wealth and economic success.

   - Problem Identification: Provide a written analysis that assesses, based on what you have determined over the last twelve weeks, how the issue of poverty is presented to the American public. Specifically, how is this issue being framed in terms of:

   - Causality

   - Severity

   - Incidence

   - Proximity

   - Crisis

   - Conclusion: Given your research, what conclusions, if any, can you draw as to how the issue of poverty is currently being framed? Is poverty a public or private problem?

SUGGESTED READINGS

Berger, P. L., and T. L. Luckmann. *The Social Construction of Reality.* Garden City, NY: Doubleday, 1967.

Davenport, T. H. *The Attention Economy.* Boston: Harvard Business School Press, 2001.

Elder, C. E., and R. W. Cobb. *The Political Uses of Symbols.* New York: Longman, 1983.

Iyengar, S. *Is Anyone Responsible? How Television Frames Political Issues.* Chicago: University of Chicago Press, 1991.

Rein, M., and D. A. Schon. "Problem Setting in Policy Research." In Carol H. Weiss, ed., *Using Social Research in Public Policy Making.* Lexington, MA: Lexington Books, 1977.

Rochefort, D. A., and R. W. Cobb. *The Politics of Problem Definition.* Lawrence: Kansas University Press, 1994.

Schneider, A., and H. Ingram. "Social Construction of Target Populations: Implications for Politics and Policy." *American Political Science Review* 87 (1993):334–347.

ENDNOTES

1. C. J. Bosso, "The Contextual Basis of Problem Definition," in D. A. Rochefort and R. W. Cobb, *The Politics of Problem Definition* (Lawrence: Kansas University Press, 1994), 182–183.

2. E. Werner, "A Changed Landscape and Lingering Problems a Decade after Los Angeles Riots," Associated Press Wire, April 26, 2002.

3. P. G. Gosselin, "Jobless Rate to Highest Since 1995," *Los Angeles Times,* May 4, 2002. A1.

4. Ibid., A1.

5. For an understanding of why clarity is lacking, and the differing frames by which we understand politics and policy, see D. A. Stone, *Policy Paradox: The Art of Political Decision Making* (New York: Norton, 1997). Also, for a discussion of how social construction is theorized as affecting politics, policy, and policy making, see A. L. Schneider and H. Ingram, *Policy Design for Democracy* (Lawrence: University Press of Kansas, 1997).

6. One could argue that as the world increases in technological, communicative, and cultural interdependence within a modern and global media, our social reality has achieved a global level. In contrast, previous generations, because of limitations, may have been unable to expand their social reality beyond their immediate circle of actual experiences. Ironically, for other cultures, such a statement may still be true. For an interesting perspective on how such perceptions affect the economy and society, see T. H. Davenport, *The Attention Economy* (Boston: Harvard Business School Press, 2001).

7. J. E. Combs, "A Process Approach," in D. D. Nimmo and K. R. Sanders, *A Handbook of Political Communication* (Beverly Hills, CA: Sage, 1981), 55.

8. M. Rein and D. A. Schon, "Problem Setting in Policy Research," in Carol H. Weiss, ed., *Using Social Research in Public Policy Making* (Lexington, MA: Lexington Books, 1977), 235–252.

9. Benjamin I. Page and Robert Y. Shapiro, *The Rational Public* (Chicago: University of Chicago Press, 1992).

10. Ibid., 15.

11. Michael Kammen, "The Contrapuntal Civilization," in Ann G. Serow, *The American Polity Reader* (New York: Norton, 1990), 24.

12. Graduate Institute of International Studies, *Small Arms Survey Yearbook 2002* (Geneva, Switzerland: Graduate Institute, 2002).

13. Bureau of Justice Statistics, *FBI Uniform Crime Reports,* retrieved from (http://www.ojp. usdoj.gov/ bjs/glance/guncrime.htm).

14. Ibid.

15. For a review of recent studies on small arms use, see Graduate Institute, *Small Arms Survey.*

16. Bosso, "The Contextual Basis," 185.

17. D. A. Rochefort and R. W. Cobb, "Problem Identification: An Emerging Perspective," in Rochefort and Cobb, *Politics,* 15–20.

18. Ibid., 16.

19. Ibid., 20.

20. A comparison of this is between Canadian and U.S. reactions to mass shootings at schools. In Canada, a mass shooting at the University of Montreal led to substantial changes in gun ownership laws and further restrictions on access and possession. No significant U.S. federal legislation has materialized to restrict gun ownership, even with significant shootings at schools.

21. Rochefort and Cobb, *Politics,* 21.

7

Agenda Setting

A Theoretical Understanding

This chapter explores the process of agenda setting—the theoretical and practical process by which issues emerge onto the political and policy agenda. Underscoring the process of agenda setting are various theoretical interpretations of the dynamics by which issues gain attention and enter onto the agenda. These theoretical perspectives are critical to appreciating how an issue may develop from relative obscurity and capture significant political and policy attention. The process of agenda setting can also be described as a series of broad stages in which issues develop and emerge within a public or government agenda.[1] Overall, a study of the agenda-setting stage will help the student of public policy understand the dynamics by which diverse policy issues, and various potential policy problems are narrowed into a specific set of topics that various policy actors focus on. It is this set of issues that enter and survive on the agenda that are eventually considered for some type of policy action.

WHAT IS AGENDA SETTING?

How would one define the phenomenon of agenda setting? Quite simply, the agenda represents those issues that gain specific attention from the various institutional and noninstitutional actors. The issues that garner attention are perceived to be public policy problems. However, as discussed in Chapter 6 on problem identification, it is the rare and extreme issue that is clearly and immediately seen by all policy actors as a definitive public problem. Thus, the agenda-setting process helps explain the manner by which the vast number of issues emerge on the public and political agenda.

The sheer number of issues that may enter onto the agenda are theoretically broad and diverse—reflective of a wide number of potential issues that compete for critical attention among the relevant policy actors. In part, this vast agenda of issues is narrowed by the set of competing policy actors whose interest may favor one issue over another at particular times. For example, environmental interest groups may focus on an array of issues, but may fixate on an issue such as global warming or ocean pollution during certain political cycles. Certain issues may capture wide public and political attention, as well as increased agenda status, by their sheer significance and severity. Again, problems that are high in cost and scope are more easily perceived as important issues facing the polity. Nevertheless, the process by which certain issues gain attention and enter onto the policy agenda, at the expense of other issues, remains an important dynamic that is open to differing theoretical interpretation.

Essentially, many difficult questions are confronted when attempting to understand the agenda-setting process. First, what explains how the agenda-setting process occurs and develops? Second, why do certain issues receive a high degree of attention and priority within the policy agenda whereas other issues remain mired in a lack of attention—even though one could objectively argue that both issues are of equal importance for society? Finally, what explains why certain issues can dramatically attract attention, yet, seemingly within a short time are off the public and political agenda?

For answers to these difficult questions we can look to different theories of agenda setting. Three theories of agenda setting—Downs's issue-attention cycle, Kingdon's multiple streams, and Cobb's and Elder's model of agenda setting—are briefly discussed to help illustrate various theoretical perspectives on the dynamics and process of agenda setting.

DOWNS'S ISSUE-ATTENTION CYCLE

The agenda-setting process, from Anthony Downs's perspective, can be understood as the central dynamic by which a private issue gathers increasing attention and is transformed into a public issue demanding some kind of policy action. This "issue-attention cycle" helps explain which issues enter onto the agenda, and how an issue may leave or lose its status within the agenda.[2] Based on Downs's model of agenda setting, an issue undergoes a life cycle that is marked by a period in which attention builds and fixates on a specific issue, but then attention is quickly mitigated and diminishes over time. Downs's issue-attention cycle has five critical stages that help explain how an issue evolves (see Box 7.1).

During the initial pre-problem stage an issue of concern exists related to a certain socioeconomic or political condition. The issue may be either domestic or international in nature. Focused public attention at this stage, among various institutional and non-institutional actors, is absent. Although general and wide public awareness may not exist at the moment, certain groups or actors are

---

Box 7.1 Stages of Downs's Issue-Attention Cycle

1. Pre-problem stage
2. Alarmed discovery
3. Realization of cost
4. Gradual decline
5. Post-problem stage

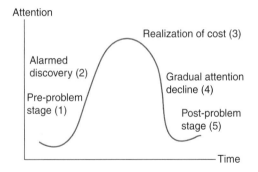

FIGURE 7.1 Downs's Issue-Attention Cycle.

active and concerned with the issue. Such interest groups and activists may attempt to build wider awareness of the issue, as well as foster greater support for some kind of governmental action. Still, in the absence of greater public awareness, the issue remains marginalized and limited in terms of the policy actions that may result (see Figure 7.1).

The second stage, as derived from Downs's model, is that of "alarmed discovery."[3] During this stage, new information emerges or an event occurs to incite focused attention by the policy actors on a particular issue. The nature of the event or condition that sparks this alarmed discovery must be sufficient to result in greater awareness among the wider public and across policy actors. Arguably, such an event must be severe or significant enough that it cannot be easily marginalized or diminished. For example, the school shootings at Columbine High School in 1998 was a classic example—severe in kind and shocking in nature. This event clearly focused the entire nation—and almost all policy actors—on the issue of school violence and guns. Yet, the initial emotional euphoria that leads to substantial increases in public attention, coupled with the placement of the issue on the public agenda, is confronted by a subsequent realization that formulating a legislative solution may prove difficult, taxing, and costly. As a result, dramatic as the event

might be, the attention span among policy actors is assumed short, and interest may wane as the reality of how complex this problem is to address manifests.

As the Columbine shootings help demonstrate, initial issue attention shifts away from identifying the problem to a discussion of what is the exact nature of the problem and how is it best resolved. Whereas initial attention may build quickly depending on the significance of the event in question, programmatic and ideological complications associated with defining a prospective policy solution can dampen both the demand for policy action and the attention granted the issue. For example, policy proposals to address gun violence, whether in schools or in society, could require considerable restrictions on personal use or access to firearms. As a result, additional concerns over the regulation of guns may entail fundamental changes in the judicial and political interpretation of the Second Amendment. Simply put, an issue that emerges to capture the attention of various policy actors does not operate in a vacuum. When an issue such as guns in school is both identified and defined as a public problem, policy proposals to solve such a problem can lead to an array of additional concerns over other issues such as the appropriate role of government, personal freedom, and crime and punishment.

For Downs, as an issue enters onto the agenda so does the sobering realization that the problem is a formidable one to solve and policy solutions may be difficult to accept for some of the policy actors concerned with the issue. As the political and policy reality begins to set in around the issue, a decline of interest and attention begins to occur. In the absence of a clear understanding of the problem and acceptable policy solution that can be easily implemented, many policy actors—whose interests are not solely fixed on this issue—may become increasingly frustrated, bored, or distracted. With respect to gun violence in schools, the often-heated debate over the appropriate understanding of the nature of the problem, its supposed pejorative effects, and the consequences of policy action may only further dissipate attention.

During stage four, Downs's issue-attention model helps emphasize that agenda setting does not happen in the absence of other competing issues. To the contrary, multiple issues may be evolving within and across the polity. As a result, for those policy actors who are not focused solely on such a specific issue, such as interest groups, the emergence of other issues will inevitably compete for the finite attention span of the policy actor.

The last stage of the Downs model is the post-problem stage. During the final stage of the issue-attention cycle, the waning of attention leads to a decrease in concern among policy actors toward the respective issue. Proposed solutions to the identified problem may further lessen concern, as such actions suggest that policy actors are addressing the issue. With respect to school gun violence, proposing additional regulations, increasing government oversight, or adopting a more aggressive stance toward prosecuting gun-related crimes may lead to less attention as such policy actions may pacify the concerns that initially mobilized various policy actors. During this stage, traditional policy actors, such as interest groups, government officials, or lobbyists, again supplant those actors who were initially mobilized by the importance of the issue. As is expected, such actors will continue to pay attention and remain active on this issue irrespective of whether there is greater public attention given.

Downs's issue-attention model offers an interesting explanation of the dynamic within the agenda-setting process. As discussed, the model provides a perspective on why certain issues dominate policy actors' attention, are readily identified as problems, and become the focus of the polity—and over time why such issues fall from attention and become supplanted by other competing issues. Of course, the Downs model is a simplification of a complex agenda-setting process, but offers a basis with which to understand how fickle our attentions may be with regard to setting the agenda of issues perceived important for the society.

KINGDON'S MULTIPLE STREAMS MODEL

As discussed in Chapter 5, for John Kingdon the policy process is best explained by the interplay of multiple streams. These three streams—problems, policies, and politics—reflect the defining dynamics that underscore the foundation of the agenda-setting process for Kingdon. Each stream reflects the significance and influence that the nature of the problem, the character of policy solutions, and the defining temper of the surrounding politics has on the setting of the agenda. Kingdon's model adds to the explanation of agenda setting by highlighting the profound and often ignored role of timing in explaining the impact of certain policy and political participants. The three streams interact within an opening of a policy window that allows the confluence of specific issues and solutions to capture the agenda at a particular period. Each of the three streams, and the notion of the policy window, will be briefly discussed below (see Figure 7.2).

Problem Stream

Problems represent the stream of issues that various policy actors may fixate and focus on. For Kingdon, the identification of specific issues over others depends on the following factors: indicators, focusing events, and feedback.[4] "Indicators" can suggest the

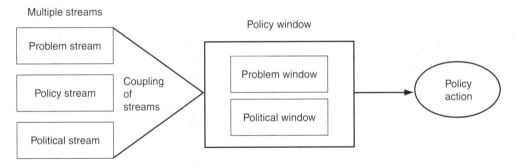

FIGURE 7.2 The Agenda-Setting Process—Kingdon's Three Streams.

severity of the problem. Underscoring the impact of specific indicators is the role played by focusing events. "Focusing events" represents the proverbial spark that focuses and fixates attention on a specific issue. "Feedback" helps explain how an actor's attention on certain issues is reinforced within the political process:

> Problems are often not self-evident indicators. They need a little push to get attention of people in and around government. That push is sometimes provided by a focusing event like a crisis or disaster that comes along to call attention to the problem.[5]

Policy Stream

The policy stream represents the essential ideas and solutions debated and bantered among the various policy-making actors and policy entrepreneurs. Policy entrepreneurs propose certain policy positions over others. The significance of the policy stream for agenda setting is that it is the path by which ideas, solutions, or alternatives are matched with identified problems.

The source for such ideas, according to Kingdon, is the policy entrepreneur who acts as an "advocate for proposals or for the prominence of an idea."[6] The policy entrepreneur is the essential proponent of a particular solution. Such entrepreneurs are motivated by a desire to receive some reward from successfully matching the problem issue and policy solution within the agenda. This reward, whether it is prestige, prominence, wealth, power, or idealistic satisfaction, justifies the energy these actors expend in seeking to set the agenda.

The policy stream, however, does not include a reflective discussion on which problems and solutions are the most deserving or most important. Rather, a selection process leads to a preference for those issues and ideas that can compete given the constraints of the political and public policy process. For Kingdon, these survival constraints are as follows:[7]

- Technical feasibility
- Value acceptance within the policy community
- Tolerable cost
- Anticipated public acquiescence
- Political acceptability

Technical feasibility explains how theoretical or infeasible ideas may quickly lose prominence within the agenda. The minutia of details, for instance, of how an identified public problem will be solved is critical to understanding which ideas are favored. Ideas that seem infeasible, given current resources within the government or society, may prove difficult to promote. Of course, such notions of technical feasibility depend to a great extent on how important the solution is within the greater political arena. Some advocates, for example, suggested that a manned-moon mission was initially infeasible. Similar claims have been made about current research into missile defense technologies. Absent the political or societal support, however, technical infeasibility proves a constraint on whether an issue may gain wider attention and support.

Value acceptability refers to whether proposed policy solutions are deemed acceptable in light of widespread individual, societal or institutional values. Such values act as a basis with which to evaluate both problems and proposed policy solutions. Values, such as a preference for a more egalitarian society or for a smaller role for government, may foster the creation or support of policies that reflect one's preferred policy solution.

Tolerable cost refers to whether a problem or policy issue can be resolved in light of certain budgetary or political realities. In budgetary terms, lack of fiscal resources can place severe limitations on how a problem is defined, as well as the viability and acceptability of a particular solution. Policy ideas that entail considerable cost may diminish political support or become marginalized within the agenda.

Public Acquiescence refers to the clear importance and impact the *public* has in accepting or rejecting specific policy proposals. The policy community may often react and shape proposals based on the influence and interests of the general public or even a narrower slice of the wider public. Although the public at large may have a limited role in actively developing new policy ideas, it is quite evident that the public's degree of support (or lack of support) for certain policy initiatives is often integral to explaining which issues enter and survive the agenda-setting process.

Political acceptability represents the degree of broad political support required to promote attention for an issue. At a minimum, a policy idea must have sufficient support if it is to survive the agenda-setting process. Lack of political support among policy actors for a particular policy position may foster increased favor for a more accepted course of action. As the political composition of the governmental arena changes, for example, so does the likely support for certain policy issues.

Political Stream

The final stream is the political stream. For Kingdon, the political stream represents the "electoral, partisan, or pressure group factors," indicative of the classic political motivations held by the critical institutional policy actors.[8] The importance of this distinction, of emphasizing a notion of real politics, is to reflect that the policy agenda does not develop in a vacuum. This means that the broad political context comprised of the interplay between partisan, public, and group interests is essential to agenda setting. Additionally, which issues gain political recognition is influenced by the national mood shared by the public, organized political forces, and members of the government.

The national mood captures the notion that shared concerns or interests can predominate throughout the public. As this national mood changes, as indicated by swings in public opinion, it affects the context of the public policy process. The specific consequences are that it pushes certain issues into greater prominence, emphasizing those issues that are of seemingly more importance for the American public. Additionally, the national mood, as it changes, can serve as a constraint by minimizing the prominence of certain issues on the agenda. Similarly, issues that once held great importance for the public at a specific period may quickly lose favor and be replaced by a competing perspective. For example, anti-immigration propositions, popular in the early 1990s in California, quickly lost political favor among the California public as socioeconomic and political conditions changed.[9]

Organized interests, in comparison, reflect the classic interpretation of the influence and sway of interest groups. According to Kingdon, interest groups help define the agenda and specify alternatives. As for the role played by members of government, the nature of American politics ensures some level of consistent change. The composition of government, whether it be the elected members of government, the personal and committee staff, the appointed executive members, or the bureaucracy, are all subject to change in due time. Each newly elected presidential administration, for example, will bring a sea of change by appointing upward of 6,000 members of the executive staff, leading to the replacement of previously appointed members. This results in the transfer of senior staff from Congress to the executive branch, and leads the staff of the losing party to seek out new employment in corporate, lobbying, or other policy-making circles. As such, a cycle of change permeates and ripples through the government as the seats of power change. The effect from these types of political changes often helps to redefine the issues that fall on the agenda.

Finally, bureaucracies also shape and mold the agenda. For Kingdon, these so-called administrative turf battles are indicative of the differing agendas and jurisdictional battles held by the various bureaucratic agencies operating within the American political system. Each agency, for instance, may prioritize certain issues and actions over others. Given budgetary, organizational, or political climates, the preference of an agency for a particular issue can change over time. Overall, according to Kingdon, these three streams—political, policy, and problem—influence agenda setting and policy action by interacting and flowing through a particular window that may have opened.

Policy Windows

Policy windows that may open due to political forces or the nature of the problem are by no means fixed and can be fleeting in terms of the opportunity to address a specific policy issue through some kind of government action:

> These policy windows, the opportunities for action on given initiatives, present themselves and stay open for only short periods. If participants cannot or do not take advantage of these opportunities, they must bide their time until the next opportunity comes along.[10]

The focus of these policy windows is not on a broad agenda of issues, but on a much narrower and more definitive decision agenda. For Kingdon, the decision agenda represents the specific set of issues that the government is aware of and considers important enough to warrant consideration for action. Such a window can open predictably at regular intervals as reflected by the budget cycle and the appropriation bills designed, formulated, and adopted for each fiscal year. In comparison, other policy windows may be open as a reaction to a dramatic problem or the alignment of specific political forces. For example, events such as terrorism, airline disasters, natural disasters, or a riot may represent problems that lead to a dramatic opening of a policy window. In addition, the election of President Clinton in 1992, coupled with a democratically controlled Congress, provided the ideal political environment for a "window" to open that permitted dramatic attempts at health care reform.

Overall, although policy windows may open, the issues that are seriously considered within this decision agenda remain limited. Essentially, no policy actor possesses the means to address all issues equally. Selections must be made. Consequently, decision agenda windows can be opened as the agenda itself is changed by either politics or the nature of the problem.

Thus solutions come to be coupled with problems, proposals linked with political exigencies, and alternatives introduced when the agenda changes. Their advocates hook them onto the problem of the moment, or push them at a time that seems propitious in the political stream. This is why, as one bureaucrat said, "Issues keep reemerging in other forms. You think you'd buried it one year, but it comes up the next year in a different place. The issues get packaged differently, but they are just about the same."[11]

Kingdon's model of agenda setting offers an added approach with which to understand how a variety of dynamics affect which issues emerge on the government's and public's agenda. In particular, this theoretical work helps highlight how the nature of the problem, the activities of policy entrepreneurs, and base politics all affect the process of agenda setting. Nevertheless, whereas Kingdon's theory adds a rich theoretical complement to Downs's model of the issue-attention cycle, there are additional approaches to understanding the agenda-setting stage.[12] For example, Roger W. Cobb and Charles D. Elder provide a theory of agenda setting that illustrates the evolution and development of policy issues.[13]

COBB AND ELDER AGENDA-SETTING MODEL

Roger Cobb and Charles Elder identify two broad categories of agendas—the systemic and the institutional—by which issues evolve from obscurity into a wider public agenda, and then can enter into a narrower policy-making agenda.[14] Cobb and Elder la-

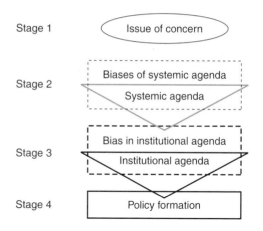

FIGURE 7.3 Agenda Setting—An Explanation of Policy Issue Development.

bel the public agenda as systemic and the policy-making agenda as institutional. Potential issues, if there is to be potential policy action, must evolve within and through these two agendas (see Figure 7.3).

The first stage of the Cobb and Elder agenda-setting model is defined by the emergence of an issue that warrants concern or attention. This issue of concern represents the spark to the agenda-setting process.[15] Such a potential problem is seen as having a negative effect on some segment of the society, group, or individual. Depending on the significance of the problem, real or perceived, wider attention can be justified beyond the segment of society, group, or individual directly affected. The failure of previous attempts to resolve the issue privately may also raise further attention as to the wider importance of the problem.

During the first stage, initial identification of a potential problem represents the instigating element that helps initiate the agenda-setting process. At a minimum, as discussed in Chapter 6, this issue must represent an identifiable and costly problem for some definable segment of society. Issues that have little societal relevance or significance may not warrant attention at a specific period. For example, although racial segregation and discrimination was policy in many southern states after the Civil War, this was not held as an issue of concern for either the white majority or the governing elites. For the groups that supported such racist policies, this was not an issue that demanded or justified civil rights actions or other types of public policy action by either the state or federal government. Such a moral failing of public policy may be understood in the context of this agenda-setting model provided by Cobb and Elder. Specifically, the problem of racial inequality was clearly a problem for African Americans in the South, made more severe by the legitimization of it by state policies, but it was clearly stymied from entering the agenda by the power of perceptions and beliefs held by the greater public within the systemic agenda.

The second stage of the Cobb and Elder agenda-setting model is the systemic agenda. Within this agenda, widespread beliefs and perceptions, popular among the public and governing elites at a given time, help diminish and narrow which issues are important. Although certain issues may indeed have a negative impact on a definable group, the power of beliefs held by the wider public, coupled with the possible lack of resources by this group that could be used to publicize their concerns, may affect the public perception of whether this issue is important. Consequently, because the public may fail to consider an issue as a public problem, a significant lag may result between the time an issue materializes and the moment when the wider public identifies such issues as public problems.

Within the systemic agenda, the dynamic of agenda setting is complicated by the set of individual, group, and societal beliefs that help frame and interpret the many issues that emerge for consideration. Identifying an issue as a public problem is complicated because of the power of such beliefs to subjectively redefine an issue into one of less or more significance. The systemic agenda is replete with a variety of complex issues of varying significance, all competing for attention. Certain issues may garner greater attention because of the role certain noninstitutional and institutional actors have in advocating the importance of the issue to the public. Nevertheless, at any one time within the systemic agenda, the media, the public, interest groups, members of Congress, the president, elements of the bureaucracy, or individual citizens can attempt to highlight the significance of a particular socioeconomic issue they believe is both important and a public problem.

Environmental interest groups, for example, attempt to highlight the consequences of global warming and other environmental threats. The media, through investigative reports, may spur attention to abuses in senior home care or the propensity of certain cars to have deadly malfunctions.[16] In comparison, a member of Congress or a president may become fixated on a particular issue, such as civil rights or the environment.[17] The public, during times of recession, may emphasize the importance of economic growth and unemployment. The bureaucracy may stress the need for greater resources in dealing with issues such as homeland security. Individual citizens whose children have been kidnapped may identify the need for increased penalties or better means of coordinating public and police responses to such crimes.

The dynamics of systemic agenda also help explain why not all issues will be considered for policy action. Basically, not all issues can survive the filter of perceptions that exists and reduces which issues are of importance within the systemic agenda. However, if an issue is thought to be of grave importance by the public, if the issue qualifies as a crisis, if interest groups and other policy actors mobilize to advocate for the issue, or if powerful institutional actors seek to emphasize the seriousness of the issue, there is an increased chance that this issue will move onto the institutional agenda. For Cobb and Elder, the perceptions that help spark the agenda-setting process are referred to as "triggering devices."

The systemic agenda is marked by a screen of assumptions, facts, values, and overarching beliefs held by the various actors operating within it. Certain issues may indeed be of great consequence, but it is seldom clear which issues are the most important for the public. Entrance and survival within this systemic agenda depends greatly on the array of beliefs held, the actors involved in setting the issue within this agenda, as well as the resources held by the respective actors. As the beliefs, actors, and resources change over time, the position of an issue within the systemic agenda can also change. Issues deemed radical or insignificant at a certain period, as once were many environmental, civil rights, or gay rights issues, can be seen quite differently as changes occur within the broad systemic agenda. The rethinking of issues can occur because of dynamic changes in attention and perception that are possible within the systemic agenda.

The dynamic character of the systemic agenda arises from the shifts in beliefs, resources, and the array and power of actors involved in this initial agenda-setting process. These shifts are a byproduct of a competition within the systemic arena to garner concern or attention to certain issues at the expense of others. Although in some cases such competition may indirectly lead to the diminishment of other issues of concern, in other cases it may be a strategic gambit by certain actors who wish to limit or redefine the importance and understanding of a given issue at the expense of others. In sum, issues that spark public attention help mobilize greater public awareness. It is these issues that enter and persevere within the systemic agenda. Among these issues

within the systemic agenda, an additional agenda-setting process will help narrow the issues that undergo consideration within the institutional agenda.

For Cobb and Elder, the third stage of the agenda-setting process involves the setting of the agenda within the institutional or policy-making realms of the government. At the federal level, this refers to the three branches of the government and the bureaucracy. This institutional agenda involves the set of issues that are to be considered for some subsequent kind of policy actions. The policy-making importance of this agenda emerges in light of the fact that only issues that enter the institutional agenda can expect consideration for policy action.

As with the systemic agenda, the institutional agenda is also framed and defined by a set of beliefs, actors, and resources. Within the elected branches of the federal government, for example, the need for reelection, ideological perspective, and political affiliation, represent a set of beliefs that further define which issues should be considered for policy action. Within the bureaucracy, organizational and agency culture can foster a preference for certain issues. At the judicial level, legal and ideological beliefs help define how certain issues are understood. Yet, eventhough many beliefs may exist, the institutional arena operates within a realm of politics and policy making.

The institutional agenda-setting process is marked by the defining reality that this is a strikingly political process. This process is served by the prominence of elected actors within the institutional agenda, and the necessity for political victories and accomplishments. Therefore, issues that carry with them greater political harm or threat may be quickly diminished in significance or redefined in a manner that lessens the political damage from them. In contrast, issues that are believed to hold great political and electoral favor may rise in prominence within the institutional agenda.

The significance of an issue within the institutional agenda depends greatly on the political calculations of the various policy actors. In particular, the ideological and political perspective of certain institutional actors can define and redefine which issues are deemed important. A conservative skew to Congress, for example, may favor issues and initiatives that reduce or alter the role of government, lessen rates of taxation, or increase defense spending. In contrast, a more liberal Congress may favor issues and initiatives that promote a more intrusive role for government, increased income redistribution, increased education or health care spending, and support for decreases in defense spending. These ideological beliefs can also clash with additional beliefs influenced by party affiliation, the preferences of constituents, as well as their respective national vision for which issues demand their attention and action. Beliefs, however, represent only one set of biases that can skew the institutional agenda.

The actors involved within the institutional agenda reflect both the traditional series of institutional and noninstitutional actors. The distinction in this particular stage is the particular prominence and importance of the institutional actors. Institutional actors represent the critical players that will make the defining decisions as to which issues will be focused on at the expense of others. Although noninstitutional actors, such as the media, lobbyists, interest groups, or constituents, can have a considerable effect on the decision-making process, the institutional actor makes the final selection of which issues are to be explored and discussed. As such, the vagaries of the institutional agenda will further narrow which issues are of concern to the critical policy actors.

Traditional issues, for example, may dominate the agenda at the expense of new issues. In part, this can be explained by the expertise and experience of the institutional actors in dealing with these older issues. Ad-ditionally, the procedures of the budget cycle, highlighted by an authorization and appropriation process that extends from February to October of each fiscal year, may further limit attention to the most pressing issues beyond those related to the federal budget. Lack of critical political support within the party or committee can only delimit the concern for an issue. In sum, institutional actors, because of well-recognized political constraints, confront the "reality" that they must be selective in applying their attention to an issue because constraints do exist.

Another factor in understanding which issues gain importance within the institutional agenda is that of resources. Regardless of the resources—fiscal, time, or political—institutional actors are constrained by the reality that resources are finite and not all issues can be deemed equally critical for policy action. As such, institutional actors must calculate which issues matter the most to them. For elected institutional actors, the political cycle compels them to expend finite political resources on issues that are deemed most important for their political health. Other nonelected institutional actors, such as the bureaucracy or judiciary, must also focus on the set of issues that they believe to be most important. The Supreme Court, for instance, does not hear every potential case, but chooses which cases hold greater significance for the political society. In comparison, noninstitutional actors attempt to influence the institutional agenda by lobbying and engaging in grassroots movements, as well as providing or restricting campaign or party donations to various elected institutional actors.

Within the institutional agendas, as issues penetrate and survive the set of biases unique to this agenda, the set of institutional actors will begin to focus and fixate on a narrow set of issues that are perceived—both in political and nonpolitical terms—to be the most important. It is these issues that are then considered for policy action, this in turn leads to the formulation of alternatives that would best resolve the issue under question.

The final stage of the practical understanding of agenda setting is policy formulation. Issues that have emerged and survived the biases of both the systemic and institutional agenda will become the foci for policy action. Such policy actions result from an intrinsic understanding of the issue or problem as it has been defined throughout the agenda-setting process. The manner in which an issue is framed and understood affects the resulting kind of possible policy action. The design of a proposed solution to a problem is developed and matched with the respective understanding of the issue. Significant and dramatic types of policy formulation, for instance, will require an acceptance that the issue or problem discussed is of particular extreme importance for the society. Absent such extreme significance, as highlighted by those issues that have high cost and scope for society, the process of policy formulation may reflect a more varied and muted course of action where competing proposals are put forth to reflect competing interpretations as to how to best solve the problem or issue. The following chapter on policy formulation will expand on the process and influences that help shape and structure the various proposals put forth to redress an identified policy problem that has survived each of the agendas.

SUMMARY

The previous discussion presented three theories with which to understand the complexity of the agenda-setting process. As noted, this integral predecision stage of the policy process reflects the dynamic process by which an issue rises from obscurity to garner public and political attention. In particular, agenda setting helps us understand how a far larger set of important issues and problems compete for attention within the public and political arenas. More important, this process helps us understand how the agenda of issues to be considered for policy action become limited in number.

The agenda-setting stage highlights an important realization: Some issues may be recognized as important, but not all important issues will enter onto the policy agenda. Practically, institutional and noninstitutional actors can consider only a select number of issues at any given period. The attentions, energies, and sheer interests of the many policy actors will vary. Thus, not all issues are given equal attention, regardless of their merit. This agenda-setting process is by no means fair or just, but captures the competitive dynamic whereby even morally important issues can be ignored if perceived and deemed insignificant by the sets of actors within the public and political arenas.

This unfair and competitive process was explained theoretically through Downs's issue-attention cycle model and by Kingdon's streams theory. Aside from these theoretical interpretations, an additional and more comprehensive perspective on agenda setting was emphasized by discussing the Cobb and Elder model. The Cobb and Elder theory of agenda setting explained the process as an interaction between two policy agendas—the systemic and institutional agenda—and helped highlight how an issue must survive multiple policy agendas before it is considered for policy action.

In summary, agenda setting represents a stage marred by the brutish competition among beliefs, perceptions, and attention. This competition is flamed by policy actors that, given their respective beliefs and perceptions, will also attempt to persuade which issues, events, or actions justify subsequent policy formulation and action. The significance of agenda setting for the policy process can be stated quite simply: Without the issue entering the agenda, in particular the institutional agenda, there can be no consideration for policy action. Again, policy solutions and actions are developed only for issues that are recognized as public problems. Many potential public problems will not enter any policy agenda. The negative consequences from these ignored problems will perpetuate until they enter and survive the agenda-setting process. In the end, how well one understands the dynamics of this stage in the policy process can prove critical to whether one's policy interests and concerns are eventually considered as public problems.

DISCUSSION QUESTIONS

1. What does the process and dynamic of agenda setting suggest for the ebb and flow of the policy-making process? Does this agenda-setting dynamic help or threaten the goal of making "good" public policy? Discuss why.

2. Kingdon suggests that agenda setting involves three streams. Which, in your opinion, is the most and least important stream determining whether a given issue enters the agenda or not? Discuss.

3. Cobb and Elder suggest that two interrelated agendas—the systemic and the institutional—help us understand which issues enter and rise on the nation's public and political agendas. What biases within each of the agendas do you believe hinder greater attention being given to the plight of the homeless or the right of gay people to marry?

4. Describe how an issue, such as the shooting deaths of thirteen teenagers and a teacher at Columbine High School, rose and fell within the systemic (public) and institutional (government) agenda.

   a. First, research, using one or two media sources (CNN, MSNBC, YAHOO news wire service, or Lexis-Nexus),

   assess the agenda prominence of the school violence issue two weeks before the shootings in April 20,1999. Was this issue of any prominence on the systemic agenda prior to April 20?

   b. Second, using both the http://www.thomas.loc.gov Web site and other news sites (e.g., Lexis-Nexus), research and record any specific political statements made by institutional actors concerning gun violence, and the date or number of pieces of gun-related legislation introduced within two weeks of April 20, 1999. Determine if this issue had any prominence on the institutional agenda at that time.

   c. Third, after the events of April 20, 1999, and using the same research resources as stated above, track the evolution of the coverage and political attention given the Columbine deaths. Assess how much focus and attention was given this issue in the two weeks following the shootings. Did the issue of gun violence remain prominent on both agendas during this period?

   d. Finally, what dynamics or factors may explain why the issue of gun violence does not have more prominent status within the policy agenda?

SUGGESTED READINGS

Anderson, James E. *Cases in Public Policy-Making.* New York: Holt, Reinhart & Winston, 1982.

Baumgartner, F. R., and Bryan D. Jones. *Agendas and Instability in American Politics.* Chicago: Chicago University Press, 1993.

Cobb, R. W., and Charles D. Elder. "The Politics of Agenda Building." *Journal of Politics* 33, no. 4 (1971): 892–915.

Downs, Anthony. "Up and Down With Ecology: The Issue-Attention Cycle." *The Public Interest* 28 (1972): 38–50.

Kingdon, John. W. *Agendas, Alternatives, and Public Policies.* New York: Longman, 1995.

ENDNOTES

1. S. T. Theodoulou, "How Policy Is Made," in S. T. Theodoulou and Mathew A. Cahn, *Public Policy: The Essential Readings* (Englewood Cliffs, NJ: Prentice Hall, 1995), 87.

2. Anthony Downs, "Up and Down With Ecology: The Issue-Attention Cycle," *The Public Interest* 28 (Summer 1972): 38–50.

3. Ibid.

4. John W. Kingdon *Agendas, Alternatives, and Public Policies* (New York: Longman), 1995.

5. Ibid., 94–95.

6. Ibid., 122.

7. Ibid., 131.

8. Ibid., 145.

9. Immigration policies in California highlight the rise and fall of issues on the public and political. In the early 1990s, fed by a slowing economy, issues such illegal immigration, welfare, and loss of jobs fed the public support for proposition. For example, Proposition 187, which passed in 1994 with 60 percent support, and which was supposed to end social service assistance for illegal immigrants, was effectively disregarded by Gov. Gray Davis in 1999 with little public uproar. See Reuters Wire "California Governor Gives Up Immigration Measure," CNN Web site, July 24, 1999.

10. Kingdon, *Agendas,* 166.

11. Ibid., 173.

12. Additional theories can be used to understand the agenda-setting process. These include F. R. Baumgartner and Bryan D. Jones, *Agendas and Instability in American Politics* (Chicago: Chicago University Press, 1993). Also, P. A. Sabatier and H. Jenkins-Smith, *Policy Change and Learning: An Advocacy Coalition Framework* (Boulder, CO: Westview Press, 1993).

13. R. W. Cobb and Charles D. Elder, "The Politics of Agenda Building," *Journal of Politics* 33, no. 4. (November 1971): 892–915. See also R. W. Cobb and Charles D. Elder, *Participation in American Politics: Dynamics of Agenda Building* (Baltimore, MD: Johns Hopkins University Press, 1983).

14. R. W. Cobb and C. D. Elder, "Issues and Agendas," in Theodoulou & Cahn, *Public Policy,* 98.

15. G. Starling, *Strategies for Policy Making* (Chicago Dorsey Press, 1988), 69.

16. For an analysis and review of the power and influence of interest groups, see J. R. Wright, *Interest Groups and Congress: Lobbying, Contributions, and Influence* (Needham Heights, MA: Allyn & Bacon, 1996); C. Wilcox, *The Interest Group Connection: Electioneering, Lobbying, and Policymaking in Washington* (Seven Bridges Press, 1997).

17. For insight into the motivations, political and otherwise of members of Congress, see W. Oleszek, *Congress and Its Members,* 8th ed. (Washington, DC: CQ Press, 2001); Lou Frey, Michael T. Hayes, eds., *Inside the House: Former Members Reveal How Congress Really Works* (University of Press of America, 2001).

8

Policy Design
and Formulation

Public policies do not just appear; they have to be created or designed. If policies are solutions to perceived problems or identified issues that emerge, then there has to be analysis of what is the most appropriate course of action to deal with the problem or issue. This involves policy makers choosing between alternative courses of action. Inherent in this process is the fact that policy makers must deal with the question of selecting the correct set of instruments that can actually be adopted and "best" match the problem. Simply, what is needed for successful policy formulation is that a policy must be adoptable politically. Ideally the best policy formulation would solve the identified problem. In actuality, policy formulation is a political exercise in which the best policy is often sacrificed for an adoptable policy. In sum, it must be acceptable to those who adopt policy as well as to target populations. Thus, policy formulation is influenced heavily by policy makers' need to win support for their proposed policy. In this chapter we examine how policies are formulated, and we identify the major actors and the different types and models that have been developed to explain policy formulation. The discussion starts with defining exactly what is meant by policy formulation.

WHAT IS POLICY FORMULATION?

Once a problem or issue is on the public agenda, then remedies or solutions to it must be seriously considered. It should be noted that in certain instances formulation can and does occur prior to agenda setting. Kingdon focuses on the role of broad-based policy communities that over time may sometimes develop a consensus on a solution to a particular problem. When the problem becomes more salient, a solution is then already available.[1] Policy formulation is the development of remedies that deal with a specific problem or address a particular issue within the institutional agenda. It takes place before legislation is enacted and theoretically ends once the policy is implemented. However, in reality formulation often becomes reformulation because once policy is implemented and then evaluated, it is often redesigned to address inadequacies either politically or policy wise. This then is the iterative nature of formulation. The policy process itself is also iterative in nature.

Inherent in formulation is the notion of bargaining and compromise. Often concessions will be made in order to win the most political support among the relevant policy-making actors for a particular solution. It is an incredibly political process from start to finish. There are many competing realities to the process of formulation. The essential reality of policy formulation is that there can be multiple actors designing different remedies or mechanisms for solving the same problem at the same time. In Congress, for example, numerous policy proposals compete with each other for adoption. This often results in competing proposals fighting for political support. Another reality is that formulation can occur over a long period and with it comes a continuous process of coalition building behind certain policy proposals. A final reality is the recognition that formulation does not necessarily result in adoption, even though the expected result of policy formulation is that it is a solution to a problem.

GENERIC POLICY SOLUTIONS OR INSTRUMENTS

Most authors, when discussing the nature of policy solutions, refer to the work of Deborah Stone.[2] Professor Stone's policy solutions are displayed in Box 8.1. Policy solutions may come in the form of legislation, executive orders, judicial decisions, or other policy outputs. When discussing what policy solutions may be developed, it is beneficial to acknowledge that they are a composition of instruments or tools with which to achieve the objectives of a proposed policy.

In addition to Stone, various other authors offer classification schemes of policy instruments (see Box 8.2).[3] The schemes may vary in the types of categories of solutions but what all schemes, including Stone's, have in common is they are mechanisms by which government seeks to alter the behavior of specified target populations. In reality such change might not have occurred without the government providing the target populations with the ability to do so. The schemes are also used to demonstrate that policy solutions are meant to achieve policy goals.

All of these schemes share common dimensions. The first dimension is a focus of activity. Thus, we can get a general sense of what government is attempting to achieve with the policy. The second dimension is a delivery system through which the level of complexity of implementation can be gauged. The third dimension is the program's administrative level of centralization. The final dimension is the degree to which the program requires detailed administrative action. Overall, these dimensions help us to better appreciate just how similar these schemes are regardless of the labels used by each author.

Box 8.1   Stone's Policy Solutions

SOLUTION	OBJECTIVE	COMMENT	EXAMPLE
Inducements	Influences behavior	Can be negative or positive	Tax penalties Tax credits
Rules	Mandates or requires specific behavior	Often used in conjunction with other solutions such as inducements	Rules attached to successful grant applications
Facts	Provision of information to persuade target populations to behave in a particular way	Provision of information allows for informed judgment on part of targets	Just Say No campaign
Rights	Gives rights or duties to certain individuals and groups	Are claims backed by government power	Civil rights legislation
Powers	Charges decision-making bodies with specific powers	Culturally changes way decisions are made	Changing size or membership of a body such as National Council on Education

SOURCE: Adapted from D. A. Stone, *Policy Paradox and Political Reason* (Glenview, IL: Scott Foresman, 1988).

When choosing a policy solution, policy makers must take into account four factors. First is political feasibility; even if a policy proposal has technical feasibility it will not work without political support. The second factor is the amount of resources available to implement the solution. If there are insufficient resources to carry out the proposed course of action, then it is not a viable option. A third consideration is to know if the program can be successfully established and managed. This can be referred to as administrative feasibility. The final factor policy makers should consider is the reaction of the target population. Policy makers should investigate the receptivity of the target population to changing their behavior or complying with the policy. A policy that fails to change a target population's behavior fails by definition.

ACTORS INVOLVED WITH POLICY FORMULATION

The institutional and noninstitutional actors discussed in terms of formulation have been referred to in the earlier discussion of the *who* of policy making. It should be realized that one of the difficulties in formulating policy is that there are large numbers of actors involved in the process. Adding to this problem of multiple actors is the fact that there are few rules guiding formulation. In other words, solutions to problems have to be created and designed, and there is no map for the policy actors to follow in reaching the best solution. B. Guy Peters argues that this absence of rules is responsible in part for the complexity of formulation.[4] These two factors combine to ensure that

Box 8.2   Policy Solutions and Instruments Classification Schemes

ANDERSON SCHEME	LEVINE, PETERS, THOMPSON SCHEME	PETERS SCHEME	SCHNEIDER AND INGRAM SCHEME	OBJECTIVE	EXAMPLE
Directive power	Law and regulation	Law	Authority Tools	Carry the force of law; compel particular behavior	Environmental regulations; antitrust laws
Services	Direct provision of services or goods	Services		Services provided directly by government to users	Air traffic control; mail services
Benefits	Transfer payments	Money		Transfer of money from government to various interests	Social security; food stamps
Contracts	Contracting out			Contracts with private firms to provide goods and services	Contracts to run prisons and hospitals
General expenditures				General spending by government every day on people, services, and goods it needs to function	Personnel costs; supplies; utilities
Market and proprietary operations				Government activities that have private counterparts; have economic and policy consequences	Public corporations; Federal Reserve Bank
Taxes	Tax system and expenditures	Taxes		Policies that levy cost on targets to make some activities more or less economically desirable	Tax credits and deductions
Loans	Loans and loan guarantees	Other economic instruments		Induce economic activity or other desirable activity	Small business loans; student loans
Subsidies				Payments to ensure economic viability of an activity	Farm subsidies
Sanctions			Inducements and sanctions	Induce quasi-voluntary or coerced actions based upon tangible payoffs	Fines for violating regulations
Inspection and licensing				Need permission to carry out an activity	Driver licenses; professional licenses

---

Box 8.2   Policy Solutions and Instruments Classification Schemes

ANDERSON SCHEME	LEVINE, PETERS, THOMPSON SCHEME	PETERS SCHEME	SCHNEIDER AND INGRAM SCHEME	OBJECTIVE	EXAMPLE
Informal procedures				Procedures not specified in laws or regulations to regulate behavior	Plea bargaining; taxpayer and IRS correspondence to resolve dispute
		Suasion			
		Horatory tools		Attempts to persuade desirable behavior or avoid undesirable behavior	Just Say No campaign
	Intergovern-mental grants			Provision of funds	Arts grants
	Insurance				
		Provision of insurance when not available through market		Cobra; flood insurance; federal deposit insurance	
		Capacity-building tools		Training and technical assistance	Technology transfer and provision of information products
		Learning tools		Help people understand relevant aspects of the problem	

SOURCE: Adapted from T. A. Birkland, *An Introduction to the Policy Process* (Armonk, NY: M. E. Sharpe, 2001), 168–173.

---

formulation is fraught with political and policy difficulties. What follows is a discussion of the more important actors at the national level of government. It should be noted that some actors are more important than others and that the policy domain dictates in many respects who may be actively involved with any given issue. However, all actors involved in the different venues of policy design can and may attempt to influence formulation at varying points.

The President

The president and the executive offices associated with the White House are often very active in policy formulation. In recent years presidents have created commissions and task forces to solidify their participation in formulation of policy. An example of this would be Bill Clinton's task force on health care reform. In the modern era it is common for presidents to actively take a personal interest in policy formulation. For example, the staffs of both Ronald Reagan and Bill Clinton were often involved in the preparation of legislation for congressional review. More often than not, presidents are part of the process because they were elected to office with a policy agenda. Such an agenda is the establishment of policy goals and priorities for an administration. Presidents are often publically judged on the success of their agenda which often means they are assessed on which policy solutions are pursued and the policies that are enacted. The advantage of having presidential participation in the policy formulation process is that the president is the only actor with a national constituency and national political recognition. This allows presidents to formulate policies with the national interest as their focus and to redefine the national interest to serve their policy agenda. This can also prove to be a drawback as presidents tend to define national interests in line with the interests of those who elected them into office and not always the public at large. For example, many critics will argue that George W. Bush in his first months of office has tended to initiate policy proposals in areas such as the environment that reward his electoral backers in the energy and oil industry. However, President Bush is really no different than any of his predecessors who also had to contend with the political and policy implications of their individual policy agendas.

Congress

Members of Congress are a significant source of draft legislation and thus are most often associated with policy formulation. The principal ways members of Congress participate in formulation are through the development of new legislation, legislative oversight, and legislative review. Additionally, the involvement of members of Congress in the formulation of policy is facilitated by the integral role played by their personal or committee staffs. These staffs not only research possible policy proposals but also design them.

The implication of congressional involvement in the development of policy proposals is that partisan or political influence pervades the choice of what type of remedies are formulated. Each member of Congress confronts the political reality that the best politically formulated policy is not necessarily the best solution to a problem. Often it's the one that has or will receive the most political support. A further implication is that legislators tend to formulate detailed policy proposals that often require micromanagement of programs. An example of this would be recent laws that removed discretionary exclusions from the hands of the Immigration and Naturalization Service. This policy action was taken as members of Congress formulated and adopted a policy that returned control over a critical area of immigration back to policy makers and thus away from the day-to-day implementers of policy.

The Bureaucracy

Many policy proposals are developed initially by governmental agencies. Bureaucrats often have more expertise and involvement in policy issue areas than many elected office holders and may possess the relevant information and data resources necessary to formulate proposals that can be possible policy solutions. Additionally, bureaucrats understand implementation procedures and what can and cannot be done. Such characteristics place the bureaucracy in a strong position in the race to formulate possible remedies to problems. This allows bureaucrats to have significant responsibility in the overall policy formulation process. The implications of such prominence can be serious for the types of solutions that are formulated. For example, because of their desire to maintain their agency's survival, bureaucrats might lack the initiative to develop dramatic or innovative policy solutions. Moreover, the political necessity to achieve accountability, efficiency, and effectiveness places even greater constraints on the type of policy design conducted by bureaucrats. Thus, there is a tendency for bureaucrats to formulate incremental proposals.

Interest Groups

Interest groups are major actors in policy formulation and often propose or initiate policy solutions. Such groups are also key facilitators in the bargaining, negotiations, and compromises that occur around various alternative policy proposals. Interest group primacy in policy formulation can best be understood by realizing that it is a reflection of their group resources and level of influence. Many authors such as Schnattschneider and Lowi would argue that American interest groups have undue power in the policy process and often structure formulations that reflect their interests rather than the common good.[5] Critics of interest groups' activities in this stage of the policy process argue that powerful groups have significant impact on the direction of legislation. Those who support significant interest group participation in policy formulation would argue that in spite of disparities between groups in terms of their resources and their influence, interest group participation enhances the democratic process because it allows for more grass-roots participation in the policy-making process. As such we could argue that policy formulation is a reflection of the mobilization of the more influential interest groups in American society.

Think Tanks and Policy Entrepreneurs

Over the last thirty years there has been an explosion in the number of organizations and individuals who attempt to influence the direction of policy solutions through their expertise. Such actors often initiate policy proposals and push other actors to support their policy preferences. The implication of such behavior is debatable. Any degree of influence will largely be determined by the groups' and individuals' level of influence with key legislators and other policy formulators. Think tanks, either independent or associated with institutions of higher learning, often provide vital research on the feasibility and possible effects of particular policy proposals. Theoretically, they operate without any particular agenda. However, over the last few years it has become more and more evident that many such organizations are linked to specific ideological platforms. Hence, think tanks are taking a much more active role in influencing policy formulation.

Policy entrepreneurs are distinguished by their motivation to initiate dynamic policy change within society.[6] Their presence and actions can significantly affect the probability that particular policy proposals will be considered in the formulation process. They identify problems, network in policy circles, shape the terms of policy debates, and build coalitions behind certain proposals. These activities attract the attention of decision makers and can encourage them to initiate appropriate policy responses.[7] Through networking, entrepreneurs can determine what arguments will persuade others to support their policy ideas, and this allows them to shape the debate around their preferred policy solution.[8] Simply, entrepreneurs know which issue to push and how to sell it to different audiences.

Policy entrepreneurs who successfully engage in such activity will be in a good position to build leverage when it comes to coalition building and in the long run be more effective in getting their ideas approved as viable policy solutions. Policy entrepreneurs are in many ways similar to business entrepreneurs acting as "brokers" making the most of any opportunity that comes their way. It is not always going to be the case that policy entrepreneurs' activity will lead to the adoption of a policy, but whether it does or does not, the significance of these actors in policy innovation and the formulation of policy proposals is great.

HOW POLICY IS DESIGNED

For some authors, designing policy is not just determining what type of policy or instruments; it is also a reflection of the role that perceptions of deservedness and political power have on influencing both the design of policy and its justification. In "The Social Construction of Target Populations," authors Schneider and Ingram show how pervasive stereotypes and policy making are connected through a social construction model.[9] Schneider and Ingram argue that the justification and substance of any policy can be understood through a recognition of how groups targeted by a given policy are socially constructed. Social construction is how society perceives a group. In short, it is the image held of a group by others within both the political arena and society in general.

In essence, the social construction perspective argues that within society there are groups of individuals (target populations) endowed with culturally constructed images. Such images can be positive or negative. Policy makers are influenced by these images with respect to the types of benefits and burdens they are willing to distribute to the groups through policy. Authors such as Donovan and Herek and Capitanio argue that the effects of such image construction is that in electoral periods incumbents hope to maximize their electoral advantage through prior policy choices.[10] Thus, the ideal is for positively constructed groups to receive benefits while their negative counterparts receive burdens. The danger for policy makers is they can incorrectly perceive the social construction and political power of some target populations and thus give benefits and burdens to the wrong groups. One possible consequence of such misperception is policy makers' electoral success could be affected. Thus, policy makers ideally hope to distribute the most benefits to those groups with the most political power and most pos-

itive social construction. Of course, in reality the ideal is often not achieved. In the real world there are groups that are positively constructed but powerless and other groups that are negatively constructed but historically powerful due to their economic and political resources. Thus, the distribution of benefits and burdens is not as straightforward as the ideal suggests. Often the influence a group wields through its actual or attributed power will dictate the distribution of benefits and burdens of the group to maximize the electoral ambitions of policy makers. In order to justify this behavior, Schneider and Ingram argue that policy makers utilize a number of believable rationalizations to justify their policy actions.[11] Thus, policy makers exploit rationalizations that maximize the benefits and minimize the burdens targeted at favored groups.

In the social construction model four types of target populations are identified through a typology that measures the interrelationship between social construction and political power (see Figure 8.1). Social construction can be positive or negative,

Constructions

Power	Positive	Negative
Strong	Advantaged The elderly Business Veterans Scientists	Contenders The wealthy Unions Minorities Cultural elites The moral majority
Weak	Dependents Children Mothers	Deviants Criminals Drug addicts Communists Gangs

FIGURE 8.1 Social Construction and Political Power: Types of Target Populations.

whereas power can be high or low. What determines each group's labeling is the manner in which they mobilize their members, the perception by the public at large of their deservedness to be helped based upon general assumptions of lifestyle, and their general political fortunes which are based upon the group's level of resources. The resources that are available to groups are economic, political, motivational, and organizational.

Schneider and Ingram's four types of target populations are advantaged, contenders, dependents, and deviants. Advantaged social populations are positively constructed and are highly powerful, whereas contenders are negatively constructed but also very powerful. Dependents have little power but are positively viewed, whereas deviants are not only powerless but also negatively constructed. The net effect of this balance between image and power is that advantaged groups tend to have a good deal of influence and thus a greater likelihood of receiving benefits when targeted by policies. They are also likely to have a high level of control over the way policy is shaped. In the case of contenders, they have little influence over the distribution of benefits but a relatively good deal of control over the substance of policy burdens. In comparison, dependents are more likely to receive burdens than benefits. However, dependents, because of their image, can exercise some influence over the policy process so they may also be targeted for benefits. Finally, deviant populations receive burdens rather than benefits and have little or no influence over policies that may affect them. The significance of a deviant social construction is that policies will be created that are punitive rather than rewarding.

Groups and individuals seek policy changes to achieve benefits while minimizing costs or transferring costs to other groups or individuals. Thus, if we accept that when policy is designed who benefits is always kept in mind and that there is an interplay of factors such as economic analysis, societal values, policy makers' belief systems, the structure of the policy process, and the distribution of power within the structure, how do we judge one particular policy solution against another policy solution that deals with the same issue? It is clear from the earlier discussion that policy makers are not monolithic or neutral, so one should bear in mind that the choice of policy solutions is often fought among a group of policy makers pushing their own alternatives within the institutional agendas. This battle is theoretically the process of examining and evaluating alternative policy proposals that are intended to lessen or resolve a problem and is generally referred to as policy analysis.

POLICY ANALYSIS

The term *policy analysis* was first used by Charles Lindblom in 1958 when he used it to refer to a type of quantitative analysis involving incremental comparisons in which nonquantitative methods are included in the recognition of values and policy.[12] Over the years it has come to be defined in other ways. What we can say today about policy analysis is that it provides the use of reason and evidence to allow decision makers to choose the best policy from a number of alternatives. It is a body of concepts and principles aimed at helping decision makers make more intelligent, more ethical, more effective, and more efficient choices. Policy analysis, however, is not an exact science because it cannot ensure that chosen proposals will be in the best interest of the public or even solve the problem completely. We can find such policy analysts on legislative staffs, in think tanks, in consultant firms, in nonprofit organizations, and in universities.

Prior to any analysis of any policy issue, the analyst must ask certain questions. For example, who am I serving? Is it the client, is it elected officials, an interest group or groups, or the general public? Once the analyst answers this question, then he or she is ready to undertake the steps of policy analysis.

THE POLICY ANALYSIS STEPS

Most authors would agree that there is a series of steps undertaken when conducting a piece of policy analysis. There might be disagreement on how many steps there are in the sequence, but it is clear from reading the policy analysis literature that there is a sequence of activities that must be carried out for effective analysis.[13] Each step is clearly linked to the next, and if the sequence is dramatically broken, then the likelihood of the analysis being flawed greatly increases. The objective of this discussion is to provide readers with a quick overview of the practical sequence of steps, but not a detailed methodological breakdown of policy analysis.

Most practical policy analysis is based upon the work of Patton and Sawicki, MacRae and Wilde, and Bardach.[14] The sequence is illustrated in Figure 8.2. At each step certain activities must be undertaken in order to move successfully to the next step.

Also, at the completion of each step the analyst should review to see if the activities of the current step relate basically to what was done in the previous steps. The objective of any piece of policy analysis is the development of alternatives (policy proposals) that can be judged as to how well they meet the problem as it is identified and understood.

Problem Definition

The objective in this step is the creation of a problem statement that defines the problem being addressed. It is in effect verifying, defining, and detailing the problem. The analyst attempts to frame the problem in concrete terms and create a statement that allows the client to have a firm understanding of the problem's dimensions. This requires that the analyst understand how others see the problem, thus the analyst must be able to identify the causes of the problem.

Problem definition is crucial to the overall analysis because if the problem is defined incorrectly or poorly, then the chances are great that any developed and selected solutions will be inappropriate. In order to arrive at a definition of the problem, all relevant actors from the most affected to the least affected must be identified and the problem must be defined from each of their perspectives. Additionally, all influencing factors must be identified and taken into account.

Establishing Evaluation Criteria

Criteria are needed if alternatives are to be compared and evaluated as to their effectiveness in dealing with the problem. Criteria allow for alternatives to be judged as acceptable to relevant constituencies as well as effective in addressing the problem. There are common categories of criteria that may be applied to all alternatives and issue areas. Other more particular criteria can be developed and operationalized as needed according to the problem definition. Each criteria category is

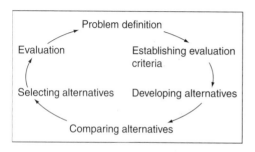

FIGURE 8.2 Policy Analysis Steps.

SOURCE: Adapted from C. Patton and D. Sawicki, *Basic Methods of Policy Analysis and Planning* (Englewood Cliffs, NJ: Prentice Hall, 1986), 2, 26.

operationalized according to the problem at hand. In order to operationalize the criteria, analysts must define the goals of any policy and its objectives. The categories are[15]

- Technical feasibility, including effectiveness and adequacy
- Economic feasibility, including costs, benefits, and cost effectiveness
- Political viability, including acceptability to actors and stakeholders
- Administrative viability, including the ability to implement and manage
- Legality and ethics—is it legal, is it ethical?

Developing Alternatives

Once criteria have been established, a series of alternative policies should be identified. The ideal is to identify all possible options, but that is seldom feasible. Thus, the goal of this step is to generate sufficient alternatives so that there really is a choice. A common error is to generate alternatives that do not deal specifically with the problem. Once the alternatives have been identified, the analyst should check them against the problem statement to ensure that they indeed address the problem.

Alternatives can be generated in a number of ways. For example, alternatives may be identified through researched analysis of existing policies that deal with similar problems, surveys of experts, experiments, and brainstorming. Brainstorming is simply a quick way of listing all possible alternatives of dealing with a problem from the "do-nothing" option to more ambitious solutions. It is a freewheeling process by which analysts can finalize a list of alternatives to be evaluated against established criteria. Once alternatives have been identified and finalized they should be refined, modified, altered, adapted, and omitted until the analyst is left with a list of final alternatives that will

be evaluated against the established criteria. The analyst should leave this stage with anywhere from four to twelve serious alternatives. The refining and modification process is achieved through applying each generated alternative to the problem statement.

Comparing and Selecting Alternatives

In these two steps the alternatives that have been identified are evaluated and compared against the established criteria. This necessarily involves the ranking of criteria in terms of importance. In order to present decision makers with the best solution or solutions, the analyst must be able to identify differences among alternatives in terms of their ability to solve the problem and decide which alternatives are superior to others. The goal is to develop a rough ranking of which alternatives might be preferable given the criteria employed.

Evaluation

The process has come full circle, and this step allows for the inclusion of feedback in all considered alternatives in order to see whether the policy, if adopted, is doing what it is supposed to and if not, why it is not. Evaluation is basically providing possible evaluation models that might be utilized if an alternative is implemented.

THE SIGNIFICANCE OF POLICY ANALYSIS

Policy analysis represents a critical thread that ties all of the implications derived from the previously discussed predecision stage. In essence, policy formulation represents the proposed solution to the identified problem. How one understands and analyzes the problem, its nature, and its dynamics is critical to developing appropriate, effective, and efficient policy solutions. Real-world politics often ensure that because problems are not always identified correctly, generated policy solutions are not always as effective as they could be. More important, the most politically feasible solution is often the one that can be adopted and this causes the incorrect matching of solutions to the nature of the problem.

MODELS OF POLICY FORMULATION

There are many different models of policy formulation, and each model depends upon the criteria used for classification. B. Guy Peters developed a scheme to classify particular approaches taken in preparing policy solutions.[16] Peters argues that in order to formulate policy, policy makers must be well versed in the nuances of politics and policy and understand the problem at hand.[17]

In his models, Peters essentially demonstrates the interaction between knowledge of causation and the level of factual information. For Peters, policy formulation is based upon two interacting factors—how much factual information is available to the formulator and how well he or she understands the problem's causes.[18] Figure 8.3 shows Peters's classification scheme, which ranges from simple to complex formulation models: routine, creative, conditional, and craftsman.

	High knowledge of causation	Low knowledge of causation
High information	Routine	Conditional
Low information	Craftsmen	Creative

FIGURE 8.3 Peters's Formulation Models.

SOURCE: Adapted from B. Guy Peters, *American Public Policy: Promise and Performance* (New York: Chatham House, 1999).

Routine

Routine is the simplest type of formulation. It requires high levels of knowledge about causation and high levels of factual information. The types of policy that result from routine formulation are incremental changes on policy issues that are common to the legislative agenda. In other words, formulation is the routine adjustment of existing policies. There can be shifts in routine policies if underlying theories of causation change. Examples of routine formulation are defense spending during the Cold War years and social security changes.

Creative

Creative is the second formulation model. In this type, formulators lack sufficient information and causal understanding and therefore any policy proposals that emerge are doubtful in terms of their effects. Creative formulation occurs because of decision makers' low knowledge levels of causation and low factual information levels. Policy makers not only need to be creative but also cautious when they match individuals' needs with the needs of the implementing agency. Often this requires that policy makers build in reversible policy choices that can be called upon if the creatively formulated policy is unworkable or needs correction.[19] This can result in formulators being influenced by bureaucratic claims of expertise and knowledge of the issue area. An example of creative formulation is personal social services, such as counseling.

Conditional

Conditional formulation is the third model. In this type of formulation decision makers have sufficient information but lack causal knowledge. Thus, policy proposals are based on the likely effects of the policy. Such proposals often allow for possible modification of the policy as it is being implemented and as conditions change. A good example of conditional formulation is fiscal policy.

Craftsman

Craftsman is the final formulation model. In this type, decision makers clearly understand the causes of the problem but lack supportive information. Thus, a formulated policy relies heavily on probability of outcome. More often then not it is poorly formulated because even if causes are known, the decision makers know little of the facts of the situation and errors are inevitable. An example of craftsman formulation is a policy that dictates use of military force.

SUMMARY

Once policy has been formulated and alternative solutions have been thoroughly examined, a preferred proposal emerges. This preference must then be formally adopted. Policy formulation is complex. It is a constant battle that never ends even if a policy is adopted. The relationship between formulation and adoption is clear: The nature of a problem affects how solutions are formulated as well as what solution is finally adopted as law. Crucial to policy adoption is whether a majority coalition can be put together to support one particular proposal. Thus, often the policy adopted is the most feasible and not necessarily the best in terms of solving or dealing effectively with the problem. Feasibility is defined as the one that has the most consensus behind it. The process of policy adoption is discussed in Chapter 9.

DISCUSSION QUESTIONS

1. The president and senior advisors are in the process of determining what policy actions should be taken to address the terrorist threat posed by the FARC group in Colombia. Your tasks are as follows:

   a. Define and determine the nature and scope of the threat (problem definition).

   b. Determine and describe various policy instruments you recommend and how they could be utilized to address the specific nature of the threat.

   c. Make two basic recommendations for formulation of policy:

      i. A policy recommendation without any consideration of domestic political or international constraints.

      ii. A policy recommendation with consideration of domestic political or international constraints.

   Note: Your answer to question 1 should be three pages long. It should be single-spaced and clearly written, with the president and staff as your intended audience.

2. The problem of secondhand smoke is a serious problem that affects the common good. Develop four well-articulated problem statements that identify the problem from the perspective of a parent, a bar owner, a smoker, and the CEO of a large tobacco manufacturing corporation.

3. In one sentence each, develop ten different alternatives for solving the following problem. Do not worry about real-world constraints.

   The state of California experiences an energy shortage every summer, and every summer the shortage gets worse.

SUGGESTED READINGS

Behn, R. D. "The Big Questions of Public Management." *Public Administration Review* 55 (July/August 1995):313–324.

deHaven-Smith, L. *Philosophical Critiques of Policy Analysis.* Gainesville: University of Florida Press, 1990.

Dowding, K. "Model or Metaphor? A Critical Review of the Policy Network Approach." *Political Studies* 43, no. 1 (1995):136–158.

Dunn, W. N., and R. M. Kelly. *Advances in Policy Studies Since 1950.* New Brunswick, NJ: Transaction, 1992.

Fischer, F. "Reconstructing Policy Analysis: A Postpositivist Perspective." *Policy Sciences* 25, no. 3 (1993):333–339.

Gray, V. "Competition, Emulation, and Policy Innovation." In L. C. Dodd and C. Jillson, eds., *New Perspectives on American Politics.* Washington, DC: CQ Press, 1994.

Munger, M. *Analyzing Policy.* New York: Norton, 2000.

Weissert, C. "Policy Entrepreneurs, Policy Opportunists, and Legislative Effectiveness." *American Politics Quarterly* 19 (1991):262–274.

Wilson, J. Q. *Bureaucracy: What Government Agencies Do and Why They Do It.* New York: Basic Books, 1989.

ENDNOTES

1. John W. Kingdon, *Agendas, Alternatives, and Public Policies* (Boston: Little Brown, 1984).

2. D. A. Stone, *Policy Paradox and Political Reason* (Glenview, IL: Scott Foresman, 1988).

3. A. L. Schneider and H. Ingram, *Policy Design for Democracy* (Lawrence: University Press of Kansas, 1997). and J. E. Anderson, *Public Policymaking,* 4th ed. (Boston: Houghton Mifflin, 2000), 233–244.

4. B. Guy Peters, *American Public Policy: Promise and Performance* (New York: Chatham House, 1999), 59–67.

5. E. E. Schattschneider, *The Semisovereign People* (New York: Holt, Rinehart & Winston, 1960); T. Lowi, *The End of Liberalism* (New York: Norton, 1979).

6. F. R. Baumgartner and Bryan D. Jones, *Agendas and Instability in American Politics* (Chicago: University of Chicago Press, 1993); Kingdon, *Agendas.*

7. Kingdon, *Agendas;* G. Majone, "Policy Analysis and Public Deliberation," in R. B. Reich, *The Power of Public Ideas* (Cambridge: Harvard University Press, 1988), chapter 7.

8. S. Kelman, *Making Public Policy* (New York: Basic Books, 1987); Kingdon, *Agendas;* W. Riker, *The Art of Political Manipulation* (New Haven, CT: Yale University Press, 1986).

9. A. L. Schneider and H. Ingram, "The Social Construction of Target Populations: Implications for Politics and Policy," *American Political Science Review* 87 (June 1993):334–347.

10. M. Donovan, "The Politics of Deservedness: Ryan White and the Social Construction of People with AIDS," *Policy Studies Review* 12, no. 3/4 (Autumn/Winter 1993); G. M. Herek and J. P. Capitanio, "AIDS Stigma and HIV-Related Beliefs in the United States: Results from a National Telephone Survey," paper prepared for presentation at 1998 World AIDS Conference in Geneva, Switzerland, June 28–July 3, 1998.

11. Schneider and Ingram, "The Social Construction," 336.

12. C. E. Lindblom, "The Science of Muddling Through," in S. Z. Theodoulou and Mathew A. Cahn, *Public Policy: The Essential Readings* (Englewood Cliffs, NJ: Prentice Hall, 1995).

13. C. Patton and D. Sawicki, *Basic Methods of Policy Analysis* (Englewood Cliffs, NJ: Prentice Hall, 1986), 29.

14. D. MacRae and T. Wilde, *Policy Analysis for Public Decisions* (Belmont, CA: Wadsworth, 1985), 7–11; Patton and Sawicki, *Basic Methods,* 35; E. Bardach, *A Practical Guide for Policy Analysis* (Chatham, NJ: Chatham House, 2000), 20–26.

15. Patton and Sawicki, *Basic Methods,* 156–157; Bardach, *A Practical Guide,* 20–26.

16. Peters, *American Public Policy,* 66–67.

17. Ibid., 66–67.

18. Ibid., 66–67.

19. Ibid., 66–67.

9

Policy Adoption

Decisions and Strategies

The initial predecision stages of the policy process lead to the identification of problems, the setting of agendas, and the formulation of policy solutions. During these initial stages, issues of concern emerge, ideas are debated, issues enter and leave the agenda, and alternatives are designed to best address a policy problem. Once policy alternatives are designed, however, some kind of governmental decision must be made regarding the direction and type of governmental action that will follow. This seemingly simple act of making the decision to adopt a proposed course of policy action represents a defining moment in the policy process.

The significance of the decision stage is highlighted by a simple realization that only adopted policies can have an intended effect on society. Moreover, only by adopting policies can a proposed course of action garner legitimation within the political and public arena. In sum, the policy adoption stage represents the process by which alternatives are politically explored in the lawmaking arenas, debate and negotiation transpire within the legislative process, and actions are taken to promote specific legislative positions over others.

DEFINING POLICY ADOPTION

In order for a policy to be adopted it has to be accepted by those actors and groups with the power and authority to make decisions. The key to adoption is political feasibility. Political feasibility can be defined as a policy that has a consensus of support

Box 9.1 Forms of Policy Adoption	
Forms	**Example**
Regulations	Regulation of trucking industry
Executive orders	President Clinton's 1995 loan to stabilize Mexican peso
Executive agreements	NAFTA
Judicial action	1954 *Brown v. Topeka Board of Education*
Legislation	2001 Patriot Act
Approval of referendums or initiatives	California's Proposition 187

behind it. It might not be the best or the correct policy to solve the problem, but it has the most support. Policy adoption is the formal approval by institutional actors of a policy proposal. The process of the adoption of laws or policies by a legislature, such as Congress, is also referred to as *policy legitimation*. Legislation is one of the most important and publicized means of adoption and will be discussed in more detail in the next section. Box 9.1 highlights the forms that policy adoption may be achieved through.

POLICY ADOPTION DECISION CRITERIA

The decision to adopt a proposed policy is a seemingly simple choice—to vote to adopt or not. In actuality, policy adoption is the byproduct of the decisions made by the critical institutional actors who have the authority to approve a proposed government action. All institutional actors are influenced by a variety of decision criteria during the decision-making process. These criteria, as

highlighted by James E. Anderson, reflect the various influences and factors that actors may consider when deciding whether to adopt a specific policy alternative.[1] Criteria that can influence policy-makers' decisions include values, political party affiliation, constituency interests, and deference.[2]

Values

Values represent a general set of beliefs and norms that shape and affect the kind of policy action, if any, that should be taken. For Anderson, these values reflect organizational, professional, personal, policy, and ideological perspectives that an individual may adhere to or be influenced by. In many circumstances, some or all of these values will interact and affect the preference of the decision maker for certain policy actions over others.

Organizational Values. Every agency or institution develops its own culture that reflects the mandate, mission, and history of that organization. Within any bureaucratic agency, for instance, actors confront a culture defined by the goals, interests, and power of the agency within the overall policy-making arena. The mission and goals specific to each government agency can shape how officials evaluate certain policy proposals. Competing interests may fail to penetrate the power of these organizational values that place a high premium on organizational loyalty and adherence. Missions of various bureaucratic agencies can overlap, functions assigned can conflict, and the purpose of an agency can foster an environment that impedes bureaucratic cooperation and coordination. In the end, such values can greatly influence decisions on proposed regulations and legislation.

Professional and Personal Values. Values also appear as the result of professional and personal proclivities. Professionally, the particular backgrounds of certain professions, such as engineers at the National Aeronautics and Space Administration (NASA), scientists at the National Institutes of Health (NIH), policy analysts at the General Accounting Office (GAO), or lawyers at the Justice Department, can favor a specific course of action over others. Specifically, "professionally trained people carry these preferences or values with them into the organization, some of which become dominated by particular professions."[3] In comparison, personal values reflect the general motivations and influence that each individual may harbor when determining the appropriate course of action.

Each decision made by a political actor is a decision made without the luxury of controlling for personal values. The influence of specific moral or ethical visions, of career or financial advancement, and of an interest in a historical legacy or political significance can all have an effect on how a decision is made by a specific political actor. The decision not to invade and occupy Iraq as part of the 1991–1992 Persian Gulf War may be explained by the array of competing values affecting then President George H. Bush. For instance, the president's personal concern for the moral standing of the United States or his preference of ensuring his future moral standing may explain why he decided to end the war sooner than some of his own military commanders preferred.[4]

Policy and Ideological Values. Policy and ideological values have an additional influence on the decision making of government officials. Elected and appointed policy leaders must decide on a course of action that also redresses part of or the entire problem identified. Issues that are left to perpetuate and fester represent risky political vulnerabilities. Elected leaders are especially sensitive to the notion that an important issue of public concern was needlessly ig-

nored. Decision makers must place a value on taking credible policy action because allowing a problem to persist is not always a politically viable option. Although surprising to some cynics, policy decisions are made out of a genuine desire to pursue actions that are believed will best solve the policy problem.[5]

Ideological values, in comparison, reflect the set of political beliefs that help define one's vision of the political and policy-making worlds. The notion of defining a political actor as liberal, moderate, or conservative captures the role ideology has in influencing how an issue is perceived and a decision is calculated. Such a belief system helps to define and clarify the complex world for many in and out of government. Decisions as to what action should be taken on a prospective piece of legislation can be shaped by one's basic vision for society and the political world.

Conservatives, for instance, may hold general positions of less government and greater liberty for the individual. Liberals, in contrast, may believe that government can indeed be an instrument that resolves social failings. Moderates, however, whether somewhat conservative or somewhat liberal, may be more varied in their position, holding to a more pragmatic view of policy making. In short, each set of ideological values, held by each policy actor, represents a powerful instrument with which to determine what course of action best addresses the perception of the policy problem and serves the actor's vision for society. The passion and strength of conviction underscoring such ideological beliefs can lead to political conflicts over which ideological vision best serves the policy problem and society. Between 1994 and 2000, the various budgetary and policy fights between President Clinton and the Republican-controlled Congress highlight the striking political and policy divisions that can emerge from differences in political ideology.

Political Party Affiliation

Political parties represent an explicit influence on the decisions made by the various actors within the policy-making process. Although recent victories by independents suggest a new era for third parties, American policy making operates within a two-party system dominated by Republicans and Democrats. These two political parties continue to have an indelible impact on the decision-making process by helping set the institutional agenda, defining the process by which legislation is adopted, as well as serving as a considerable influence and constraint on the decisions taken and supported by the various legislative actors.

Political parties affect policy decisions because of the obvious role the parties play in the political life of an elected policy maker. Legislatively, because the support of various majorities is required for the passage of legislation, members rely on and foster party loyalty. Political parties provide an immediate and potential source of majority political support for one's own agenda or policy initiative. However, the strength of the political parties rises and falls depending on the degree of cohesion and party voting that exists. Historically, the party unity and polarization between the two dominant political parties has steadily grown since 1970 in both the U.S. Senate and House of Representatives.[6] Since 1992, for instance, over 50 percent of all recorded votes reflected a majority of Democrats opposed by a majority of Republicans in both chambers of the legislative branch.[7] Moreover, the Republican revolution of 1994 has reinvigorated the role of the party whips in attempting to ensure and coerce party discipline.

Overall, every elected member of Congress confronts the real threat of political retaliation, of political isolation, and of the long-term political consequences that may come from the lack of a member's support for his or her party's preferred policy positions. From the passage of legislation within committees, to the structure and composition of committees, to placement of legislation on the various calendars, to the votes and debate on the floor, an elected member must often rely on the support of his or her party members to survive and thrive politically.

The advantage of the political party is that loyalty will be rewarded. As a member rises in seniority more prominent positions on committees are available. With loyalty and seniority come the opportunities for senior party positions. Additionally, the parties represent a potentially powerful group to rely on to pass legislation that aids the political agenda of a respective member. In terms of future elections, the political party offers the political resources and organizational structure that greatly aids the next campaign for reelection. In short, the political party can be a significant influence on the decisions taken by the various institutional actors. Still, the nature of the particular issue may be even more significant in explaining how institutional actors decide or whether they can side with the preferences of the party and senior political figures.

Certain issues, because of their intrinsic political nature or sensitivity, can diminish the influence of the political party on decision making. Issues that are of special importance for constituents within the district, state, or nation may compel an actor to stray from stated positions of his or her political party. The 2002 McCain-Feingold legislation dealing with campaign finance reform represented a legislative issue that many members of the Republican Party preferred to support—even though widespread opposition existed within the party.[8] Similarly, a number of Senate Democrats dissented with the majority of their party to support President George W. Bush's 2001 tax cut plan. Hence, decisions regarding whether or not to formally support a policy proposal reflect a mixture of the dominance and cohesion of the party, coupled with the political realities that may surround the institutional actor as related to a given issue. At some point, policy makers will have to decide between the wishes of their political party and the demands of their respective constituents. How elected officials decide depends, in part, on the interests of their constituencies.

Constituency Interests

Elected decision makers, whether at the local, state, or federal level, must decide between the sometimes-conflicting motivations of their constituents, their political party, and their own preferences for a particular course of policy action. The political realities of the electoral process, however, suggest that all elected representatives are first and foremost political animals. As such, constituency interests must predominate over all other interests.

The notion of constituency interest suggests, however, that what one's constituents prefer is clear and readily discerned. In actuality, such clarity seldom occurs for decision makers. Certain significant events or issues may indeed develop within a respective political arena and reflect a degree of popular interest that provides clarity for the decision maker. Yet, effectively and consistently determining the constituency interest can prove difficult. Constituency interests are by no means fixed and the preferences of one's respective public can and does change over time as new circumstances and issues emerge. Moreover, some policy makers within divided political districts confront the added difficulty of attempting to discern what the majority may prefer even when no clear majority interest may exist among the constituency. Still, given the sheer number and varied nature of hearings, resolutions, bills, and legislation considered within a given political session, the political reality is

that the impact of constituent interests may be exaggerated in light of the day-to-day realities of policy making.

The impact of constituency interests may depend on how the term is defined. A narrow definition may focus on a vast segment of the public. A broader definition would include the constituent role of interest groups, associations, lobbyists, citizen activists, as well as the general public. In actuality, a broad definition of constituency interests would include actors that play an active role in the policy-making process. The public's interest, attention, and activism in the policy-making process will vary greatly depending on the issue. In the absence of an active and consistent role by the public, decision makers must make decisions based on their own preferences, as well as the information, positions, and preferences outlined by those actors that are active in the process. Arguably, the role of constituency interests varies depending on how an issue is perceived within the public and political agenda.

Many policy actions, such as those dealing with detailed regulatory changes, budgetary appropriations, or other detailed legislation, may hinder a wider role by the constituency. Essentially, the more detailed and obscure the proposed policy action, the more unlikely it is that the broad spectrum of the public will become active participants in the legislative process. Other proposed policy actions, such as those dealing with emotional issues like civil rights, the environment, education, or abortion, can be more sensitive to the direct pressures of constituents. Even though such emotional issues may spark responses in the overall positions among constituents, the detailed minutiae of writing legislation may further obscure the positions a legislator should or should not take because proposed legislation may include a variety of initiatives and actions designed to deal with a respective policy problem.

Deference

Decisions within the policy-making process are also influenced by the deference decision makers can have for the interests of certain policy, political, and administrative authorities. The technical complexity of certain issues may increase the role and influence of various policy groups both within and outside the government. Governmental policy groups, such as the General Accounting Office (GAO) or the Congressional Budget Office (CBO), may affect the analysis, understanding, and positions that policy makers take on specific issues. At a minimum, such governmental policy agencies provide a useful source of information and analysis. Aside from governmental policy research groups, decision makers may also take into consideration the analysis and position favored by think tanks, such as Rand, CATO, the Urban Institute, or Brookings. Such think tanks offer policy expertise and analysis of both specific issues and broad policy areas. The deference to such policy actors, however, is a product of the willingness of the decision maker to accept the findings and analysis of such government institutions or think tanks.

Aside from these governmental or research think tanks, various political associations and interest groups provide additional policy expertise and analysis. Decision makers may pay attention to the views offered by key political associations and interest groups. Interest groups, such as the American Association of Retired Persons (AARP), the National Rifle Association (NRA), the Sierra Club, provide both analysis and understanding of policy problems. Additionally, associations such as the National Governor's Association (NGA), the National League of Cities (NLC), or the National Education Association (NEA) also conduct independent policy research and analysis.

Policy research provided by interest groups and associations will inevitably favor certain positions and decisions on key policy issues. When addressing particular issues of importance to them, these organizations may have considerable influence on policy makers' decisions. These groups amass further influence by the sheer political weight that their stated policy positions carry within the broad political arena. For instance, decision makers may defer to such groups out of a reluctance to publicly oppose the positions of politically powerful interest groups.

Aside from the political influence of interest groups or associations, decision makers can and do accommodate senior legislative authorities on certain issues. Within Congress, for instance, newer representatives may defer to the party leadership or senior members of the committee. To some extent policy-making reality compels legislative actors to defer to the expertise of members that sit on the respective committee responsible for the proposed piece of legislation. That is not surprising, given the sheer numerical size of some proposed pieces of legislation, coupled with the scope of various programs and services that are discussed. Aside from policy and political deference, additional guidance is provided by various administrative agencies.

The hierarchical nature of the administrative agency leads officials within the agency to follow the guidance and dictums of both administrative and political superiors. The effectiveness of the agency requires that officials follow the directives of their administrative authorities. Deference is based on the authority accorded certain agency officials and political appointees. Such deference, however, can lead to conflicts between the stated positions preferred by the political appointees and the preference of career agency officials. Additionally, agency oversight by congressional actors further complicates decision making as agency officials, vulnerable to the regulatory and budgetary role of Congress, may have to defer to the preferences of respective members of Congress. Conversely, during the policy formulation and adoption stages, members of Congress may also decide to defer to the positions preferred by senior administrative officials within various agencies.

Overall, deference reflects the interpersonal role that persuasion and influence can have on the policy decisions made by the various institutional actors. As stated, deference may be based on the hierarchy of authority established within an administrative agency. In other cases, however, deference reflects the political power of senior party officials, senior committee members, policy actors, and interest groups to compel other actors to defer to their positions. Still, the real weight of such deference depends on the extent to which other factors—whether values, political party affiliation, or constituency interests—affect the decision-making process of the legislative actor.

THE LEGISLATIVE PROCESS AND POLICY ADOPTION

The adoption of policy proposals winds through an institutional process that helps structure and define the course of action undertaken by the respective political actors. The path of policy adoption varies among and within each institution with degrees of policy-making power. The courts, the executive branch, and Congress all have unique environments and contexts in which various government actions are considered for adoption. Institutionally, the policy process is fragmented and divided among all three branches of the federal government. Formulation and adoption of proposed policy actions occur within the executive and legislative branches, and constitutional oversight is afforded to the

judicial branch. The focus of the following section, however, is on the prominence of Congress and its central role in decision making throughout the legislative process.

The primary responsibility for the formulation and adoption of federal policy proposals rests within the legislative and executive branches. Within this legislative process, the bicameral chambers of Congress, coupled with the additional role played by the executive branch in guiding policy proposals, are critical to effectively understanding the origins of policy proposals, as well as the particular kinds of policy action that can be taken. Within the legislative branch, four kinds of legislative actions can be taken by Congress: bills, joint resolutions, concurrent resolutions, and simple resolutions.[9] Each is summarized in Box 9.2.

The fragmented nature of American public policy provides a wide forum for the ideas and opinions that become the sources of legislation. Constitutionally, the separation of powers ensures a multiple path by which individuals, groups, and institutions can attempt to influence and shape the beginnings of the adoption of legislation. In theory, no one institution, individual, or group possesses greater influence than any other, and no one policy actor can be prevented from proposing a piece of legislation and pursuing its adoption. Interestingly, any citizen can draft and propose a piece of legislation to be considered for submission by an elected representative. In reality, depending on the issue, various institutions, groups, and individuals can have considerable influence in how decisions are made within the legislative process.

To what extent any one actor can influence policy adoption depends, to some degree, on how well the formal legislative process is understood. This process, by which a bill becomes law, represents the main policy battleground for the formulation and adoption of a proposed legislation. In other

---

Box 9.2   Kinds of Legislative Actions

Bills: Bills are the most common type of legislation and can be either public or private. A public bill is one that affects the wider public, whereas a private bill affects a specified individual. A bill originating in the House of Representatives is designated by the letters *H.R.* followed by a number that it retains throughout the legislative process. A Senate bill is designated by an *S* followed by a number that it retains throughout the legislative process. The term "Companion Bill" describes a bill that is identical to a bill introduced in the other house of Congress.

Joint Resolutions: Joint resolutions may originate in either the Senate or the House—not jointly in both houses. Joint resolutions are similar to bills, requiring approval by both chambers and the president, except when dealing with constitutional amendment issues when approval by the president is unnecessary if two-thirds congressional supported is garnered. A joint resolution originating in the House is designated as "H.J. Res." followed by a number. A joint resolution in the Senate is designated as "S. Res." followed by a number. Such joint resolutions become law in the same manner as bills.

Concurrent Resolutions: Concurrent resolutions address matters affecting the operations of both houses and are not equivalent to a bill. These actions are not presented to the president for veto or signature. Such resolutions are used to express facts, principles, opinions, and purposes of the two houses. Such resolutions in the House are designated "H. Con Res." followed by a number, and "S. Con Res." in the Senate followed by a number. On approval by both houses they are signed by the Clerk of the House and the Secretary of the Senate.

Simple Resolutions: Simple resolutions concern the rules, operation, or the opinion of either house alone. Simple resolutions are considered only by the body in which they are respectively introduced. In the House, simple resolutions are designated as "H. Res." together with a number. In the Senate, simple resolutions are designated as "S. Res." together with a number. Upon adoption, simple resolutions are attested to by the Secretary of the Senate or Clerk of the House and are published in the *Congressional Record*.

---

words, the legislative arena can be recognized as a theater for political war in which the battleground includes advocates, both in and out of government, who hold to competing positions as to what decisions should be made and what policy should be adopted.

THE LEGISLATIVE PROCESS— FROM BILL TO LAW

The legislative process is a fragmented and conflict-prone process by which competing bills must survive innumerable institutional and political obstacles in order to be adopted. The basic legislative process is outlined in Article 1, Section 7 of the U.S. Constitution. In reality, the modern-day legislative process extends beyond the framework outlined by Article 1 and includes the significant role of committees, parties, and rules that are not specifically articulated within the Constitution. In particular, within the bicameral Congress, the legislative process is structured and divided between the dominant legislative roles played by committees and subcommittees within both chambers, as well as the party structure that establishes key party positions accorded specific legislative roles.

Any member of Congress can introduce legislation. Although some bills can be described as symbolic and political in value, only a few can or will become laws. In fact,

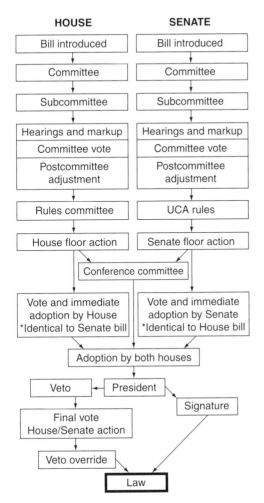

HOUSE   **SENATE**

Bill introduced   Bill introduced

Committee   Committee

Subcommittee   Subcommittee

Hearings and markup   Hearings and markup

Committee vote   Committee vote

Postcommittee adjustment   Postcommittee adjustment

Rules committee   UCA rules

House floor action   Senate floor action

Conference committee

Vote and immediate adoption by House *Identical to Senate bill   Vote and immediate adoption by Senate *Identical to House bill

Adoption by both houses

Veto ← President

Signature

Final vote House/Senate action

Veto override

Law

FIGURE 9.1 The Legislative Process.

of the total number of acts, bills, and joint resolutions introduced between 1789 and 1998, no more than 1 percent became law.[10] These statistics make resoundingly clear the circuitous and obstacle-ridden path that legislation must follow if it is to become law (see Figure 9.1).

House of Representatives

The legislative process begins with the introduction of a proposed piece of legislation or bill (see Figure 9.1). Every member

may introduce prospective legislation at any time while the House is in session, and is formally recognized as the sponsor of the legislation. An unlimited number of members may cosponsor a respective piece of proposed legislation. The legislative process begins once a bill is dropped into the hopper and it is formally introduced by its HR title and assigned a number. Once introduced, the bill is referred, with the consent and certain discretion of the Speaker, to a specific committee. It is at this stage that the "real business" of policy adoption occurs.[11]

A bill is assigned to the committee that deals with its subject matter. The House rules include over 200 classifications for determining which committees will handle various legislative measures and proposals. Box 9.3 shows, for example, the legislative responsibilities for the Armed Services committee.

In practice, because proposed legislation addresses a variety of subjects it can be assigned to multiple committees. This process

---

Box 9.3 Legislative Responsibilities of the Committee on Armed Services

- Ammunition depots, forts, arsenals, and Army, Navy, and Air Force reservations and establishments
- Common defense generally
- The Department of Defense
- Military applications of nuclear energy
- Tactical intelligence and intelligence-related activities of the Department of Defense
- Strategic and critical materials necessary for the common defense
- Size and composition of the Army, Navy, Marine Corps, and Air Force

SOURCE: Adapted from information found on the Armed Services Committee Web site, available at http://www.house.gov/hasc.

is known as *multiple referrals*. In general, one committee is assigned the primary committee based on the discretion of the Speaker of the House. Most complex bills, such as those dealing with the fiscal-year federal budget, will be introduced and assigned to more than one committee. Since the 1980s, about "three out of ten major [legislative] measures were multiply referred, [while] in the 104th Congress half" of all legislative proposals were referred to multiple committees.[12] The consequence of multiple referrals on decision making is that it requires a significant degree of cooperation among policy actors in order to ensure that proposed legislation is ready for floor action. At times, divergent interests between members within various committees will only complicate the legislative process.[13] Overall, the committee stage of the legislative process represents a key forum where an array of decisions must be made concerning the structure and content of the legislative proposal.

After being introduced, and assigned to the relevant full committees, a bill can be further divided among relevant subcommittees. Interestingly, many pieces of legislation will die at this stage because further consideration is not granted by either the full committee or subcommittee. If the committee or subcommittee chooses to take up the legislation for consideration, the relevant subcommittees will begin the initial critical examination, conduct hearings and investigations into the proposed legislation, as well as gather testimony and input from relevant institutional and noninstitutional actors. Following such testimony and hearings, a markup session will occur. Markup is the formal process by which the content of a proposed legislation, its language and structure, is determined.[14] During this stage, ensuring adoption of the bill may require significant rewriting and reworking of the legislative language in order to conform to the interests of the majority or senior members of the subcommittee. After markup in

the subcommittee, a vote will be taken to decide whether to pass the bill for consideration by the entire committee. Failure to attract sufficient subcommittee support is a severe blow to a policy proposal and will most likely result in the legislative death of the bill. If the subcommittee adopts the bill, it is passed on to the full committee for additional consideration.

The full committee, once receiving the proposed legislation, may conduct further hearings and markup sessions or may simply choose to adopt the decision of the subcommittee. If the full committee decides in favor of the bill, prospective legislation is passed on for floor action coupled with a written report. The report will describe the purposes and scope of the bill; explain committee revisions; note proposed changes to existing law; and include views of the executive branch agencies, the specific positions of minority or dissenting views held by the members of the committee, as well as estimates of expected cost and regulatory impacts of the bill.[15] If submitted for consideration to the entire House, additional changes in the content of the legislation are expected in the postcommittee stages.

Postcommittee adjustment refers to substantive changes made to the language and content of legislation in order to increase the viability of policy adoption by the House. According to Barbara Sinclair, over a third of major legislation is subjected to postcommittee changes, and quite often "changes will be negotiated and then incorporated into a substitute bill or an amendment."[16] Such postcommittee adjustments have also increased in light of disagreements arising from multiple referrals to various committees.[17] According to Sinclair, postcommittee tweaking proves essential if the legislative process is to avoid a contentious floor battle:

> To pass a big rescission bill (a bill cutting already appropriated spending) in 1995,

the leadership had to agree to drop restrictive anti-abortion language and to accept a lockbox provision dictating that savings go to deficit reduction and not to fund tax cuts. The first was necessary to get the votes of the GOP moderates, the second to pick up some votes from Conservative Democrats.[18]

The next step in the legislative process is the scheduling of legislation for floor action by placing the bill on one of the House calendars. Although the calendar may timetable floor action, priority can be given to proposed legislation by the suspension of rules or special rules. Within the House, the majority party and the Speaker of the House effectively control the various rules that are used to structure and time the legislative schedule. Such rules can outline and restrict time for debate, method of amendments, and the order by which legislation may be considered. The purpose of rules is to provide the majority party with the means to control the method and manner in which the adoption of policy is considered within the House of Representatives.

Floor action begins with debate over the rules assigned to a specific piece of legislation. Such debate involves whether the rules assigned are appropriate or too restrictive. If the House approves the rule, debate and amending of the legislation begins within the formal setting of the Committee of the Whole (COW). The COW is, in actuality, the House of Representatives but operates under looser quorum rules where only 100 members need be present. Amending of the bill follows after the debate, but is again restricted by the set of rules that may or may not allow germane amendments. When debate and amending is completed, the COW reports back to the House of Representatives where the House *finally* votes on the bill in the final manner in which it was approved by the COW. Final vote requires 218 members to be present.

In the end, during the final vote, the opposition to the legislation may motion to recommit the legislation to committee with or without committee. This motion to recommit is the last attempt by the opposition to stymie the adoption of the legislation by the House. Legislation that has survived through these series of legislative hurdles, especially in light of the necessary support by the majority party, has a reasonably good chance of being adopted.

In sum, the description of the legislative process in the House of Representative reflects the significant obstacles that exist within just one part of the legislative process. Policy adoption, in this single chamber, requires a bill to essentially survive numerous roadblocks designed to effectively thwart dramatic legislative initiatives. Given the House's unique institutional context, advantages and disadvantages emerge. For example, the majority party, through control of rules and the committee process, can structure the legislative process in the House to favor the adoption of its own specific policy interests. In contrast, legislation introduced by a member of the minority party, for instance, will confront a difficult path ahead unless the legislation appeals to members of the majority—preferably senior members of the party in leadership positions. Nevertheless, this discussion has explored only the legislative process in the House, and possible adoption of a policy proposal necessitates the added approval of the Senate.

The Senate

A similar legislative process occurs in the Senate when a bill is introduced. The bill is referred to committee, and then, if it survives, is considered for floor debate and voted on. The Senate is a unique legislative chamber in light of the greater power and status afforded each senator irrespective of seniority or party. In reality, this is a function of its size (100 senators) and the length of a senator's term. Within the Senate, an individual senator can at times effectively stymie a majority of his or her colleagues, can propose endless nongermane amendments, and can even attempt to talk a piece of legislation literally to death. In terms of policy adoption, the added power of each member of the Senate results in a more complex political game in which a single senator can substantially alter the character and content of legislation.

The legislative process begins with the introduction of legislation. A member of the Senate can introduce as many pieces of legislation as desired, and can also introduce legislative proposals at the behest of outside parties. Once introduced, the bill is assigned to the committee of predominant jurisdiction. In comparison to the House, multiple referrals are less frequent, and when they do occur, they are done by unanimous consent as negotiated by the relevant committee members.[19] In general, "only a little more than one in ten major measures were sent to more than one committee in recent Congresses."[20] At times, multiple and committee referral can be bypassed because prospective legislation in the Senate can be introduced as an amendment to another bill.

Assuming the legislation is assigned to a committee, a similar process to what transpired in the House develops. Prospective legislation is assigned to a particular committee and further divided among relevant subcommittees. The respective Senate subcommittees analyze and address the bill through a series of hearings, witness testimony, and expert analysis. Once the subcommittee has completed all hearings and testimony, a report is provided to the full committee for consideration. The full committee decides whether to adopt the bill proposed in light of subcommittee recommendations, reject these changes entirely, or completely redraft the piece of legislation. During the critical markup session in the full committee, decisions are made as to the nature of changes to the bill, whether the bill will be voted on favorably, submitted with an adverse report, or fail to be voted on altogether. Once completed, the bill is presented to the entire Senate for consideration, with the possibility for postcommittee adjustments.

Once adjustments to the proposed legislation are complete, the scheduling of floor action begins. Floor action in the Senate, which includes debate, the amending process, and voting, is made far more difficult in light of the power afforded each individual senator. Specifically, the filibuster provides each senator with the power to hold the floor indefinitely on any debatable motion. Stoppage of the filibuster requires a vote of cloture and the support of two thirds of the Senate. In short, the filibuster can prove a considerable weapon in preventing the passage of controversial legislation that may lack the requisite sixty votes of support.[21] To assist in the smooth passage of legislation in the Senate, the Unanimous Consent Agreement (UCA) is used to move legislation to the floor, establish the rules for debate and amendment, and specify time for votes. The UCA ensures a more ordered scheduling of legislative business.

Once legislation proceeds to the floor, the amending and debate related to the bill can be endless unless limited by the UCA. The power to offer nongermane amendments, for example, can prove considerable in altering the support for any given piece of legislation. Such amendments, or riders as they are referred to, can prove to be powerful legislative and political weapons for a senator. For instance, a senator may wish to add an amendment on a bill that is heavily supported to essentially piggyback on a winning piece of legislation. Additionally, a senator who desires to kill a piece of legislation may decide to add an amendment in the hope of breaking the coalition of support within the Senate. As a consequence of nongermane amendments, senators must build a base of political support and must remain sensitive to that support.

Policy adoption, when discussed within the institutional context of the Senate, is especially vulnerable to the divisions that may exist between senators and the parties. The resulting reality is that adoption of legislation can require a de facto supermajority of sixty votes to ensure a vote cloture, as well as to stymie additional procedural obstacles. Yet, the greatest impact of the divisions between the House and Senate is to ensure that legislation will not be adopted in identical form.

The Conference Committee

Before it may become law, a bill must emerge from both chambers of Congress with the identical wording. Given the institutional realities of the legislative process, such a possibility would be rare except in an emergency or highly cooperative situation. According to Sinclair, "in recent Congresses (103rd, 104th, 105th), 78 percent of major measures that got to the resolution stage were sent to conference.[22] The *simple* goal of the conference committee is to hammer out differences between the versions that pass the Senate and House, and to develop a single bill that can be adopted by both chambers. Reconciling differing versions of legislation, however, can prove difficult because the very institutional character and politics can differ between the Senate and House. If stark differences exist between the versions of the bill, achieving reconciliation becomes difficult. If the politics within each chamber differ, because of the differences in party control or degree of partisanship, the process of reconciliation can become even more contentious. In cases where reconciliation is at an impasse, party leaders may attempt to mediate differences and spur a negotiated settlement.[23] If the majority of conferees from both the House and Senate agree to a compromise, they sign the eventual confer-

ence report that is the final proposed version of the bill to be voted on. The resulting bill is sent back to both the Senate and House floor for a final vote by the entire chamber without additional amendment.

The President's Role

A piece of legislation that is adopted by majorities in both chambers continues its path to either law or extinction when it is transmitted to the president for consideration. A president has the power to approve or veto the bill. A bill becomes law if signed by the president, or if left unsigned for more than ten days while Congress is in session. A vetoed bill, however, is then sent back to the House and Senate where a two-thirds majority in both chambers can override the presidential veto. But, if a session of Congress formally ends within the ten-day window that a president is considering a piece of legislation, by not signing the bill, the president vetoes it by means of the pocket-veto. Although the president's legislative power is seemingly limited in nature, essentially signing or vetoing a bill, the threat of veto represents a powerful force in the formulation and adoption of policy throughout the legislative process in Congress.

A president has considerable influence over the formal legislative process through the threat of the veto. The two-thirds override established by the Constitution represents a formidable obstacle, and such large majorities are rare within each of the chambers. Thus, the mere threat of veto can reshape the legislative agenda in both chambers to better reflect the legislative interests of the president. Basically, a president may choose to veto a legislative proposal if it is considered unconstitutional, an encroachment on presidential authority, ill-advised policy, or unacceptable for political or ideological reasons.[24] Historically, the use of the veto has declined significantly from President Franklin D. Roosevelt's record of

---

Box 9.4   Key Points of the Legislative Process

Introduction

- Legislation originates in the House, Senate, White House, or federal department or agency

Committee Stage

- Representative or senator submits proposal to clerk of the House or Senate
- The bill is referred to proper committee, which refers it to subcommittee for research and hearings; bill can be amended at this point
- Subcommittee sends bill back to committee, and it may proceed without further review or be subject to more hearings
- Bill may now be amended or killed; most bills introduced in Congress die in committee
- If bill survives, it's sent to Rules committee (majority leader in Senate), which decides whether bill will be subject to open or closed rule; under open rule, a bill sees more debate and can be amended to a greater degree

Floor Action

- Following this, bill is placed on the calendar for discussion on the floor and ultimately on the other chamber floor
- If bill fails to pass on the floor, it's dead; if it passes, it must then repeat this process in the other chamber

Adoption

- If same version of bill is adopted, it's sent to president for consideration
- Different versions of bill can result in a call for joint conference committee
- If conference report is favorable, the bill is sent back to both chambers for final vote, with no possible changes to the final version of the bill
- President must then review the bill; if president does nothing in ten days, bill becomes law
- President may veto bill, in which case it goes back to House and Senate, where two-thirds majority is needed to override presidential veto

---

635 vetoes over his tenure.[25] More recently, President Clinton performed 25 vetoes between 1993 and 1998.[26]

The previous discussion of the legislative process highlights aspects that are valuable to understanding the stage of policy adoption. Specifically, the legislative process ensures that this aspect of policy adoption will prove difficult. Because of constitutional and institutional procedures, the legislative process provides an array of points where members of Congress, as well as those who seek to influence them, must decide what actions should be taken. Box 9.4 summarizes some of the key points of the legislative process.

In sum, what the entire legislative process reflects are the multiple points where institutional actors must decide whether to adopt or reject a policy proposal. The decision is seldom a simple one. At various points throughout the legislative process, a member must calculate whether or not he or she supports the proposed legislation. Dramatic and immediate attempts at policy adoption, although possible, require the effective cooperation of majorities in both the House and

Senate, party leadership, the committee members, senior members of the committee, and the president—as well many noninstitutional actors that seek to influence these institutional actors. Given the challenge posed by this circuitous legislative process, it is important to recognize that policy adoption is not limited to a single theater of action, such as the Congress, but involves an array of arenas that prove instrumental to the policy adoption stage.

THEATERS OF ACTION

The process of policy adoption develops within and across an array of avenues or so-called *theaters of action*. Within these theaters, proposed policies are debated, formulated, and considered for adoption. Moreover, such theaters are by no means isolated, but often intermingle to mutually frame the manner in which policy positions are adopted. The most significant theaters include the public, executive, congressional, and political theaters.

Public Theater

American policy making occurs within a public theater in which public opinion can directly shape many legislative positions, strategies, and the voting behavior of elected officials. The public theater can directly influence the behavior of legislative actors by constraining or encouraging actions by decision makers. Attempts at hindering or encouraging policy adoption will inevitably be affected by the extent to which a decision maker is concerned with the reactions of the public. The fickle nature of public opinion makes measured responses particularly difficult for decision makers.

Within the public arena, various advocates for a particular issue will attempt to mobilize public opinion to influence the passage or obstruction of legislation. Elected officials, quite obviously, are especially sensitive to the public opinion of their respective constituent base. Every elected decision maker remains cognizant of the positions favored or opposed by their constituents. The difficulty, however, is that formulation of public opinion can be shaped and changed as new information and events develop.

Executive Theater

The president, the cabinet, and the agencies that fall under the responsibility of the executive branch represent an additional theater of action. Legislative proposals often develop under the direction or guidance of the president. The preparation of the fiscal-year federal budget that covers all proposed federal spending represents the most consistent example of a presidential policy proposal. Within the executive branch, cabinet and agency officials also play an integral role in the development of the budget, offer policy initiatives, as well as develop their own regulatory proposals to address areas of agency responsibility. As a theater of action, the president, the cabinet, and agency officials will not only prove essential to the development of policy proposals but also their support—or lack of it—can directly affect whether a policy is adopted.

Congressional Theater

The significance of Congress as a theater of action extends beyond the two chambers and includes both the formal and informal sets of actors who influence and affect policy adoption. Clearly, within this theater, it is the voting positions of the 535 members of Congress that are the most important to consider when attempting to ascertain the likelihood of policy adoption. However, the ability of a member of Congress to explicitly affect whether a policy is adopted or not also depends on party seniority, position on committee, whether the member is part of the party leadership, as well as whether the member's vote is critical to developing a majority for or against the policy.

Political Theater

Through the policy adoption stage, intermingling within all of the previous theaters of action is the effusive role of the various political players. These sets of noninstitutional actors, such as party organizations, interest groups, political associations, lobbyists, and citizen activists, represent how intrinsically political the business of policy making is in modern American politics. Each of these actors plays a constant role in attempting to influence the positions of elected officials critical to the adoption of a policy. For such political actors the goal remains a desire to maximize their self-interests, or the interests of their clients or members, at the expense of those with differing interests. The goal for such actors is seldom the adoption of the best policy.

National party organizations, such as the Republican National Committee (RNC) or the Democratic National Committee (DNC), provide elected members and would-be representatives fiscal and electoral resources. During the election cycle, and especially in what are expected to be close and contentious congressional elections, many members of Congress will depend on the financial monies and election infrastructure necessary to run a modern media-driven campaign. For members of Congress, their future in politics can be affected by the extent to which they can garner the necessary party support. Therefore, how a national party organization stands on key policy proposals, as well as the dependence of the member on the party, can provide insight as to the positions a representative may take during policy adoption.

Interest groups and associations, in comparison, remain engaged in the legislative process from the moment a piece of legislation is even considered for introduction. Initiatives and proposals for policy solutions will be readily made by such actors seeking to further their legislative goals. More important, associations and interest groups are extremely active in mobilizing and building coalitions to further their legislative interests. Interest groups can also be essential to influencing the legislative positions of members of Congress. These groups not only offer policy analysis and proposals but also actively recruit members of their association to lobby members of Congress or the executive branch in support of their preferred policy position.

Lobbying campaigns are the hallmark strategy by which such noninstitutional political actors attempt to influence policy adoption. Lobbying campaigns include media campaigns, attempts to mobilize members' voting behavior, letter and advocacy campaigns, the building of political coalitions with other policy, as well as the use of monies to foster access and influence with critical members essential to policy adoption in Congress and the executive branch. To what extent these actors can influence policy adoption depends on the strategies they employ during the policy process.

INFLUENCING POLICY ADOPTION

The previous description of policy adoption and the legislative process suggests that it is so complex, and so institutional, that only the professional political actors can affect the votes of critical decision makers in government. In actuality, average citizens can—if they choose—successfully influence which policy actions are adopted by decision makers. How such influence develops involves a process and strategy that can be adopted by an array of policy actors (see Figure 9.2).

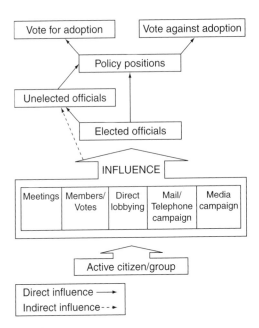

FIGURE 9.2 Process of Influencing Policy Adoption.

Some of the means that are available to influence policy adoption include the following:

- Mobilizing members and votes
- Direct lobbying
- Focused mail and telephone campaigns
- Aggressive multimedia campaigns

Mobilizing Members and Votes

For the political activist, influencing elected decision makers depends on the ability to mobilize politically like-minded individuals, such as members of one's interest group, to display a show of political force. Mobilizing requires seeking out individuals who are willing to actively participate in the political process. Participation may first come in the form of joining a grassroots movement or a more organized interest group. Critical to effective mobilizing, however, is whether members seek to directly influence elected officials.

The power of mobilizing within a democratic system is that it provides a clear political message that members will vote for elected officials that support their legislative positions. Because elected officials are especially cognizant of the political power of disaffected voters, a well-organized mass of potential voters can affect whether a decision maker will support a specific policy position.

Instrumental to mobilizing the ultimate political power of members of an interest group or movement is the size of the group. In general, more political influence is obtained as the size of the group increases relative to the size of the electorate. Clearly, sheer numbers of supporters can translate into both potential votes and potential political influence. To what extent a decision maker may be influenced roughly depends on the size and cohesion of the membership, and whether a group's support is essential for reelection. Still, a small, well-organized group can acquire influence if it is extremely impassioned, organized, well financed, and focused in its advocacy efforts. For example, Mothers Against Drunk Driving (MADD) began as an especially small interest group. With passion and organization, MADD has become extremely successful in influencing the adoption of policies designed to reduce drunk driving.

Direct Lobbying

Direct lobbying represents an explicit attempt to influence the voting or decisions of elected or other political decision makers. Either through hiring a lobbyist or by developing and engaging in a lobbying campaign, direct lobbying promotes specific policy positions. Overall, lobbying is an exercise that exploits money, knowledge of the issue, and access to key officials in order to obtain the desired legislative outcome.

Lobbyists, through fundraisers for candidates and contributions to candidates and the parties, can utilize monies to develop contacts and access. Although money does not necessarily translate into direct influence on policy positions, it represents a powerful tool for the lobbyist to garner access, be able to meet with staff and decision makers, and present positions to policy makers instrumental to policy adoption. Money also helps finance the campaign, via the fostering of meetings, presentation materials, and other research, that allow the lobbyist to establish knowledge and a clear position for an issue during a meeting with a decision maker.[27]

The knowledge of an issue, and the ability to provide clear and factual information, is an ingredient of influence in direct lobbying. With greater information and knowledge of an issue, direct lobbying can move from being merely a source of influence to a source of information for the decision maker.[28] Lobbyists prove to be essential sources of information for the decision maker and the staff when formulating policy, when evaluating the consequences of a proposal, as well as when determining whether or not to adopt a specific public policy position.

Direct lobbying may rise and fall, depending on the access that can be gained and exploited by the lobbying campaign. Access provides the basic opportunity to directly meet and influence the opinions and positions of decision makers. Such direct access and meetings provide lobbyists the opportunity to build interpersonal relationships with staff and decision makers, establishes them as knowledgeable experts on the issue, and allows them to communicate a political and policy relevance of the position they prefer the decision maker take when deciding whether to adopt a policy proposal.

Focused Mail and Telephone Campaigns

The notion of a letter or telephone campaign may seem antiquated in an era of modern technologies such as faxes and e-mails. However, a well-designed and focused mail and telephone campaign, according to former government officials and staffers in Congress, represents a potent weapon with which to influence the opinions of the decision maker.[29] When conducted appropriately, a personal letter and mail campaign can reflect the emotion and passion that can affect how issues and policy proposals are perceived by the actors in the political process.

A letter campaign can be either handwritten, a pro forma letter, or in e-mail form. According to former officials, representatives, and staffers, a well-designed campaign can have an impact on how decision makers see an issue vis-à-vis their constituency. In particular, the personal and handwritten letter reflects an action by a constituent that is increasingly rare, but is seen as an authentic emotional expression. An e-mail or pro forma letter has less emotional significance, but can resonate if a large number of citizens participate. Similarly, a telephone campaign garners influence depending on the number of calls received from constituents in favor of a given issue position. For the elected official, the relative dearth of letters and calls received from constituents concerning many of the issues debated within Congress suggests that a well-organized and mobilized campaign can and does have great influence on the course of policy adoption.[30]

Aggressive Multimedia Campaigns

Modern advocacy requires not only the exploitation of traditional tools but also a realization that politics and policy operate within a society in which perceptions and issues are framed by a variety of media sources. Accordingly, successful advocacy requires a strategy with which to build attention and support among a wide swath of the public and political arena. An aggressive media campaign provides a path with which to mobilize the disinterested and uninformed public and political decision maker, as well as to further mobilize the already politically active. Some of the elements of a successful media campaign include

- Press releases
- Letters to the editor and opinion pieces
- Radio talk-show call-ins
- TV news interviews
- Handouts, fliers, and leaflets

Press releases, for example, would raise awareness to new policy analyses, special reports on the problem, and public marches or forums that would hopefully lead to coverage by local or national news services. Letters to the editor and opinion pieces represent an attempt to influence newspaper positions or to interject preferences for certain policy positions within the public debate. Further, radio talk-show call-ins are an organized attempt to frame and structure the public debate surrounding an issue. Similarly, TV interviews of advocates or the encouragement of special reports on an issue of concern represent the goal to influence opinions of the public through the most commonly used communication medium. Finally, the distribution of handouts, fliers, and leaflets is a basic grassroots strategy to build public attention by raising awareness on an individual-by-individual basis.

SUMMARY

Policy adoption is the stage in the policy process where decisions are made as to what type of policy action, if any, should be taken. As the discussion of the legislative process highlighted, it is a constant battle, seemingly never ending, to see a specific policy adopted. Crucial to policy adoption is whether a majority coalition can be put together to support one particular proposal. A more efficient legislative process proves generally unlikely given differences among critical institutions and institutional. Moreover,

policy adoption is also not limited to a single institution or policy actor, but involves a multiple of theaters where policy adoption is influenced and affected. Finally, the diverse and pluralistic nature of American government provides the opportunity for a variety of noninstitutional actors to directly influence and affect the decisions that determine what policy action is adopted. Thus, because of this political and institutional context, the policy adopted may not be the *best* policy to solve the problem, but simply the most practical and feasible policy that can escape this stage of the policy process.

DISCUSSION QUESTIONS

1. The legislative process is marked by a series of structural twists and turns. Is the American legislative process conducive to efficient and effective policy making? If not, how should it be changed?

2. Are committees essential to making "better" policy? Do you believe committees make it easier or harder for the average citizen to influence the policy-making process? Discuss.

3. If you had to choose just one, which of the theaters identified in this chapter do you think plays the most important role in the stage of policy adoption?

4. In your opinion, which of the values discussed is the most and least important when decisions have to be made by the various policy-making actors? Discuss.

5. It is a common opinion in Washington, and among many in the nation, that members of Congress serve only their reelection interests by ensuring that their constituents are pleased. Find out whether members of Congress, both the Senate and the House, will respond to you if you are not from their district but hold prominent positions on committees or the party.

   a. Select twenty prominent national senators and House representatives who are not from your state. Prepare the same e-mail on any issue that you are interested in or concerned about that is occurring at the national level. Be sure to emphasize that you would like a written response and information as quickly as possible to a series of questions (at least two) or concerns you have about this issue.

b. If one week (seven business days) passes between your e-mail and a response, send the e-mail one more time.

c. Prepare a one- to two-page analysis of whether they responded, how quickly they responded, the amount of information provided, and the quality of information.

6. Lobbying, it is often said, it both an art and a science. Because of your knowledge of the legislative process, you have decided to become more active in attempting to influence the legislative process. Your tasks are as follows:

a. Identify a current legislative issue being considered for policy adoption (go to http://www.Thomas.loc.gov).

b. Specify what your legislative goals are with respect to this proposed legislation:

  i. Stop or kill it.

  ii. Change it.

  iii. Ensure its adoption as is.

c. Develop a strategy to achieve your goal by doing the following:

  i. Telephone—Which members of Congress do you want to call?

   1. Prepare a statement of what you will say.

  ii. Letter-writing campaign

   1. Prepare a draft letter that outlines what your position is on the issue.

   2. Identify who of importance will receive this letter.

  iii. Personal meetings

   1. You can meet with no more than ten members of Congress or other officials; who will they be?

   2. Write a one-page paper that outlines what you want to communicate to the decision maker.

  iv. Mass mobilization

   1. You want to mobilize others who may interested in this issue. Prepare the following:

    a. A sample letter to the editor

    b. A sample flier to hand out at public arenas

SUGGESTED READINGS

Bosner, C., E. B. McGregor, Jr., and C. V. Oster, Jr. *Policy Choices and Public Action*. Upper Saddle River, NJ: Prentice Hall, 1996.

DeKieffer, D. E. *The Citizen's Guide to Lobbying Congress*. Chicago: Chicago Review Press, 1997.

Dye, T. *Politics in America*. Upper Saddle River, NJ: Prentice Hall, 2002.

Gray, V. "Competition, Emulation, and Policy Innovation." In L. C. Dodd and C. Jillson, eds., *New Perspectives on American Politics*. Washington, DC: CQ Press, 1994.

McKay, D. *Essentials of American Government*. Boulder, CO: Westview Press, 2000.

Oleszek, W. J. *Congressional Procedures and the Policy Process*. Washington, DC: CQ Press, 1999.

Schneier, E. V., and B. Gross. *Legislative Strategy: Shaping Public Policy*. New York: St. Martin's Press, 1993.

Sinclair, B. *Unorthodox Lawmaking*. Washington, DC: CQ Press, 2000.

Tarr, D. *How Congress Works*. Washington, DC: Congressional Quarterly, 1998.

Weissert, C. "Policy Entrepreneurs, Policy Opportunists, and Legislative Effectiveness." *American Politics Quarterly* 19 (1991): 262–274.

ENDNOTES

1. J. E. Anderson, *Public Policymaking,* 3rd ed. (Boston: Houghton Mifflin 1997), 140–152.

2. As noted by Anderson, the entire set of decision criteria include values, political party affiliation, constituency interests, public opinion, deference, and decision rules. These are by no means the only basis for determining how members of Congress decide whether to adopt an issue. The expected utility model discussed in Chapter 5, for example, has had remarkable success forecasting the decisions of policy makers based on three criteria: political or policy power, policy position, and salience of the issue. For additional insights, review Jacek Kugler and Yi Feng, eds., "The Expected Utility Approach to Policy Decision Making: Assessments, Forecasts and Strategies," *International Interactions* Special Issue, No. 3–4, 1997.

3. Anderson, *Public Policymaking,* 142.

4. For more background on this decision, and other similar presidential decisions during war, see G. Hess, *Presidential Decisions for War: Korea, Vietnam, and the Persian Gulf* (Baltimore, MD: Johns Hopkins University Press, 2001); C. Kegley and G. A. Raymond, *From War to Peace, Fateful Decisions in International Politics* (Boston: St Martin's Press, 2002).

5. W. Oleszek, *Congress and Its Members* (Washington, DC: CQ Press, book interviews, 2001).

6. H. W. Stanley and R. G. Niemi, *Vital Statistics on American Politics 1999–2000* (Washington, DC: CQ Press, 2000), 211.

7. Ibid., 211.

8. H. Gleckman, "Campaign-Finance Reform, the Right Way," retrieved February 12, 2002, from http://www.Businessweek.com.

9. Based on public information provided on THOMAS Legislative Information Web site, available at http://www.thomas.loc.gov.

10. Stanley and Niemi, *Vital Statistics,* 207.

11. This insight is based on numerous conversations one of authors has had with congressional staffers in professional and personal settings.

12. Barbara Sinclair, *Unorthodox Lawmaking: New Legislative Processes in the U.S. Congress* (Washington, DC: CQ Press, 2000), 11.

13. Ibid., 14.

14. W. J. Oleszek, *Congressional Procedures and the Policy Process* (Washington, DC: CQ Press, 1999), 105.

15. Ibid., 119.

16. Sinclair, *Lawmaking,* 17.

17. Ibid., 18–19.

18. Ibid., 19.

19. Ibid., 36.

20. Ibid., 36.

21. This reflects the threat of filibuster, and the failure of possessing enough votes to override the veto. Also, this assumes that all 100 seats are filled. See D. Tarr, *How Congress Works* (Washington, DC: Congressional Quarterly, 1998).

22. Sinclair, *Lawmaking,* 59.

23. Ibid., 63.

24. Oleszek, *Congressional Procedures,* 294.

25. Stanley and Niemi, *Vital Statistics,* 256.

26. Ibid., 256.

27. E. Schneier and B. Gross, *Legislative Strategy: Shaping Public Policy* (New York: St. Martin's Press, 1993), 140–158.

28. See H. Smith, *The Power Game: How Washington Works* (New York: Ballantine Books, 1988), 89–119; R. T. Sherrill *Why They Call it Politics,* 6th ed. (Fort Worth, TX: Harcourt, 2000), 168–233.

29. Based on interviews conducted in Washington, DC, between 1999 and 2001 by Kofinis. It is surprising how many congressional staffers, former members of the House, and professional lobbyists highlighted the influence of a mail/letter campaign. In particular, one story of a lobbyist who worked for a member of Congress told of how the member would ask for impassioned letters from a constituent so that the member could personally call or address the issue.

30. Based on interviews conducted in Washington, DC, between 1999 and 2001 by Kofinis. More commonly, many congressional offices will tally the calls, e-mails, and letters to roughly evaluate the issue positions from constituents.

10

Policy Implementation

Execution of
Policy Solutions

U ntil now our focus has been on the identification of problems, the setting of
the agenda, the formulation of policies, and the solutions adopted. These aspects we have categorized as falling into the predecision and decision phases of the
policy process. The discussion will now begin to center on the postdecision phases,
which include the stages of implementation, evaluation, and policy termination or
change. In this chapter we will consider the initial postdecision stage of policy implementation.

WHAT IS POLICY IMPLEMENTATION?

Policy implementation represents the stage where government executes an
adopted policy as specified by the legislation or policy action. At this stage, various government agencies and departments, responsible for the respective area of
policy, are made formally responsible for implementation. Until policies are implemented, no insight can be derived as to what effects they may have on a target population or for the society, or whether the policy can be judged a success
or failure.

Experts have offered various definitions of policy implementation. For James
E. Anderson, policy implementation "can succinctly be defined as what happens after a bill becomes law."[1] In comparison, Donald S. Van Meter, describes implementation as the "continuation of politics by other means."[2] Thomas R. Dye
determines that "policy implementation is all of the activities designed to carry out

Box 10.1   Definition of Policy Implementation

- Policy implementation is the stage in the policy process where policy action occurs to address a recognized policy problem.
- At this stage, the design of a policy proposal is put into effect.
- Policies are executed by respective administrative agencies.
- Selected instruments are applied reflective of the legislative mandate, bureaucratic interpretation, and capacity.
- Specified target populations, and the society, experience the first tangible effects of the policy once implemented.

the laws enacted by the legislative branch of government."[3] For Paul Sabatier and Dan Mazmanian, "implementation is the carrying out of a basic policy decision, usually made in a statute (although also possible through important executive orders or court decisions)."[4] As shown in Box 10.1, our definition summarizes the broad components that we feel are essential to understanding policy implementation.

The rest of the chapter will explain why the stage of policy implementation matters, the direct relationship between policy design and implementation, an identification of the most critical factors that influence and affect implementation, and a brief discussion of the theoretical and practical challenges to effective policy implementation.

IMPLEMENTATION— WHY IT MATTERS

Why does policy implementation matter? The answer to this question did not gain significance until the seminal work on imple-

mentation by Jeffrey L. Pressman and Aaron Wildavsky.[5] Prior to Pressman and Wildavsky, little attention had been paid to the role of government agencies or to the impact that administrative actors had on the effectiveness of public policies. Implementation, it was believed, was an administrative or bureaucratic issue, not a public policy issue. Such assumptions, however, ignored the importance of implementation to public policy.

Pressman and Wildavsky evaluated a federal jobs creation project that was being administered by the Economic Development Administration (EDA) in the city of Oakland, California. The policy goal of the program was to address unemployment in the inner city. Pressman and Wildavsky, however, identified gaps between the initial design and goals of the policy and the effects of implementation.[6] As their case study indicated, successful implementation is made difficult if the intent of the policy is ambiguous. Their study also indicated that cooperation is necessary among administrative actors to ensure the success of a policy.

Until the work of Pressman and Wildavsky, concern for the implementation stage was seen as secondary, even unnecessary, to a more effective understanding of the public policy process. We now realize that effective and efficient policy actions require consideration be given to the constraints and challenges of implementation—preferably even as the policy is formulated. In other words, how well a policy is implemented has much to do in determining if it is successful or not.

THE RELATIONSHIP: DESIGN AND POLICY IMPLEMENTATION

As a stage in the policy process, policy implementation is especially important because no adopted policy action, whether a law, an

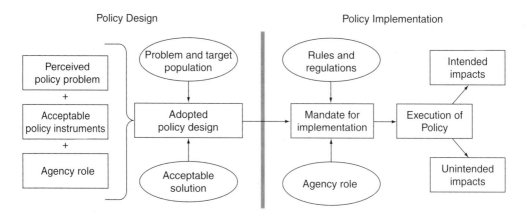

FIGURE 10.1 The Relationship between Policy Design and Implementation.

executive order, or a court decree can, in and of itself, alter the nature of the problem that it was designed to solve. Policy implementation is the intervening stage between the desire for change and actual change in the problem. Hence, all policies, regardless of how well they are designed, and irrespective of the political and policy goals, depend on policy implementation. This relationship between design and implementation is described graphically in Figure 10.1.

Figure 10.1 represents a graphic description of the relationship between policy design and implementation. As discussed in Chapter 8 on policy formulation, the phase of formulating a policy design involves a trade-off between what is acceptable politically and what is the appropriate policy solution. To be successful, a public policy must be designed to address the actual nature of the problem. Also, a well-designed policy, if it is to aid implementation, must assign the appropriate agency and instruments with which to change the target population's behavior. Therefore, a poorly designed policy not only may fail to solve the problem but also, once implemented, may result in unintended impacts.

The relationship between policy design and implementation can be illustrated very

simply in a 2-by-2 table. As Figure 10.2 indicates, poor policy design and poor implementation is the worst-case scenario. In this case, the design of the policy did not address the logic of the problem, and implementation is poorly executed. In contrast, the policy with a good design and good implementation is the best-case scenario as it achieves the goals of the policy, is executed well, and is by definition effective policy. If a policy is poorly designed, but implemented well, it results in unintended impacts or unknown effects. In terms of policy with a good design and poor implementation, that policy will prove ineffective. In this case, because the policy was poorly implemented, the positive impacts from the well-designed policy solution fail to materialize. In general, such policies will have little or no impact on the specific policy problem.

In sum, the point that Figures 10.1 and 10.2 seek to convey is the inescapable interrelationship among policy design, implementation, the impacts of a policy, and the consequences that follow the execution of the public policy solution. Again, each policy includes a design of how a public problem will be resolved. This design will define, in varying detail, the goal(s) of the policy,

Implementation

	Poor	Good
Poor	"Very poor" Negative impacts intended and unintended	"Unintended impact" Unknown effects
Good	"No impact" Ineffective	"Effective policy" Intended impact achieved

Policy Design (row label)

FIGURE 10.2 Policy Implementation and Design.

the set of policy instruments to be used, the agency responsible for implementation, possible timetables, and the target populations. The point of policy design is to match the correct set of instruments with the identified problem. The ideal is to develop a policy that, when implemented, achieves the desired goals and solves the identified problem. However, as discussed in Chapters 8 and 9, the political realities of formulation and adoption may result in less than perfect policy design. The consequence of poor policy design for successful implementation is significant, however.

For example, a policy that is too vague can lead to confusion over the policy's goals, the responsibility of the implementing agency, and the identity of the target population. In contrast, a policy too specific and restrictive in its design may limit necessary agency discretion, and can prevent changes that could improve the success of implementation. The most negative consequence for the policy process, however, arises if the solution that is to be implemented is not appropriate for the problem identified. In other words, the problem is misunderstood, the instruments assigned do not match, and the agency responsible may be incapable or unwilling to execute the policy.

If a policy design cannot alter the problem behavior, successful implementation proves irrelevant.[7] Basically, a poor policy design that is implemented will not miraculously become good policy in the future. A poor policy design and poor implementation merely accentuate the failures of policy. Only a well-designed policy and effective implementation will achieve the impacts that were intended by the policy. In a perfect world, policy designers would objectively define a problem, determine the best applicable instruments with which to change the target population's behavior, and would assign the policy to the appropriate set of governing agents to implement this solution. The reality, however, is that policy problems are often misspecified, the selection of instruments may be more determined by ideological or political beliefs, the determination of the target population may reflect a bias for or against certain groups, and the agency assigned responsibility for the policy may lack the resources to implement.

In sum, understanding the relationship between design and implementation does indeed matter. If one desires to avoid implementation problems there must be recognition that policy design affects both the success of implementation and, more important, the success of the policy. Therefore, better policy can result if policy designers and implementors address some or all of the following questions during the policy process:[8]

- Was the design of the policy appropriate given the nature of the problem?
- Does the design assist or complicate policy implementation?
- Is the agency organizationally capable of administering the program or policy?
- Can the instruments be effectively implemented?
- Are there political obstacles to effective and efficient implementation?

- What impact will the policy solution, once implemented, have on the target population(s)?
- How essential are the administrative actors to success of the policy?
- Have political factors prevented or made difficult policy implementation?

THE MAJOR ACTOR IN POLICY IMPLEMENTATION

According to Majone and Wildavsky, implementation is not a neat and clean process, but an evolution in which "at each point we must cope with new circumstances that allow us to actualize different potentials in whatever policy ideas we are implementing."[9] What may explain this evolutionary process is that implementation is always affected by politics. Rather, the evolution of policy implementation is defined and redefined, in part, because of the constancy of the actors that intervene throughout the course of policy implementation.

As with every stage in the policy process, a variety of institutional and noninstitutional actors are involved in shaping the evolution of policy implementation. The role of such policy actors can be roughly divided into two categories—those that implement policy and those that influence the implementation of policy. Among these actors, the bureaucracy represents the major actor responsible for implementation. The second set of actors includes the president, the Congress, the courts, and interest groups.

Bureaucracy

The bureaucracy represents the executive arm for official decision makers. These vast and sweeping governmental organizations are accorded the responsibility to define and

execute policy decisions. No governmental decision can be implemented without administration and execution by the bureaucracy. Woodrow Wilson, in 1887, effectively summarized the obvious importance of the bureaucracy:

> Administration is the most obvious part of government; it is government in action; it is the executive, the operative, the most visible side of government, and is of course as old as government itself.[10]

For Wilson, the performance of the bureaucracy was essential for both government effectiveness and efficiency. Max Weber, in comparison, stated that an increasingly complex society would necessitate the growth and size of the bureaucracy. Weber's ideal bureaucracy has defined the structure and role of the modern bureaucratic organization.[11] Specifically, one can construe certain implications from Weber's notion of the ideal bureaucracy for both modern government and policy implementation (see Box 10.2).

Overall, the ideal role of the bureaucracy is to ensure the effective implementation of government policies. Bureaucratic implementation, as Weber suggests, is not intended to be a democratic exercise, as that would ensure a political and varying pattern of implementation. Instead, it is to be direct, unemotional, and the methodical execution of the policy decision. The power of the bureaucracy, however, is not simply based on its administrative function of implementing policy decisions.

The real power of the bureaucracy, it could be argued, lies in its ability to define the details of the policy and the details that will affect the method of implementation. It is highly unlikely that any given policy action will define all aspects critical for implementation by the bureaucracy. As James Anderson states, "administration agencies often are provided with broad and ambigu-

---

Box 10.2 Weber's Ideal Bureaucracy

WEBER'S IDEAL BUREAUCRACY	ROLE OF THE BUREAUCRACY	IMPLICATIONS FOR GOVERNMENT AND IMPLEMENTATION
Administration is carried out in a continuous basis, not simply at the pleasure of the leader	Apolitical implementation	Increased stability, minimize corruption
Tasks in the bureaucratic organization are divided into functionally distinct areas each with requisite authority and sanction	Power to implement	Ensure effective governing
Offices are arranged hierarchically	Disciplined implementation	Ensure bureaucratic authority
Resources of the bureaucratic organization are distinct from those of the members as private individuals (i.e., administrators do not own the means of administration)	Public-owned agency	Accountable agency, limit agency corruption
Control in the bureaucratic organization is based on impersonally applied rational rules	Aemotional implementation	Equitable implementation

---

ous statutory mandates that leave them with much discretion to decide what should or should not be done."[12] The ambiguity of legislation, and the necessity to establish rules for how policy will be implemented, grants the bureaucracy the power of rule making—the process by which rules and regulations are subject to the constraints of the Administrative Procedures Act of 1946. Rule making involves the following:

- *Proposed rules*—Proposed changes to rules are published in the *Federal Register.* Public comments and suggestions on the changes are requested.

- *Interim rules*—Rules and regulations are issued on an emergency or temporary basis. Public comment is possible before issuance of final rule.

- *Final rules*—Formal decisions on new rules alter existing regulations. Public comments introduced previously may result in modifications.

Rule making is significant because seldom, if ever, will an adopted policy action, such as a law, encompass all of the necessary details of how, when, and where the policy is to be implemented. Rules define the basis and conditions in which a policy will be implemented by the given agency. Because of such real power over implementation, the bureaucracy enjoys considerable discretion in interpreting the actual intent, method, and scope of a policy decision. This means that the bureaucracy can, to some extent, redefine the intent of a policy action—thereby becoming de facto policy makers in the process. Hence, considerable power lies within the fifteen major departments that comprise the executive branch and the federal bureaucracy (see Box 10.3).

In addition to the fourteen executive departments, other government organizations can also be described as part of the federal bureaucracy. First, the Executive Office of the President (EOP) represents the various

Box 10.3 Executive Departments with Cabinet Status

Department and Year Established	Principal Mission	Important Subagencies	Budget Outlay (in millions of dollars) ACTUAL 2001	Budget Outlay (in millions of dollars) PROJECTED 2002
State (1789)	Promote peace and stability, create and expand markets, conduct treaty negoti- ations, coordinate international activities	Bureau of Arms Control, Bureaus of Political Affairs, Democracy, Human Rights and Labor, Diplomatic Security	7,524	11,132
Treasury (1789)	Promote prosperous and stable American/ world economy, manage government finances, safeguard financial system	Secret Service, Bureau of Public Debt, Secret Service, Bureau of Engraving and Printing, Internal Revenue Service	390,569	382,616
Interior (1849)	Land conservation, fire management, service to Native Americans	Bureau of Land Management, Fish and Wildlife Service, National Park Service, Bureau of Indian Affairs	8,249	10,290
Justice* (1870)	Enforce law, defend interests of United States, administer and enforce immigration laws, supervise federal corrections	FBI, Bureau of Prisons, Immigration and Naturalization Service, Civil Rights Division	21,296	23,073
Agriculture (1889)	Ensure safe food supply, support sound development, expand markets, reduce hunger	Food and Safety Inspection Service, Forest Service, Animal/ Plant Health Inspection Service, Food Safety and Inspection Service	68,759	76,565
Commerce** (1913)	Promote U.S. competi- tiveness, enhance economic competitive- ness, provide effective management of nation's resources	Bureau of Census, Bureau of Economic Analysis, National Weather Service, Patent and Trademark Office, National Oceanic Atmospheric Administration	5,137	5,495
Labor (1913)	Promote welfare of job seekers, improve work conditions, protect retirement and health care, promote collective bargaining	Bureau of Labor Statistics, Occupational Safety and Health Administration, Pension and Welfare Benefits Administration	39,367	58,579

Box 10.3   Executive Departments with Cabinet Status

Department and Year Established	Principal Mission	Important Subagencies	Budget Outlay (in millions of dollars)	
			ACTUAL 2001	PROJECTED 2002
Defense*** (1947)	Deter war and protect the security of the United States	Departments of Army, Air Force, Navy, Joint Chiefs of Staff, National Security Agency	293,995	330,553
Housing and Urban Development (1965)	Create opportunities for homeownership, enforce nation's fair housing laws, help homeless people, spur economic growth	National Mortgage Association, Office Healthy Homes, Public and Indian Housing Agencies, Office of Fair Housing	33,994	30,948
Transportation (1966)	Ensure a fast, safe, efficient, accessible and convenient transportation system that meets vital national interests	Federal Aviation Administration, Transportation Security Administration	67,175	64,371
Energy (1977)	Enhance national security through energy policy, ensure integrity and safety of nuclear weapons, increase domestic energy production	Federal Energy Regulatory Commission, Office of Nuclear Energy, Energy Information Administration	16,490	19,093
Health and Human Services**** (1979)	Protect health of Americans, provide essential social health and welfare services	Food and Drug Administration, Centers for Disease Control, NIH, Administration for Children and Families	426,767	459,366
Education (1977)	Ensure equal access to education, promote educational excellence	Federal Student Aid, Office of Elementary and Secondary Education, Office for Civil Rights	35,748	47,587
Veterans Affairs (1988)	Serve America's veterans, provide medical care, benefits, social support	Veterans Health Administration, Center for Minority Veterans, Veterans Benefit Administration	45,839	51,451
Homeland Security (2002)	Manage homeland defense, respond to domestic attack or disaster, manage immigration	Customs, Secret Service, FEMA, Bureau of Immigration	n/a	n/a

* Formed from the Office of Attorney General (1789)
** Formed from Office of Commerce and Labor (1903)
*** Formed from the Department of War (1789)
**** Formed from Department of Health, Education and Welfare (1953)

agencies, offices, and councils that lack cabinet status, but often serve powerful roles within the executive branch. New offices, for example, will emerge under each president as occurred with the Office of Faith-Based and Community Initiatives under President George W. Bush. Other offices within the EOP, such as the National Security Council (NSC), tend to have a consistently prominent role in serving the modern president.

Second, legislative organizations, such as the General Accounting Office (GAO), Congressional Research Service (CRS), and the Congressional Budget Office (CBO), provide critical information and expertise to members of Congress and their staff. Such actors can be very helpful in the designing of policy. The CRS, for instance, provides critical background and research on policy issues and legislative proposals. The GAO conducts and provides policy analyses and formal program evaluations that help determine problems and weaknesses in policy or program implementation. Similarly, the CBO provides budgetary projections and assistance to the Congress as it prepares its yearly federal budget.

Third, independent agencies, regulatory boards and commissions, and public corporations are additional examples of the dozens of governmental entities within the bureaucratic realm. Examples of independent executive agencies include the National Aeronautics and Space Administration (NASA), the General Services Administration (GSA), and the Social Security Administration (SSA). Independent regulatory boards, which operate outside the direct authority of the political arena and are created to regulate some aspect of the economic or political arena, include the Federal Elections Commission (FEC) and the Federal Communications Commission (FCC). Government corporations, which are unique organizations created to fill a specific mission within the society that is currently not filled by the private market, include the

Tennessee Valley Authority, the U.S. Post Office, and Amtrak.

Overall, all of the organizations comprise various parts of the American federal bureaucracy. The current organizational structure of the federal bureaucracy is described in Figure 10.3.

The bureaucratic structure described in Figure 10.3 complicates effective administration and implementation by placing a high premium on interagency cooperation. Interagency conflicts emerge, for example, because agencies and departments struggle to define their purpose, clientele, function, and areas for which they are responsible. The consequence for the implementation of policy is that such "interagency conflicts put a heavy burden on higher officials, particularly the president and department agency heads, who must attempt to coordinate the agencies under their charge."[13]

Although the role and structure of the bureaucratic actor is clearly fundamental to the success of policy implementation, it is not the only policy actor that affects and shapes the stage of policy implementation. Rather, many other policy actors, including the president, Congress, the courts, and interest groups, also play important roles throughout the stage of policy implementation.

OTHER ACTORS INVOLVED IN POLICY IMPLEMENTATION

The President

One of the broad roles of the president is that of chief executive of the bureaucracy. As chief executive, the president has the power to appoint a series of officials from heads of agencies to undersecretaries and deputy undersecretaries. Such appointments represent the desire of every president to control the method of policy implementation. This

```
                        ┌─────────────────────┐
                        │  U.S. Constitution  │
                        └─────────────────────┘
┌──────────────────┐    ┌─────────────────────┐    ┌──────────────────┐
│ Legislative Branch│   │  Executive Branch   │    │  Judicial Branch │
└──────────────────┘    └─────────────────────┘    └──────────────────┘
```

Legislative Branch	Executive Branch	Judicial Branch
Congress Senate House	**President and Vice President** Executive Office of the President	**Supreme Court**

General Accounting Office
Congressional Research
   Service
Library of Congress
Congressional Budget
   Office
	Council of Economic Advisers
	Council on Environmental
	   Quality
	USA Freedom Corps
	President's Critical
	   Infrastructure Protection
	   Board
	Domestic Policy Council
	National Economic Council
	National Security Council
	Office of Homeland Security*
	Office of Science and Technology
		President's Foreign
		   Intelligence Advisory
		   Board
		Office of Management
		   and Budget
		Office of National Drug
		   Control Policy
		Office of National AIDS
		   Policy
		Office of U.S. Trade Rep
		White House Military
		   Office
			U.S. federal courts

Department of Agriculture	Department of Defense	Department of Education	Department of Energy	Department of Health and Human Services	Department of Commerce	Department of Housing and Urban Develop
Department of Interior	Department of Justice	Department of Labor	Department of State	Department of Transportation	Department of Treasury	Department of Veterans Affairs

Select Independent Establishments and Agencies

Advisory Council on Historic
   Preservation
Commodity Futures Trading
   Commission
Environmental Protection Agency
Federal Communications
   Commission
Federal Emergency Management
   Agency
Federal Maritime Commission
Federal Trade Commission
National Aeronautics and Space
   Administration
National Council on Disability
National Endowment for the
   Humanities
National Railroad Passenger
   Corporation
National Regulatory Commission
Peace Corps
Securities Exchange Commission
Social Security Administration
U.S. Agency for International
   Development
U.S. Office of Government Ethics
Voice of America
	American Battle Monuments Commission
	Consumer Product Safety Commission
	Equal Employment Opportunity
	   Commission
	Federal Deposit Insurance Corporation
	Federal Energy Regulatory Commission
	Federal Reserve System
	General Services Administration
	National Archives Record Administration
	National Credit Union Administration
	National Indian Gaming Commission
	National Science Foundation
	Nuclear Waste Technical Review Board
	Office of Federal Housing Enterprise
	   Oversight
	Pension Benefit Guaranty Corporation
	Selective Service System
	Tennessee Valley Authority
	U.S. Arms Control and Disarmament
	   Agency
	U.S. Postal Service
		Central Intelligence Agency
		Corporation for National Service
		Farm Credit Administration
		Federal Election Commission
		Federal Labor Relations Authority
		Federal Retirement Thrift Board
		Merit Systems Protection Board
		National Capital Plan Commission
		National Endowment for the Arts
		National Mediation Board
		National Transportation Safety Board
		Occupational Safety and Health
		   Administration
		Office of Personnel Management
		Postal Rate Commission
		Small Business Administration
		Thrift Savings Plan
		U.S. International Trade Commission
		U.S. Trade and Development Agency

*Will become the Department of Homeland Security as of 2003.

FIGURE 10.3 Organization of Federal Bureaucracy.

control is established, at least in theory, by appointing officials who share similar ideological, political, management, and policy preferences as the president. As such, a president can achieve some control and influence over bureaucratic implementation through the power to appoint and replace various officials within a given agency. Arguably, the degree of control a president has depends on the policy area.

With defense and national security policy, a president enjoys considerable influence because of his position as commander in chief. In these defense-related areas, the president possesses considerable power in directing the implementation of various policy decisions. Nevertheless, internal agendas can emerge within the defense and intelligence agencies to weaken presidential authority over implementation. In comparison, within domestic policy, the presidential policy agenda must be implemented in a bureaucratic environment that can be readily co-opted by internal agency divisions, competing agencies and agendas across the government, and pressures arising from domestic politics. In reality, however, a presidential preference for successful implementation of any policy or program, foreign and domestic, requires the cooperation of the entire bureaucracy from top to bottom, including political appointees and professional civil service.

A president gains further control and influence over the bureaucracy and implementation through preparation of the yearly federal budget proposal. The federal budget proposal represents the fiscal framework for how funding will be allocated to specific federal agencies and departments. Thus, the budget allocation can demonstrate how a president can fiscally force an agency to change its method of implementation. Through cuts in an agency's resources, the president can diminish the role and capacities of the agency to meet its mandated responsibilities. In comparison, with increases

in budget allocations, an agency can gain the means to further execute new programs and initiatives.

In addition to political appointments or budgetary control, a president can also propose more dramatic management or organizational reforms. Specifically, the entire bureaucracy, or a particular agency, may be restructured or face reform. Such reforms attempt to alter the method and conditions by which bureaucracies function and implement policy decisions. For example, President Reagan wanted to abolish the Department of Education, the Department of Energy, as well as merge the Commerce and the Labor Departments. Under President Clinton's tenure, management reforms seeking to "reinvent government" were proposed to reduce the minutia of bureaucratic rules and regulations. In 2001, the Bush administration made its management goals quite clear—rethink how government operates, reduce waste, and achieve a government that is more effective and efficient.

The difficulty, however, is that such dramatic organizational and management reforms may fail. President Reagan's proposal for the abolishing and merging of the energy and education departments confronted an unsupportive Congress and an unwilling bureaucracy. President Clinton's management initiatives confronted a less than cooperative bureaucratic environment. In sum, presidential influence over implementation depends on whether the policy area, the appointees, their preferred budget, and their reforms are able to collectively create the conditions that enhance control over the bureaucracy and implementation.

Congress

The role of Congress includes shaping and overseeing the implementation of policies and programs. From determining the appropriations accorded to each agency, program, and service, to the critical function of oversight that seeks to ensure the accountability of the bureaucratic agency, Congress continues to play an active role that affects how policy decisions are executed. Even though the bureaucracy is seen as an extension of the president and executive branch, "overseeing the bureaucracy is . . . as much a congressional prerogative as an executive one."[14] It is this oversight function that captures the significant role that Congress has in affecting the manner and method by which programs and services are implemented by the various bureaucratic organizations.

Ideally, congressional oversight is a formal exercise that requires a purposeful evaluation in order to determine the efficiency, effectiveness, and accountability of various bureaucratic agencies during the implementation. Among the purposes of congressional oversight, according to Fesler and Kettle, are the following:[15]

1. Assure the intent of Congress is followed during implementation.

2. Investigate instances of inefficiency, ineffectiveness, and lack of accountability.

3. Collect information necessary for future changes in policy, programs, and services.

4. Evaluate program effectiveness and impacts.

5. Defend agencies, programs, and services supported by congressional members.

6. Reverse unpopular implementation.

The specific oversight role played by Congress develops within the committees. In general, committees that are organized along policy lines provide an oversight function as they prepare and formulate new legislation. Hearings that address various domestic and international issues and the performance and impact of federal agencies in addressing these issues serve as direct and indirect oversight of how well the bureaucracy is executing its mandate. Additional oversight power is garnered by budget authorization and appropriations committees, as well as committees on governmental reform. Supporting this oversight function are the CBO, CRS, and the GAO.

The difficulty confronting Congress, however, is that the power and promise of oversight does not necessarily translate into effective oversight of the bureaucracy. The problem is that "oversight is best intermittent" or results in excessive intrusion by members of Congress "to promote their own self-interest."[16] Simply put, differing political agendas can lead members of Congress to use oversight power as a weapon against disliked agencies or policies that are being implemented. Finally, political interests, such as those presented by constituents, lobbyists, or interest groups, can lead members of Congress to attempt to stymie agency implementation. As a result, oversight can be a weapon used for or against effective implementation.

Courts

The role of the courts provides a legal basis by which citizen activists, interest groups, or state and local governments can attempt to effectively regulate the regulators. In particular, the Administrative Procedure Act (APA) provides for judicial review of both rule making and adjudicative decisions. Rule making involves the establishment of regulatory guidelines that can be enforced on a case-by-case basis or lead to an industry or sectorwide rule. Adjudication represents the action to address disagreements with an agency decision or in the citation of an alleged violator whose actions are contrary to existing law and regulations.

Whether rule making or adjudicative decisions, the courts can and do become involved in reviewing agency actions as they affect the public or target populations. Overall, the courts play an instrumental role in regulating and mediating the inevitable clash of interests that emerge as the bureaucracy defines the scope and nature of its regulatory actions during the stage of implementation. Fesler and Kettle summarize this role by the courts as one that reviews agency actions to determine whether or not the agency is fulfilling its mission as mandated by the statute, or whether agency actions may extend beyond the legal scope of the statute.[17]

Interest Groups

The relationship between interest groups and the bureaucracy can, at times, be either cooperative or conflictual. Depending on the policy area, and the regulatory function of the bureaucratic agency, the array of interest groups can span a wide ideological and policy spectrum. Based on the type of organization, and its administrative or regulatory purpose within the policy arena, the number and nature of the interactions between interest groups and the bureaucracy can be quite substantial.

The importance of policy implementation, coupled with the bureaucratic discretion in determining rules and procedures for implementation, can result in an increasingly close relationship between a given bureaucracy and interest groups. Various theories, such as iron triangles, issues networks, and policy subsystems, help explain how various circles of interest groups, political actors, and bureaucracies can develop such relationships. Ironically, these relationships are basically ensured given current federal agency procedures.

When developing new initiatives or gathering additional information, various agencies may call upon interest groups to offer perspective, guidance, and expertise.[18]

Further, because of the rule-making procedures outlined by the APA, interest groups often become involved by commenting within the thirty-day window that follows publication of the proposed rules published in the *Federal Register*.[19] Additionally, interest groups become involved, even mobilized, by the release of proposed federal rules in order to persuade regulatory actors to favor decisions and interpretations beneficial to their respective interests. In general, bureaucracies will operate closely with an array of interest groups whose interests are affected by the respective agency. Again, the overall purpose of interest group involvement is to create a more favorable regulatory environment during eventual policy implementation.

A bureaucracy, such as the Department of Transportation, will often interact with a number of interest groups from the cross section of the policy or regulatory sector. Interest groups that attempt to influence and shape how the Department of Transportation implements policy, for example, may include not only corporate interest groups, such as those representing airlines, railroads, shipping or trucking associations, but also groups that represent local and state governments, employee unions, and environmentalists. Irrespective of the basis for the interest group, each of these actors will attempt to influence regulatory decisions that favor their specific interest and policy agenda. According to John R. Wright, the extent to which interest groups become active during implementation can also influence their future role during subsequent stages of policy implementation:

> Groups with extensive experience with issues . . . will be recognized not only for their expertise about technical aspects of policy but also for their knowledge of the political considerations necessary for successful implementation or adjudication of policies.[20]

CHALLENGES TO IMPLEMENTATION

The challenge posed by implementation is in determining how to best execute policy decisions so that the intended impacts are achieved. Ensuring effective implementation, as has been discussed, is critical to the policy process but remains a complicated task. The implementation stage is affected by the nature of the policy design, by the bureaucracy, and by the various other policy actors that seek to influence the manner in which policies and programs are executed. Because no blueprint exists for how policies should be implemented, the student of public policy, the analyst, and the various political actors must rely on theory to derive practical insights on how to improve the success of implementation.

Theoretically, the study of policy implementation is a relatively new field, but theoretical approaches have emerged with which to understand the dynamics of and the obstacles to the effective execution of policy decisions. Because disagreement exists within the field over what is the "better" theoretical model for understanding the stage of implementation, it is valuable to consider various approaches to exploring the process of implementation.[21]

In general, the approaches to studying implementation can be broadly classified as top-down, bottom-up, and synthesized (i.e., bottom and top). Each of these theoretical approaches provides differing perspectives on the implementation process, as well as on the factors and dynamics that affect implementation. Each of the schools of thought will be briefly discussed here, and an example of one approach—the Mazmanian and Sabatier conceptual framework of a top-down model—will illustrate the theoretical and practical insights that can be derived from such theories to improve the process of implementation.

THEORIES OF IMPLEMENTATION

The theories of implementation emerged out of the early case study work that first recognized that problems consistently existed in the execution of policies and programs. Early scholars of implementation, such as Derthick, Bardach, and Pressman and Wildavsky, concluded that policies and programs simply did not meet their objectives because of unforeseen or unrecognized problems during implementation.[22] From these early insights emerged the various theoretical approaches and models that are currently discussed within the field of implementation studies.

Top-Down Approach

The top-down approach considers implementation to be a function of the government decision, government management and oversight, and the resulting execution by the bureaucracy. Hence, effective implementation requires an understanding of which factors and dynamics impact the ability of the bureaucracy and government to execute decisions effectively.[23] Overall, the purpose of the top-down approach is to focus the attention of the policy designers and implementors toward those elements that, when recognized and addressed, can improve the success of implementation.

Examples of the top-down approach include the pioneering work by Meter and Van Horn, as well as the more encompassing conceptual model by Mazmanian and Sabatier.[24] The value of the models developed by Meter and Van Horn, and especially Mazmanian and Sabatier, is that they recognize various elements and dynamics that help explain the complexity of implementation, the obstacles to implementation, and the manner in which the success of implementation could be improved (see Figure 10.4).

However, the criticisms of this approach are that too many factors are emphasized within the theory as being relevant, that ideas of managing implementation from the top are overly optimistic, and that other actors outside the strict arena of policy designers, decision makers, and government officials are important to the success of implementation.

Bottom-Up Approach

The bottom-up approach focuses on the critical role played by the various actors specifically responsible for or able to influence implementation. Basically, "the Bottom-Up approach starts by identifying the network of actors involved in the service of deliveries in one or more local areas and asks them about their goals, strategies, activities, and contracts."[25] This approach, as developed by Richard Elmore and others, emphasizes the importance of the network of actors directly responsible for policy execution, the explicit bargaining and accommodation that determines the path by which policies are implemented, and the important role played by the front-line or "street-level" agents directly responsible for implementation.[26]

The criticisms of this approach, not surprisingly, center on what some suggest is an exaggeration or overemphasis on the bottom level of implementation, and a minimization of the importance of factors such as political management and administrative control, broad socioeconomic and political factors, and how the language of the policy action, or statute, can affect the success of implementation.

Synthesis: A Top-Down, Bottom-Up Approach

Assumed weaknesses with the previous approaches to understanding implementation have led to what can be generally referred to

as a synthesis of the two approaches.[27] Richard Elmore, for example, expanded on his previous work to emphasize the importance of top-level factors, such as policy makers, the design of policy, and the instruments selected, and bottom-level factors, such as the nature and capacity of the target population to change its behavior.[28] In comparison, a synthesis by Paul Sabatier, which is emphasized within the ACF (advocacy coalition framework) model that was discussed in more detail in Chapter 5, also focuses on bottom- and top-level aspects to implementation. For Sabatier, political, socioeconomic, and policy elements interact with the various actors within a subsystem to affect how policies are implemented.[29]

APPLYING A THEORY OF IMPLEMENTATION

Each of the theoretical perspectives on implementation offers valuable insight as to how implementation may indeed occur. No one theoretical approach perfectly explains the process of implementation. However, this book focuses on one approach, not because it is the better or only theory with which to explore implementation, but to provide some perspective on how such theories can aid our practical knowledge of how to improve implementation. The approach we use is an example of the top-down school of thought—the Mazmanian and Sabatier framework.

Mazmanian and Sabatier Top-Down Implementation Model

For Daniel Mazmanian and Paul Sabatier, "the crucial role of implementation analysis is the identification of the variables which affect the achievement of legal objectives throughout the entire process."[30]

The Mazmanian and Sabatier theoretical framework emphasizes three categories that affect why policy decisions may not have the desired results the decision makers or other policy actors may have forecasted. These three categories are (1) tractability of the problem being addressed by the statute; (2) ability of the statute to favorably structure the implementation process; and (3) the net effect of a variety of political variables. Each of these three broad categories, and the intervening elements within them, provides a theoretical description of the complex interrelationship and challenge to effective policy implementation (see Figure 10.4).

Intrinsic to the challenge of implementation is the realization that the tractability of the problem, according to Mazmanian and Sabatier, can complicate the implementation process from beginning to end. Tractability of the problem reflects the difficulty of developing and measuring the technical evidence that a program or policy is having the desired impact. Such technical limitations may further be negatively affected by the diversity of behavior change required, the size of the target population, and the degree of behavioral change reflected within the problem. Essentially, policy implementation is made more difficult the more diverse the behavior that is regulated, the larger the size of the target population, and the greater the amount of the behavioral change required of the target population.

The second category emphasizes how a statutory decision can further address the

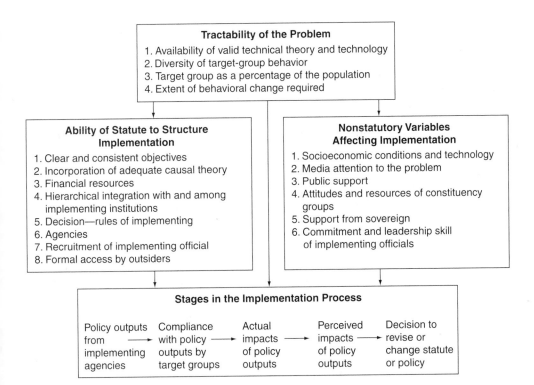

FIGURE 10.4 Mazmanian and Sabatier Conceptual Framework.

SOURCE: Adapted from Daniel A. Mazmanian and Paul A. Sabatier, "A Conceptual Framework of Policy Implementation," in S. Z. Theodoulou and Mathew A. Cahn, *Public Policy: The Essential Readings* (Englewood Cliffs, NJ: Prentice Hall, 1995).

intrinsic challenge to implementation. Sabatier and Mazmanian emphasize that a policy design and resulting statute may complicate implementation if it fails to provide a clear focus or goal. As a consequence, policy directives and goals may ultimately fail if it is unclear what the policy objectives are for the administrative agencies. Furthermore, if the statute fails to provide sufficient resources, does not take into consideration the effect of a lack of cooperation among agencies, is assigned to unsupportive implementing agencies or officials, or provides for too much or too little oversight, it will complicate future implementation.

The third category of the framework emphasizes how any statutory policy design, if it is to be successfully implemented and achieve the desired behavior change, must "receive constant and/or periodic infusions of political support" and develop within a favorable socioeconomic and political environment.[31] Clearly, public and political support can ebb and flow as external circumstances change. A statute with considerable and constant public and political support may better weather the difficulties that arise during implementation.

Such public and political support can motivate administrative actors to ensure that the policy is successfully implemented. Moreover, positive media attention to the issue and to the importance of its implementation, support from the relevant constituents and decision makers, as well as the commitment and skill of the implementing officials will add to an issue's successful implementation. Such elements also are affected by the overarching socioeconomic and political conditions that exist. Clearly, the greater environment in which a policy is designed and implemented can have a considerable impact on the resulting support and involvement the public, political, and administrative actors may have during the implementation process.

The Mazmanian and Sabatier theoretical model provides a description of the factors and dynamics relevant to the implementation process. In particular, we can see how implementation is complicated by the interaction between the nature of the policy problem, the statutory design, and the environment in which implementation transpires. Theoretically, the Mazmanian and Sabatier model helps emphasize the array of factors that are assumed to complicate the process of implementation. Still, one can also utilize the insights of Mazmanian and Sabatier's model to improve the success of implementation (see Box 10.4).

THE PRACTICE OF IMPLEMENTATION

Although it is important to understand some of the theories of implementation, in the end, policy implementation remains a practical exercise of planning for and executing a policy decision. Hence, the following section explores, in general, some of the areas that we believe can further help one prepare for and better understand the actual practice of policy and program implementation. These areas include (a) the basic challenges to implementation, (b) the role of strategic planning, and (c) the start-up and execution planning phases.

Challenges and Pitfalls of Implementation

The implementation stage, as discussed throughout this chapter, is an action phase of the public policy process. Successful implementation, therefore, requires a general base of knowledge of what challenges and pitfalls can emerge to hinder the execution of a policy or program. Some of the major challenges to effective implementation are

---

Box 10.4 Mazmanian and Sabatier Model—Theory and Practical Insights	
Theoretical Insight	**Practical Insight for Policy Implementation**
1. Availability of valid technical theory and technology	Develop/utilize technologies that measure changes in problem
2. Extent of behavioral change required	Forecast degree of behavioral change required; if necessary, consider more modest goals
3. Clear and consistent objectives	
4. Financial resources	Evaluate the degree of statutory clarity; ensure clear objectives are specified
5. Public support	Assess the organizational capacity/resources of achieving implementation goals
6. Support from sovereigns	Gauge pubic opinion; undertake steps to build public awareness/support
	Assess opinion of sovereign responsible for oversight; undertake steps to build authority awareness/support

---

posed by the following: clarity of policy goals, implementation intelligence, and the strategy or model adopted for implementing the policy or program.

Clarity of Policy Goals. Clear policy or program goals help specify the ends or objectives desired from the policy action. Ideally, policies should be formulated with consideration of what the actual and specific goals of the policy are. In reality, policy decisions often lack any direction or specific goals. The difference between specific and ambiguous goals is substantial. A goal stated with clarity and specificity not only provides direction but also improves the basis by which policies can be evaluated for accountability, efficiency, and effectiveness. As Pressman and Wildavsky suggested, a clear goal is critical if one is to judge the effect and success of policy implementation.[32] For Mazmanian and Sabatier, the clarification of objectives and priorities is a critical aspect of the statute and has a profound impact on the possible success of implementation.[33]

Majone and Wildavsky comment on the irony of what is more important—"the chicken of the goal or the egg of implementation."[34] In other words, without obvious goals or precise objectives, a policy is unlikely to be easily or successfully implemented. The practical challenge, however, is in dealing with the inevitable realities that the goals are seldom clear or specific, that they may change over time and evolve through the implementation process.[35] Yet, a policy without a specific goal can never truly fail or succeed, because it operates in a perceptual trap where goals can be defined and redefined by the various actors involved.

Finally, goals, even if specified, do not operate in a static societal or administrative environment. Over time, the goal of a policy can change because of organizational, policy, or political factors. For example, the initial goals of the 1996 Welfare Reform were to reduce user dependence on welfare. However, as socioeconomic conditions worsened in 2001, the discussion of the reauthorization of the 1996 Welfare Reform

Act has led to concerns over whether the goal of reducing the number of welfare recipients is achievable or even desirable.[36]

In the ideal world of administration and policy implementation, a clear or specific goal would provide direction, as well as a basis of determining the success or failure of the program. However, as Fesler and Kettle suggest, ambiguity in goals may persist because it allows for greater political manipulation during implementation, in terms of allowing for the redefinition of a program's success and failure, as well as providing implicit discretion for the agency when implementing.[37] The consequence, however, is that program implementation is executed without direction, and a clear basis for evaluation is lacking.

Information Intelligence. Information intelligence refers to the strategic necessity for constant feedback as to how implementation is progressing, as well as, when possible, preliminary assessments of impacts. Such information is essential for administrative agents and policy makers if they are to judge the success and impact of implementation. Timely, accurate, and relevant information is essential so that strategic changes in implementation can be made as the policy is being executed. Given the increasing reliance on multiple bureaucracies, information and feedback is essential to gauge the degree of interagency and intergovernmental cooperation or conflict, which may be affecting policy implementation. Again, the goal is to obtain information that helps identify where implementation is being successfully accomplished or where problems may exist. The importance of such information intelligence is highlighted by the enormous administrative and policy responsibilities confronted by the newly created Department of Homeland Security (DHS).

A key responsibility of the DHS is to manage and coordinate the "implementation of a comprehensive national strategy to secure the United States from terrorist threats or attack."[38] The success of the DHS is dependent on the extent to which this new agency can effectively analyze, coordinate, and communicate the information from dozens of agencies that will be part of this new federal agency. In addition, effective implementation will require effective communication with a number of additional federal agencies, including the Departments of Defense, Health and Human Services, Transportation, the Central Intelligence Agency (CIA), and the Federal Bureau of Investigation (FBI). If the DHS is to achieve its multitiered mission of detecting, preparing, preventing, and protecting against future domestic attacks, a high level of information intelligence must be obtained.

Information intelligence requires a high level of communication and feedback not only from the agencies involved in policy implementation but also, when applicable, from the populations affected by the policy action. Implementation can be improved only if the implementors have insight as to how a policy or program is affecting a target population. The challenge is in developing a positive path for communication between agencies and the target populations that allows for valuable feedback. However, with certain target populations, such as deviant types (e.g., criminals), there may not exist an administrative or political desire for gathering such information.

Strategic Planning

The purpose of strategic planning, within the context of policy implementation, is to highlight the importance of assessing the capacity of an agency to meet specific implementation tasks and goals mandated by the policy decision. Essentially, strategic planning is a tool with which the agency can evaluate its ability to achieve the goals of the policy, as well as plan for how the policy will be executed. It is also a tool with which an implementor can "match its objectives and capabilities to the anticipated demands of the environment to produce a plan of action that will ensure achievement of objectives."[39] Finally, it allows for the implementing officials and the agency to assess potential near-term challenges that could affect the success of policy implementation. The basic steps to strategic planning are described in Box 10.5.

Start-Up and Execution Phases

The practical realities of implementation require an understanding of the necessary steps and actions that must occur to execute a policy decision. The decision to go to war, for example, is not simply an order that leads to action (see Figure 10.5). Rather, with every policy decision, regardless of its scope or purpose, a series of events must be executed in some logical order if a policy is to be implemented effectively. Basically, if a policy is going to be successfully implemented, or in order to critique the implementation of a policy, one must be aware of the start-up and execution phases.

The start-up phase represents the realization that a lag-time exists, sometimes substantial, between the adoption of a policy decision, the implementation of the policy, and the resulting impacts of the policy.[40] In effect, the more complex the policy decision, the more administrative actors involved; the

---

Box 10.5 Strategic Planning Steps and Values

Steps to Strategic Planning	Value for Implementation
1. Statement of agency goals, mission, or vision	Define the mission or purpose of the agency; clarify the area of administrative responsibility.
2. Adoption of a time frame	Define the overall planning horizon for the agency; what are the critical dates to achieve agencywide goals?
3. Assessment of present capabilities	Assess the agency's capabilities; critical assessment of financial and human capital strengths or weaknesses; determine overall capacity of the agency for successful implementation of programs or services.
4. Assessment of organizational environment	Evaluate the environment confronting the agency; will changes in the administrative environment tax or improve future implementation?
5. Development of a strategic plan	Outline the method by which the agency will achieve goals, mission, or vision; provide direction and focus on implementation responsibilities; clarify where agency must shift resources/focus in order to achieve implementation.
6. Organizational integration	Provide direction and tasks for specific actors within the agency; motivate the agency on specific tasks to improve organizational environment critical to implementation.

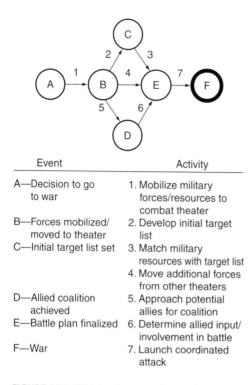

Event	Activity
A—Decision to go to war	1. Mobilize military forces/resources to combat theater
B—Forces mobilized/ moved to theater	2. Develop initial target list
C—Initial target list set	3. Match military resources with target list
	4. Move additional forces from other theaters
D—Allied coalition achieved	5. Approach potential allies for coalition
E—Battle plan finalized	6. Determine allied input/ involvement in battle
F—War	7. Launch coordinated attack

FIGURE 10.5 CPM Implementation Technique— Going to War.

more complex the problem, the more obdurate the target population; the more political the implementation environment, the more the policy decision requires new regulations, rules, and programs; the longer it may take before a policy achieves any level of impact— intended or unintended. Simply put, a policy decision will seldom be implemented in a day—or even two for that matter.

The notion of a start-up phase helps emphasize that an indeterminate amount of time will pass between the policy decision, implementation, and impacts from the policy. In terms of certain issues, such as war, disease, economic decline, or terrorism, many in the public and political arena fail to realize that every policy will take time to start up before it can effectively address any policy problem.

Start-Up Phase. The start-up phase, as it is has been described, is "a traumatic time in the life cycle of a program, since it is at this time that the separate elements considered in formulation must be brought together and begin to function as a system."[41] The challenges from this start-up phase confront each and every policy decision. However, a learning curve is possible whereby administrative agencies and actors, consistently responsible for specific program areas and policies, learn to overcome the obstacles posed by this initial phase during policy implementation.

The assumption of a learning curve suggests that in the initial phase of implementation, the impact of a program may be slow to develop. It will also take some time for agency officials to develop the necessary level of training and knowledge of the program. Further, the target population itself may be slow to change its behavior or slow in conforming to the intent of the program. With any new program, it is to be expected that the policy's benefits and impacts may be minimized until implementation reaches an optimal level.

This learning curve is made even more complicated if the policy decision deals with an entirely new area of policy making. For example, with respect to the DHS, or the new Transportation Security Administration (TSA), given the infancy of these agencies, it is expected that the learning curve will be very high and successful implementation of the programs within these agencies will suffer. One method with which to possibly address issues of how to implement a policy is to correctly plan out its execution.

Execution Phase. One method of forecasting problems with implementation, even before the start-up phase, is to plan the execution of the policy decision by using tools such as the Critical Path Method (CPM).[42] The basic value of CPM, also described as Network Analysis or PERT (for Performance Evaluation Review Technique), is to delineate, graphically, the various "steps required to implement a policy decision."[43] The purpose of CPM is to provide a visual basis by which the implementor can better plan for the policy's execution, as well as forecast potential obstacles even before actual implementation. Again, the difficulty of policy implementation is made strikingly obvious through the use of the CPM technique.

The CPM method represents an articulation of the series of steps expected to put a policy into effect (see Figure 10.5). Accordingly, CPM utilizes two elements: events (represented by circles) that describe the start or completion of a specific task, and activities (represented by arrows) that represent the resource-eating actions that must occur in order to accomplish the task. The value of this exercise is that it "identifies the set of events that must occur to implement a policy and links them together in the proper sequence with activity arrows . . . [which] represent the amount of time (or other resources) that must be consumed to produce an event."[44] Again, the analytical value of this exercise is that it forces one to realize the difference between the rhetoric of policy action and the realities of policy action. In other words, implementation is far more difficult to plan than it may seem or as various policy actors describe it. Consider the following *simple* example of the United States deciding to go to war with another state, and follow the basic steps involved in implementing this decision.

As the example in Figure 10.5 illustrates, implementing a decision involves a number of critical steps, all of which prove essential to the successful execution of a policy decision. Although the example of going to war is grossly simplified, it helps highlight the critical tasks and activities that are associated with such a policy decision. More impor-

tant, it emphasizes that a policy can fail even if one step is not accomplished during implementation. Additionally, if one or two tasks are performed poorly early on, the effects ripple through the entire implementation process.

MODELS OF IMPLEMENTATION

Given the intrinsic difficulties in implementing public policy, it is helpful to adopt models where implementation has already been successful. Such models of implementation sometimes offer a strategy for executing implementation, provide a blueprint for how a program should be constructed, and may even identify potential obstacles in the implementation process. Welfare reform, for example, before it was even adopted by many U.S. states, and the federal government in 1996, had already been proposed and implemented in the State of Wisconsin under then-governor Tommy Thompson. The success of the Wisconsin program served as a model and helped persuade other states that significant welfare reform was possible and could be successfully implemented. Clearly, successful models of implementation can prove to be quite helpful.

The value of researching previous models of implementation requires insight to be gained concerning not only the success, but also failures of such implementation. In terms of success, one must determine why the program was successful. Such administrative factors as the nature of the statute, the character of the target population, the agencies responsible or involved, the tools utilized, the rules and regulations governing implementation, the financial resources allocated, the leadership of officials, and public or political support, should all be considered. With respect to failures, one must also research why and where implementation may have failed, and what the consequences were from such failures. Overall, whereas utilizing a model from a previous case of implementation proves very useful, wide generalizations given the difference in the character of the problem, politics, and agencies, across states or regions can question how well a program can be successfully implemented in other parts of the nation.

SUMMARY

It is fair to state that an understanding of implementation must begin with an appreciation of the complexity and significance this stage has for the policy process. No one should expect that policy implementation will be easy and perfectly successful. Rather, as has been stressed throughout this chapter, implementation matters for the student of public policy because it is at this stage in the policy process where words get translated into action and where design leads to execution and impact. Our understanding of the stage of implementation also offers some telling lessons as to how interrelated the policy process is. Clearly, all policy actors must consider the challenges that arise in effective and efficient implementation. Still, one important area not addressed in this chapter is that of the normative questions that may surround all aspects of policy implementation. For scholars like Martin Levin, administration and implementation of policy cannot be removed from the ends and values established within policy design:

> The public policy schools must stress for their students the importance of ends. We should ask our students to try to make the trains run better and faster. But even more important, we should ask them to worry about the trains running in the right direction.[45]

Although questions of whether the right policies are being implemented are significant, it seems just as significant to ask whether the right *types* of policies are being implemented. Many of the woes of society, as well as the failings of public policy, will continue unless future policy implementation becomes more effective. The challenge for policy actors is in appreciating the importance of implementation before policies are simply designed with the expectation that effective policy execution is a given. As this chapter sought to emphasize, better policy design and a stronger foundation of knowledge that recognizes the value of implementation will, over time, lead to better policy. The challenge, of course, is in first recognizing how important this policy stage is for the entire policy process.

DISCUSSION QUESTIONS

1. Within the public and political arenas, why is so little attention given to the practical realities of policy implementation?

2. Is the bureaucracy ultimately responsible for the effectiveness of government?

3. Is it possible, given the array of policy actors involved, that effective implementation of policy is not a goal because of a lack of confidence in what the intended or unintended impacts should be?

4. The perception of ineffective government and ineffective implementation seem paramount. Explore this presumption further:

   a. Using Weber's tenets for an ideal bureaucracy, which of the fourteen executive departments noted in Figure 10.2 do you believe is the most ideal?

   b. Research how that department has been recently evaluated by the General Accounting Office, using the resources on the department's own Web site, http://www.Whitehouse.gov. Evaluate how "ideal" that agency or department is in reality.

5. Take any recently adopted policy and map out, using the CPM method described in Figure 10.4, the steps and estimated time to effectively implement this policy. Include each step that you can logically deduce is relevant to successful implementation from beginning to end.

SUGGESTED READINGS

Bardach, E. *The Implementation Game: What Happens After a Bill Becomes a Law.* Cambridge, MA: MIT Press, 1977.

Edwards, G. C. *Public Policy Implementation: Introduction.* Greenwich, CT: JAI Press, 1984.

Fesler, James W., and Donald F. Kettle. *The Politics of Administrative Process.* New York: Chatham House, 1996.

Lipsky, M. *Street-Level Bureaucracy.* New York: Russell Sage, 1990.

Mazmanian D., and P. Sabatier. *Implementation and Public Policy.* Lanaham, MD: University Press of America, 1989.

Mazmanian, D., and P. Sabatier. "The Implementation of Public Policy: A Framework for Analysis." *Policy Studies Journal* 8 (1980): 538–560.

Pressman, J. L., and A. Wildavsky. *Implementation.* Berkeley: University of California Press, 1994.

Sabatier, P. A. "Top-Down and Bottom-Up Approaches to Implementation Research: A Critical Analysis and Suggested Synthesis." *Journal of Public Policy* 6, no. 1 (1986): 22–48.

Shafritz, J. M., and A. C. Hyde. *Classic of Public Administration.* Fort Worth, TX: Harcourt Brace College, 1997.

ENDNOTES

1. J. E. Anderson. *Public Policymaking,* 3rd ed. (Boston: Houghton Mifflin, 1997), 214.

2. D. S. Van Meter, "The Policy Implementation Process," *Administration and Society* 6 (February 1975): 447.

3. T. R. Dye, *Top-Down Policymaking* (New York: Chatham House, 2001), 137.

4. P. A. Sabatier and Daniel Mazmanian, "A Conceptual Framework of the Implementation Process," in S. Z. Theodoulou and Mathew A. Cahn, *Public Policy: The Essential Readings* (Englewood Cliffs, NJ: Prentice Hall, 1995), 153.

5. J. L. Pressman and A. Wildavsky, *Implementation* (Berkeley: University of California Press, 1994).

6. Ibid.

7. G. C. Edwards, *Public Policy Implementation: Introduction* (Greenwich, CT: JAI Press, 1984), ix.

8. These questions build on the work and insights of other implementation scholars.

9. G. Majone and A. Wildavsky, "Implementation as Evolution," in Theodoulou and Cahn, *Public Policy,* 150.

10. Woodrow Wilson, "The Study of Administration," in J. M. Shafritz and A. C. Hyde, *Classic of Public Administration* (Fort Worth, TX: Harcourt Brace College, 1997), 13.

11. M. Weber, "Bureaucracy," in Shafritz and Hyde, *Public Administration.*

12. Anderson, *Public Policymaking,* 216.

13. James W. Fesler and Donald F. Kettle, *The Politics of Administrative Process* (New York: Chatham House, 1996), 114.

14. Ibid., 319.

15. Ibid., 322–323.

16. Ibid., 338.

17. Ibid., 340–362.

18. J. R. Wright, *Interest Groups and Congress: Lobbying, Contributions, and Influence* (Needham Heights, MA: Allyn & Bacon, 1996), 52.

19. Ibid., 52.

20. Ibid., 53.

21. P. A. Sabatier, "Top-Down and Bottom-Up Approaches to Implementation Research: A Critical Analysis and Suggested Synthesis," *Journal of Public Policy* 6, no. 1 (1986), 22–48.

22. Martha Derthick, "Defeat at Ft. Lincoln," *The Public Interest* 20 (1970): 3–39; Pressman and Wildavsky, *Implementation;* E. Bardach, *The Implementation Game: What Happens After a Bill*

Becomes a Law (Cambridge, MA: MIT Press, 1977).

23. Dye, *Policymaking,* 138.

24. See D. Mazmanian and P. Sabatier, *Implementation and Public Policy* (Lanaham, MD: University Press of America, 1989).

25. James P. Lester and Joseph Stewart, Jr., *Public Policy—An Evolutionary Approach* (New York: West, 1996), 103–105.

26. Richard Elmore, "Backward Mapping: Implementation Research and Policy Decision," *Political Science Quarterly* 94 (1979), 606–616; Sabatier, "Top-Down and Bottom-Up Approaches," 22–48.

27. Lester and Stewart, *Public Policy,* 106.

28. Elmore, "Forward and Backward Mapping: Reversible Logic in the Analysis of Public Policy," in K. Hanf and T. Toonen, *Policy Implementation in Federal and Unitary Systems* (Dordrecht, The Netherlands: Martinus Nijhoff, 1985), 33–70.

29. Paul A. Sabatier and Hank C. Jenkins-Smith, *Policy Change and Learning: An Advocacy Coalition Framework* (Boulder, CO: Westview Press, 1993), 18.

30. Mazmanian and Sabatier, *Implementation,* 21.

31. Mazmanian and Sabatier, "A Conceptual Framework," 162.

32. Pressman and Wildavsky, *Implementation.*

33. Adapted from Mazmanian and Sabatier, "A Conceptual Framework."

34. Majone and Wildavsky, "Implementation as Evolution," 140.

35. Fesler and Kettle, *Administrative Process,* 387.

36. M. Bustillo, "Time Is Running Out for Thousands on Welfare," *Los Angeles Times,* April 20, 2002.

37. Fesler and Kettle, *Administrative Process.*

38. See the 2002 Official Mission Statement, available at the Office of Homeland Security Web site, http://www.Whitehouse.gov.

39. J. M. Shafritz and E. W. Russell, *Introducing Public Administration* (New York: Longman, 1999), 246.

40. G. Starling, *Strategies for Policymaking* (Homewood, IL: Dorsey Press, 1988).

41. Ibid., 510.

42. Mark W. Huddleston, *The Administration Workbook,* 4th ed. (New York: Longman, 2000), 306.

43. Ibid., 406.

44. Ibid., 307.

45. Martin Levin, "The Day After the AIDS Vaccine Is Discovered: Management Matters," *Journal of Policy Analysis and Management 12* (3), 1993, 450.

11

Policy Evaluation

The Assessment
of Executed
Policy Solutions

Concerns over accountability, efficiency, and effectiveness in policy making are intensifying at all levels. Elected officials, policy makers, community leaders, bureaucrats, and the public at large want to know what policies work and what policies are not working, and why. More often than not, policies and the programs they create often fail to achieve their intended effects and have unintended outcomes. The purpose of evaluation is to determine whether an implemented program is doing what it is supposed to. If it is, then evaluation will assess how well it is achieving its intended objectives and goals. If the program or policy is not performing well, evaluation will determine what effects the program is having. Through evaluation we can determine whether a policy's effects are intended or unintended and whether the results are positive or negative for the target population and society as a whole.

Over the years evaluation has become more commonplace, although it is not new for governments to assess whether their programs are cost effective and are achieving desired benefits. For example, in the Roman Empire, it was common to alter tax policies in response to fluctuations in revenues. This was an early form of policy evaluation. American policy makers became more concerned with judging the effects of policies in the 1960s with the advent of the War on Poverty programs. Specifically, policy makers became more concerned with whether the different welfare and antipoverty programs were having the effect they were supposed to have and whether tax dollars were being spent efficiently and effectively. From the late 1960s, requirements for program evaluation were written into almost all federal programs.[1] Subsequently, Congress established evaluating organizations such as the Congressional Budget Office and the General Accounting Office. Funding support for such organizations has varied with each subsequent presidential administration. For example, the Reagan administration made deep budgetary cuts that affected the federal government's ability to conduct program evaluation.[2]

In this chapter we will identify the different types and approaches to evaluation, discuss the process of evaluation, identify who carries out evaluation, and the obstacles that face evaluators. The chapter's objective is to offer a brief, simple, and clear introduction to program or policy evaluation. It is not intended to point to any one approach or type of evaluation over another. The best evaluation is the one that meets the needs of the program or policy that is being evaluated. We begin by distinguishing program evaluation from other related forms of assessment activity.

WHAT IS POLICY EVALUATION?

Policy evaluation consists of reviewing an implemented policy to see if it is doing what was mandated. The consequences of such policies' programs are determined by describing their impacts, or by looking at whether they have succeeded or failed according to a set of established standards.[3] Within the field of public policy a number of perspectives exist as to what evaluation is. The first perspective defines evaluation as the assessment of whether a set of activities implemented under a specific policy has achieved a given set of objectives. Thus, overall policy effectiveness is assessed.[4] A second perspective defines evaluation as any effort that renders a judgment about program qual-

ity.[5] The third perspective defines evaluation as information gathering for the purposes of making decisions about the future of a program.[6] A final perspective found in the literature views evaluation as the use of scientific methods to determine how successful implementation and its outcomes have been.[7]

The General Accounting Office (GAO) defines program evaluation as the provision of sound information about what programs are actually delivering, how they are managed, and the extent to which they are cost effective.[8] None of these definitions are necessarily unacceptable. However, policy evaluation can be better defined as a process by which general judgments about quality, goal attainment, program effectiveness, impact, and costs can be determined.

What differentiates policy evaluation from other informal types of assessment is, first, its focus on outcomes or consequences.[9] Next, evaluation is done postimplementation. In other words, the program must have been implemented for a certain period. Third, the goals of the policy or program are provided to the evaluators. The main purpose of evaluation is to gather information about a particular program's performance to assist in the decision to continue, change, or terminate.

THE USEFULNESS OF EVALUATION

One way that programs or policies may be assessed in terms of their accountability is through formal evaluation. Thus, the real value of program or policy evaluation is that it allows for accountability to be measured empirically. Conducting an evaluation allows policy makers to be provided with accurate information on key policy questions that arise from the implementation of any policy or program. This information is of course provided by an evaluation study within a given set of real-world constraints, such as time, budget, ethical considerations, and policy restrictions. The usefulness of conducting an evaluation study of a program or policy is that it provides information to policy makers on whether the policy or program in question is achieving its stated goal and at what costs these are being achieved. The effects of a program or policy will also be ascertained and if the evaluation is conducted correctly policy makers will be able to determine whether those effects are intended or unintended. Of course, policy makers want to know if programs are being administered and managed in the most efficient, accountable, and effective manner. An evaluation study can determine if this is true or not. Evaluation is also useful because it can eventually stimulate change. Finally, the utility of conducting an evaluation is that it can discover flaws in a program that policy designers were never aware of in the abstract.

TYPES OF POLICY EVALUATION

There are a variety of models or frameworks that fuse theoretical content with practical guidelines for conducting a program or policy evaluation. Most models arose in the 1960s and 1970s and were early attempts to conceptualize what evaluation was and how it should be conducted. Thus, they offer varying understandings as to the goals of an evaluation, the role of the evaluator, the scope of an evaluation, as well as how it is organized and conducted. Subsequent practitioners have taken the models and adapted them to changing times, contexts, and needs. Often two or more models will be used in conjunction with each other. The result is that there are several different types of evaluation models that vary in complex-

ity.[10] There are, however, four types that are most commonly applied: process evaluation, outcome evaluation, impact evaluation, and cost–benefit analysis.

Process Evaluation

This type focuses on the concrete concerns of program implementation. It assesses how a program or policy is being delivered to target populations or how it is being managed and run by administrators. A process evaluation should

- determine why a program or policy is performing at current levels
- identify any problems
- develop solutions to the problems
- improve program performance by recommending how solutions should be implemented and evaluated once carried out.

With this type of evaluation the focus is not on whether the program is meeting specified goals, but is to develop recommendations to improve implementation procedures. This type of evaluation is best suited to the needs of program managers and has the objective of helping managers overcome barriers to achieving the goals of the program or policy being implemented.

Outcome Evaluation

This type of evaluation focuses on the degree to which a policy is achieving its intended objectives with regard to the target population. It is concerned with outputs and whether the policy is producing the intended results. This can lead to assessment of effectiveness, including cost. Outcome evaluation is not well suited to the needs of program-level managers because it does not provide operational guidelines on how to improve the implementation of the program. Rather, it is best suited to the needs of policy designers because it identifies whether there is consistency between policy outputs and program intent. An outcome evaluation must determine the following:

- legislative intent
- program goals
- program elements and indicators
- measures of indicators
- program outcomes and outcome valences (whether they are positive or negative)

Impact Evaluation

Impact evaluation focuses on whether a program is having an impact on the intended target population. The major difference between impact evaluation and outcome evaluation is that the latter is solely concerned with whether the program or policy's goals and objectives are being achieved. In comparison, impact evaluation is concerned with assessing whether the target population is being affected in any way by the introduction and implementation of the policy. There is also concern with the impact of the program on the original problem being addressed. The benefit of impact evaluation is that it is suited to the needs of both program-level managers and policy designers, for it is important for both to ascertain whether target populations are appropriately receiving delivery of a program. Successful impact evaluation must help identify the following:

- theoretical goals of the program or policy
- the actual goals
- program or policy objectives
- program or policy results and whether they are intended, unintended, positive or negative in effect

Cost–Benefit Analysis

This type of evaluation focuses on calculating the net balance of the benefits and costs of a program. Essentially, cost–benefit analysis is a method with which to evaluate and assess the effectiveness of a policy's costs, benefits, and outcomes. Evaluators identify and quantify both the negative costs and positive benefits in order to determine the net benefit. For many it is a controversial evaluation technique because of the difficulty of applying it to the public sector. It ignores qualitative concerns at the expense of quantitative information. For example, if we take a cost–benefit analysis approach to assessing certain policy issue areas, it is sometimes easier to calculate the immediate real-dollar costs than the tangible benefits. For certain types of programs such as education or the environment, one could argue that the real benefits do not materialize for years or decades. Hence, a cost–benefit analysis may evaluate a program for being inefficient in terms of monetary expenditures when it may in fact be effective in realizing its long-term goals and in delivering benefits that in the long term far exceed the dollar costs. There are simply some things, such as quality of life, that cannot be quantified. If used alone, cost–benefit analysis can color discussion on whether a program or policy is successful. It is most useful as a tool in conjunction with one of the other types of evaluation.

HOW POLICY IS EVALUATED

Evaluation of policy is fairly complex and includes initial activities that must be undertaken to ensure the success of the overall evaluation. Intrinsic to this success is the duty of the evaluator to communicate findings and conclusions to the client. Evaluation can be viewed as a three-stage sequence:

Box 11.1   Essential Activities in the Evaluation Process

- Identification of goals and objectives of the program or policy to make measurement possible
- Comprehension of the mission statement or noting the absence of one
- Construction of an analytic model of what the program or policy is expected to achieve; this includes a set of theoretical propositions about means-end relationships
- Development of a research design to distinguish program or policy goals from what is actually achieved
- Collection of data or actual measurement
- Analysis and interpretation of data

9. Are we measuring what we are supposed to?

10. What are we doing, how are we doing it, and who cares what we tell them?

STAGES IN THE EVALUATION PROCESS

Stage One—Planning

This stage consists of three steps. Step one is familiarity with the program. Step two is deciding the focus of the evaluation, and step three is developing evaluation measures. In step one evaluators must become aware of and familiar with the program or policy being evaluated. This can be accomplished by the evaluator asking himself or herself a series of questions. The first question attempts to clarify the goals and objectives of a program or policy. This is not always easy to do because the legislative mandate for the policy may have ambiguously expressed goals, or multiple goals, or conflicting goals. Next, the evaluator must determine the relationship of the program being evaluated to other similar programs. Third, the evaluator must identify the major stakeholders in and the target populations of the program.

Stakeholders are individuals, agencies, or groups that hold stakes in the outcome of the evaluation. Target populations are those whom the policy affects. Nontarget groups should also be considered because they may potentially be affected by the policy.[12] Finally, the evaluator must learn the ongoing and recent history of the program. Once all of these questions have been answered, then the evaluator can move on to the next activity in the planning stage.

In step two of the planning stage evaluators must decide what they are assessing. Specifically, what is the focus of the evaluation? Is it the policy's impact, is it its

planning, data gathering, and dissemination. Across these three stages a series of essential activities must take place (see Box 11.1).

According to Sylvia, Sylvia, and Gunn, we can ensure that an evaluation is being planned correctly by running a ten-point check:[11]

1. Is the program experimental or is it ongoing?

2. Who is the audience?

3. Are the measures, indicators, and the design appropriate for the needs of the audience?

4. Are we interested in outcome or impact?

5. What is the purpose of the evaluation?

6. Are we trying to build theoretical knowledge or in seeing if maximum service is provided?

7. How will the study affect funding of the program?

8. Can we realistically produce a valid design given our resources?

outcomes, is it the costs and benefits, or is it the way the policy is being delivered? Once the focus is decided upon the evaluator can conduct step three, which is the development of measures for the focus. Such measures should include estimating the cost of the policy, in both dollar and nondollar terms.

Stage Two—Data Gathering

Two types of data must be collected by evaluators. First, data must be collected that allows for the program's overall configuration and structure to be better understood. Thus, information on how the program is delivered, to whom, and how many clients are served must be gathered. The second type of data gathering deals with the degree to which program goals and objectives are being achieved. The evaluator must also collect data on other effects, both intended and unintended, that can be attributed to the policy. How data is gathered will be determined by the evaluator's decision to apply quantitative or qualitative methods. Quantitative methods refer to a range of techniques that involve the use of statistics and statistical analysis for systematically gathering and analyzing information. Qualitative methods are aimed at understanding underlying behavior through comprehending how and why certain actions are taken by implementors, clients, and target populations. Box 11.2 highlights the differences between quantitative and qualitative methods of analysis.

There is no agreement on which type of analysis to utilize. Often the best way to determine which methods to apply is to look at the program's size and scope, the intended audience for the evaluation, the program's goals, the evaluator's own skills, and the resources available to conduct the evaluation. Once the methods have been determined, the evaluator must develop the research design and confirm the instruments (data-collection devices) that will be applied (see Box 11.3). Research de-

---

Box 11.2   Differences between Qualitative and Quantitative Analysis

Quantitative	Qualitative
Counting	Interpreting
Measuring	Experiencing
Confirming	Understanding
Determining	Arguing
Testing	Exploring
Observing	Experiencing
Finding what is real	Exploring multiple realities

Box 11.3   Research Instruments

Quantitative Method	Qualitative Method
Subject knowledge tests	Case studies
Attitude surveys	Personal interviews
Samples	Personal observations

---

signs can be seen as strategies that can help the evaluator improve the validity and reliability of the evaluation. Designs must be rigorous to avoid validity or reliability threats, but must also be appropriately applicable to the complexity and needs of the program. Once a research instrument is selected and data gathered, the evaluator may use a number of statistical techniques to analyze and interpret the data. Such techniques allow the evaluator to determine the potential associations or correlations of the variables under analysis.

Stage Three—Dissemination

The final stage in the evaluation process involves dissemination of the findings of the evaluation to those who commissioned the evaluation, specifically the client. In some cases evaluation findings are also forwarded to stakeholders, target groups, or the public at large. The goal of any evaluation is to provide useful information. Usefulness depends upon a number of factors, including timeliness, accuracy, and completeness. All evaluation reports should report assumptions as well as real indicators that affect data interpretation. In sum, every evaluation will include the perceptions and assumptions that the evaluator derives from the assessment. Additionally, there should be alternative explanations for all observed outcomes, the separation of fact from opinion, and the findings should be clear and unambiguous. Finally, an evaluation should, when appropriate, include recommendations for the policy's continuation, change, or termination.

Another dimension critical to effective dissemination is the relationship between the evaluator and the client. In many ways clients can influence an evaluation study's outcome by bringing pressure to bear. For example, a client may have already made up his or her mind about the program and may pressure the evaluator to produce an assessment in accord with a predetermined finding. In response to such concerns, professional organizations in recent years have clarified the rights and responsibilities of evaluators in publishing standards and guiding principles for program evaluation practitioners.[13] The standards are principles rather than rules that evaluators should adhere to. They simply highlight what are acceptable and unacceptable practices; thus, they are a benchmark for practitioners. Evaluators must decide for themselves what practices are ethical and justifiable.

WHO EVALUATES?

The choice for any agency or group that wishes to be evaluated is who should conduct the evaluation. In many ways this is the most critical decision in the evaluation process. The choice is between internal and external evaluators. Neither choice is inher-

ently better than the other. The key to who should be used as an evaluator depends upon the needs of the organization that is commissioning the evaluation study. Both types of evaluators have their strengths and weaknesses. Internal evaluators have an overall advantage of being familiar with the program, the organization, the actors, and the target population. This can save time in the planning stage of the study. However, it can also prove to be a disadvantage in that internal evaluators, because of their ties to the organization, might be "too close" to identify problems, to place blame, or to recommend major changes or termination.

External evaluators are individuals who have no internal connection or ties to the organization being evaluated. They are perceived as "outsiders." External evaluators are often used when the evaluation is authorized by an entity other than the organization itself. For example, if the City of Los Angeles wanted to evaluate the Los Angeles Police Department, it would be an authorizing entity outside of the organization being evaluated. In this case it is more than likely the city would use external evaluators on the assumption that external evaluators would provide objective information because they have no vested interest or agenda to fulfill. The major advantage of external evaluation is that it is perceived to be impartial because evaluators supposedly have no stake in the outcome of the evaluation. This is particularly useful when controversial programs or policies are being assessed. A further strength of utilizing external evaluators is that they are usually professional consultants who are trained in the requisite skills and methods of evaluation techniques. In the past this was undoubtedly true. Recently, however, many individuals working in the public sector are educated in administration and management programs that train students in both policy analysis and program evaluation and are capable of conducting an evaluation.

The major disadvantage of opting for an external evaluation is cost, in both money and time. Some would also argue that it can prove costly in terms of organizational politics because of its potentially disruptive nature. A further disadvantage could be that external evaluators also have an agenda. For instance, they may wish to please the client in order to secure future jobs. This is potentially a dilemma. However, in theory professional ethics ensure that evaluators, although mindful of client needs, should stay true to their impartiality. Another weakness of utilizing external evaluators is they may face resistance from within the organization and between actors and other stakeholders who might have a vested interest in the outcome of the evaluation.

In conclusion, it is interesting to consider two general laws formulated by James Q. Wilson, which put into perspective concerns about the evaluation process.[14] Wilson's first law is that all policy interventions in social problems produce the intended effect—if the research is carried out by those implementing the policy or by their friends. Wilson's second law is that no policy intervention in social problems produces the intended effects—if the research is carried out by independent third parties, especially those skeptical of the policy. Wilson's laws help explain just how difficult the evaluation process is.

OBSTACLES AND PROBLEMS IN EVALUATION

Several factors pose serious problems during the evaluation of a policy.[15] The first factor is ambiguity in the specification of the objectives and goals of a policy. It is common for objectives and goals to be sometimes unclear or equivocal and this can cloud the assessment of whether the goals and objectives have been met. A second problem can occur when objectives have been stated, but there is no clearly defined way to measure the success of the objective. A third problem is the presence of side effects from other policies that interact with the program being evaluated. In essence, the problem is how to weigh outside factors relative to the operation of the program being evaluated. A fourth problem is that the necessary data is often not available, or if it is available, it is not in a suitable state for the purposes of the study. Fifth, the politics of the situation will often interfere with the evaluation process. For example, there may be resistance by administrators or other policy actors to an evaluation being conducted or to its findings. A sixth problem is determining if sufficient resources are being allocated to conduct the most appropriate type of evaluation. Finally, the need for validity can prove to be a problem for evaluators.

There are three broad categories of validity that evaluators must be concerned with: internal, external, and programmatic. Box 11.4 highlights each of these factors in achieving a valid design. If evaluators do not pay close attention to such factors in the formulation and conduct of an evaluation, then the very findings of the evaluation will be invalidated. The obstacles to validity are numerous and range from elements within the environment to methodological errors by the evaluator.

Overall, obstacles to evaluation are important factors that can prevent successful evaluation and hinder the evaluator's recommendations being utilized by policy makers. Quite often, because of contextual factors, human factors, or technical factors, decision makers may be prevented from utilizing the results of the study. Contextual factors involve factors within the environment that will be affected in unacceptable ways if decision makers act on the recommendations of the evaluation. Technical factors refer to the

---

Box 11.4   Validity Types

Internal Validity	**External Validity**	**Programmatic Validity**
Does evaluation measure what it intends?	Can findings be general-ized?	Does evaluation generate information that is useful to program officials?
Does evaluation require correct identification and measuring of program goals?	Can findings be replicated?	Is evaluation designed to be acceptable to all audiences?

SOURCE: Adapted from R. D. Sylvia, K. M. Sylvia, and E. M. Gunn, *Program Planning and Evaluation for the Public Manager*, 2nd ed. (Prospect Heights, IL: Waveland Press, 1997), 117–127.

---

problems caused by methodological consid-erations. Human factors are obstacles posed by the personality and psychological profile of the decision makers, evaluators, the client, and other internal actors. In reality, evalua-tion is fraught with problems and weaknesses.

SUMMARY

In this chapter, we have discussed what pol-icy evaluation is, how it is carried out, who does it, the problems that may be encoun-tered, and the obstacles to the utilization of recommendations made by program or pol-icy evaluation studies. Over the past thirty years, policy evaluation has attracted consid-erable interest among policy makers at all levels in the public sector. It is important to remember that evaluation is essential, for it often tells policy makers what is working and what is not working.

DISCUSSION QUESTIONS

1. Design an impact evaluation for a public sector program that provides basic medical services to homeless people.
2. In 2001, the State of California attempted to increase the number of

elementary teachers, encourage relocation of teachers to rural areas, and improve the practical teaching experience during training. To accomplish these goals the state opened a new regional campus of its state university and appointed a provost to run it. The first three years of the provost's tenure in office were marked by continual pressure and criticism from the local school board, the teachers' union, the local community, and the media. In response to such lobbying and criticism the provost redefined the original goals of the initiative. He developed the more operational goals of recruiting former teachers as university faculty, established working relationships with all elementary schools in the immediate area, and created programs for currently employed teachers to enhance their teaching skills.

How would you evaluate this particular program, and why?

SUGGESTED READINGS

Albaek, E. "Knowledge, Interests, and the Many Meanings of Evaluation: A Developmental Perspective." *Scandinavian Journal of Social Welfare* 7 (1998): 94–98.

Albaek, E. "Why All This Evaluation? Theoretical Notes and Empirical Observations on the Functions and Growth of Evaluation."

Canadian Journal of Program Evaluation 11, no. 2 (1996): 1–34.

Bingham, R. D., and C. L. Felbinger. *Evaluation in Practice: A Methodological Approach.* New York: Longman, 1989.

Fisher, F. *Evaluating Public Policy.* Chicago: Nelson Hall, 1995.

Haverman, R. "Policy Evaluation Research After Twenty Years." *Policy Studies Journal* 16, no. 2 (Winter 1987): 191–218.

Nachimas, D. *Public Policy Evaluation: Approaches and Methods.* New York: St. Martin's Press, 1979.

Sylvia, R. D., K. M. Sylvia, and E. M. Gunn. *Program Planning and Evaluation for the Public Manager,* 2nd ed. Prospect Heights, IL: Waveland Press, 1997.

Weiss, C. *Evaluation: Methods for Studying Programs and Policies,* 2nd ed. Upper Saddle River, NJ: Prentice Hall, 1998.

ENDNOTES

1. R. Haverman, "Policy Evaluation Research After Twenty Years," *Policy Studies Journal* 16, no. 2 (Winter 1987): 191–218.

2. M. E. Rushefsky, *Public Policy in the United States* (Belmont, CA: Wadsworth, 1990), 16.

3. M. J. Dubnick and B. A. Bardes, *Thinking About Public Policy* (New York: Wiley, 1983), 203.

4. J. S. Wholey et al., *Federal Evaluation Policy* (Washington, DC: Urban Institute Press, 1970), 15.

5. Haveman, "Policy Evaluation Research," 191–218.

6. R. D. Bingham and C. L. Felbinger, *Evaluation in Practice: A Methodological Approach* (New York: Longman, 1989), 4.

7. Ibid., 3.

8. General Accounting Office, *Federal Evaluation Issues* (Washington, DC: GAO, 1989), 4.

9. F. G. Caro, ed., *Readings in Evaluation Research,* 2nd ed. (New York: Russell Sage, 1977), 6.

10. J. R. Sanders, *The Program Evaluation Standards* (Thousand Oaks, CA: Sage, 1994), 8–12.

11. R. D. Sylvia, K. M. Sylvia, and E. M. Gunn, *Program Planning and Evaluation for the Public Manager,* 2nd ed. (Prospect Heights, IL: Waveland Press, 1997), 171–174.

12. E. R. House, *Evaluating with Validity* (Thousand Oaks, CA: Sage, 1980), 20–33.

13. Sanders, *Evaluation Standards,* 8–12.

14. J. Q. Wilson, "On Pettigrew and Armor," *The Public Interest* 30 (Winter 1973), 132–134.

15. B. W. Hogwood and L. A. Gunn, *Policy Analysis for the Real World* (New York: Oxford University Press, 1984), 220–227.

12

Policy Change or Termination

Once a policy has been implemented, it becomes prey to all sorts of political realities and dynamics that constantly affect and shape how the policy is viewed as time passes. Interest groups mobilize, target groups complain, funding fluctuates, and sometimes there are legal challenges. Such real-world dynamics force policies to evolve and change. Under certain circumstances policies can also just end. One of the natural consequences of evaluating policies or the programs they create is that sometimes decision makers act upon the evaluation findings and force change, although, as discussed in Chapter 11, this is not always the case. Policy does not always change radically because many political actors and much of the public may not support rapid change. We should also realize that sometimes policies remain essentially the same. There are various factors that can account for the absence of policy change. Among these factors are favorable evaluations, lack of evaluation, or extensive political support strong enough to overcome unfavorable evaluations.

In spite of wide acknowledgment of the effects of real-world dynamics, until recently, political scientists paid little attention to this stage of the policy cycle.[1] For many the stages-heuristic approach ended with policy evaluation. Some authors suggested that as part of the evaluation stage feedback occurred. This in turn allowed policies to be simply reformulated and reimplemented. With the addition of the change and termination stages, the feedback process has been encompassed and formalized into the stages-heuristic approach.

During the policy change and termination stages, policies are assessed, sometimes change occurs, and sometimes, although it is rare, policies are terminated completely. More often than not, changes to policies will occur rather than outright policy termination.[2]

POLICY CHANGE DEFINED

When a policy is replaced or modified in some respect or repealed in parts, then policy change has occurred. Policies are rarely maintained exactly as adopted. Change inevitably starts to occur as soon as a policy is implemented because of the intrinsic ambiguity of legislation. Thus, policies are constantly evolving and the policy cycle is an ongoing dynamic process. Policies are formulated, adopted, implemented, evaluated, reformulated, and reimplemented, and the cycle continues. Why is this the case? It is because when policies are designed they have as their goal the solving of a particular problem or the achievement of specific objectives. Whether objectives are achieved or not, policy makers will respond by altering or modifying the original policy. In the following chapters discussing the various substantive policy areas, the cycle of change is evident. For example, antipoverty policies today are very different in many aspects than they were in the 1960s. Whether the evolution is good or bad is not relevant to our discussion; what is germane is the fact that these policies have been reshaped over time and have evolved through change. Such change can be referred to as policy succession.[3] Policy succession can essentially be realized as taking one of the following three forms:

1. Modification of existing practices
2. Enactment of new legislative statutes
3. Major shifts in goals and direction of objectives

REASONS FOR CHANGE

There are eleven factors that can account for policy change. First, there might be changes in societal dynamics that force a policy to change to meet new conditions or facets of the same problem. Second, new policies may contradict or invalidate an existing policy. Third, a policy is challenged constitutionally or lawsuits are pursued against it. Fourth, technological changes alter a policy's feasibility or relevance. Fifth, new discoveries or revelations alter public support for the policy. Sixth, economic and political conditions change, thereby altering the environment in which the policy operates. Seventh, elections bring into office officials with very different ideological agendas and interpretations of what a particular policy should or should not be doing. Eighth, the problem is solved, thereby negating the need for the policy. Ninth, those implementing may lack the skills to manage the policy effectively. Tenth, once implemented a policy may show its defects and weaknesses. Finally, target groups simply refuse to comply with or they mobilize strongly against the policy.

Hogwood and Gunn suggest adding three further reasons for change to the policy cycle.[4] They argue that there are relatively few new areas of policy making in which modern governments can become involved. Thus, most new policies will overlap with or be extensions of existing policies and programs. This seems to reconfirm Charles Lindblom's classic characterization of American policy making as being incremental in nature.[5] The authors also contend that because of inadequacies or unintended effects, existing policies create conditions necessitating change. Finally, Hogwood and Gunn believe that changing policy is easier than terminating policy. Economic conditions may change and certain policies may be considered unnecessary, wasteful, or inappropriate; however, there will always be groups that support such policies. Therefore, politically it is easier to modify them than end them.

PATTERNS OF POLICY CHANGE

Policy change may follow several patterns. The most common patterns of policy change are listed below:[6]

Linear Change: With linear change, one policy is replaced with another or the location of an existing policy is changed. For example, the Aid to Dependent Children Act was replaced with Aid to Families with Dependent Children (AFDC). An additional example would be the conversion of the 1973 Comprehensive Employment and Training Act into the 1982 Job Partnership Training Act.

Consolidation Change: This type of change combines two or more programs with similar goals and objectives into a single new policy. When several environmental regulatory programs are fused or rolled together under one general policy consolidation has occurred. For example, under the1992 Energy Policy Act several environmental regulatory programs were joined together.

Split Change: Split change divides an agency that is responsible for a particular policy or program into smaller organizational units, each of which are responsible for part of the original policy. Examples include the splitting of the Atomic Energy Commission in 1974 into two new agencies, the Nuclear Regulatory Agency and the Energy Research Development Agency, and the splitting of the Immigration and Naturalization Service into service and enforcement branches.

Nonlinear Change: This type of change reflects drastic or major policy change. It usually comes about because new social conditions develop, there are technological advances, or simply because political office holders desire change for ideological reasons. An example is the Clinton administration's reversal of the "gag rule," which forbade family-planning clinics from discussing abortion with their clients. A more recent example would be the 2001 Patriot Act which by some standards is a dramatic expansion of government powers in the areas of law enforcement and domestic security.

IMPLEMENTING POLICY CHANGE

The implementation of policy change is complex and often uncertain. Any policy change must go through the usual policy-making process. Each stage presents new difficulties for policy makers because established organizations, target groups, and stakeholders firmly entrench themselves in the process, attempting to block or control any changes. This extension of the policy cycle reflects how the policy process does not simply begin or end but is continually evolving. Figure 12.1 outlines the process of policy change throughout the policy cycle. It highlights the complexity of policy change at each stage of the cycle.

UNDERSTANDING WHY POLICY CHANGE OCCURS

The reasons for policy change have previously been discussed, but understanding why major changes in policy occur in the United

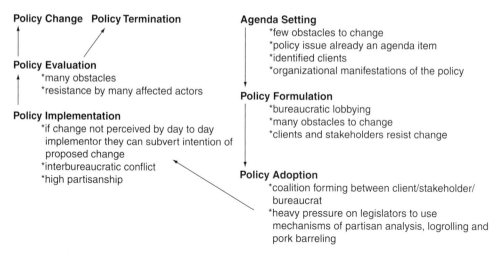

FIGURE 12.1 Policy Change and the Policy Cycle.

States can best be understood through the use of policy change frameworks. There are three major frameworks that can be found within the literature: the cyclical thesis, the evolutionary or policy learning thesis, and the backlash or zigzag thesis.

As stated earlier in regard to policy implementation and evaluation, there is no single framework that can best explain policy change over time. Rather, each framework should be applied to specific policy areas to see whether change in a particular policy reflects policy learning, shifts in national mood, or transferal of benefits to new target populations.

The Cyclical Thesis

Arthur Schlesinger is the main proponent of this particular framework.[7] Schlesinger and his followers argue that when American politics is analyzed it should be understood that there is a continuing shift between public purpose and private interest. In essence, what Schlesinger argues is that there are periods when the national mood is conservative and

there are other periods when it is liberal; in other words, policy making is cyclical in nature. In terms of policy making this means when the national mood is conservative the public supports the notion that the private sector and individual responsibility is the best way to deal with national problems. When the national mood is liberal, then the public supports more government involvement and a commitment to public sector intervention. Such mood swings represent approximately thirty-year cycles. For example, from the Harding–Coolidge years until Franklin Roosevelt's election in 1932, the national mood was conservative and there was little public support for large-scale government intervention to deal with the nation's problems. Franklin Roosevelt's New Deal, however, was supported by a liberal national mood that demanded reform and affirmative government to deal with the depression era problems. This national mood was similarly evident in the Kennedy–Johnson years. The retrenchment of the Ronald Reagan years was supported by a national mood swing back to conservatism in the early 1980s.

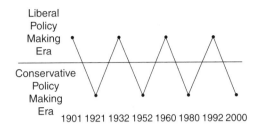

FIGURE 12.2 Conservative and Liberal Policy Making Cycles.

SOURCE: Adapted from A. Schlesinger Jr., *The Cycles of American History* (Boston: Houghton Mifflin, 1986).

Schlesinger argues that the mood swings represent a generation span, each generation bringing with it individual values and beliefs, which are shaped by experiences. Hence, the change in national mood ushers in policy making of a certain ideological direction. In sum, the cyclical thesis basically proposes that the evolution of American public policy can be understood through a cyclical perspective alternating between periods of conservative policy making and periods of liberal policy making. This makes American public policy fairly predictable. Figure 12.2 illustrates how these cycles have produced eras of liberal and conservative policy making. We believe that the weakness of this thesis is that the national mood in recent years seems much more volatile than Schlesinger's thirty-year span suggests.

A further way to understand why national mood swings occur is to use Samuel Huntington's argument that voters become disillusioned with what government enacts and move in the opposite direction.[8] According to Huntington, the United States has periods of "creedal passion" which lead to eras of constitutional reform and eras of societal calm. Essentially, what Huntington is arguing is that there are periods when a dominant societal creed dictates change and other periods

when such a creed is less than dominant and consequently there is no impetus for change.

The Evolutionary or Policy-Learning Thesis

Paul Sabatier and Hank Jenkins-Smith argue that policy change is a function of three factors that are based upon three premises.[9] The three factors are the interaction of competing "advocacy co-alitions" within a policy community; external changes outside the policy community; and stable policy community parameter effects. The three premises are as follows: (1) To understand policy change it must be studied over a minimum of a ten-year period, because that is the length of the policy cycle. (2) Policy communities must be focused upon because they are networks of institutional and noninstitutional actors that are interested and affected by the policy. (3) Public policies can be conceptualized as "belief systems."

In sum, policies are composed of value priorities and causal assumptions on how to achieve such priorities. Certain advocacy groups push certain policies based on their belief systems. As time passes, groups may change their beliefs and alter their demands depending upon the context and the information they receive. However, groups and their belief systems are fairly stable over time. In fact, the belief system is set for at least a ten-year period or more.

Major policy change normally occurs when there is large-scale societal change in socioeconomic conditions or in the dominant governing elite. Such change forces the advocacy coalitions to learn to adapt to changing times and needs. Thus, policy makers revise policy based on the policy learning that has been brought about by external events such as conflict or widespread changes in how society perceives its resources should be directed.

The Backlash or Zigzag Thesis

Authors such as Edwin Amenta and Theda Skocpol argue that American policy making is erratic.[10] Rather than viewing policy making in the United States as being dependent on shifts in national mood, the authors state that it is dependent upon shifts in perceptions about who benefits from policies. The zigzag is basically seen as a stimulus and response cycle which is a backlash against the group or groups that have been benefiting from the policies. In short, policies from one period benefit certain groups and provide the stimulus for other groups to react against particular policies and force policy change in the next period. So policies change from time to time because the group that perceives themselves not to be benefiting seeks to bring about different policies to become policy beneficiaries. This then forces past beneficiaries to become policy "losers."

In the preceding discussion, the cyclical thesis, the policy-learning thesis, and the backlash thesis were used to explain why policy change may occur. What we must now ask is what happens if policy is not changed but is ended? In the following section we will define exactly what termination is and how it may occur.

WHAT IS POLICY TERMINATION?

Policy termination is a rare phenomenon and there are few real-life examples. Thus, much of the scholarly discussion is theoretical and abstract and in spite of its importance in the policy process there is little research done on the dynamics of policy termination. Policy termination has been defined as "the deliberate conclusion or cessation of specific public sector functions, programs, policies, or organizations."[11] In essence it is the dissolution of an agency, the redirection of pol-icy, the elimination of a program, or fiscal retrenchment.[12] Termination is not easy. Indeed, because often the costs, both political and economic, are so high there is reluctance on the part of decision makers and beneficiaries to terminate policies or programs.[13] For these reasons and more, policy termination faces powerful obstacles.[14]

WHY IS POLICY TERMINATION SO RARE?

One factor explaining the rarity of policy termination is the desire of organizations to survive. It is a dynamic conservatism that induces organizations to pursue new goals to achieve once original policy goals are accomplished. The creation of new goals helps legitimize the organization's continued existence. It is also true that administrators will change program goals rather than terminate a program when they face difficulties, such as weak evaluations. This desire to survive also accounts for administrators' vested interest in seeing their organization continue. Quite simply, they do not want to lose their jobs.

Another factor inhibiting termination is legal obstacles. Some programs must exist based upon current laws. Thus, whether they fulfill their goals and objectives is irrelevant to their continuance. For example, there is general consensus that public education is not working. Thus, it can be argued that it is not achieving its goals. However, legally, even though some individuals and groups would like the government to withdraw from the provision of education, it legally cannot. A third factor blocking termination is the high start-up costs of new programs. Ironically, it is often cheaper to keep a program than terminate it. Fourth, administrators and staff can seek to stop termination by joining forces with political actors, individuals, and groups opposed to termination.

DeLeon calls such unions antitermination coalitions.[15] Finally, decisions to terminate are often political. As such, policy termination is often embedded in ideological struggles that occur within the political arena.

REASONS FOR POLICY TERMINATION

Policies can be ended for one of the following reasons or a combination of them. First, a policy can be terminated because it is no longer effective, it is not meeting its specified objectives and goals, or it is simply not "solving" the problem it is supposed to address. Second, the need for the program simply disappears. Third, budgetary requirements force the end of a policy or program. Cuts in the space exploration program or recent attacks on affirmative action programs at the individual state level are good examples of termination based upon budgetary requirements. Fourth, an evaluation study makes the case that the policy is unsatisfactory in impact or outcome. For example, airline deregulation came about because the 1978 Commercial Regulation Act was terminated because evaluation after evaluation found that airline regulation was not achieving what it was supposed to. Fifth, the political environment may no longer support the goals of a policy. The change in welfare policies came about largely because of the wholesale societal belief that the welfare system was malfunctioning and needed major reform. Finally, certain policies or programs are terminated for purely ideological reasons.[16] The election of a conservative president or a liberal Congress will undoubtedly affect not only what becomes policy but also what remains as a policy or program. For example, Ronald Reagan essentially eliminated the Maternal Infant Care program and Supplemental Women, Infants, and Children Feeding program through reduced funding. He argued such programs were not appropriate areas for the federal government to be involved in. However, evaluations showed them to be cost effective and to have a favorable benefit–cost ratio, ultimately saving society money. Reagan's ideological opposition drove him to cut the programs because he believed they encouraged women to be single mothers or indigent through the provision of extra food and medical resources. Similarly, President Bill Clinton oversaw a significant reduction in defense spending based upon his ideological stance of favoring expenditure on nondefense policy areas and his ideological commitment to cutting deficits.

TYPES OF POLICY TERMINATION

There are four main types of termination that can occur:[17]

Functional Termination: This is dramatic and a complete ending of government responsibility as stipulated in a particular policy or program. It is extremely rare, but there are cases of it. An example is the privatization of a responsibility that was once the exclusive province of the public sector, as when California allowed energy to be supplied by private companies. More recently in Philadelphia the city government lost control of twenty-two schools that now fall under the control of a private education corporation.

Organizational Termination: This is the elimination of an entire organization or agency—for example, the elimination of the Congressional Office of Technology Assessment in 1995. It is not very common. Rather than terminate an agency, government mostly chooses to reorganize and split an agency into multiple units of responsibility.

Policy Termination: This is the complete abandonment of a policy because the principles underlying it no longer have common societal agreement. For example, the Jim Crow laws were discarded in the South with the advent of civil rights legislation in the mid-1960s.

Program Termination: Program termination is the elimination of a particular program that is implemented by a particular policy. However, the overall policy remains in effect. It is the most common type of termination because the number of actors involved or affected is limited. For example, in 1986 the Reagan administration terminated revenue sharing programs that were adopted during the Nixon administration. Revenue sharing channeled revenues to state and local governments with few requirements. President Reagan, however, terminated revenue sharing because of large federal deficits and because of public pressure.

APPROACHES
TO TERMINATION

Once a type of termination is selected, policy makers must then decide how they wish to carry it out. Eugene Bardach states there are basically two approaches that decision makers can take when terminating policy.[18] The first approach is to terminate swiftly. Termination is quick and decisive. Bardach calls this "Big Bang" termination. The policy or program is ended quickly with no phasing-out process. It is usually accompanied by a long political struggle between multiple actors. Essentially there is public articulation by government of the desire or intention to end a policy or program. Groups mobilize when government announces the end of the program. In contrast, the second approach is a process by which the decision to terminate is announced

by government as a phasing out over a fixed period. Bardach calls this "Long Whimper" termination. It can be achieved in a number of ways. For example, government can announce that a program will no longer be in place by a certain date or the allocated budget for a program will be slowly reduced over a period. Inevitably, termination is accomplished because the program will no longer be able to function effectively due to insufficient funding. This will mostly occur when one policy is replaced with a completely new one.

SUCCESSFUL POLICY
TERMINATION STRATEGIES

Policy termination can be made more viable if decision makers pursue certain strategies.[19] First, decision makers can control the flow and level of publically available information until they have developed comprehensive justification for termination. A second strategy is for decision makers to enlarge the termination constituency beyond the policy's clientele base. The goal is to create sufficient support among policy actors to end the policy or program. Another strategy would be for decision makers to publically demonstrate that termination is not solely based upon inefficiency or ineffectiveness, but that the policy is also producing harmful effects. In doing so, decision makers should be prepared to take advantage of ideological shifts in the public mood that would benefit termination.

Decision makers could also choose to pursue a strategy whereby they refuse to compromise. Agreeing to such compromise would surely allow for policy change rather than the ending of the policy. A fifth strategy is for legislative votes to be avoided on the termination as legislators will always favor change over termination because it is less costly electorally. Policy makers could also choose to stop termination becoming a fight between the executive and legislative branches. A further strategy is for decision makers to be prepared to go outside an agency for management of its termination. Also beneficial to decision makers is to ensure the costs of termination are not higher than a policy's continuation. If so, it is sometimes better to compensate individuals who will suffer because a policy is being terminated. A further strategy often used by decision makers is to sell termination as not the ending of a particular program but the means of adopting a new more necessary policy that is better than existing practices. Finally, decision makers should always be very clear why a policy or organization is being terminated in order to justify the ending of the program publically.

TYPES OF TERMINATORS

Those terminating policies or programs can be classified as to type based upon their motivations for termination.[20] The first type of terminator is an *oppositionist*. Such individuals are decision makers who feel that a policy or program should be terminated because it is simply bad. Their reasoning for perceiving a policy or program in this manner is mainly ideological. *Economizers* are the second type of terminator. This type sees termination as a way to cut government expenditure in times of need. The third type of terminator is a *reformist*. Such individuals see termination as the only choice if a better and more useful policy, program, or organization is to be created. In reality, termination is so rare that it is difficult to clearly distinguish types of terminators.

SUMMARY

Policy change and termination are both troublesome endeavors for government. Policies are developed to address certain problems or issues; however, they rarely do so and are often perceived to have failed. Box 12.1 lists the

> ### Box 12.1   Policy Failure Explanations
>
> - The problem is around for too long and loses urgency
> - Inadequate resources
> - The vagaries of implementation
> - The impact of changing circumstances
> - Repudiation by target population
> - Unclear or incompatible goals
> - Uncertainty on how to achieve goals
> - Cannot change everything
> - Conditions are not conducive
> - Failure of political institutions
> - Ineffective policy tools
> - Not based upon sound causal theory
> - Unrealizable expectations
> - Unclear political boundaries of responsibility
> - Relationship of policy to other policies not taken into account
>
> SOURCE: Adapted from H. Ingram and D. Mann, "Policy Failure: An Issue Deserving Attention," In *Why Policies Succeed or Fail*, H. Ingram and D. Mann, eds. (Beverly Hills, CA: Sage, 1980).

most common explanations for policy failure. All too often, however, the policy remains on the books and uses scarce resources. If the policy is changed or terminated, it creates an opposition from those actors that have a vested interest in its continuation. Although it is far more common for policy to change than be terminated, there will be times when a policy or program is ended. Termination is costly and can have negative consequences. Thus, termination is difficult and troublesome. It is far more rewarding to change policy than end it.

DISCUSSION QUESTIONS

1. If the federal government decided to privatize social security arrangements, under what pattern would you classify the policy change? Why?

2. Opponents of national missile defense suggest this program is infeasible both in terms of cost and technology. Advocates of the program argue the future benefits outweigh the current costs. Research both sides of the issue and develop a recommendation to terminate or not.

SUGGESTED READINGS

Brewer, G. D. "Termination: Hard Choices, Harder Question." *Public Administration Review* 38, no. 4 (July/August 1978): 338–344.

Daniels, M. R. *Terminating Public Programs: An American Paradox.* New York: M. E. Sharpe, 1997.

Frantz, J. E. "Reviving and Revising a Termination Model." *Policy Sciences* 25 (May 1992): 175–189.

Sabatier, P. A. "Toward Better Theories of the Policy Process." In *PS: Political Science and Politics* 24, no. 2 (June 1991): 147–156.

ENDNOTES

1. P. DeLeon, "A Theory of Policy Termination," in J. V. May and A. Wildavsky, *The Policy Cycle* (Beverly Hills, CA: Sage, 1978), 279–300; B. W. Hogwood and L. A. Gunn, *Policy Analysis for the Real World* (Oxford: Oxford University Press, 1984), 241–260; P. A. Sabatier, "Top-Down and Bottom-Up Approaches to Implementation Research: A Critical Analysis and Suggested Synthesis," *Journal of Public Policy* 6, no. 1 (1986): 21–47.

2. J. E. Anderson, *Public Policymaking: An Introduction* (Boston: Houghton Mifflin, 1990), 257; B. W. Hogwood and B. Guy Peters, *Policy Dynamics* (New York: St. Martin's Press, 1983), 75; B. Guy Peters, *American Public Policy: Promise and Performance,* 4th ed. (Chatham, NJ: Chatham House, 1996): 184.

3. Peters, *American Public Policy,* 100–161.

4. Hogwood and Gunn, *Policy Analysis,* 241–251.

5. C. Lindblom, "The 'Science' of Muddling Through," *Public Administration Review* 19 (1959): 161–163.

6. Peters, *American Public Policy,* 161–163.

7. A. Schlesinger Jr., *The Cycles of American History* (Boston: Houghton Mifflin, 1986); A. Schlesinger Jr., "America's Political Cycle Turns Again," *Wall Street Journal,* December 10, 1987.

8. S. P. Huntington, *American Politics: The Promise of Disharmony* (Cambridge, MA: Bellnap/Harvard University Press, 1981), 284.

9. P. A. Sabatier, "Knowledge, Policy-Oriented Learning and Policy Change: An Advocacy Coalition Framework," *Knowledge: Creation, Utilization, Diffusion* 3, no. 4 (June 1987): 649–692; P. A. Sabatier and H. Jenkins-Smith, eds., *Policy Change and Learning: An Advocacy Coalition Approach* (Boulder, CO: Westview Press, 1993); P. A. Sabatier, "An Advocacy Coalition Framework of Policy Change and the Role of Policy-Oriented Learning," *Policy Sciences* 21, nos. 2–3 (1988): 129–168.

10. E. Amenta and T. Skocpol, "Taking Exception: Explaining the Distinctiveness of American Public Policies in the Last Century," in F. G. Castles, *The Comparative History of Public Policy* (New York: Oxford University Press, 1989).

11. G. D. Brewer and P. DeLeon, *The Foundations of Public Policy* (Homewood, IL: Dorsey Press, 1983), 385.

12. P. DeLeon, "Policy Termination as a Political Process," in D. Palumbo, *The Politics of Program Evaluation* (Beverly Hills, CA: Sage, 1987), 184.

13. Hogwood and Gunn, *Policy Analysis,* 247–248.

14. DeLeon, "A Theory of Policy Termination," 279–300.

15. DeLeon, "Policy Termination as a Political Process," 173–202.

16. J. M. Cameron, "Ideology and Policy Termination: Restructuring California's Mental Health System," in J. V. May and A. Wildavsky, *The Policy Cycle* (Beverly Hills, CA: Sage, 1978), 300–328; DeLeon, "Policy Termination as a Political Process," 173–194.

17. J. P. Lester and J. Stewart Jr., *Public Policy: An Evolutionary Approach,* 2nd ed. (Belmont, CA: Wadsworth, 2000), 156–157.

18. E. Bardach, "Policy Termination as a Political Process," *Policy Sciences* 7, no. 2 (June 1976): 123–132.

19. R. Behn, "How to Terminate a Public Policy: A Dozen Hints for the Would be Terminator," *Policy Analysis* 4, no. 3 (Summer 1978): 393–413.

20. Bardach, "Policy Termination," 123–132.

Case Study One   An Illustrative Case of the Policy Process: Terrorism and Aviation Security

How was it possible, Americans would ask on the morning of September 11, 2001, that four passenger airliners could be hijacked by terrorists and crashed into the World Trade Center in New York City, the Pentagon building in Washington, DC, and into farmland in the state of Pennsylvania? How was it possible that airline security was so vulnerable to foreign terrorists? How could public policy and programs dealing with aviation security fail so dramatically? Since that day, the answers to these questions continue to be explored.

The factors precipitating the hijackings and attacks continue to be debated. Were the attacks the result of an intelligence failure, anger toward American foreign policy, the failures of an open immigration policy, lack of sufficient policing and surveillance powers for the government, lack of governmental oversight over the airline industry, or specific failures in aviation or airline security? The dramatic nature of this policy failure has led to a wealth of policy actions dealing with issues related to the events of September 11. Without question, each of the policy actions represents an important area for investigation and analysis. The focus of this analysis, however, is on the failures in airline security and to illustrate the evolution of policy action through the stages-heuristic framework.

It is quite clear that on September 11, 2001, the programs and policies dealing with aviation security failed. As a result of this failure, dramatic policy actions would follow. All domestic flights were grounded within the United States, all airports were closed, and normal operations did not resume for weeks. This was the first time that the Department of Transportation had ever ordered such a dramatic action. In the days, weeks, and months that followed, airline travel and aviation security was to change fundamentally.

One of the key changes was the passage of the 2001 Aviation and Transportation Security (ATS) Act, and it serves as an important example of how the stages-heuristic approach can be used to help better understand the evolution, execution, and effects of public policy. The ATS Act represents a dramatic example of a policy that evolves through a series of policy stages from problem identification to policy termination or change. Although by no means did the evolution of the ATS policy follow in a mechanical step-by-step manner, it is evident that this policy did evolve across the various phases and stages identified by the stages-heuristics approach. The analysis begins with a brief discussion of the history associated with aviation security.

Aviation Security—A Brief History

The concern with aviation security grew out of the spate of hijackings that occurred in the late 1960s and lasted well into the early 1970s. However, with the "installation of metal detectors and attendant pre-boarding inspection of passengers and their carry-on items," the number of hijackings declined significantly. Overall, "the annual number of hijackings similarly declined from an average 50 per year for 1968–1969 to 18 per year for both the 1970s and 1980s before decreasing still further during the first half of the 1990s to the lowest level since 1968: an average of only 14.4 per year."[1] Prior to September 11, it may be fair to generalize that although incidents of terrorism—such as the bombing of PAM 103, and suspected terrorism, such as TWA 800—occurred, the predominant perception was that airline security was effective. Yet, even a cursory analysis of airline security raises doubts as to whether airline travel was ever truly safe.

Prior to September 11, numerous international airports within the United States recorded thousands of incidents in which airports failed to abide by Federal Aviation Administration (FAA) guidelines. From 1991 to 2000, in Los Angeles, for example, over 2,700 incidents were recorded.[2] At Boston and New York, during this same period, over 2,000 total serious incidents were recorded, and in Washington, DC, more than 500 serious incidents occurred.[3] Including all 25 of the busiest U.S. airports, over 18,000 incidents were recorded.[4] Department of Transportation reports dating back to 1997 and 1998 found repeated failures by the FAA in correcting

Continued

known deficiencies in airport security, baggage check, and violations or problems with airline security firms.[5] In sum, strong evidence existed, far prior to September 11, regarding the failures of airline security and the risk to airline travel.

During the Clinton administration, in order to address weaknesses in airline security, the 1997 White House Commission on Aviation Safety and Security proposed fifty-seven recommendations concerning safety, security, air traffic control and disaster response. However, as additional GAO analyses determined in 1998, only thirty-one of these recommendations were implemented, and the overall performance of the implementation was mixed. In short, the recent history of airline security was consistently marred by programmatic failures. Hence, one could argue that prior to September 11, airline security was clearly an issue of concern, but neither clarity nor consensus—either within the government, the public, interest groups, or the airline and airline security industries—emerged as to what was the exact problem or what policy actions were required.

Problem Identification—The Evolution of a Classic Public Problem

Airline security is not a new problem or issue of concern. For over three decades, studies, reviews, and actions have been ordered in light of failures with airline security. Prior to September 11, the issues of failures surrounding airport security were long established among circles of political actors and government agencies, such as the FAA, airline experts, the airlines, and airline security firms. In other words, the issue of airline security, its failings and faults, was not an unknown issue.

Aside from some government studies, as well as the federal commission set up after TWA 800, little evidence exists to suggest that many policy actors were extremely concerned with the severity of the security problems associated with airline travel. In contrast, for those few policy actors interested in or connected to the issue of airline security, the persistent failures, problems, and vulnerabilities within this industry were well known. Reynold Hoover, an aviation antiterrorism consultant and former Alcohol, Tobacco and Firearms (ATF) agent, stated, "What happened on [September 11] . . . is something we in the aviation security business knew could happen for years."[6] Between the beginning of 1997 and April 2000, for example, aviation security was the topic of eleven GAO studies that highlighted issues dealing with poor training of airport security staff, lack of sufficient bomb-detection equipment, and the general failings of aviation security.[7]

Within the Department of Transportation (DOT), the agency ultimately responsible for aviation security, numerous studies made it clear that it was aware of a "serious" problem. Dating as far back as 1997, the DOT looked at the role and added necessity of air marshals on American carriers. In 1998, the difficulty in deploying bomb-detection devices was documented. In 1999, weaknesses were found in the use of explosives-detection devices, and it was found that "some passengers were not properly processed for additional security measures."[8] However, because of questions surrounding the oversight by the FAA, the lack of significant and valid evaluative studies, the advocacy of interest groups representing the airlines and aviation security firms, a debate over what was *the* problem with aviation security, and how serious it was, complicated perceptions and perspectives of what should be done to address this issue of concern.[9] Of course, on September 11, 2001, the perception of the failings related to airline security would change fundamentally.

The events of September 11 represent a classic example of a national crisis—or a classic public problem. The day of the events, and in subsequent days following, there was no debate or discussion of whether there was or was not a public problem in airline security. In the time prior to September 11, however, debate did occur over what problems existed, as well as what was the appropriate role for government. Because of the dramatic cost and scope associated with the attacks, the relevant institutional and noninstitutional policy actors easily perceived that this was a public issue. Even though other issues and problems still affected the nation, in the hours and days following the events of September 11 no other issue was perceived to be as important as terrorism, the safety of airline travel, and threats to the national security posed by failings in airline security.

Such public and political perceptions justified immediate and dramatic action by the federal government from grounding all airline travel into and out of the United States, initiating air combat patrols over American skies, to the presidential order that if another plane was hijacked it was to be shot down if it could not be diverted. On September 11, 2001, the private or public issues related to airline security were not debated or discussed; rather, immediate and dramatic public intervention occurred. The question, however, is why was this the case.

The obvious answer would emphasize that it was a severe problem or a crisis. However, was it not also a crisis and a severe problem before September 11, 2001? The more valid answer may well be that after September 11 it was no longer open to perceptual redefinition. This "crisis" had long been recognized by some policy actors, it had already led to the loss of hundreds of lives with Pan Am 103, and it was clear that the United States had long been the target of terrorists. Given these facts, why was airline security not seen as a clear problem even though millions of Americans fly every year? The answer may lie in recognizing that prior to September 11 relatively little attention was given this issue because so few had been affected, the costs—economic and personal—were relatively limited, and the perception endured that airline security was, for the most part, effective. This perception fundamentally changed on September 11, as the cost and scope of the event made it clear that this was a public problem of such magnitude that it required immediate recognition as a public problem (see Figure CS1.1).

Agenda Setting

The events of September 11 represent a tragic example of a crisis and a classic public problem. As understood through the Cobb and Elder model of agenda setting, the crisis nature of the terrorist attacks "triggered" the issue across the systemic and institutional agenda (see Figure CS1.2). In what were minutes after the events, the issue of airline security became one of the most important on both agendas for most—if not all—of the policy actors interested or active within this policy area.

Irrespective of the biases that had previously stymied the placing of the aviation se-

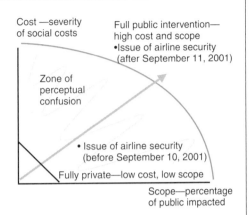

FIGURE CS1.1   September 11—The Path to Perceptual Clarity.

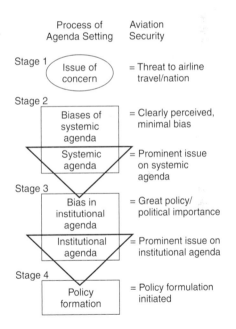

FIGURE CS1.2   Agenda Setting under Crisis Conditions—Aviation Security.

curity issue high on either agenda, September 11 represented a crisis that quickly overcame the intrinsic politics of the agenda-setting process. Consequently, addressing the problem of aviation security became the focus for policy formulation.

Continued

Policy Formulation and Adoption

The process of policy formulation and adoption associated with September 11, and specifically the airline security issue, can be broken down into two rough stages. The first stage of policy formulation was immediate, decisive, and required little politicking, as critical policy actors achieved immediate consensus that significant actions would have to be quickly formulated, adopted, and implemented to address an issue this severe in nature. The action taken by the federal government was the immediate grounding of all airline travel, both commercial and private, as well as the closure of all airports. Such dramatic policy action had never been taken before in the history of American aviation.

With respect to the policy actions immediately following the attack, policies were quickly formulated, adopted by presidential order and support of Congress, and implemented effectively by the Department of Transportation. More important, among other relevant and interested policy actors, there was no public attempt to alter, redefine, or minimize the policy action. As Figure CS1.3 highlights, legislative efficiency emerged because of the coalition of support that emerged among all institutional and noninstitutional actors due to the nature of the threat. In the initial response to the crisis, policy actors sought to cooperate as best possible to ensure the requisite policy actions were undertaken. The political and policy cooperation that emerged represents a powerful example of how efficient the policy process can be under extreme conditions. This was possible, even though American policy making is constitutionally designed to be structurally inefficient under "normal" circumstances. Under such crisis conditions, this same governmental structure, fueled by greater cooperation among institutional and noninstitutional actors, can and does prove remarkably conducive to efficient policy making.

However, the second round of policy formulation and adoption related to the events of September 11, involved the more difficult process of developing ideas, proposals, and solutions in the absence of crisis. During this phase, the various policy actors, with their respective beliefs and interests, had to cooperate to formulate and adopt policy actions in light of what was the perceived problem in aviation security. As Figure CS1.4 indicates, a number of laws were enacted to address a diverse set of issues arising from the terrorist attacks. From issues related to relief for victims, stabilizing the airline industry, to authorizing the use of military force, substantial policy actions were formulated and adopted in the weeks and months after September 11. Yet, dramatic changes to aviation security would take weeks of politicking, debate, and negotiation—even as the threats and problems persisted.

The politics intrinsic to all policy formulation erupted when it became clear, among many policy actors, that members of Congress were considering extremely significant changes to aviation security. In particular, as the debate began to focus on federalizing airport security, those actors that disagreed with this policy proposal quickly mobilized. In this case, the airlines, airline associations, and private aviation security firms quickly mobilized to prevent or stymie dramatic changes in aviation security policy.[10]

The political and policy debates surrounding the changes to aviation security centered around two basic proposals: first, whether airport security should now fall totally under fed-

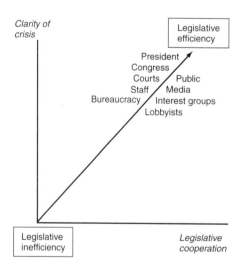

FIGURE CS1.3   September 11 and Legislative Efficiency.

Bills and Joint Resolutions Signed into Law

HR2882: Public Safety Officer Benefits bill

HR2883: Intelligence Authorization Act for Fiscal Year 2002

HR2884: Victims of Terrorism Relief Act of 2001

HR2888: 2001 Emergency Supplemental Appropriations Act for Recovery from and Response to Terrorist Attacks on the United States

HR2926: Air Transportation Safety and System Stabilization Act

HR3162: Uniting and Strengthening America by Providing Appropriate Tools Required to Intercept and Obstruct Terrorism (USA PATRIOT ACT) Act of 2001

HR3986: To extend the period of availability of unemployment assistance under the Robert T. Stafford Disaster Relief and Emergency Assistance Act in the case of victims of the terrorist attacks of September 11, 2001.

S1424: A bill to amend the Immigration and Nationality Act to provide permanent authority for the admission of "S" visa nonimmigrants.

S1438: National Defense Authorization Act for Fiscal Year 2002

S1447: Aviation and Transportation Security Act

S1465: A bill to authorize the president to exercise waivers of foreign assistance restrictions with respect to Pakistan through September 30, 2003, and for other purposes.

S1573: Afghan Women and Children Relief Act of 2001

S1793: Higher Education Relief Opportunities for Students Act of 2001

S.J.Res. 22: A joint resolution expressing the sense of the Senate and House of Representatives regarding the terrorist attacks launched against the United States on September 11, 2001

S.J.Res. 23: Authorization for use of military force

FIGURE CS1.4   September 11 and Adopted Legislative Actions.
SOURCE: Adapted from information found on the Thomas Legislative Information Web site, available at http://www.thomas.loc.gov.

eral control and management, and second, whether government oversight of the privately managed security firms responsible for airline security should be increased. In other words, the question was whether aviation security should continue to remain under some private or public control or become entirely public in nature. Given the scope of policy actions that were being considered, the debate over formulating aviation security policy quickly became mired by various ideological, political, and administrative agendas among the policy actors over what direction policy should go—public or private (see Figure CS1.5).

The extent to which differing political and policy interests affected the debate and policy formulation is highlighted by the realization that airline security reform was not adopted until November 19, 2001. Interestingly, it took over eight weeks to formulate and adopt a policy to address airline security, but less than two weeks to adopt policy that

provided loans and grants to benefit the airline industry. Obstacles to "quick" policy formulation and adoption can be explained by the politics and advocacy efforts that quickly emerged after September 11. Aviation security firms began an aggressive lobbying campaign to prevent dramatic changes, such as federalizing control, in aviation security policy. Airlines were concerned that added security arrangements, if too tedious, could reduce future travel and the economic viability of the airlines. Certain policy actors, such as the Republican leadership in the House of Representatives, simply opposed the need for a new federal agency for airline security on ideological and political grounds. Finally, other activists were hesitant as it was not clear that a new federal bureaucracy would perform any better than private actors in improving airport security.

Overall, the second round of formulation and adoption is a classic example of how an

Continued

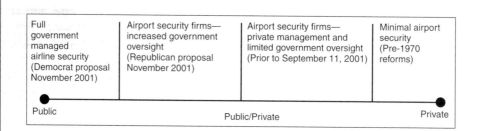

Full government managed airline security (Democrat proposal November 2001)	Airport security firms— increased government oversight (Republican proposal November 2001)	Airport security firms— private management and limited government oversight (Prior to September 11, 2001)	Minimal airport security (Pre-1970 reforms)

Public   Public/Private   Private

FIGURE CS1.5   Public vs. Private Policy Solutions—Issue of Airport Security.

issue, perceived initially as a crisis, and serious in consequence, cannot entirely avoid the politics intrinsic to the policy process once the perception of the instigating crisis begins to dissipate. Nevertheless, the Aviation and Transportation Security (ATS) of 2001 was signed into law. The effectiveness of this legislation, however, depends on how well the policy is implemented.

Policy Implementation, Evaluation, and Change

The implementation of the ATS Act represents a formidable task for the federal government. As a result of the adoption of the ATS, a new bureaucracy, the Transportation Security Administration (TSA), was created under the Department of Transportation. This new administration is to have wide programmatic responsibility over a number of areas (see Box CS1.1):

The ATS legislation mandated the implementation of significant changes by modifying security measures to prohibit access to the cockpit, place air marshals on high-risk flights, institute air measures to reduce security threats within all airports, require screening of all persons and baggage, establish a 911 emergency call capability for all airplane telephones serving passengers, strengthen detection against all potential explosives, and transfer direct oversight and management of baggage screening from the FAA and private security firms to the TSA. Although such expansive implementation goals were to be expected, problems in executing such a broad mandate have quickly materialized—problems not taken into consideration during formulation or adoption.

During the ongoing implementation of the TSA's mandate, significant problems have already arisen. These problems include meeting the deadline for implementing all of the programmatic responsibilities emphasized within the legislation. Allocating resources, hiring and training a staff of over 30,000, creating new management positions, supplying bomb-detection devices—all of these tasks are taking longer than expected. Overall, implementation of these initiatives will likely be marked by continuing and persistent difficulties.

The most recent assessment of airport security in early 2002 continued to find dramatic and widespread failures. Critical areas of airports and planes were still not secure and airport screeners failed to detect weapons in carry-on baggage. As of April 2002, no formal and comprehensive evaluation has been conducted of the new policy initiatives, as the implementation of the TSA is still ongoing. Nevertheless, future evaluations will be vital. It may be fair to state that it is unlikely that airline security will improve dramatically—regardless of whether or not it is under complete government control—unless systematic efforts are made to critically and comprehensively evaluate the programs related to these new airline security initiatives. Without evaluation, failures, problems, and weaknesses will continue to persist.

In terms of policy change, it is apparent that dramatic policy action was taken that has fundamentally reshaped airline security within the United States. At a minimum, a radical shift in the role of government did occur. What remains open to question, however, is whether the scope and immediacy of policy actions taken have addressed the pol-

---

Box CS1.1   TSA Areas of Responsibility

1. Civil aviation security, and related research and development activities
2. Security responsibilities over other modes of transportation that are exercised by DOT
3. Day-to-day federal security screening operations for passenger air transportation and in-trastate air transportation
4. Policies, strategies, and plans for dealing with threats to transportation
5. Domestic transportation during a national emergency (subject to the Secretary of Transportation's control and direction), including aviation, rail, and other surface transportation, and maritime transportation, and port security
6. Management of security information, including notifying airport or airline security officers of the identity of individuals known to pose a risk of air piracy or terrorism or a threat to airline or passenger safety

---

icy problem or the political problem. Is airline travel actually safer, or have these policy actions simply attempted to change the perception? At a minimum, the impact and effect of federalizing airport security, as well as the many other changes that occurred, have impacted airline travel. What will be debated in the years to come is what real effect these changes have had, if any, on airport security.

SUMMARY

Overall, the human cost from the terrorist attacks now stands at roughly 3,000 lives—American and foreign residents. Since the terrorist attacks, the ripples of the events of September 11 have expanded across the spectrum of public policy. Aside from changes in aviation security, the federal government has increased powers of surveillance, increased immigration oversight, increased defense spending, established an Office of Homeland Security and the Transportation Security Administration, gone to war in Afghanistan, and initiated a wider global war against terrorist groups. The issue that this case study attempted to briefly explore was that of aviation security. The goal of the case study, however, was to utilize the stages-heuristic model to better understand the sometimes dramatic nature of the policy process.

How can a student better understand the public policy process and the evolution of issues such as aviation security? The answer lies in the framework that one adopts to understand the complexity of the policy process. We believe that this exercise illustrates the analytical value of the stages-heuristics approach. The stage-heuristics method, discussed throughout this book and in this case study, offers a conceptual framework to guide our analysis and understanding of the manner in which aviation security policy evolved. More important, this framework is an especially useful approach to better understand how policy develops and the dynamics within each stage and phase of the policy process—from problem identification through change or termination.

ENDNOTES

1. B. Hoffman, "Aviation Security and Terrorism," Center for the Study of Terrorism and Political Violence, CIAO working papers, 1997.

2. See "Analysis of FAA Enforcement Information database," CNN special report on Airport Security, available at *http://www.cnn.com/SPECIALS/2001/trade.center/flight.risk/airpo.*

3. Ibid.

4. Ibid.

Continued

5. Department of Transportation Report, *Administration of Security Guard Contracts,* April 17, 1998; Department of Transportation Report, *Security of Checked Baggage Flights within the United States,* July 16, 1999.

6. E. Wieffering, "Experts Doubt Security Measures Will Be Effective," retrieved September 16, 2001, from http://www.startribune.com.

7. "Security Long a Concern at United States Airports," *New York Times,* September 12, 2001, A17.

8. Department of Transportation, government documents, available at http://www.oig.dot.gov/docs.

9. See R. Aloso-Zalivar, "FAA Culture of Bureaucracy Stymies Security Reform Efforts, Critics Say," *Los Angeles Times,* October 27, 2001, A14; Christopher Drew and Mathew L. Wald, "Security Long a Concern at United States Airports, *New York Times,* September 12, 2001, A17.

10. An association was quickly formed of the various private security firms to lobby Congress within weeks of September, 11, 2001.

Case Study Two   Social Construction and Agenda Setting: AIDS

Human immunodeficiency virus (HIV) and acquired immunodeficiency syndrome (AIDS) were first acknowledged in the United States in 1981 and ever since have had an unprecedented effect upon society (see Box CS2.1). It would be hard to identify many other diseases in the twentieth century that have had such an impact and been greeted with such hostility. It is obvious that the HIV/AIDS epidemic in the United States and globally is a disease that is unconcerned with politics, social status, or sexual preference. It is a health crisis that illuminates troubling biases and discriminating practices in economic, political, social, and health care systems.[1]

As the epidemic enters its third decade, the rate of HIV infection for Americans has stabilized at roughly 40,000 annually. This is a reduced overall HIV infection rate compared with the previous decade. However, the reduced infection rate is not reflected in the HIV/AIDS rate for African Americans, Hispanics, and women.[2] By December 2002, approximately forty million adults in the world were living with AIDS.[3] By December 2002, the total number of individuals reported as dying from AIDS in the United States was 467,000, including 462,653 adults and 5,257 children.[4] Table CS2.1 shows a breakdown of the HIV/AIDS epidemic in the United States. From

Box CS2.1   AIDS in America

1981	First CDC warning about a rare disease, eventually known as acquired immunodeficiency syndrome (AIDS)
1984	Viral agent that causes AIDS is identified, later named human immunodeficiency virus (HIV)
1985	Rock Hudson announces he has AIDS
1986	First panel of the AIDS Memorial Quilt is created
1987	AIDS Coalition to unleash Power (ACT UP) is established; FDA approves AZT, the first antiviral agent for the treatment of AIDS; the first comprehensive needle exchange program is established in the United States
1990	Congress authorizes the Ryan White Comprehensive AIDS Resources Emergency (CARE) Act of 1990
1991	Earvin "Magic" Johnson announces he is HIV-positive; Kimberly Bergalis is reported to have been infected by her dentist
1992	Mary Fisher, who is HIV-positive, addresses the Republican National Convention; U.S. Open & Wimbledon winner Arthur Ashe announces he has AIDS
1994	U.S. Public Health Service recommends use of AZT by pregnant women; AIDS is the leading cause of death for all Americans ages 25–44
1996	Eleventh International Conference on AIDS in Vancouver highlights promising new treatment protease inhibitors; *Time* magazine names AIDS researcher David Ho "Man of the Year"
1998	African American leaders declare an AIDS "state of emergency" in the African American community; Congress establishes the Congressional Black Caucus/Minority HIV/AIDS Initiative
1999	CDC reports the death rate in the United States due to HIV/AIDS dropped by about half as a result of the combination drug, or "cocktail," therapy
2002	Top ten states with highest number of cumulative cases in order of highest to low are: New York, California, Florida, Texas, New Jersey, Pennsylvania, Illinois, Puerto Rico, Georgia, Maryland; top ten cities with highest number of cumulative cases in order of highest to low are: New York City, Los Angeles, San Francisco, Miami, Washington, DC, Chicago, Philadelphia, Houston, Newark, Atlanta

Continued

Table CS2.1 U.S. HIV/AIDS Epidemic Demographics for 2002

CUMULATIVE NUMBERS OF AIDS CASES	816,149
Adult and adolescent AIDS cases	807,075
Number of males	666,026
Number of females	141,048
Number of children under 13	9,074
Number of adults 20–49	712,133
Number of whites	343,889
Number of African Americans	313,180
Number of Hispanics	149,752
Number of Asian/Pacific Islanders	6,157
Number of Native Americans	2,537

Table CS2.1 it is clear that HIV/AIDS is far from being a white gay person's disease as it was considered to be in the early 1980s. It is a disease that does not discriminate on the basis of race, gender, class, geography, or sexuality.

The AIDS issue is a good example of how to use social construction theory to explain many of the inequities found in the distribution of policy benefits and burdens. Indeed, some authors contend that the nature and intensity of AIDS stigmas are shaped by the epidemic's social construction in different locales.[5] The theory of social construction helps us understand the development of policy design regarding AIDS. Herek and Capitanio argue on the basis of a longitudinal national survey that AIDS-related stigma has affected societal responses to the epidemic.[6] They conclude that AIDS stigma persists in the United States and that AIDS stigma is a strong symbolic issue—a stigma most strongly expressed against those individuals who contract HIV sexually.

AIDS and the Policy Agenda

AIDS is a policy issue that has been explored in multiple ways. Many of the aspects of the issue have not been adequately addressed. The search for a cure still continues, and the dollar amount for research increases daily. The primary direction of policy solutions has been in the caring for victims and preventive programs. However, policy has been slow to address the epidemic in certain ethnic and racial groupings. A brief overview of the epidemic shows that despite the substantial financial and health effects of AIDS, it took considerable time for the federal government and its scientific agencies to recognize the epidemic for what it was.[7]

It could be argued that it took even more time for the government to treat the epidemic seriously. Until the late 1980s the AIDS story was one of policy delay. The reason for the delay was quite simple—politics. Many authors have written of the failure of leadership at the national level to formulate and implement AIDS policy in the early days.[8] When AIDS first hit America, it affected most deeply groups outside of mainstream America. As it progressed, it had a disproportionate effect on groups such as gay men, drug users, African Americans, and Hispanics who have few political representatives and fewer policy advocates.[9] Consequently, little policy was enacted.

In the early 1980s AIDS became a litmus test by which candidates for offices were judged.[10] If an electoral candidate was not perceived by voters as tough on AIDS, then such a candidate was clearly in favor of a gay lifestyle, drug use, immorality, and decadence. In the first half of the 1980s Republican and Democratic candidates took such a hard line on AIDS that, coupled with sensational media coverage and a frenzy of misinformation and noninformation, no administration would act to formulate and adopt a coherent AIDS policy.

Change came by the late 1980s because conservatives found it more difficult to obtain the sort of political capital from AIDS that they had previously. Thanks to Rock Hudson, Ryan White, and Magic Johnson, it became acceptable to suggest that AIDS was a public health problem that needed to be addressed. Essentially, one could argue that the social construction of AIDS victims had changed.

AIDS policy also suffers from the problems of cost and access. Certain fiscal constraints limit the abilities of government to adopt new AIDS programs or expand existing ones. Added to this are the ever escalating costs of health care. The problem of access affects those groups within society who typically suffer from "rotten outcomes."[11] Such groups, because of their low degree of political power and lack of policy leverage, are at a disadvantage in terms of opportunities to influence the policy making process. As such it disadvantages them in the policy formulation stage and policy design fails to take into account their needs and sensitivities.

When looking at AIDS policies, it is useful to look at John Kingdon's agenda-building model.[12] The Kingdon model, as discussed in Chapter 7, states that there are structures of opportunity for issues to become part of the policy agenda. The policy agenda is gauged by the priority of issues in legislative debates or government spending programs. Kingdon refers to such structures as policy windows. These opportunities must be taken advantage of quickly, for windows open and close as changes occur in what he describes as the problem and political streams. Over time the sense of urgency and commitment to the feeling that AIDS is a problem has declined, thus affecting the primacy of the issue in the policy attention cycle. Nevertheless, there was and still is the general societal feeling that something has to be done about AIDS.

Why is AIDS less of a perceived problem now than previously? One could argue it is no longer seen to be at epidemic levels. Another factor could be that, just as in the early years, it continues to hit hardest in certain marginalized groups, such as gays and drug users. It also strikes heavily racial and ethnic minorities who are politically marginalized and who have little political resources at their disposal to influence policy making. One also cannot dismiss the impact of declining media coverage on the problem status of AIDS as an issue.[13] The media constructs a social reality for societal understanding of AIDS in America. Since the mid-1990s, media coverage has decreased dramatically. The message being picked up is that AIDS is no longer an epidemic due to declining AIDS related deaths.[14] The public at large no longer perceives AIDS to be a significant problem. This reflects Anthony Downs's issue-attention cycle thesis.[15] He suggests that the rise, peak, and decline of interest in a policy issue are subject to its importance or its crisis status. After the media heavily bombards the public with an issue, its attention will slowly decline. This seems to be the case today with AIDS in America.

The net effect is that although there might be policies that are, as Kingdon would argue, being floated, waiting in a sense for some-

thing to happen, the politics stream and its participants continue to affect formulation, adoption and implementation away from AIDS policy solutions. In the case of access to HIV/AIDS health care programs, such as the AIDS Drugs Assistance Program (ADAP), the relative policy weakness of racial or ethnic groups cannot be overlooked. Such groups are disadvantaged at every level of the policy cycle. They have low levels of political power which in turn affects the amount of leverage they can try to bring on the policy-making process. Not only are they marginalized in terms of having a stake in the type of policy being designed, but they will also be overlooked by implementors as key stakeholders. This essentially means they will not benefit from policy as they should.

One can safely assume that women and racial or ethnic AIDS victims are not being perceived as "deserving" of policy benefits. Consequently, it is inevitable that inequality in the distribution of policy benefits and burdens will occur and these groups will be disadvantaged even though they clearly should be the targets for benefits if the rate of incidence is taken into account.

The incidence and transmission data of the last eight years reinforces a myth that many want to believe, that most Americans need not fear exposure to AIDS. It is a myth, however, because HIV/AIDS is an equal opportunity disease. Data clearly show that no group is immune to the virus, although it does hit in certain groups more than others.[16] Actors who push the myth use the actual number of infections in certain groups compared to other groups. Rather, one should be specifically concerned with the growth rate of infection within groups. In short, to look at how many cases there are (i.e., the raw numbers of infected) through a particular type of transmission and ignore the relative increase or decrease in that particular type of transmission amongst specific groups is dangerous and can have serious policy ramifications. For example, current data demonstrate that the rate of growth of new infections is increasing faster among heterosexuals than gay people, even though more gay people are infected in total numbers.[17]

Apart from the obvious health care ramifications of an AIDS epidemic in groups such as

Continued

African Americans, Hispanics, and women, and particularly among low-income individuals within these communities, it is also troubling that these groups are disproportionately represented among those living without adequate access to health care services in general.[18] Such inequalities have undoubtedly contributed to the growth and spread of HIV/AIDS in these communities. Thus, not all groups in America are benefiting equally from treatment advances. Also, many ADAP programs, which assist low-income HIV/AIDS persons with drug therapy, have capped or restricted enrollment due to lack of resources and display enrollment disparities among such populations.

A further complicating factor is that many women and minorities are without private health care insurance. A 1994 AIDS Cost and Services Utilization Survey (ACSUS) conducted by the Department of Health and Human Services addresses the issue of HIV and health insurance coverage.[19] The data are clear that public coverage is not available to those who could benefit from treatment the most.[20] Additionally, the 1996 changes in federal and state welfare provision have led to increased cuts in resources devoted to treatment and prevention of HIV/AIDS.[21]

Why Inequities—The Social Construction Explanation

In the previous chapter on policy formulation the social construction of target populations theory was introduced to illustrate what some authors believe to be the relationship between pervasive stereotypes and policy making. The theory suggests that within society there are groups of individuals (target populations) endowed with positive or negative culturally constructed images. Such images influence policy makers with respect to the types of benefits and burdens they are willing to distribute to the groups through policy design.

Previous studies have demonstrated how people with AIDS were socially constructed in the first decade of the epidemic and show that such populations were publicly grouped and characterized in ways that had important implications for how they were regarded by the public and consequently by policy makers.[22] Using the Schneider and Ingram model

of social construction in the United States, gay men and women living with AIDS can initially be labeled a deviant target population. This social construction shifted by the late 1980s to gay people being a dependent group. We argue that, by the late 1990s and early 2000s, gay people are perceived as a contender population. Why this shift? It is our assertion that due to the mobilization of gay people by groups such as Act Up, AIDS Project Los Angeles, and the Gay Mens Health Care Crisis Group, gay men and women in general became more visible and overtly active in American political life. The 1980s was a period of political resurgence by many gays who perceived that "straight" America was content with their destruction by the AIDS virus.[23] They believed that they would not receive public assistance in this time of crisis unless they forced America and its policy makers to take action. In contrast, women with AIDS started off and continues to remain a dependent population, whereas African American and Hispanic people living with AIDS are socially constructed as deviants.

The Schneider and Ingram framework is by no means without weaknesses and critics. However, it does provide a framework that might explain the inequities in the distribution of policy benefits and burdens to people with AIDS. AIDS stigmas, although still strongest against gays with AIDS, have been offset by the increasingly visible political mobilization of gay men and women. This has increasingly positive effects on their social construction. Thus, gay people living with AIDS are now receiving more benefits than burdens. However, AIDS stigmas continue to be layered upon preexisting societal stigmas toward groups considered outside of mainstream America. The net result is that you cannot separate AIDS stigmas from cultural stigmas associated with drug use, a gay lifestyle, poverty, and racial minority status.

SUMMARY

The AIDS epidemic has led to some public policy changes: increased assistance for the purpose of medications through the AIDS Drug Assistance Program (ADAP), increased funding of research, and the Ryan White Act. However, at the start of the twenty-first century AIDS is still a problem the polity must deal with. Unfortunately, it currently appears that the urgency to do so may be lacking. There are some individuals who argue that what has occurred is the routinization of the epidemic, that AIDS is no longer in the crisis stage. It is true that with decreasing numbers and premature declarations that the epidemic is over, comes decreasing media and public attention. This undoubtedly will affect the position of the issue on the policy agenda. With this comes the likelihood that active consideration of the issue will become less likely. Thus, HIV/AIDS and its treatment will increasingly fail to receive serious attention from policy makers.[24] With the decrease in media attention comes the inevitable perception that HIV/AIDS is no longer a problem, and the window of opportunity for policy adoption may be closing. Thus, with the changing problem status of the disease, the strategic choices open to those who attempt to set the agenda on the issue will be limited. The net result will be the prevention of serious consideration of the issue by policy makers. This will be accompanied by a general decline in perceived support of the issue based upon the assumption that HIV/AIDS is no longer at epidemic levels and therefore no longer a threat to public health. Consequently, the issue will be excluded from the institutional agenda and perhaps even the systemic agenda. The systemic agenda covers all issues that are generally recognized to deserve public attention and are matters within the government's legitimate jurisdiction. The institutional agenda involves all issues explicitly up for active and serious consideration by the authoritative decision makers. The real problem is not that we might fail to get actual policy, but that AIDS will be removed from the list of topics that America as a society feels should always be of concern. Thus, those groups most in need will not have policy formulated for them or targeted at them; the marginalized will become more marginalized. This is already happening. The disease is becoming an epidemic within poor and nonwhite America and eventually will have serious ramifications on a series of societal levels.

What remains disturbing for poor and nonwhite Americans is that they continue to be overlooked in the AIDS policy-making arena and suffer in the distribution of policy benefits and burdens. This is partly due to their social construction which, in time, affects their degree of political power and ultimately their level of policy leverage. If African Americans with AIDS, Hispanics with AIDS, and women with AIDS wish to reap the full benefits of policy and lessen the burdens targeted at them, they must learn from their gay counterparts. Some may argue that the window of opportunity has passed. Whether this is true or not depends on whether mobilization by women with AIDS, African Americans with AIDS, and Hispanics with AIDS is still possible. It might be the case that it is too late and that they will never gain influence in the decision-making process. We leave you with a question: If this is the case, should we tell such groups to simply give up and accept their fate as sealed? Or should we encourage them to mobilize and take action for themselves as gay Americans have on this issue of AIDS?

ENDNOTES

1. S. Z. Theodoulou, *AIDS: The Politics and Policy of Disease* (Upper Saddle River, NJ: Prentice Hall, 1996), 2.

2. CDC Briefs, December 2002.

3. Ibid.

4. Approximately 388 people died from AIDS, whose age at death was unknown.

5. G. Herek and J. P. Capitanio, *AIDS Stigma and HIV-Related Beliefs in the United States: Results from a National Telephone Survey.* Paper presented at the 1998 World AIDS Conference in Geneva, Switzerland, June 28–July 3.

6. Ibid., 1.

7. S. Epstein, *Impure Science: AIDS, Activism and the Politics of Knowledge* (Berkeley: University of California Press, 1996), 4–7.

8. Theodoulou, *AIDS*; K. L. Kirp and R. Bayer, *AIDS in Industrialized Democracies* (New Brunswick, NJ: Rutgers University Press, 1992).

9. S. Epstein, *Impure Science,* 10.

Continued

10. Theodoulou, *AIDS,* 7.

11. L. Schorr, *Within Reach: Breaking the Cycle of Disadvantagement* (New York: Doubleday, 1988).

12. J. W. Kingdon, *Agendas, Alternatives, and Public Policy* (New York: HarperCollins, 1984).

13. Theodoulou, *AIDS,* 48–67.

14. Ibid., 64.

15. Anthony Downs, "Up and Down With Ecology—The Issue-Attention Cycle," *The Public Interest* 28(1972), 38–50.

16. National Institute of Allergy and Infectious Disease, May 2002, "Fact Sheet: Minorities and HIV Infection"; National Institute of Allergy and Infectious Disease, January 2002, "Fact Sheet: Women and HIV."

17. Ibid.

18. Agency for Health Care Policy and Research, December 1997 and December 2001, *"AHCPR News and Notes: Access to Care."*

19. Ibid.

20. Ibid.

21. S. Z. Theodoulou, *Policy and Politics in Six Nations* (Upper Saddle River, NJ: Prentice Hall, 2002), 166–173.

22. M. Donovan, "The Politics of Deservedness: The Ryan White Act and the Social Construction of People with AIDS," *Policy Studies Review* 12, no. 3/4 (Autumn–Winter 1993).

23. One only has to scan the gay press, such as the *Advocate,* in this time period to see such arguments.

24. R. W. Cobb and C. D. Elder, *Participation in American Politics: The Dynamics of Agenda Building* (Baltimore/London: Johns Hopkins Press, 1983); John. W. Kingdon, *Agendas, Alternatives, and Public Policies* (New York: Longman, 1995).

PART III

Policy Arenas

Exploring the Policy Process

13

Environmental Policy

Defining and Identifying a Problem

In all industrialized countries since the early 1980s environmental issues have become increasingly prominent on policy agendas.[1] The political importance of such issues for policy makers is reflected by the number of political parties and political leaders that represent themselves as "green." The dimensions as well as the sheer number of environmental problems are vast. The dimensions include but are not limited to global warming, global destruction of the ozone layer, global deforestation, and global overpopulation. Among the numerous issues are air, water, ground, and noise pollution; radioactivity; toxic waste; pesticides; and endangered species. As a result, the possible policy solutions that governments may formulate and implement are also numerous. Thus, governments may define their environmental problems in various ways. This partly explains why in the last decade substantial environmental gains have been achieved in most industrialized countries, but the process of environmental protection has been costly, frustrating, and fraught with difficulties.

Due to nations defining environmental problems differently, the environmental agenda differs from nation to nation. However, all nations are interested in developing environmental policy for the long term. All nations also have to formulate policy that deals with specific issues relevant to their own environment. Increasingly, many nations are implementing environmental policy on the basis of sustainable development. Sustainable development promotes social and economic progress that is consistent with environmental protection and technological growth.

There is no commonly agreed definition of *sustainable development*. The most commonly cited definition is "development that meets the needs of the present without compromising the ability of future generations to meet their own needs; it should also meet the needs of the poor in the world, and economies should take into consideration the impact of human activity on the surrounding environment."[2] Sustainable development, then, is development that encourages long-term production and consumption patterns that do not degrade the human or natural environment.

What then is environmental policy? It is a governmental action taken to solve the problem of society's relationship to its physical environment, which includes elements of air, water, and soil. Environmental problems refer to the result of human and societal actions that are perceived as undesirable and harmful to the physical environment and citizens' physical well-being.

CONTEMPORARY ENVIRONMENTAL POLICY IN THE UNITED STATES

Concern with the environment in the United States has been a matter of public concern since the late 1800s and the start of regional urbanization. Conservation policy was first introduced by President Theodore Roosevelt at the start of the twentieth century. This laid the foundation for federal government coordination of policy activity concerning the environment in the 1930s. The Franklin Roosevelt administration coordinated environmental activity and established new federal agencies to oversee specific resources.[3] In spite of such agencies, until the mid-1960s environmental policy making was fragmented and characterized by limited numbers of actors and incremen-

tal bargaining and compromises. Policy formulation was the prerogative of a few members of Congress, and there was no consistent presidential commitment.

In 1962, Rachel Carson published her groundbreaking text on the environment, *Silent Spring*. This work warned Americans of the health dangers posed by DDT and other pesticides. It is from this point that many Americans' environmental awareness surfaced. *Silent Spring* alerted the public to the environmental damage caused by industrialization. The book was a key catalyst in identifying environmental degradation as a problem for American policy makers to deal with. The first real piece of legislation enacted in the environmental policy arena was the 1963 Clean Air Act. Although President Kennedy and the Democrat-controlled Congress supported and passed the act, it was strongly opposed by corporate lobbies. It is generally considered to be a weak piece of legislation. The enforcement procedure was too complicated in that it required state action to initiate lawsuits against polluters. The 1960s witnessed further environmental policy enactment. Examples of legislation protecting the environment are the 1965 Water Quality Act, the 1966 Endangered Species Conservation Act, and the 1967 Air Quality Act. These acts established standards and made federal grants available to states that wished to comply.

It is with the adoption in 1969 and enactment in 1970 of the National Environmental Policy Act (NEPA) that a national environmental policy was launched. This legislation provides the foundation for future policy action in dealing with the environment. Among the act's main provisions is the requirement that all major federal construction must complete an Environmental Impact Statement (EIS). An EIS requires demonstration that a government project does not significantly harm the environment. If the EIS shows to the contrary, and if damage was done, procedures and mechanisms are in place to correct that damage.

The reasons for the increase in environmental policy activity in the mid- and late-1960s are the growth of environmental interest groups, renewed congressional interest, and the spotlight on episodes such as offshore oil spills in California. Environmental problem identification was fueled by the sociopolitical changes of the 1960s. For example, changes brought about by the civil rights movement's mobilization demonstrated to many individuals that those with little power can change policy through grassroots activity. The net result was that the federal government began to redefine the way it looked at the environmental problem; from the 1970s on, the problem was no longer defined in piecemeal fashion. Rather, it was felt that environmental degradation was a national problem, thus there should be federal coordination of policy. In 1970 the Environmental Protection Agency (EPA) was created by President Richard Nixon. The EPA was given the job of coordinating and enforcing all environmental laws. Prior to its establishment, several agencies across several federal departments were responsible for monitoring and regulating different aspects of the environment.

As a result of the EPA's creation, a series of laws were adopted in the early 1970s. For example, the 1970 Clean Air Act, the 1972 Federal Environmental Pesticide Control Act, the 1972 Federal Water Pollutants Control Act Amendments, the 1976 Resource Conservation and Recovery Act, and the Toxic Substances Control Act of 1976. The magnitude of this legislation is impressive, and each act provided in some way federal support of environmental protection. For example, the Clean Air Act set national standards for ambient air quality through National Ambient Air Quality Standards (NAAQS). All states had to develop plans, be approved by the EPA, and meet NAAQS requirements. In the situation where a state

plan did not meet federal requirements, the EPA was authorized to prepare and enforce a plan for that state. Additionally, the EPA was mandated to set exhaust emission standards for the auto industry and develop plans for the introduction of catalytic converters and fuels with reduced lead levels. The 1972 Water Pollution Control Act set targets to be achieved by 1985 for the amount of discharged pollutants in navigable waters. It also provided $23 billion in grants for the construction of water treatment plants and installation of the best available technologies by local governments by the year 1983. Under the 1976 Resource Conservation and Recovery Act, the regulation of hazardous waste storage was mandated, and the EPA was given authority to establish hazardous waste disposal standards. Although many of these acts were groundbreaking, they were weakened by the requirement that state and local government compliance had to be sought by the EPA. The EPA simply did not have the resources, including the workforce, to enforce compliance.

As a result of the 1970s frenzy of environmental legislation activity, a strong industrial and business coalition grew opposing proenvironmentalism. Many critics argued that environmental protection was helping to increase costs and inflation and thus was responsible for slowing economic growth. It was argued that the burden on business was too large; compliance with strict environmental regulations increased costs and thereby damaged profits. This influenced later administrations, led by strong presidential involvement in policy formulation, in defining and dealing with environmental problems.

During Jimmy Carter's tenure in the White House, superficial legislation was adopted in 1980 that set aside approximately $1.6 billion in emergency funds to deal with environmental spills or dumping. In addition to defraying corporate costs, the legislation also allowed the EPA to shift its emphasis from conventional pollutants and increased the agency's budget by 25 percent. By 1980 and Ronald Reagan's election to the White House, it was clear that business complaints about excessive environmentalism had been heard. Reagan was strongly opposed to additional legislation regulating the environment. He promoted what he felt was "reasonable" environmentalism and called for bureaucrats to stop exceeding their authority in the environmental sector. In essence, Reagan was calling for a new definition of the United States' environmental problem. He felt that previous policy had led to too much government, too much regulation, and was antibusiness and antigrowth. He argued that business was responsible environmentally and should stop being treated as if it was not. Businesses should be encouraged to voluntarily protect the environment and not interfere with their ability to be competitive. Reagan's policy agenda focused on reducing government regulation and reversing the federal government's role in environmental protection. Consequently, the Reagan years saw reduced budgets for environmental policy implementation, repeal of environmental legislation, and the appointment of policy makers that were antienvironment.[4] This led to hundreds of dismissals of EPA staff including the firing of the entire staff of the President's Council on Environmental Quality.

When identifying environmental problems the Reagan administration took into account cost, containment, and introduced cost–benefit analysis in environmental policy design. Any new EPA regulation had to submit to a cost–benefit analysis. Publically, the government claimed that it was attempting to ensure that any money spent on proposed regulation would result in increased benefits rather than increased costs to taxpayers. Most new environmental regulation failed the cost–benefit test because a dollar amount could not easily be assigned to the benefits of environmental esthetics or increased life span for endangered species or humans. Reagan achieved his objective of promoting industrial growth through reduced regulation of the environment.

Reagan's successor George Bush was faced with increased public support in favor of stronger environmental protection. This support was mobilized by militant environmental interest groups. In the face of such environmental consciousness, George Bush made environmental policy a key issue in his 1988 campaign for the presidency, announcing that he wanted to be known as the "environmental president." Although it can hardly be argued that Bush was characterized as an activist environmental president, he did deliver somewhat on his promise. His administration enacted two major pieces of legislation: the 1990 Clean Air Act Amendments and the 1992 Energy Policy Act. Both were much closer to congressional desires than Bush's own wishes. They were much stricter and imposed more costly regulations on industry. The combined legislation mandates that air quality throughout the United States meet certain standards through reduction of emissions from industrial processes and cars, including pollutants that cause acid rain. They also introduced standards for phasing out chemicals that attack the ozone layer. In the latter years of his administration, Bush approved an increase in the EPA's budget and supported areas of America's coastline being declared off-limits for oil exploration. However, he refused to support the 1992 Rio Earth Summit environmental treaty, until its provisions aimed at slowing global warming were modified and weakened. Additionally, he refused to sign a treaty protecting endangered species. Both actions created much opposition from environmental groups.

In 1992, Bush sought reelection against Dem-ocrats he labeled "environmental crazies." Bill Clinton and his vice presidential candidate Al Gore perceived there was general dissatisfaction with Bush on the environment. They criticized the president for not being committed to controlling environmental damage and for allocating minimal funds to environmental cleanup and protection—thus, challenging Bush's identification of the environmental problem. Clinton and Gore promised to be active environmentally and vowed to reverse the record on environmental protection. Gore promised that being tough on environmental protection did not mean being tough on business.[5]

The Clinton–Gore years attempted to balance the demands of economic growth while protecting the environment from increased damage. Some would argue that this meant being too generous to business at the cost of not producing tougher environmental legislation.[6] The focus of Clinton's environmental policy was on provision of more generous funding of environmental mandates. There were also attempts to make the system less bureaucratically rigid. Additionally, by the end of Clinton's first year in office, major changes were made in the leadership of all the main environmental agencies involved in formulating and implementing policy. Although a number of measures were implemented toughening standards, for the most part, Clinton's environmental policy agenda was frustrated by a Republican-controlled Congress determined to reduce federal government regulation. The existence of a divided government from 1994 to 2000 proved to be a formidable obstacle to stricter environmental policy. For example, congressional Republican opposition to discussion of global warming issues meant executive–legislative gridlock on the issue and thus blocked Clinton's attempts to address the issue.

In Clinton's second term in office the administration pushed the idea of cost-effective environmental reform. In 1997 the Clinton administration acted as a signatory to the Kyoto Protocol, a global environmental agreement on global warming.[7] However, the Senate has yet to ratify it. The Kyoto accord requires industrial countries to cut back greenhouse gas emissions to 1990 levels. Signing the Kyoto Protocol placed the reduction of CO_2 emissions squarely on the institutional agenda. At this time, the problem of CO_2 emissions required a policy remedy. This is evident by data that shows in 1995, 85 percent of net greenhouse gas emissions in the United States was due to CO_2 emissions.

Bill Clinton's true success in the environmental policy sector was to shift the focus of environmental initiation from Congress to the White House, thus ensuring the president took control of problem definition. This was symbolized by his replacing the Council on Environmental Quality with the White House Office on Environmental Policy and by the support his cabinet showed for the EPA.

It is still too early to analyze the environmental policy of the first president of the twenty-first century; however, it appears the stage is set for an assault on much of the Clinton environmental record. Although President George W. Bush campaigned as "environmentally friendly," his first ninety days in office generated much concern from environmental groups. During the presidential campaign, Bush accused Al Gore and the rest of the Clinton administration of not doing enough to control CO_2 emissions. He went on to infer that he would support mandatory reductions similar to those that had been introduced in his home state of Texas. However, in March 2001 he publically reversed his pledge to limit CO_2 emissions by rejecting proposed limits, justifying his turnaround on the issue by arguing such limits could lead to major increases in energy prices. This is a very clear reversal by Bush. Only a month earlier his EPA director Christine Todd Whitman at the G-8 Environment Summit in Trieste, Italy, publicly outlined a stance that the Bush administration would be a dependable ally in the war against the greenhouse effect. Whitman also publicly backed emissions control as central to Bush's proposals on climate change. Backed by strong lobbying from coal and utility companies, Vice President Dick Cheney persuaded Bush to contradict Whitman, whose job as EPA director, in theory, has the greatest influence in determining the nation's environmental policy. In doing so he also managed to get Bush to contradict the president's own previously defined position in favor of emissions control. The reversal has not only upset environmental groups in the United States but also has led to criticism internationally. European Union leaders issued a statement expressing concern about the change of heart and fears for the future of the global agreement made in Kyoto, Japan, in 1997. Some articulated they would go ahead with the Kyoto accord without the participation of the United States.

The problem of CO_2 emissions has not been reduced, but what has increased is American industry's opposition to limiting CO_2 emissions. Such opposition argues industry will be hurt by more stringent emission standards and resulting increased transportation costs. In short, industry argues that its international competitiveness will be affected and ultimately will result in lost jobs. The best policy would be to use voluntary standards, but most supporters of environmental control argue this will achieve little. Conservatives and energy industry supporters argue that the Kyoto Protocol imposes costly environmental controls on domestic businesses while giving developing countries an unfair competitive advantage by easing restrictions facing them. This is especially alarming because they believe the idea of global warming is based on "fuzzy" science and in truth might be an environmental problem that does not exist. In the early summer of 2001, President Bush, speaking to reporters before he departed for a European state visit, declared the Kyoto global warming agreement "fatally flawed." He announced that more scientific research must be done before the world can devise a workable strategy for dealing with climate change. Bush went on to state the Kyoto agreement is based on inconclusive scientific evidence and would require unattainable reductions in greenhouse gas emissions.

Soon after the CO_2 emissions reversal, President Bush seemed to make it clear that his first term in office would be a strategic assault on the environment after he announced plans to rescind a Clinton-era regulation limiting the amount of arsenic allowed in drinking water. President Clinton reduced the standard, set in 1942, allowing a maximum of fifty parts arsenic per billion to ten parts per billion. He was responding to EPA recommendations calling for a maximum of five parts per billion. The Bush administration is returning the standard to the pre-Clinton maximum.

ENVIRONMENTAL PROBLEM DEFINITION AND IDENTIFICATION

The way governments define the environmental problem is complicated by the fact that, unlike other policy areas such as health or welfare, environmental policy does not provide specific benefits or services to citizens. Regulation of behavior is particularly salient in the environmental policy sector. Environmental regulation of behavior occurs without producing immediate tangible services and benefits. Common to most industrialized nations' environmental problem definition is the acquiescence that environmental problems are the result of many activities of modern industrial society—activities that are vital to growth and economic well-being. In many ways, environmental policy making curbs activities that benefit society and therefore is a postmaterialist political concern.[8]

Problem identification in the environmental policy sector is complicated by citizens' definition of their rights and freedoms with respect to the environment. Such rights will be reflected in widely held social values.

For example, in the United States, social values such as the right to own and drive an automobile and the importance of the open road will ultimately influence the government's definition of the environmental problem. This, in turn, will affect the type of policy solution that is formulated and implemented. In the long run it will eventually hinder the adoption of more restrictive environmental policies. Some authors argue that if something is viewed as right and proper, then it is rarely challenged when it comes to making decisions about environmental policies.[9] Environmental problem definition in the United States often takes into account public opinion and priorities. Often policy adoption is easier to pursue if policy makers define the environmental problem in the same way as the American public.[10]

Environmental problem identification may also be affected by economic factors. Economic pressures arising from globalization and increased international competitiveness have affected how American policy makers perceive a specific environmental problem in any given context of time. For example, how willing the government is to identify air pollution as a result of poor emissions standards will influence its concern with not damaging the nation's international competitiveness. The way the government defines an environmental problem will influence the range and type of possible policy solutions developed to meet the problem. It will not create policy solutions that will render domestic industry less competitive and less profitable in the global marketplace. Cost considerations undoubtedly influence the environmental problem identification process in the United States. Policy makers will be reluctant to encourage cost-prohibitive policy solutions. The economic costs of achieving carbon dioxide (CO_2) emission targets have clearly determined how the U.S. government has defined the need for clean air.

Problem identification in the American environmental policy sector is further complicated by the absence of definitive evidence supporting many environmentally related issues. For example, in the last few years many individuals and groups in the United States have argued that the problem of global warming has been overstated.

Central to defining and identifying a problem is policy makers clearly identifying policy goals. In the United States in the last two decades, environmental policy goals can be identified as security, efficiency, and cost effectiveness. How different administrations pursue these goals is affected by their ideological beliefs surrounding the role and nature of government intervention in society. In the following section we focus on a discussion of contemporary American environmental policy dynamics to see how these goals have been advanced by different administrations. The existing research on environmental policy is largely due to case studies; thus, there is a general absence of theorizing. Most work on environmental policy is highly descriptive, as is this discussion.

THE POLICY PROCESS AND ENVIRONMENTAL POLICY MAKING

Environmental policy formulation and implementation is complex in the United States because it occurs at multiple points in the government system. A variety of executive branch offices, departments, and agencies, including the EPA, are responsible for the development of environmental policies. The creation of the EPA in 1970 in effect ensured the federal government the primary responsibility for environmental protection policy. Previously Congress was the major institution responsible for formulating environmental policy. Kraft suggests that decreased congressional responsibility is understandable given congressional "grid lock" and the general absence of progressive sentiments on Capital Hill.[11] Switzer argues that Congress simply failed to lead the environmental agenda-setting process and thus lost the initiative in formulating policy.[12] Problem definition was done at the executive level. Among the reasons for such failure, according to Switzer, are the fragmented committee system, congressional members being cross pressured from probusiness and proenvironment lobbies, insufficient resources such as time and expertise, and finally, a concern with the "local" rather than the "national."

On occasion, Congress, under its constitutional jurisdiction to regulate interstate commerce and control activities on federal lands, may also adopt specific, detailed (rather than framework) environmental policies. These laws will then be implemented, depending on their specific provisions, by either the executive branch or the states. Additionally, implementation and enforcement of environmental legislation may be pursued through criminal and civil actions pursued in the courts. Indeed, federal environmental management in the United States is characterized by strong compliance and enforcement.

Since the early 1980s some states have increasingly become environmental policy initiators and formulators and taken away much of the federal government's traditional responsibility in environmental regulation.[13] The response of particular state governments to environmental issues is dictated by factors such as severity of environmental damage, urbanization levels, the fiscal resource base, who controls the state legislature, and the prevalence of professional legislators and administrators.[14] Additionally, the level of influence of an individual state's environmental interest groups and strength of industry will affect state government responses. In those states

where formulation and implementation have become more of a state government responsibility, state bureaucratic structures have been created to develop and implement environmental policies. In such situations state policies under strict federal oversight can extend, or possibly supersede, federal mandates. In other states, laws are in place that prevent the toughening of federal standards. However, in spite of some states' increased assertiveness in the area of environmental policy implementation and enforcement, there exists in the United States a general policy of shared authority and cooperative arrangements between federal and state governments, often with state governments having to comply with federal regulations in the environmental policy sector.

Generally, local governments play a minor role in implementing current regulations. The exception would be in areas where the environmental movement is visibly strong, such as the Western states.[15] In such areas local policy makers are often pressured into implementing stricter rules than required by the state or federal protection laws.[16] In response to growing state assertiveness in recent years, some authors predict that in the coming years it would be more correct to argue that states and localities act autonomously in the area of environmental protection.[17]

ENVIRONMENTAL POLICY INSTRUMENTS

Various instruments have been used by American policy makers in their pursuit of environmental management. Environmental policy in the United States primarily takes the form of direct regulations that set strict standards. Stiff penalties and noncompliance fees have been handed down to those who do not comply with standards and regulations. Economic instruments and voluntary agreements are also commonplace to control environmental degradation, though to a much lesser degree than direct regulations.

American policy makers have increasingly addressed environmental problems through the use of economic incentives that stress market mechanisms—for example, environment-specific subsidies, tradable discharge permits, or tax breaks for corporations that implement pollution controls. There are limitations to the use of such incentives, however. First, the effectiveness of economic incentives depends on both consumers and polluters accepting shared responsibility and accurately informing each other about what they are doing. Second, it is difficult to administer and monitor such incentives. Third, it is not easy to assess whether goals and targets have been reached.

The government and industry have entered into voluntary agreements to reduce environmental degradation and pollution levels. These agreements are normally used in conjunction with other policy instruments. Voluntary agreements either may be directly negotiated by government and industry, or industry may independently develop programs that demonstrate its concern with the environment it operates in. When voluntary agreements are entered into, they are not legally binding. Government and industry mutually agree to set goals, targets, and target dates. The problem with such agreements is they are difficult to monitor and enforce. Additionally, there are limitations with how sanctions imposed for a noncompliance are carried out.

Like other industrialized nations dealing with the globalization of many environmental problems, the United States has used international environmental agreements as an environmental policy instrument. In the 1980s and 1990s the United States was a strong advocate of and participant in international environmental policy making. Indeed, the United States was in the forefront of industrialized nations promoting the development, implementation, and encouragement of global environmental agreements, particularly with respect to air quality. For example, the United States is party to both regional and international agreements to reduce air-contaminant emission levels. One of the earliest of these agreements was the 1987 Montreal Protocol on Substances That Deplete the Ozone Layer. The United States also joined the 1992 United Nations Framework Convention on Climate Change (FCCC) and the Convention on Biological Diversity, also drafted in 1992. Agreements also exist between the United States and Mexico, such as the 1992 Integrated Border Environmental Plan and the 1996 Border XXI Program. The 1997 Kyoto Protocol on global warming is one of the more controversial international agreements that the United States has considered, which may account for the Senate's lack of ratification.

SUMMARY

One of the items at the forefront of the American policy agenda in recent years is the environment. The importance of the issue is clearly seen in public opinion polls, which regularly demonstrate the public's concern over environmental degradation and the need for government to be more responsive to environmental protection.[18] Constant media exposure of urgent environmental problems intensifies these societal feelings. However, American policy makers and the American public are faced with a dilemma: Environmental protection requires more government intervention and interference in citizens' daily lives. How the dilemma plays out will determine how American policy makers identify and eventually formulate and implement problems in the environmental policy area.

Due to the necessity of consensus building in the American policy process, American environmental policy making has been predominantly incremental and adaptive. Environmental policy development was pioneered through command-and-control measures and later through voluntary and market-based approaches. As one of the most active nations in developing and complying with global environmental agreements, the United States can be characterized as a nation with extensive experience in the environmental policy sector. Although policies are not always successful, compared to many other nations, the United States has a strong record of commitment. This record is partly due to the creation of effective institutions responsible for implementing environmental policies. What allows one aspect of environmental regulation to be successful and another to fail is not apparent. However, future success is more likely to be achieved by policies that are based in a sound socioeconomic and ecological context. The ramifications of such policies should be understood over time, as should interactions across geographical areas, and the interests of the various stakeholders, from community to business.

The ongoing struggle between environmental reform and the realities of conducting business in the United States will continue to raise policy-making challenges. The tone set by President George W. Bush appears to be one that will continue dealing with the environment through policy design that takes into account cost effectiveness, voluntary action, and consensus building. Such policies will call for flexibility and more public–private partnerships. Public–private partnerships are crucial to the American perception of sustainable development. It seems more than likely that sustainable development principally will be responsible for creating objectives, targets, and strategies for environmental policy.

The costs of environmental protection and its role in government budget deficits will continue to emphasize government's need to be accountable through cost-effective measures. The need for new types of environmental policy will continue and policies that were passed in the first years of the twenty-first century will more than likely be the path taken over the next decade. There may be more tax incentives to phase out environmentally damaging activities, such as ozone deflecting substances; business may more than likely be asked to publicly articulate its activities that harm the environment; and there will be increased emphasis on reporting performance, and subsidization to various sectors such as agriculture to create incentives to comply with environmental consciousness.

Several formidable obstacles to stricter environmental regulation exist. First, cultural values ensure that many Americans will continue to strongly oppose policies that increase their cost of living. Next, public opinion in the United States is weakly mobilized around the issue of global warming. Thus, there is limited support for stronger immediate action. Third, the adoption of economic instruments to reduce environmental degradation has been strongly fought by industry and consumer advocacy groups. The opposition argues that the costs of such regulation are too high and the results would be damaging to U.S. economic competitiveness. It is likely such opposition will continue. Fourth, the lack of a strong formal environmental party in the United States reduces the likelihood that Congress will address environmental issues. Finally, although American environmental policy making is fragmented due to political realities, such as the two-party system, these same realities allow for flexibility and responsiveness to market considerations.

DISCUSSION QUESTIONS

1. Should environmental concerns be nonpolitical and above party politics and ideological concerns?

2. What should be the true goals of environmental policy?

3. How would you define the United States' environmental problem?

SUGGESTED READINGS

Berry, R. J. *Environmental Dilemmas.* New York: Chapman & Hill, 1993.

Burnes, P. M., and I. G. Barnes. *Environmental Policy in the European Union.* Cheltenham, England: Edward Elgar, 1999.

Caldwell, L., and R. Bartlett. *Environmental Policy: Transnational Issues and National Trends.* Westport, CT: Quorum Books, 1997.

Collier, U., and R. Lofstedt. *Cases in Climate Change Policy.* London: Earthscan, 1997.

Jameson, A., R. Eyerman, and J. Craner. *The Making of the New Environmental Consciousness.* Edinburgh, Scotland: Edinburgh University Press, 1990.

John, D. "Environmental Policy and Policy Reforms." *International Political Science Association Proceedings,* Seoul, South Korea, August 17–21, 1997.

Rosenbaum, W. A. *Environmental Politics and Policy,* 4th ed. Washington, DC: CQ Press, 1998.

Scheberle, D. *Federalism and Environmental Policy: Trust and the Politics of Implementation.* Washington, DC: Georgetown University Press, 1997.

Tsuru, S. *The Political Economy of the Environment.* London: Athlone Press, 1999.

Vig, N. J., and M. E Kraft, eds. *Environmental Policy: New Directions for the Twenty-first Century.* Washington, DC: CQ Press, 2000.

ENDNOTES

1. A. Heidenheimer, H. Heclo, and C. Adams, *Comparative Public Policy* (New York: St. Martin's Press, 1990), 308.

2. V. Bhaskar and A. Glyn, *The North, The South and the Environment: Ecological Constraints and the Global Economy* (Tokyo: United Nations University Press, 1995), chap 2.

3. For example, the 1933 Tennessee Valley Authority, the 1937 Social Conservative Service, and the Civilian Conservation Corps.

4. Examples include Gorsuch Burford as the head of the EPA and James Watt as Secretary of the Interior. Bolter was openly hostile to a strong federal government role in the environment.

5. A. Gore, *Earth in the Balance: Ecology and the Human Spirit* (Boston: Houghton Mifflin, 1992).

6. S. Tsuru, *The Political Economy of the Environment* (London: Athlone Press, 1999).

7. See the *Kyoto Protocol to the United Nations Framework Convention on Climate Change,* available at http://www.unfccc.de/resource/docs/convkp/kpeng. html.

8. H. McCormick, *The Global Environmental Movement* (London: Bellhaven Press, 1989).

9. J. Switzer, *Environmental Politics: Domestic and Global* (New York: St. Martin's Press, 1974), 40–65.

10. E. Laverty, "Legacy of the 1980s in State Environmental Administration," in M. S. Hamilton, ed., *Regulatory Federalism, National Resources, and Environmental Management* (Washington, DC: American Society for Public Administration, 1990).

11. M. Kraft, "Environmental Gridlock: Secondary for Consensus in Congress," in N. S. Vig and M. E. Kraft, eds., *Environmental Policy in the 1990s* (Washington, DC: CQ Press, 1990).

12. Switzer, *Environmental Politics.* 40–65.

13. J. P. Hays "The New Environmental West," *Journal of Policy History* 3, no. 3 (1991): 223–248; B. G. Rabe, "Power on the States: The Promise and Pitfalls of Decentralization" in N. J. Vig and M. E. Kraft (eds.), *Environmental Policy: New Directions for the Twenty-first Century,* (Washington D.C.: CQ Press, 1999), 32–54.

14. Vig and Kraft, *Environmental Policy,* 1–31.

15. Laverty, "Legacy of the 1980s," 110–119.

16. Hays, "Environmental West," 223–248.

17. Ibid., 223–268.

18. D. Rapp, "Special Report," *Congressional Quarterly Weekly Report,* January 20, 1990.

14

Education Policy

Setting and Building an Agenda

All industrialized nations in the twenty-first century have witnessed a greatly expanded role for the state in the provision of education. Since 1945, education expenditures have represented the fastest growing area of public spending.[1] A comparison of public expenditures on education as a percentage of gross domestic product (GDP) in nations of the Organization for Economic Cooperation and Development (OECD) shows national investment in education varies (see Table 14.1). In general, studies show that higher income nations spend more public funds per student than lower income nations.[2] These studies rank the United States at the upper level of public per-pupil expenditures. The prominence of education on the national political agenda is a result of its budgetary requirements and the essential function it performs in society. In the provision of public education there is a mix of both formal institutional activity and informal activity. State activity is integrated with family, market, and community involvement. The mix and the level of integration vary greatly from nation to nation.

The difficulty in analyzing public programs of education is that, although there is general theoretical support for it, there is usually intense controversy over what interests and values should be represented in policy design. On one hand, some individuals argue that public education should promote social mobility and encourage greater equality in society.[3] Others state that public education should contribute to the well-being of the economy.[4] An efficiently run economy requires an educated workforce; the more educated an individual is, the more he or she can contribute to society. Education also provides individuals with skills that allow them

Table 14.1 Public Direct Expenditures on Education as a Percentage of Gross Domestic Product

Selected Nations 1985–2000			
Nation	1985	1990	2000
Australia	5.4	4.3	4.8
Canada	6.1	5.4	5.7
France	5.0	5.1	6.0
Germany	4.6	4.5	4.6
Greece	3.4	3.7	3.5
Ireland	5.6	4.7	4.5
Italy	4.7	5.8	4.9
Japan	3.7	3.6	3.5
Mexico	3.0	3.2	4.2
Norway	5.1	6.2	7.7
Russia	3.2	3.4	3.4
Spain	3.6	4.2	4.5
Sweden	5.2	5.3	6.0
Switzerland	4.9	5.0	5.5
Turkey	3.1	3.2	3.0
U.K.	4.9	4.3	4.9
U.S.	4.7	5.3	5.1

SOURCE: Adapted from the National Center for Education Statistics, "International Comparisons of Education," *Digest of Education Statistics, 2001* (Washington, DC: National Center for Education Statistics, Institute of Education Sciences, U.S. Department of Education, 2001).

to be financially autonomous from the state. The more educated the workforce, the more competitive a nation will be in the international marketplace.

The state's role in the provision of education in industrialized nations is to be a regulator, a funder or purchaser, and a provider or planner. Data suggest that in most nations the private sector is comparatively small.[5] The most common state role is that of provider or planner. However, nations do vary in the level of their educational systems' administrative centralization; that is, control of the public education system varies from nation to nation. Other differences also exist. For example, there are differences as to when compulsory education starts and finishes, although all education systems are divided along age lines.

Also, different forms of educational specialization are available from nation to nation. Finally, some systems stratify by age and ability.[6]

What is remarkably similar in the vast majority of nations today is the demand for national education reform. Behind such demands is the belief by both politicians and corporate leaders that the way to solve society's most pressing problems is through school reform. Essentially, if obstacles to economic development and progress, individual success, social harmony, and international competitiveness are to be removed, then there must be changes in how schools educate children. The demand for reform in the United States and many European nations is fueled by the belief that their respective educational systems have produced workers who cannot solve problems or compete on a global level.

The call for educational reform requires policy makers to deal with several policy problems. First, who should have access to schooling? Integral to this question are beliefs on equality of opportunity in society. Many individuals believe education can compensate for existing social and economic inequalities—thus, the call for universal access to education at all levels. The more restricted the access the more likely existing social or economic divisions will be perpetuated. Other individuals argue that because people differ greatly in their capabilities and aptitudes, not everyone is equally capable of benefiting from an education. To equalize education access is to waste resources. Achievement, especially at the secondary and university levels, should be the basis of access.

The second policy problem revolves around the substance of education being provided and the question of whether everyone should receive the same type of education. In essence, it's a debate over liberal or vocational education. A liberal education would provide students with a generally well rounded intellectual background in many fields of study. Such an education is directed at reducing social and economic inequalities. A vocational education provides students with job-related skills; it is essentially technical training and represents a market orientation that emphasizes education to promote global competitiveness. This leads to debates over who should get what type, and whether there should be national standards and national testing or assessment programs.

A third policy problem revolves around control of the education system. Should it be centralized or decentralized? As stated earlier, this is a major difference among nations. The debate essentially revolves around the question of whether the national government should control educational decision-making authority or delegate responsibility for education to the local levels. We will see that the United States, like other federal systems, tends to be more decentralized, delegating responsibility for education to the local level. Related to the question of control over education is the issue of who pays for schooling. Should education be publicly or privately funded? This question inevitably leads to questions surrounding parental control and choice relative to local schools.

CONTEMPORARY EDUCATION POLICY IN THE UNITED STATES

Education is the only basic provision of an advanced welfare state that is offered as a right of American citizenship. However, it should be noted the federal government has never played a central role in public education. This clearly distinguishes the United States from many other industrialized nations where the national government is the central actor in the education policy sector. Over the years, the federal government has increasingly abdicated responsibility, ensuring public provision of education is clearly a

state and local responsibility. The consequence has been disparity in the level and quality of education received by citizens from state to state. Public provision of education in the United States is highly decentralized and overseen by 50 different state education boards and at least 15,000 local school boards.[7] Any attempt to implement a coordinated provision of public education in such a situation appears fruitless to many.

The United States has had publicly financed education since the 1830s. It came about because of a reform movement that advocated "common school," and provided schooling at the elementary level. The goal of providing a basic elementary education was to prepare children to be good citizens.[8] Integral to being a good citizen was a decent standard of living and the ability to compete equally with others: Thus education was seen as a route to social equilibrium. By the 1860s, more than 50 percent of children were enrolled in elementary schools financed by property taxes levied by local authorities who were delegated responsibility for public provision of education by state governments. With the 1874 Supreme Court decision validating the use of taxes for public high schools, the 1880s saw expansion of high school education. Prior to 1874, a high school education was available only to the elite class through the private sector. With expansion came a need for more teachers.

By the start of the twentieth century a mass-based public secondary education system was in place due to the influx of large numbers of immigrants and the needs of a rapidly expanding industrializing economy. A debate over curriculum, in particular, academic or vocational training, accompanied such developments. In 1918, Congress attempted to resolve the debate and meet industry's demands by providing federal funding for vocational education programs as stipulated by the principles laid out in a report by the National Commission on the

Reorganization of Secondary Education.[9] Basically, the report advocated educating the masses to be productive members of the labor force. This is a utilitarian approach to education. Subsequently, as public secondary education developed, it became a two-track system: one track for a small elite prepared to enter into higher education and the professional class, and the other track for the masses who would be laborers performing menial but vital work in a variety of sectors of the economy.

During the Great Depression, from 1929 to 1941, it became apparent that public education was underperforming. The absence of jobs and the belief that the road to future employment was through education resulted in increased public secondary school enrollments.[10] During World War II an increase in industrialization led to reforms preparing students for the real world through the provision of both academic and practical skills. This continued into the 1950s when two events forced American policy makers to rethink both the structure and the substance of public education in the United States.

The first event was the Supreme Court's 1954 ruling in *Brown v. Board of Education of Topeka* that educational segregation was unconstitutional. Through the decision, the court stated that separate but equal education for African Americans as created by *Plessy v. Ferguson* violated the equal protection provisions of the Fourteenth Amendment. This forced the federal government to consider the need for federal assistance to minority and low-income groups. The second event forcing public education reform was the 1957 Soviet launch of the *Sputnik* satellite into space. Many individuals perceived this as symbolic of the USSR's technological superiority and American vulnerability to attack from superior communist military strength. It was felt that the only way the United States could regain its superiority over the USSR was through

better education. Congress responded by passing the 1957 National Defense Education Act which provided millions of federal dollars for math, science, and foreign language education programs.[11] The effects of this new funding were the design and implementation of new curricula, increases in the numbers of teachers trained, and a reorientation in focus to academic excellence rather than real-world skills.

The 1960s and 1970s were turbulent with demonstrations and public protesting of social ills and inequalities. Many individuals believed that the public education system negated the pursuit of equity and demanded reform in national education policy. Lyndon Johnson's Great Society and War on Poverty programs saw the enactment of laws that were the first serious attempts by government to remedy past societal inequities. They also attacked the federal government's role in the provision of education. The first law was the Elementary and Secondary Education Act of 1965. This targeted $1.5 billion in federal aid for remedial course work, research, and instructional materials to the nation's poorest schools. It was followed later in the same year by the Equal Opportunity Act. This act appropriated less than $200 million for the establishment of the Head Start program. The goal of the program was to provide cultural enrichment to preschool children from low-income families. The program took off almost immediately, and by 1966, Head Start served 733,000 low-income, mostly minority children.[12] This annual enrollment was not exceeded until after 1990.

In the desire to strengthen equal opportunity, critics argued that a number of strategies were introduced in the 1960s and 1970s that led to permissive education. As examples they cite developments such as the easing of graduation requirements; the protection through federal and state laws of increased access to higher education for minorities, women, and foreign loan students on the basis of status rather than achievement; and the general move away from a structured, disciplined learning environment to more open, freewheeling classrooms. Thomas Toch contends that public education was in a shambles during this period.[13] Authors such as James Coleman argue that the net result of permissive education was the exodus of urban whites to the suburbs in search of a good old-fashioned education for their children again.[14] It could be argued that effectively this put racial segregation in place once again.

By the late 1970s many parents felt that public schools were inferior to private, parochial schools.[15] This criticism forced demands for a move back to academic rigor. For those who were against many of the Great Society equity-based programs it also fueled even greater opposition to equity through civil rights and antipoverty measures. Two reform trends influenced American public education in the early 1980s: uniform standards and greater accountability. The assumption behind reform was the belief that academic achievement can be improved by imposing rigorous education standards, uniform curricula, and assessment tests. The intended goal of the reform was not equity, but better quality education. Local authorities responded by advocating minimum skill levels for students and demanding that standardized test scores and other performance indicators improve in public schools. Such efforts to raise public school performance, however, were hindered by lack of finances. California's Proposition 13 and Massachusetts's Proposition 2 1/2 led to tax limits being adopted in seventeen states and the capping of property taxes. This severely limited revenues for public schools. Voters were discontented with government in general and public education specifically.[16]

In 1981, President Reagan made it clear that a priority of his presidential administra-

tion was the elimination of the federal department of education. Reagan's administration was conservative and very critical of past education policies. In particular, the Reagan administration felt that previous policies were liberal equity policies that weakened curriculums, limited parental choice, rewarded participation not achievement, and resulted in children poorly educated in basic skills and the sciences. Reagan and his policy advisors argued that the only way to reform the system for the better was through the introduction of market forces. They advocated mechanisms such as school vouchers. Vouchers would allow parents to use tax dollars to pay for private education for their children. Market forces supposedly would force the system to become competitive. Other proposed policy solutions called for increased graduation requirements, enhanced standards for teacher certification, and in some areas, teachers' salaries being tied to students' performances.

The fears of so many seemed confirmed when the National Commission on Excellence in Education published its 1983 report, *A Nation at Risk*. The report claimed that American public education was in a state of crisis.[17] The report intensified concerns about education related to international competitiveness. The concluding recommendation was that vigorous reform was the only way to restore quality. It was necessary because American workers were ill-prepared for the new global competitive marketplace, and their performance was below that of the past generation. The report's authors confirmed the belief that the United States was losing its ability to compete in an increasingly competitive global marketplace. To critics of the U.S. public education system, it was obvious: the failing education system with almost two decades of declining student achievement levels was responsible for the nation's loss of economic competitiveness. The major effect of *A Nation at Risk* was to inspire a movement in the United States known as the excellence movement. The movement's primary goal was to support an intensive approach to education to introduce rigor in the nation's public schools. Supporters of the movement argued that such an approach would raise graduation standards for students and teachers and reemphasize the importance of education overall. Armed with the report's findings, the business community and public opinion quickly demanded that the report's findings be formulated as policy. The report and reaction to it acted as the necessary triggers to place education reform back on the institutional agenda.

A number of subsequent published reports confirm many citizens' views that the problem was not confined solely to public elementary and high schools but that American higher education was also failing to produce quality graduates.[18] The media carried stories of how most American graduates could not perform simple tasks such as giving change, writing letters, or understanding an article from the newspaper—stories suggesting that American higher education was producing functionally illiterate individuals. The demand for reform that revamped education at all levels in the United States grew. Critics reemphasized the need for a change in the educational system's focus. They wanted to move away from equality of access and toward equality of performance. Other demands called for further decentralized decision making, the reform of school administration, stricter accountability, and restructuring of the curriculum. The assumption behind all of these demands was that education should be more responsive to market needs. A number of states and cities experimented with such reforms. The Reagan administration responded by transferring to the states more education decision-making authority, thus reducing the federal government's role overall. By 1986, thirty-five states moved to

adopt legislation reforming educational processes and structures. Apart from the devolving of decision-making authority to the states, the Reagan administration did not develop any other comprehensive responses.

The first real attempt at policy formulation for education reform came during the Bush administration. In 1989 the president convened an education summit of business leaders, government officials, politicians, and educators. As a result of goals developed at the summit, policy proposals were formulated and submitted to Congress in 1991 as the America 2000 plan. The original plan concentrated on using market mechanisms as the impetus for change. The plan focused on government funding for parental choice between public and private schools. America 2000 was presented as a national plan for school reform. It advocated national standards of student performance and called for the evaluation of local schools through public report cards and better teacher preparation.

The America 2000 plan illustrates the problem of divided government at the national level and its implications for policy making. The Democratic-controlled Congress and the Republican-controlled White House had very different ideas about the nature of education reform, and the originally submitted America 2000 proposal underwent intense partisan debate. For the most part, Democrats strongly opposed the funding of parental school choice. The Democrat-controlled Senate rejected the administration's $30 million spending proposal on school choice programs. Other fights concerning such reforms as national standards and a national assessment system ended up in gridlock or inaction.[19]

Education reform was a prominent campaign issue in the 1992 presidential election, thus ensuring its place on the institutional agenda. By 1992 many supporters of education reform were arguing that the approach of the past two administrations had been too incremental and that the only way the education system could produce students whose achievements matched other nations' achievement levels would be through comprehensive reform. The Clinton administration responded by developing what the president and his supporters perceived to be dramatic reform proposals in Goals 2000: The Educate America Act. In reality, Goals 2000 was very similar to the America 2000 plan. The one real difference was in the replacement of school choice proposals with the pursuit of charter schools. Charter schools were new or reorganized independent public schools and would be held accountable for results agreed upon in charters authorizing their creation. President Clinton also proposed national standards and testing.

Even though there was such similarity in the America 2000 and Goals 2000 recommendations, partisan conflict on education reform continued around many of the same disputes as the 1980s and early 1990s. Many Republicans feared federal control of education if national standards were implemented. They argued that the nation's 15,000 local districts would lose their ability to choose their own curriculum and assessment methods. Democrats also opposed national tests on the grounds that such test results could be used to cut funding to areas and schools that perform poorly. This would disadvantage many students who were already attending underfunded, low-performing schools. It was further argued that such tests would be unfair to disadvantaged and non-English-speaking students. In spite of the major political parties' opposition to national standards and tests, public opinion polls indicated that the majority of Americans were strongly in favor of national assessment.[20]

Eventually, Goals 2000 was passed in 1994. Its passage was due to the support of influential Dem-ocrats, favorable public opinion, and the lobbying of powerful business groups. Goals 2000 established national education goals and voluntary national performance standards. It also authorized funding for states that agreed to comply with such standards. Under the act a number of national panels, councils, and boards were created to oversee standards. The Clinton administration saw this act as an integral part of a reform package of the American educational system. American schools were asked to achieve eight specific objectives by the year 2000.[21] Clinton also articulated, when signing Goals 2000 in April 1994, that $700 billion would be provided for education for 1995. However, the act said little about higher education reform.

The Goals 2000 Act was plagued with implementation difficulties. Opposition was such that in many localities many changes requiring curriculum control and outcomes-based education were blocked by an array of groups. For example, conservative religious groups exerted pressure on or gained control of local school boards and refused to see changes implemented. Public school bureaucrats, as well as teachers, heavily criticized the act's proposals involving curriculum control and testing and worked to block such reforms. The structure of the political system has also hindered the implementation process: separation of powers essentially has given the local level control over public education, making it difficult for comprehensive change to take place. However, most of the nation's state governments led by governors of both political parties endorsed reforms conforming to the act's requirements. Business and the public also remained steadfast in their commitment to the Goals 2000 reforms, and indeed, public opinion has subsequently called for even more far reaching reforms.

President George W. Bush campaigned as an education activist concerned with the failings of the educational system. He promised to "leave no child behind and to skip subsidizing failure." President Bush is a strong believer in the use of market forces to stimulate the public sector into better provision of education. The United States continues to struggle to remain competitive in the global economy, and the need for a highly educated workforce remains critical to this endeavor.

The barriers and obstacles facing the public education system are many. For example, there is still disparity in public school finance in spite of educational reform in the states aimed at reducing the differences in funding per pupil among school districts. The proportion of the differences in per-pupil expenditures on instruction that exists among states has increased throughout the 1990s.[22] Differences in the proportion of local to state and federal funding generally persists across the United States. On the one hand, it can be argued that local funding and control of public education are essential to maintaining public sector commitment to public provision of education and ensuring that education reflects community values and needs. On the other hand, reliance on local funding may lead to inequities in the financing of public education because of differences in local wealth. At the same time, school districts relying on higher levels of state funding are more vulnerable to funding shortfalls during economic recessions than districts with higher proportions of local funding, because property taxes provide relative stability compared to the sales and income taxes upon which states tend to depend to fund low-wealth school districts.

The net result over the years of such conflicting factors is different proportions of state and local funding among the states. Thus, the quality of public education received depends upon where a student lives. The amount of expenditure per student in public elementary and secondary schools rose significantly in the late 1980s, but increased more slowly during the early 1990s. Table 14.2 demonstrates that

Table 14.2 Current Expenditure Per Pupil in Public Schools: 1961–62 to 1999–2000

School Year	Current Expenditures in Unadjusted Dollars	Current Expenditures in Constant 1999–2000 Dollars*
1961–1962	$ 419	$2,360
1970–1971	911	3,883
1980–1981	2,502	4,889
1985–1986	3,756	5,843
1989–1990	4,980	6,639
1990–1991	5,258	6,647
1994–1995	5,989	6,741
1995–1996	6,147	6,735
1996–1997**	6,392	6,811
1997–1998**	6,657	6,973
1998–1999**	6,915	7,097
1999–2000**	7,086	7,086

SOURCE: Adapted from National Center for Education Statistics, *Digest of Education Statistics, 2000* (Washington, DC: National Center for Education Statistics, Institute of Education Sciences, U.S. Department of Education, 2000) Table 170.

* Data based on the Consumer Price Index, prepared by the Bureau of Labor Statistics, U.S. Department of Labor, adjusted to a school-year basis.
** Estimated projections for these years.

expenditures per student grew 20 percent after adjustment for inflation between 1985 and 1986 and 1989 and 1990. This could be interpreted as a reflection of the issue's prominence on the public agenda. There was a slowdown in growth to less than 1 percent from 1989 to 1990 to 1994 to 1995. Many would argue this can be correlated to a lull in its visibility as an issue on the agenda. However, as concern with the issue became more prominent in Clinton's second administration, there was a 6 percent rise in expenditure per student between 1994 and 1995 and 1999 and 2000.

In January 2002, President Bush signed into law a sweeping public education reform act, the No Child Left Behind Act 2001. This law makes more federal money available for elementary and secondary education while holding educators accountable for failures in teaching the nation's forty-eight million public school children. It basically turns federal spending on schools into a federal investment in improved student performance. Under the No Child Left Behind Act, students in grades three through eight are to be tested annually in reading and math beginning fall 2005. States must show a certain level of improvement over two years and have all schools performing at a proficient level by 2014. Schools will also have to test students in science in three grades. Those schools that fail to make adequate yearly progress could face sanctions. For example, such schools may be forced to pay transportation costs for low-income students to attend better performing schools within the districts. Under the new rules, parents of children in "failing" schools may transfer their children to higher performing public schools and school districts cannot use an excuse to keep students from transferring.

Basically the reform bill increases funding to schools to promote better performance, and penalizes schools where students need better instruction; for example, a school in which test scores failed to improve over six years can be restaffed. Under the legislation, states have to ensure that within four years all teachers are qualified to teach in their subject areas and funds are provided for such professional development. Finally, schools must develop annual report cards that show their standardized test scores compared with both local and state schools. The act's supporters argue this requirement gives parents the information about the quality of their children's schools, the qualifications of teachers, and their children's progress in key academic areas.

The No Child Left Behind Act 2001 increases federal education funding to more than $22.1 billion at the elementary and secondary levels. This is a 27 percent increase from the previous year. It also increases funding for Title 1 programs to close the gap between disadvantaged children and their peers to $10.4 billion, which is a 30 percent increase over 2000 levels. It also provides nearly $3 billion in federal funding to recruit and retain highly qualified teachers and principals and boosts funding for reading programs to nearly $1 billion. Finally, it provides an estimated $200 million for charter schools to expand parental choice for children trapped in persistently "failing" schools.

The major criticism leveled at the legislation by education specialists is that it will label too many schools unsuccessful, and in the majority of the cases, the charge would be unwarranted and impractical. For example, seven months after the legislation was signed by the president, states and school districts were scrambling to identify failing schools as defined by the law. In Connecticut, education officials were in major disagreement over which schools should be on the state's list.[23] In New Jersey, the state's 2,300 schools were ranked using test scores from 1999. This resulted in 274 schools that do not show requisite annual improvements.[24]

Only time will tell whether the United States can continue to decentralize the education system. Currently, the United States has a two-tier system of education where those who can afford it send their children to private schools, and those who cannot send their children to a public school system fraught with problems and insufficient resources.

EDUCATION POLICY AND THE AGENDA-SETTING PROCESS

Education policy in the United States in recent times is a good example of how an issue becomes part of the agenda through the conjunction of Kingdon's three streams.[25] The key to successful agenda building in the public education policy sector is the coupling of the problem stream, the policy stream, and the political stream at pivotal points or windows of opportunity.[26] Agenda setting around comprehensive education reform in the United States resulted from a set of interrelated factors. Fears surrounding the ability of the United States to compete in the global marketplace drove public attitudes on education reform and affected which agenda the issue was placed upon. Backed by the business community and public educators, there was a general societal perception that American students did not measure up to their peers in other industrialized countries and that this ultimately was detrimental to future economic strength and prosperity. This triggered the issue of large-scale education reform onto the institutional agenda.

Problem Stream

Deborah Stone argues that the problem stream in education policy depends upon numbers as symbols.[27] Numbers are perceived to be precise and objective and can establish norms, although of course numbers can be manipulated if desired. However, numbers about educational standards in the United States have been used since the 1950s to show decline and the existence of "real" problems that need to be rectified. Over the years, agenda setting around U.S. public education reform has been facilitated by public articulation of declining standards of achievement and inability to compete economically in the new global order. There have been both the perception and the recognition of the existence of problems within American public education. The publicized perception of deficiencies in curriculum, student scores, and lack of teacher and student competency have all led to the demand for public education reform. If this is combined with the fear of loss of interna-

tional competitiveness, the issue of education reform has moved from the systemic agenda to the institutional agenda.

Report after report emphasized the depth of the problem and as various actors and participants lobbied for change and publically articulated the weaknesses of the American educational system, the education reform issue moved higher on the agenda. Education reform's placement on the institutional agenda in the late 1950s, early 1960s can clearly be explained by the issue-attention cycle theory. It was an issue that garnered great public attention. However, this attention and concern were soon accompanied by sober realism over the costs and obstacles of reform. By the 1970s, the issue was no longer on the institutional agenda, but it continued to remain a prominent issue on the systemic agenda. It reemerged as an issue high on the institutional agenda by the mid-1980s. Once again the perception of problems propels the issue of education reform onto the public agenda. The return to prominence of the education reform issue in the 1980s can be best explained through the punctuated equilibria framework. Utilizing this framework, one can argue that the cycle of policy activity in the 1970s led to a period in the 1980s of public and private mobilized interest in education issues. Increased activism over education reform resulted, creating more attention that resulted in increased policy responses from both the Bush and Clinton administrations. The increased activism surrounding the issue has not dissipated and a crucial substantive policy item debated by both candidates in the presidential election of 2000 was education reform.

Policy Stream

If problems are identified, then it is inevitable that policy solutions will be advanced. However, the recognition that a problem exists does not necessarily mean that appropriate or relevant policy proposals will be offered as possible solutions. In the public education policy sector in the United States, the policy stream is complicated by the lack of a consensus around which policy recommendation will produce the desired goals of efficiency, equity, choice, and competency. In short, policies were advanced, but there was no clear sense that they would produce better educated or better prepared individuals. The last forty years have witnessed an explosion of proposed policy solutions that has only perpetuated the notion of a crisis in public education. The policy recommendations have been broad in range in terms of both goals and objectives. Some are dramatic, whereas others are incremental in substance. Some solutions advocate changes in how students are taught, others look at changing the curriculum, and other proposals recommend removing education from the public domain and allowing greater privatization. The one thing all recommended policy solutions, over the years, have in common is the acknowledgment that a problem does exist and that a better learning environment needs to be promoted.

Political Stream

Politics forced education reform onto the agenda. Although there were problems, people made the problems more of an issue than they were. Thus, the political climate changed, making education reform an issue that demanded attention on the public agenda.

The return in 1980 to classic liberal political values emphasizing smaller government and greater local control led the public and the business community to fully support reform proposals to give schools and parents greater control over education decisions. Public concern obviously led policy makers to feel the need to support public education reform. The political stream includes

changes in policy makers' receptivity to reform, changes in national mood, and heightened interest group activity. The power and activism of business interests and its political influence on the policy-making process from the early 1980s onward cannot be ignored. The objective of business interest groups was to serve their own purposes in regard to education reform. Their role and influence in setting the agenda around education reform was great. Such interest group activity was accompanied by growing media debate over falling standards and the rise of foreign economic competitors with better educated workers. As stated previously, with the election of Ronald Reagan, the federal government abdicated much of its responsibility in the area of public education. This forced a much larger role in education policy upon state governments. However, at the same time a grassroots movement advocating educational reform started to mobilize. The movement is responsible for impressing upon elected officials the large-scale dissatisfaction from taxpayers over the quality and direction of education in the United States. The issue of education reform was firmly placed on the institutional agenda at the start of the new millennium.

THE POLICY PROCESS AND EDUCATION REFORM

There is no comprehensive national education policy in the United States because of the multiple centers of decision-making power in the area of education policy. The system is a decentralized decision-making structure. This is largely due to federalism which structures education policy making at every stage of the process. According to the Constitution, education is a state responsibility. However, in most states the authority to operate and finance schools has been delegated to local school districts. The traditional role of the federal government in the governance of public education is limited to the provision of funding to states and school districts. Such funding is mostly to support special education programs. The federal government also undertakes financial aid to students in the form of scholarships and loans to participate in higher education. The majority of funding for public schools is provided by state and local school districts. This is perhaps the *real* crisis of public education in the United States, for there are insufficient resources at the state and local levels of government to provide the comprehensive reform that is required if meaningful change is to take place.

The net result of this decentralization of jurisdiction is uncoordinated policy making. Each state differs in the number of school districts and there is great variation across states and localities in terms of specific education goals, spending levels, and curriculum maintenance. Thus, the American school system is much more decentralized than other similar industrialized nations. Such decentralization makes it harder to track efficiency and effectiveness. Supporters of the Leave No Child Behind Act argue that the move to increased testing makes tracking easier. The shift recently has been to greater federal and state regulation of local districts to create greater equality and effectiveness. There are funding variations at the local level because the financing of education at the local level is usually based on property taxes. Thus, the more affluent the district the better the schools.

It is traditionally perceived that it is not the federal government's responsibility to operate the educational system. For many years the federal government has simply played a secondary role in public education provision. The net result is the negation of the federal government's ability to initiate

policy. Goals 2000 and America 2000, referred to earlier in this chapter, represent the federal government's desire to circumvent the norm that education policy cannot be directly mandated at the national level. The offering of grants and subsidies to the states, local communities, and schools that adopt federal models is a move by the federal government to influence policy through the use of economic incentives. The 2001 Leave No Child Behind Act is a return to greater local control. The act attempts to cut federal red tape, reduce the number of education programs, and create larger, more flexible programs that force decisions at the local level. In other words—decentralization is the goal.

However, with decentralized decision making it is more difficult to efficiently monitor policy outcomes, particularly in regard to national education goals. This affects the agenda in a number of ways. For example, should measurements such as standardized testing, attrition rates, or quality of teachers as demonstrated by their qualifications be utilized? Such questions dominate the measurement debate. The problem is no one can guarantee that one of these measures is better than another. Also, because of the great variations among schools and geographic regions there is no one solution that fits all. However, taxpayers still demand accountability. The decentralized nature of the policy-making process related to education allows for more involvement in education decision making by educators and citizens. Local administration also allows for greater participation by local community members in the process.

EDUCATION POLICY INSTRUMENTS

Policy makers in the United States have used several instruments to achieve education policy outcomes. The most common is di-

Table 14.3 Elementary and Secondary Education Enrollment (in thousands)

Year	1980	1990	1995	1996	1997	1998	1999*
Total	46,208	46,448	50,502	51,394	51,987	52,768	53,215
Public	40,877	41,217	44,840	45,611	46,127	46,844	47,244
Private	5,331	5,232	5,662	5,783	5,860	5,924	5,971

SOURCE: From the National Center for Education Statistics, *Digest of Education Statistics, 1999* (Washington, DC: National Center for Education Statistics, Institute of Education Sciences, U.S. Department of Education, 1999), Table 2, p. 11.

*These figures are projected.

rect provision of services. Even though the private sector is growing, with 11 percent of school-aged children enrolled in private schools, most American children are still educated in public schools (see Table 14.3).

The second type of instrument used in the provision of public education is rules. For example, it is through rules that government specifies teacher qualifications, curriculum, attendance eligibility, special service eligibility, and graduation requirements. The third policy instrument utilized by policy makers is incentives. Economic incentives were used by the Clinton administration to get local compliance to Goals 2000 objectives. A final common instrument used in education policy making is powers. Parental choice programs are an example of powers-based policy.

SUMMARY

In the last decade education reform in the United States has been a heated issue on the public agenda. As discussed earlier, the controversy has been stimulated by the perception of falling educational standards in the United States. Early criticisms of the American education system came from the business community; these criticisms in turn tapped into growing public concerns about the deteriorating quality of public schools. Critics charge that American students rate lower in skills, abilities, and aptitudes than students in other industrialized nations. The result is workers who are ill-prepared, leading to a concern over America's future competitiveness in the global marketplace. One of the most supported proposed policy solutions is the increased introduction of market forces. In the first years of the twenty-first century, a clear consensus exists that the U.S. education system is underperforming and failing to educate American children to be fully functioning, efficient workers in a global economy. The criticism in recent years of American public education is that it has fallen behind other industrialized nations in terms of student performance. Such arguments rest on educational outputs as measured by standardized achievement tests. Efforts such as America 2000 and Goals 2000 changed little. It is still too early to see the effectiveness of the Leave No Child Behind Act. Education policy at the national level remains largely symbolic policy making. There are many problems existing at all levels of the public education system. For example, dropout rates are high (20 to 30 percent) and minorities are clearly disadvantaged when higher education enrollments and graduating rates are looked at. These problems cannot be fixed with incremental policy making. The wealthier states will always do better. It seems clear that there needs to be greater coordination or centralizing of public education.

Decentralization of decision making in the education policy arena has played a significant role in defining access to educational services. Without doubt the viability and efficiency of public education regionally have been affected by the fact that states are responsible for public education funding. This has led to disparity in spending levels, with some states spending considerably more per student in public schools than other states.[28] There are real cost differentials even accounting for differences in cost of living, salaries, and materials. In the early to mid-1990s, some states were spending one-third less than other states to educate a comparable population of children.[29] In short, the decentralization of education underscores socioeconomic and cultural differences from state to state. To compensate for this inequity, the federal government does retain the right to intervene whenever state education decisions or policies are deemed to benefit outside interests and not the public interest.

DISCUSSION QUESTIONS

1. Can, and should, politics be kept out of education policy making?

2. What should be the goals of a public education system?

3. Should parents pay in any way for their children's education?

SUGGESTED READINGS

Bowles S., and H. Gintes. *Schooling in Capitalist America,* New York: Basic Books, 1976.

Chapman, J. D., W. L. Boyd, R. Lauder, and D. Reynolds, *The Reconstruction of Education: Quality, Equality and Control.* London: Cassells, 1996.

Chubb, J. E., and T. M. Moe. *Politics, Markets, and America's Schools.* Washington, DC: Brookings Institution Press, 1990.

DiConti, V. *Interest Groups and Education Reform: The Latest Crusade to Restructure the Schools.* Lanham, MD: University Press of America.

McClean, M. *Educational Traditions Compared.* London: David Fulton, 1995.

Spring, J. *Conflict of Interests: The Politics of American Education.* New York: Longman, 1998.

Wray, H. *Japanese and American Education: Attitudes and Practices.* Westport, CT: Bergin & Garvey, 1999.

ENDNOTES

1. In countries in the Organization for Economic Cooperation and Development, education spending absorbs on average 6 percent of gross domestic product and 10 to 12 percent of total public expenditures.

2. National Center for Education Statistics, "International Comparisons of Education," *Digest of Education Statistics, 2001* (Washington, DC: National Center for Education Statistics, Institute of Education Sciences, U.S. Department of Education, 2001), chap. 6.

3. A. Green, *Education and State Formation* (Basingstoke, England: Macmillan, 1990), chap. 1.

4. F. Hirsh, *Social Limits to Growth* (Cambridge, MA: Harvard University Press, 1976).

5. Green, *Education,* chap. 3.

6. NCES, *Education Statistics, 2001,* chap. 6.

7. L. Bierlein, *Controversial Issues in Educational Policy* (Newbury Park, CA: Sage, 1993), 152.

8. Ibid., 152.

9. M. W. Kirst, *Who Controls Our Schools? American Values in Conflict* (New York: Freeman Press, 1984), 30–35.

10. The number of high school students grew from 3 million in 1930 to over 6.5 million in 1941.

11. Bierlein, *Controversial Issues,* 9.

12. Committee on Ways and Means, U.S. House of Representatives, *Overview of Entitlement Programs* (Washington, DC: Government Printing Office, 1993), 1690.

13. Thomas Toch, *In the Name of Excellence* (New York: Oxford University Press, 1991).

14. Diane Ravatch, "The Coleman Reports and American Education," in A. Sovensen and S. Spilerman, *Social Theory and Societal Policy* (Westport, CT: Praeger, 1993), 129–41.

15. Ibid., 129–141.

16. J. W. Guth, W. I. Garms, and L. C. Pierce, *School Finance and Education Policy* (Englewood Cliffs, NJ: Prentice Hall, 1988) 89–93.

17. National Commission on Excellence in Education, *A Nation at Risk: The Imperative for Educational Reform* (Washington, DC: Government Printing Office, April 1983).

18. The wingspread group on higher education, *An American Imperative: Higher Expectations for Higher Education* (Racine, WI: The Johnson Foundation, 1993), 15.

19. Bierlein, *Controversial Issues,* 111.

20. In 1991, by a margin of 68 to 24 percent, Gallup polls showed the public was in favor of public schools using a standardized national curriculum.

21. Figures for 1998 projected from Statistical Abstract of the United States, 1997, no. 233, (U.S. Census Office/U.S. Government Printing Office, Washington D.C.), 153.

22. National Center for Education Statistics, *Digest of Education Statistics, 1999* (Washington, DC: National Center for Education Statistics, Institute of Education Sciences, U.S. Department of Education, 1999), 9–14.

23. *New York Times,* July 4, 2002, sec. B, p. 1.

24. Ibid.

25. John W. Kingdon, *Agendas, Alternatives, and Public Policies* (Boston: Little Brown, 1984).

26. Ibid.

27. D. A. Stone, *Policy Paradox and Political Reason* (Glenview, IL: Scott Foresman, 1988).

28. A. Heidenheimer, H. Heclo, and C. Adams, *Comparative Public Policy* (New York: St. Martin's Press, 1990), 31.

29. NCES, *Education Statistics, 1999,* 18.

15

Health Care Policy

Designing Policy Alternatives

The involvement of the state in the formulation and development of health policy is a relatively modern phenomenon. However, modern societies have consistently been concerned that citizens maintain good health, and that scientists search for cures to diseases that plague humankind. As the welfare state grew in nation after nation, more governments provided for health care, acknowledging that good health is intrinsic to human welfare. Prior to the development of the welfare state, all that most governments attempted was to slow the spread of infectious diseases. Most citizens did not look to government for help with their health. Following the expansion of state responsibilities and a number of scientific advances in the twentieth century, preventive public health initiatives grew, and governments increased their role in the curative care sector via regulation, funding, and the provision of care itself.

The relationship of good health to citizen welfare is important, for the objectives of health policy and welfare provision goes hand-in-hand. The promotion and attainment of good health require citizens to have adequate or satisfactory living conditions. Societies need healthy populations, and obviously, healthy people are more productive than unhealthy people. Sick workers take more sick days than healthy workers, even when they are self-employed. Research demonstrates the significant correlation between economic growth and better health standards. For example, studies have shown how population health affects a nation's gross domestic product (GDP) over time.[1] Other studies have highlighted the economic impact of household health. This research demonstrates a clear link between a nation's disease levels, productivity, and earnings.[2] Indicators of such a relationship are life expectancy rates, infant mortality rates, birth rates, and climate conditions.

One study shows an improvement in adult life expectancy was responsible for 8 percent of total growth in fifty-three nations between 1965 and 1990.[3] Such growth was due to the improved productivity of healthier workforces. Researchers found less absenteeism, increased incentives for investment in human and physical capital as life expectancy increases, and increases in saving rates, as workers had more need to save for retirement.[4] Pan American Health Organization studies and research conducted by the Inter-American Development Bank also support the existence of a relationship between health and economic growth. The data indicate that if male life expectancy is increased by one year, GDP will be increased by an additional 1 percent after fifteen years.[5] The correlation between economic performance and birth rate has also been shown in several studies across nations.[6] Research shows that as a population's health improves, child mortality rates increase, which leads over time to a decrease in fertility rates. After birth rates fall, economic growth increases, as the proportion of the population participating in the labor force increases. However, data also show that an increase in the number of young adults does not automatically lead to growth.[7] Clearly some dimensions of health affect workers' productivity.[8] It should be stated that the effect of sickness on individual productivity is greater in poorer nations. However, it is safe to argue that overall health will influence earnings.[9]

In the provision of health care the state may be a regulator, a funder or purchaser, or a provider or planner. In many industrialized nations the state will combine all or most of these roles. What role or combination of roles the state takes depends on the scope and extensiveness of the welfare state in any

given nation. In all industrialized nations, governments manage and provide a range of public health services; for example, health education, vaccination programs, sanitation projects, and the regulation of food and drug quality. In some nations curative care is provided directly by the government; in others there is minimal government involvement. Even in systems where government provides direct provision, individuals may still seek private health care and treatment. Likewise, in market-oriented systems the government still plays a considerable role. Since the late 1940s all nations have been seeking what they perceive to be the optimal mix of public and private activity. Consequently, there are several operating models of health care provision reflecting the different mixes of public and private activity (see Box 15.1) and there are also several different options governments can choose for cost control (see Box 15.2).

The World Health Organization (WHO) in 2000 published the first ever analysis of the world's health systems.[10] WHO measured 191 nations' health systems against the following performance indicators: overall level of population health; health inequalities within the population; overall level of health-system responsiveness (a combination of patient satisfaction and how well the system acts); distribution of responsiveness within the population (how well people of varying economic status find that they are served by the health system); and the distribution of the health system's financial burden within the population (who pays the costs).[11] WHO's analysis finds wide variation in performance and contends that citizen health and well-being depends critically on their nation's health systems.[12] The study finds performance variation even among nations with similar income levels and health expenditures.

The WHO report recommends health insurance for as many individuals as possible and refers to the need for prepayments on

Box 15.1   National Policy Models for Curative Care

MODEL	CHARACTERISTICS	EXAMPLE NATION
National health service	• Citizens guaranteed access by government to all health care services • Health care system paid for and administered directly by government, with all or most costs absorbed by government • Government pays doctors, nurses, hospitals directly to provide comprehensive care • Citizens pay into system through mandatory national health insurance contribution • Demand for services often exceeds supply—often long waiting lists for elective procedures • Citizens can go outside of system and receive treatment from private vendors	United Kingdom
Limited national health service	• Government-run hospitals staffed by government-salaried doctors and nurses • Citizens guaranteed access to government-run hospitals • High number of citizens go outside to private vendors • Quality and availability of care often insufficient	Command economies
Single payer	• Citizens guaranteed access to health care via a single insurance program run directly by government • Government negotiates best rates from hospitals and doctors • Health care provided by private vendors	Canada
Mandatory national health insurance	• Citizens guaranteed access to care by government • Multiple payers and multiple providers • Citizens receive health coverage through private insurance tied to job • Government regulates benefits and controls fees • Government provides insurance to unemployed, self-employed, and retired	Germany
Market maximized	• Citizens not guaranteed access to care by government • Government provides access for certain groups • Access to care is a choice, not a right of citizens • Some regulation by government of private health insurers • Access to services is guaranteed by citizens' ability to pay, not by urgency of need	United States

Box 15.2   Cost-Control Measures

MEASURE	OBJECTIVE	MAIN CRITICISM	EXAMPLE REGULATION
Alter behavior of those receiving services	Force individuals to monitor usage of health services	Patients' decision to receive care dependent upon economic considerations	• Requiring copayments • Requiring patients to pay in full at time care received; reimbursement at a later date
Influence physicians' behavior	Constrain number of procedures physicians provide	Patients' ability to receive services dictated by economic considerations	• Fee-for-service • Fees based upon number of patients and not services provided
Place limits on technological acquisition	Decrease likelihood of unnecessary procedures	Long waiting lists for certain technologies	• Limit what and who can buy certain equipment
Use a gatekeeper	Decrease use of specialists performing unnecessary procedures	Referrals made on basis of cost savings rather than need	• Internists make referrals only to specialists

Table 15.1 United States Health Care System Rankings by Selected WHO Indicators Rankings

Performance Overall Rank	Health Level Rank	Responsiveness Level Rank	Fairness in Financial Contribution Rank	Health Expenditure Per Capita ($) Rank
37	24	1	54*	1

SOURCE: Adapted from the World Health Organization, *The World Health Report 2000—Health Systems: Improving Performance* (Geneva, Switzerland: WHO, 2000), Annex Table 1.

* Denotes a tie with other nations.

health care in the form of insurance, taxes, or social security. In particular, nations should provide insurance to as large a percentage of low-income groups as possible. Currently, in those nations where a large number of low-income individuals do not have insurance, the poor pay a higher percentage of their income on health care than the wealthy.[13]

Table 15.1 shows how the United States' health system ranked in terms of overall quality. With the exception of the system's responsiveness and the amount of expenditure, the U.S. health system did not manage to rank among the top ten. This partly explains why health policy in the United States is such a visible issue on the public agenda.

CONTEMPORARY HEALTH POLICY IN THE UNITED STATES

In the first years of the twenty-first century health care is still a contentious item on the public agenda. However, it is highly unlikely that major reform of the system will take place in the near future. It is a system that some critics would argue is in a state of near crisis. Health expenditures continue to outpace inflation and by the year 2000 expenditure was approximately 13.1 percent of GDP.[14] The WHO 2000 report indicates the United States spends a higher proportion of its GDP than any other nation (see Table 15.2). Additionally, Table 15.2 shows the United States' expenditure on health care as a percentage of total expenditure is lower than most comparable industrialized nations. The United States ranks only 37 out of 191 nations worldwide in terms of overall performance. Most Americans receive health insurance through their employment. Thus, in times of economic recession when unemployment rates rise, health insurance is lost for those who lose their work. Today, approximately 18 percent of the U.S. population has no health insurance coverage, while millions more have such limited coverage that they would be put into economic impoverishment if serious illness hit. Working-class and middle-class families are concerned with the affordability of health care.

When discussing the history of health care in America, it may be seen as the story of fallen public expectations and lost chances. Many Americans are strongly opposed on ideological grounds to a health care system paid for and directly administered by the federal government. Such a system is viewed as "socialized" medicine and "un-American." However, since the 1980s there has been general dissatisfaction with the system, and there are demands for

change. Two issues are central to the health care reform debate in the United States. The first is cost containment. This is a concern that Americans share with many other industrialized nations' populations. The second issue is particular to the United States: it is the increasingly growing numbers of the uninsured. Many critics argue that extending coverage to all Americans is a just and necessary undertaking.

The U.S. health care system was founded upon entrepreneurial principles. Government assistance was originally aimed at informing society about activities that would improve general health or assisting people who were economically or physically disadvantaged. Government was the "safety net" for those who had no other options in health care. From 1798 and the establishment of the U.S. Public Health Service, a pattern was set: People who were well-off were afforded the very best in health care services, whereas people who were poor and disadvantaged had to compete and struggle for limited resources.

The first expansion of services and facilities for people who were poor and destitute occurred in the early 1900s. By the start of World War I approximately 4,000 hospitals were established and run by religious groups and communities. Relying on the patronage of the wealthy, these institutions subsidized charitable donations with patient fees. Over time, these facilities became "workshops" or training grounds for physicians. The Hill-Burton Hospital and Survey and Construction Act of 1946 expanded the number of nonprofit hospitals by granting a one-time federal contribution of nearly 25 percent of total costs for the construction of rural medical facilities and hospitals. The act also attracted physicians to such newly constructed facilities.

Simultaneous to this expansion of facilities was the emergence of a medical insurance industry. Any support for the

Table 15.2 Comparison of Health Care Expenditure

Selected Nations 1995–2000

Nation	Total Expenditure on Health Care as % of GDP		Private Expenditure on Health Care as % of Total Expenditure		Total Government Expenditure on Health Care as % of Total Expenditure on Health Care		Government Expenditure on Health Care as % of Total General Government Expenditure		Per Capita Total Expenditure on Health Care (U.S. $)		Per Capita Government Expenditure on Health Care (U.S $)	
	1995	2000	1995	2000	1995	2000	1995	2000	1995	2000	1995	2000
Australia	8.2	8.3	32.9	27.6	67.1	72.4	14.2	16.2	$1,686	$1,698	$1,132	$1,229
Canada	9.1	9.1	28.6	28.0	71.4	72.0	13.3	15.5	$1,821	$2,058	$1,299	$1,483
France	9.6	9.5	23.9	24.0	76.1	76.0	13.2	13.5	$2,566	$2,057	$1,954	$1,563
Germany	10.6	10.6	23.3	24.9	76.7	75.1	14.5	17.3	$3,194	$2,422	$2,449	$1,819
Greece	8.9	8.3	45.5	44.5	54.5	55.5	9.5	9.2	$998	$884	$544	$491
Ireland	7.3	6.7	27.5	24.2	72.5	75.8	12.8	16.0	$1,354	$1,692	$981	$1,283
Italy	7.4	8.1	27.8	26.3	72.2	73.7	10.0	12.7	$1,415	$1,498	$1,022	$1,103
Japan	7.0	7.8	21.8	23.3	78.2	76.7	15.1	15.4	$2,950	$2,908	$2,308	$2,230
Mexico	5.6	5.4	58.5	53.6	41.5	43.0	11.3	15.6	$177	$311	$74	$144
Norway	8.0	7.8	15.8	14.8	84.2	85.2	13.2	15.8	$2,689	$2,832	$2,265	$2,412
Russia	5.5	5.3	18.5	27.5	81.5	72.5	11.7	14.5	$126	$92	$103	$66
Spain	7.7	7.7	29.1	30.1	70.9	69.9	12.2	13.5	$1,137	$1,073	$806	$750
Sweden	8.1	8.4	14.8	22.7	85.2	77.3	10.2	11.3	$2,214	$2,179	$1,885	$1,685
Switzerland	10.0	10.7	46.2	44.4	53.8	55.6	14.5	12.7	$4,305	$3,573	$2,315	$1,988
Turkey	3.4	5.0	29.7	28.9	70.3	71.1	10.7	9.0	$93	$150	$65	$107
U.K.	7.0	7.3	16.1	19.0	83.9	81.0	13.1	14.9	$1,357	$1,747	$1,138	$1,415
U.S.A.	13.3	13.1	54.7	55.7	45.3	44.3	16.8	16.7	$3,621	$4,499	$1,639	$1,415

SOURCE: Adapted from the World Health Organization, *The World Health Report 2000—Health Systems: Improving Performance* (Geneva, Switzerland: WHO, 2000), 202–217.

introduction of a national insurance system similar to some European nations had been eroded and thus the idea was removed from the public agenda by the early 1900s.[15] The first "prepayment" system in the United States was introduced by Blue Cross in 1933 in the states of California and Michigan. These "Blue Plans" eventually spread to all states in the union. Prepayment plans calculated premiums, which applied equally to all citizens within a given community, and were based upon community ratings. Unfortunately, as high-risk groups and activities began to emerge, the Blue Plans changed to an experience rating based on individual health status to minimize risks and maximize profits. By the early 1950s it was estimated that nearly 50 percent of Americans had some form of health care insurance.[16] Such industry development was facilitated by generous tax exemptions. Concern for the uninsured led President Harry S. Truman in the 1950s to propose the replacement of private insurance with a national insurance system. However, the proposal was defeated in Congress by the American Medical Association and the insurance lobby. Supporters of national insurance were pacified by legislation, such as the Kerr-Mills Amendment to the 1960 Social Security Act, which authorized grants for insurance to the medically indigent.

The 1960s saw the health care reform issue back on the institutional agenda. Both John F. Kennedy and Lyndon B. Johnson responded by attempting to change and expand health care provision to certain sectors of the population. First, health care insurance was extended to those who qualified for social security. Second, the adoption of the Migrant Workers Act in 1962 provided federal funding of health programs for migrant workers for the first time in American history. The act also led to the creation of rural clinics designed to offer care, health care

information, and preventive programs to the migrant rural population. The success of the legislation also led to its expansion to low-income families. In 1963 community mental health centers were established to give mental health assistance. Additionally, the War on Poverty program was a direct influence on numerous amendments to the Social Security Act from 1963 through 1967. These amendments gave state governments increased funding primarily for maternal and child care activities. Through the Economic Opportunity Act of 1964 and the Comprehensive Health Planning Act of 1966, states and localities funded neighborhood health facilities and were enabled to hire medical personnel and obtain necessary resources.

The Medicare and Medicaid programs were introduced through the "war on poverty" health care reforms. Medicare was designed to provide health insurance to all older Americans and some people with disabilities as well. Medicaid provided federal grants to states for insuring selected lower income citizens. For the most part, Medicaid aided single mothers with dependent children and the elderly. Both were single-payer arrangements for health care provision. The goal of these two programs, ideally, was that they function like private insurance. Physicians and hospitals would be reimbursed for "reasonable and necessary" expenses with little interference by the federal government. Realistically, the rising costs of health care (15 percent rise in costs between the 1960s and 1970s) forced the federal government to become more involved with both Medicare and Medicaid.[17] Frustrations also rose on both sides of the Medicare/Medicaid issue. Physicians and hospitals complained of receiving fewer reimbursements than they deserved and patients criticized service in addition to limited coverage.

The 1970s saw the introduction of a managed care system in the United States. This system prohibited a move toward a system of public health provision similar to the British or Swedish or German systems. Managed care was sanctioned under the 1973 Health Maintenance Organization (HMO) Act, in which $375 million was appropriated to subsidize the formation of prepaid insurance groups. It was argued that HMOs would provide comprehensive services, greater efficiency, and improved convenience for consumers. The federal government encouraged employers to offer HMOs to employees through tax exemptions and other benefits. The net effect was to shift the burden and responsibility of health care further away from the public sector and more securely into the hands of the private sector.

One of the first companies to introduce a prepaid plan to the West Coast of the United States was Kaiser Permanente. Shortly thereafter, other managed care options were established. For example, Preferred Provider Organizations (PPOs) and Independent Practice Associations (IPAs) were created with the intention of offering more flexibility than HMOs. They discounted fees for patients with designated physicians on their plans. Both physicians and hospitals preferred PPOs and IPAs over HMOs because, they argued, PPOs and IPAs allowed them to treat insured patients while at the same time maintaining private practices. By 1978, 43 percent of physicians contracted with a PPO, although they claimed that only 12 percent of their income was derived from insurance patients.[18] The 1974 National Health Planning and Resource Development Act (NHPRD) mandated the implementation of nearly 200 health planning areas to guide hospital construction, initiate new technology, and develop master plans for health services. In addition, the NHPRD controlled hospital bed supply, hospital charges, and the monitoring of physicians and hospitals through peer review boards.

In the late 1970s and early 1980s the United States witnessed escalating health costs. Medicare costs were increasing at alarming rates, physician and hospital costs were rising dramatically, and access was becoming even more limited. At the same time, the uninsured population was expanding rapidly. As in other policy sectors, the Reagan administration defined the problem as inefficiency due to lack of competition. Policy makers argued for greater use of market forces to bring about efficiency and financial responsibility. Cost-control measures were introduced. The period was one of diminishing health care support and elimination of federal grants. It was clearly part of the Reagan privatization agenda. For example, in 1983, to curb the federal government's increased financial obligations, fee schedules were imposed unilaterally under the Medicare supplemental program. This was a uniform fee schedule based on diagnosis-related groups (DRGs). Its objective was to cut Medicare and Medicaid costs. DRGs signified America's first major national effort to identify, describe, and specify costs for categories of disease and illness. The goal of the DRGs was to contain hospital costs and achieve better efficiency in the delivery of health care. This was to be accomplished by preestablishing schedule payments for each category of illness (470 total illnesses to begin with). In addition, Resource Based Relative Value Scales (RBRVSs) were introduced to measure and develop consistent fees for physicians' services.

Such cost-cutting efforts were continued through the remainder of the decade to no avail. Expenses kept rising due to higher utilization rates per insured in Medicare and an extension of the covered population in Medicaid. In 1988 Congress passed the Catastrophic Coverage Act. This act attempted to alleviate the strain on Medicare by solving the problem of individuals spending down any resources accumulated to reach the poverty limit and thus qualify for Medicare or Medicaid assistance. Most of the act was repealed in 1989 because of the negative reaction of many prominent interest groups, including pressure from the elderly.

From 1988 to 1992, during the Bush administration, it became obvious to all that there was a need for reform. Costs were still escalating, as was the number of uninsured, and managed care was now seen to be the pursuit of profit above good health care. In response to demands for reform and the prominence once again of the issue on the institutional agenda, Congress considered a number of plans to introduce some form of national health insurance.[19] All plans had the same objective: They would increase access to health care regardless of economic or employment status, and they proposed limited cost sharing by patients. The objective was to replace private insurance premiums with public expenditures through taxes on individual households. Although opposed to national insurance, many Republicans offered alternative ways of dealing with the "crisis of care." Most of the suggestions used tax credits or vouchers to require everyone to have private insurance coverage.[20]

When Bill Clinton took office in 1993, the time seemed ripe for radical reform. The cost dimension of the American health care system was, for many individuals, out of control. From 1960, costs had increased in all areas of health expenditure (see Table 15.3). It is against this agenda-setting backdrop in 1993 that the Clinton administration pledged to create a national health insurance system that would deal with the twin problems of spiraling medical care costs and unequal access. President Clinton appointed a special task force of 500 people led by his wife, Hillary Clinton, and Ira Magaziner, an industrial policy expert. The task force was charged with developing a health reform proposal. With such presidential commitment and the growing numbers of business leaders who had publically spoken in favor of reform, many believed major reform of some sort would be enacted.

In the autumn of 1993, the Clinton administration released its Health Security Plan. The proposal was for Congress to pass a Health Security Act, which among other things required employers to provide health care insurance coverage to all employees, created an internal market device called Health Insurance Alliances to purchase coverage and services, and placed price controls on insurance premiums. The objective of the plan was managed competition in which access to both the sale of health insurance and the purchase of health care at affordable rates would be provided to everyone through the insurance alliances. Clinton's plan was an attempt to shape market forces within a framework of national health insurance. The plan was formally submitted to Congress in October 1993 and never emerged as legislation. Why, is an interesting question.

The plan failed to win support partly because of strong opposition from a variety of health sector actors, such as small health insurers, pharmaceutical companies, and small-scale businesses represented by the National Federation of Independent Business (NFIB). A fierce media campaign launched by the Health Insurance Association of America reduced popular support for the plan by charging it would reduce patients' choices, increase costs, and decrease the quality of services. For many Americans, national health care is equated with socialism and therefore it directly threatens individual rights, responsibilities, and freedom.

Other contributing factors led to the plan's failure to win adoption. First is the "bootstrap" doctrine that is ingrained in American political culture. Second, once policy formulation was seriously embarked upon, the plan was confronted with a deeply divided congressional Democratic majority. Democrats were clearly divided on which model to adopt. Third, the majority of Republican legislators were strongly opposed to Clinton's idea of managed competition. Another factor was the

Table 15.3 U.S. Health Expenditures, 1960–1993 by Type of Expenditures (in billions of dollars)

Type of Expenditure	1960	1970	1980	1990	1993
Hospital	$9.3	$28.0	$102.7	$256.5	$326.6
Physician	5.3	13.6	45.2	140.5	171.2
Dental	2.0	4.7	13.3	30.4	37.4
Other professional	0.6	1.4	6.4	36.0	51.2
Home health care	0.0	0.2	1.9	11.1	20.8
Drugs and other medical nondurables	4.2	8.8	21.6	61.2	75.0
Vision products and other medical durables	0.8	2.0	4.5	10.5	12.6
Nursing home care	1.0	4.9	20.5	54.8	69.6
Other personal health care	0.7	1.3	4.0	11.4	18.2
Program administration and net cost of private health insurance	1.2	2.8	12.1	38.3	48.0
Government public health activities	0.4	1.4	7.2	21.6	24.7
Research	0.7	2.0	5.6	12.2	14.4
Construction	1.0	3.4	6.2	12.1	14.6

SOURCE: Adapted from data obtained from the Health Care Financing Administration, Office of the Actuary, Office of National Health Statistics, 2000.

Note: Research and development expenditures of drug companies and other manufacturers and providers of medical equipment and supplies are excluded from research expenditures, but are included in the expenditure class in which the product falls.

nature of the plan itself. Generally, the plan was disliked by everyone. It seemed to offer more bureaucratization, and there was no evidence it would be cost effective. Many opponents argued it would simply not cut costs, and others opposed the proposal because they perceived it as an attempt to harness state power to extend the scope of the state in the direction of universalism. In short, it was socialized medicine in disguise.

Congressional Democrats and Republicans drew up alternative plans. Six major health reform bills were circulated during the 1993–1995 session. For example, liberal Democrats backed the Wellstone-McDermott bill which called for a move to a single-payer model. A partisan group of House moderates pushed the Cooper-Grandy bill which called for a less comprehensive managed competition plan driven by employer-mandated insurance. The Moynihan bill, backed by a group of bipartisan moderates in the Senate,

proposed an assortment of specific initiatives designed to pay for expanded insurance access for most citizens. Some moderates and some conservatives in both chambers backed the Chafee bill which called for a diluted managed competition plan with a more limited employer mandate. The Gramm bill proposed to change tax codes to expand access to some additional citizens and was favored by many conservatives in both chambers. The diversity of positions made it difficult to envision how to craft a voting majority in support of a major proposal. Finally, Senate majority leader George Mitchell led a series of bipartisan discussions in an attempt to find agreement over more limited reform. In the end, none of these proposed health care bills received a floor vote because a consensus could not be achieved, and the chance to enact radical health care reform passed.

In 1996, in response to continued criticism that the needs of the uninsured had not been met, Congress passed legislation requiring insurers to extend coverage to employees between jobs for up to one year. What was interesting about this is it was passed in a Congress that had Republican majorities in both chambers. The late 1990s saw the implementation of cost controls in the private-dominated health care sector. Many employers have contained health care costs by encouraging competition among managed care plans. Additionally, they have required or strongly encouraged employees to enroll in HMOs. In 1988 only 30 percent of the insured population was in some form of managed care; by 1998 that figure had risen to 86 percent. Insurance providers and managed care plans have increasingly been pressured to keep premiums down. In turn, managed care plans have pressured hospitals and physicians to cut costs through discounting the price of services.

The result of all this transformation of the health care system has been to place new issues of concern on the systemic and institutional agendas. For example, both physicians and patients have complained that necessary tests and treatments are sometimes not provided in the effort to control costs. This has led to public discussions surrounding perceived decreases in the quality and freedom of care, and placed insurer regulation on the agenda. It should be pointed out that it has also contributed to a slowing down in the rate of health care spending by the late 1990s. As the decade came to a close, President Clinton issued an executive order that required federal agencies to adopt, by 1999, a patient bill of rights. The order covered more than 85 million Americans (about one-third of those with insurance coverage). It gave patients direct access to medical specialists; the right to receive information on all medical options regardless of the cost; the right to appeal managed care decisions to outside panels; and the right to have emergency care paid for if a "prudent

layperson" would have deemed the visit necessary. It was intended that the executive order would lay the groundwork for future legislation.

President George W. Bush indicated in the first months of his administration that he desired to make changes in health care. One of his first attempts at change was a four-year, $48 billion measure to assist states to pay the costs of prescription drugs for low-income retirees. The Bush administration has also clearly indicated that more systematic reforms should be expected with the creation of a bipartisan commission on Medicare.

President Bush's first summer in office witnessed the fight over the introduction of a federal patients' bill of rights. The debate hinged on whether lawmakers could agree on the parameters of liability. Two versions of the bill came under consideration, one sponsored by Senators Edward Kennedy, John McCain, and John Edwards, the other by Bill Frist and John Breaux. If passed, either bill would create a whole host of new protections for patients, including guaranteed access to specialists and emergency room care. The most controversial aspect of the legislation is the expansion of the number of individuals who would be able to sue their HMOs. President Bush has urged that a cap of $500,000 be placed upon all noneconomic damages.

DESIGNING HEALTH POLICY ALTERNATIVES

By the early 1990s health care policy had moved from the systemic to the institutional agenda. As we have seen, calls for health care reform were widespread and were fueled by increased costs to both patient and provider, and a climate of increased concern over competitive market forces in the provision of health care. The attempt to introduce health care reform in the first Clinton administration provides a good arena to discuss the design of policy alternatives.

The American health care system provides individuals with curative health services through either the private market or limited insurance programs. For the most part, by the early 1990s it was obvious that reform of some kind was necessary and desired by many individuals. American policy makers were faced with the problem of designing policy that would achieve cost containment and reduce severe gaps in health coverage. Individuals without insurance coverage had restricted access to treatment for nonacute complaints. Such access was restricted by the patients' ability to pay for the services. For uninsured or underinsured individuals there was limited access to emergency services because of cross-subsidization of care by employers who provided coverage to their workers. In essence, facilities and physicians who provided care to the uninsured or underinsured offset the zero or low reimbursements they received from government insurance programs by charging higher fees to patients with private insurance. The insurance companies, in turn, passed on their cost increases to employers by increasing employee premiums. In reality, what was going on was a cost-shifting game.

Everyone was willing to play the game as long as the economy grew and business was protected from the effects of competition. However, with economic recession and changes in the structure of the American labor market the problems of cost and access became more visible. As the 1980s passed, more and more workers were employed without fringe benefits and more and more individuals were forced to pay out-of-pocket for their own health insurance. The choice for many workers was either to underinsure or not have coverage. For employers who did not provide fringe benefits, labor costs were kept down.[21] In the case of those firms that did provide benefits, they clearly felt their higher labor costs

put them at a disadvantage when competing with both American companies that did not provide benefits and overseas competitors. Employers that were providing employees with insurance started to protest the higher premiums being passed on to them to cross-subsidize the uninsured or underinsured. Some employers lobbied government to adopt a national insurance program so that all employers would have to pay their share of workers' health care costs.[22]

The Clinton administration was left with the task of designing a policy that corrected the gaps in coverage and the rising costs of provision and services. The alternatives were clear. The administration could

1. Do nothing—this would obviously not correct any of the system's shortcomings.

2. Create a national health service—this would correct access problems but would not deal with cost-containment problems; it would also result in higher taxes and meet with opposition from private insurers.

3. Build upon existing employment-based insurance—this would stop free riding from employers and would pool all risks within a national scheme.

4. Regulate the market to expand access and replace cost shifting with cost containment.

The administration combined the third and fourth alternatives in the formulation of the 1993 Health Security Plan. Policy makers advanced the introduction of both national health insurance and the regulation of health market competition. The goals of such a policy were expansion of access, cost containment, and distribution of costs across the board to all employers.

The plan proposed mandatory provision of insurance by all employers to all their employees. The government would subsidize the costs of such insurance to small businesses and those individuals who were not eligible through employment. Thus, national insurance would broaden access and eliminate cost shifting. Next, to achieve containment of health care costs, different types of insurance plans were to be allowed at different prices to the consumer. It was hoped that most individuals would opt for plans with lower premiums offered by managed care organizations such as HMOs. Such plans would be the most restrictive in terms of what they offered in coverage. It was hoped this would promote market forces to cut costs. Third, the plan required all states to join regional health alliances that would be responsible for organizing the insurance market so that small businesses and individuals would have access to affordable insurance plans. Large businesses could also join together to form alliances to manage and monitor insurance plans. In essence, the government was designing the framework under which competition would operate.

Under such a plan the federal government's powers in health care were expanded. The Health Security Act required that the government legislated the minimum comprehensive package that any plan could offer to be considered as part of the national insurance scheme. Also, the act created a National Health Board composed of presidential appointees who would be responsible for regulating the alliances and health insurance plans. Additionally, the board was given the power to limit premium increases to the rate of inflation. In short, government was setting the rules of competition within a framework of universal coverage.

As discussed earlier, the plan did not pass. However, it did help to foster the idea that change was needed. Its essential effect was to stimulate business to regulate health insurance. The net result has been for business to force competition among insurance providers that have been pressured to keep premiums down. Government has also sub-

sequently enforced incremental regulation of the insurance market to foster competition, and passed consumer protection laws governing what HMOs and other providers can and cannot do.

The reasons for the plan's failure have already been discussed, but what is left to discuss is why the Clinton administration put forward the type of plan it did. To put it simply, policy makers designed an incremental alternative based upon existing health sector arrangements. The administration perceived it as the only rational choice. Any other alternative would have been perceived as too radical. In essence, the administration designed an alternative it felt was adoptable. President Clinton and his advisors saw it as a compromise between Democratic versions of universal health insurance and conservative opposition. Questions over access and gaps in coverage could be dealt with through national health insurance. By having a national insurance that was employment based and thus a fringe benefit, the government's reach into what it provides citizens out of tax revenues was not expanded. At the same time it ensured that citizens received the most basic of social needs, health care, without requiring them to shoulder a greater tax burden.

The American health care system is a voluntary, employment-based one and, as such, employers have a large say over its operation. The Clinton administration believed business concerns over labor costs were a large part of the health care problem. This affected how the administration defined the problem, negating the prominence of other dimensions of the problem in the problem definition. Clinton felt employer-based national health insurance allowed market forces to solve access and cost problems in the American health care system. When evaluating this particular alternative the administration did not take into account that compelling all employers to provide what they believed many employers were already doing was perceived

by many in the corporate sector as under-
mining corporate autonomy. Policy designers failed to consider the economic feasibility
for smaller enterprises of providing insurance
to employees. It was clear that many employers saw national health insurance as a solution
to rising labor costs and diminished profit
margins. However, what was not clear was
the strong opposition from those employers
that saw it as placing prohibitively high labor
costs upon them.

The 1993 Health Security Plan was an
attempt at state-led reform of the health sector. It was the federal government's bid to
design policy that established a universal
health care framework that dictated how
market forces operated within the sector. Its
failure is a good example of how the design
of alternatives is crucial to not only the type
of policy that is formulated but also on possible adoption. Policy feasibility must always
take into account all actors within any given
policy sector. Although the Clinton administration felt it had designed a plan with all
the constituent groups in mind, it obviously
did not understand that constituent groups
are composed of many stakeholders who
may share common goals but have different
needs and demands. Finally, Clinton's plan
for health security demonstrates that when
policy makers design policy alternatives they
should always remember that the more complicated a policy is, the less likely it will be
favored by the public or legislators.

THE POLICY PROCESS

AND HEALTH CARE POLICY

Health care policy making in the United
States is highly diffuse. Part of the reason for
such diffusion is there is no unified national
health care policy. American health care policy is composed of a series of layers (see Box
15.3). The result is that health care reform
proposals can emerge from a variety of are-

> **Box 15.3 The American Health Care Insurance System**
>
> - Medicare—a government-mandated and managed program for the elderly
> - Medicaid—a government program for low-income people where the federal governments sets basic guidelines and the state govern-ments determine most specific standards and benefits
> - Voluntary-based insurance through private insurance providers—covers a majority of the population and is regulated by both federal and state legislation

---

nas. The decentralization of the system gives
any state government the ability to formulate
and enact health care policy. At the federal
level there are a number of executive agencies
engaged in health care policy formulation,
including the Centers for Medicare and
Medicaid Services (CMS), formerly called
the Health Care Financing Administration;
the Department of Health and Human Services; and the Surgeon General's office. Additionally, presidents can assemble groups of
interested actors to formulate policy recommendations. At the same time, Congress is
also active through its committee system in
one or more aspects of health care policy.[23]
When health care reform was high on the institutional agenda in 1993–1994 there was an
onslaught of congressional hearings on health
care.

The American health care system is financed at many different levels. The federal
government is responsible for around 56 percent of expenditures, whereas the state and
local levels pick up the other 44 percent.[24]
Federal health care revenues are collected
through income and corporate taxes. At the
state level, revenues are collected through income and sales taxes, whereas at the local
level health revenues are provided through
sales and property taxes. Additional health

care revenues are supplemented by voluntary agencies. National health expenditures in the year 2000 show that approximately just more than 50 percent of the total came from private sources, while a little more than one-third came from federal and the remainder from state and local government sources.[25] The net result is that the federal government and private employers provide programs for the middle class and above, while the state and local governments are providers of the last resort to lower income individuals and the medical needy of all social strata.

In the 1990s, many Americans still opposed health care reform, viewing it as an expansion of government. It also highlights the limitations of the American policy-making process. Citizens are wary and distrustful of government intervention. Interest groups have sufficient power to stop major reform from reaching the top of the institutional agenda. The structure of the federal system allows policy to be made and stopped at multiple levels of government. The separation of powers permits divided government and a decentralized legislative process in which multiple poles of power exist in both houses of Congress. The Clinton health care proposal failed in a Democratic-controlled legislature. This demonstrates that the ability of a president to devise major legislation depends in large part on the president's power to persuade both the public and individual legislators to support a presidential initiative.

HEALTH CARE POLICY INSTRUMENTS

It can be argued that American health policy has three generic goals.[26] The first goal is security. This can be understood as the provision of a minimum of services. The second goal is equity, which can be understood as a guarantee of access. The third goal is efficiency, which consists of the best level of services for the least amount spent. In contemporary American health care policy, the government has utilized five of the commonly recognized policy instruments to achieve its goals. First, direct provision of services. Second, rules that detail who may provide services, how services are to be provided, what services may be provided, how services will be financed, and who may receive services. Inducements or incentives both negative and positive are the third instrument used in health policy. These ensure compliance by both providers and target populations. A fourth instrument is facts that persuade the target population to undertake change in behavior. The final instrument is powers that give certain levels of government the authority to make decisions.

SUMMARY

Some critics have argued that the U.S. health care system is "the paradox of excess and deprivation."[27] The system boasts the greatest density of high-tech services, more employees per bed than any other country, and arguably the best medical research and training in the world.[28] However, the United States also possesses the highest health care costs (twice the average of industrialized nations), the largest health care expenditure of any industrialized nation, a large number of individuals (almost 44 million) who have no health insurance, and even more citizens who are underinsured.[29] Ironically, according to the WHO 2000 report the United States, one of the world's wealthiest and most powerful nations, ranks surprisingly low in many health-related areas. Why can Great Britain spend approximately 7 percent of its GDP on health services and yet rank eighteenth overall compared to America's 13.1 percent of GDP expenditure and its overall ranking of thirty-seventh (see Table 15.2)? How can the American system be so responsive and yet be so unequal in terms of financial fairness of the system? It is no wonder that recent polls have shown that 75 percent of Americans support health care reform as well as some form of national health system, even if it means higher taxes. There is also great regional variation in the quality and level of health care services, in spite of the requirement that the various states adopt federal guidelines and regulations in order to obtain necessary funds and grants. For the most part, individual states are given broad discretion in determining their own health care policies and systems.

The American health care system is a market-oriented one and it seems highly likely that it will remain so in the near future. The United States remains the lone industrial nation of its economic stature without some kind of national health insurance provided by the government through tax revenues. Public health provision is provided through Medicaid and Medicare, whereas private provision is through employer and employee contributions to fund private health insurance options or individual personal payments for health services. Greater public sector health care provision in the United States continues to be blocked by the dominance of a culture that fears "big" government. With its emphasis on individualism, self-reliance, and limited government, direct provision by government of health services is perceived to mean erosion of the individual's rights and choices. Many consider this to be much worse than the inequalities of the current system.

Costs will continue to rise and will remain an obstacle to greater public sector provision of health care. Over the past decade there has been approximately a 12 percent increase in health costs.[30] This affects every level and sector. Insurance deductibles are higher, and fees for services have increased, as have insurance premiums. Such costs are passed on to others. Prices increase so businesses can cover insurance benefits, physicians and hospitals increase their fees to cover the costs of new equipment and their malpractice and liability insurance. The consequence has been cutbacks in types of service, and lack of coverage to high-risk groups or individuals. Health care reform will continue to be heavily opposed by the private health care industry which spends millions and millions of dollars to ensure that there is not radical reform of health care provision in the United States. If there is a lesson to be learned from the battle over health care reform in the mid-1990s, it is that reform of health care can be accomplished in the United States only through small incremental changes. Reliance must be placed upon policy creators who know how to divide policy issues into palatable and thus acceptable pieces that can be explained to a small target constituency.

DISCUSSION QUESTIONS

1. When governments experiment with the introduction of market forces into health care provision, should they consider the difference between citizen and customer?

2. Should health care be a public provision and open to all regardless of income?

SUGGESTED READINGS

Altensetter, C., and J. Bjorkman, eds. *Health Policy Reform, National Variations and Globalization.* New York: St. Martin's Press, 1997.

Graig, L. *Health of Nations: An International Perspective on U.S. Health Care Reform.* Washington, D.C.: CQ Press, 1999.

Helms R. B., ed. *Health Care Policy and Politics: Lessons From Four Countries.* Washington, DC: AEI Press, 1993.

Powell, F., and A. F. Wessen. *Health Care Systems in Transition: An International Perspective.* London: Sage, 1999.

Rushefsky, M. E., and K. Patel. *Politics, Power and Policy Making: The Case of Health Care Reform in the 1990s.* New York: M. E. Sharpe, 1998.

Seedhouse, D. *Reforming Health Care: The Philosophy and Practice of International Health Reform.* New York: Wiley, 1995.

Skocpol, T. *Boomerang: Clinton's Health Security Effort and the Turn Against Government in U.S. Politics.* New York: Norton, 1996.

Tuohy, C. *Accidental Logics: The Dynamics of Change in the Health Care Arena in the United States, Britain, and Canada.* New York: Oxford University Press, 1999.

ENDNOTES

1. Mortality rates and fertility rates were used.

2. World Health Organization, *The World Health Report 1999: Making a Difference* (Geneva, Switzerland: WHO, 1999), 1.

3. D. T. Jamison, L. J. Lau, and J. Wang, "Health's Contribution to Economic Growth, 1965–90," in WHO Director-General Transition Team, *Health Policy and Economic Outcomes, 1998* (Geneva, Switzerland: WHO, 1998).

4. Ibid.

5. WHO, *The World Health Report 1999,* 5–9.

6. Ibid., 5–9.

7. D. E. Bloom and J. G. Williamson, "Demographic Transitions and Economic Miracles in Asia," *The World Bank Economic Review* 12, no. 3 (1998): 419–455.

8. J. Strauss and D. Thomas, "Health, Nutrition and Economic Development," *Journal of Economic Literature* 46 (June 1998): 776–817.

9. Ibid., 793.

10. World Health Organization, *The World Health Report 2000—Health Systems: Improving Performance* (Geneva, Switzerland: WHO, 2000).

11. Ibid., chap. 1.

12. Ibid., 3.

13. Ibid., 5.

14. *The World Bank Health Statistical Reports, 2000*—Health Systems Improving Performance (Geneva, Switzerland, WHO, 2000) 5–7.

15. The first facility to care for low-income and destitute citizens was the Pennsylvania general hospital established in 1752. Treatment was limited and resources were scarce, but local people in need were afforded some sort of health care.

16. The birth of insurance in the United States began in 1847 with the Massachusetts Health Insurance Company. The company was the first company in the United States to offer sickness insurance to employed workers. Ironically, at this point in U.S. history support for a national insurance system was great. Even President Theodore Roosevelt supported legislation to implement such a system. It is important to mention that the American Medical Association joined Roosevelt in support for a national insurance system but later joined the growing movement (business, health care workers, and insurance companies) to oppose such legislation.

17. T. Marmor, *Understanding Health Care Reform* (New Haven, CT: Yale University Press, 1994).

18. Ibid., 17–24.

19. Among the Bush-era plans considered by Congress were the Comprehensive Health Care for All Americans Act, the National Health Insurance Act, the Mediplan Health Care Act of 1991, and the Universal Health Care Act of 1991.

20. Examples of such plans include the Affordable Health Insurance Act of 1991, the Comprehensive Health Care Access Improvement and Cost Containment Act of 1991, the Health Equity and Access Improvement Act of 1992, and the Comprehensive American Health Care Act.

21. S. Giaimo and P. Manow, "Adapting the Welfare State," *Comparative Political Studies* 32, no. 8 (December 1999): 967–1000.

22. Ibid., 984.

23. From 1980 to 1991, ten House committees and seven Senate committees held hearings on health care reform.

24. Health Care Financing Administration, Office of the Actuary, Office of National Health Statistics, 2000.

25. Ibid., 77–79.

26. D. A. Stone, *Policy Paradox and Political Reason* (Glenview, IL: Scott Foresman, 1988).

27. K. J. Mueller, *Health Care Policy in the United States* (Lincoln: University of Nebraska Press, 1993), 77.

28. Ibid.

29. HCFA, 2000.

30. Ibid.

16

Welfare Policy

Formulating Policy and Legitimation of Solutions

For many individuals the provision of appropriate and sufficient standards of living to citizens is of paramount concern. Modern governments have dealt with such concerns through the formulation and implementation of social policy. Social policy covers a wide range of social and economic phenomena, from issues of self-esteem and individual rights and needs, to complex policy questions such as the relief of indigence, inequalities, and unemployment. It also includes the supply by government of goods and services, such as housing, education, and health care. How much government allocates for social policy expenditure is dictated by the extent of its welfare state. For many nations the largest portion of their governmental budget is spent on social policy—expenditures such as pension programs, unemployment and disability benefits, subsidies to support families with dependent children, and assistance to families and individuals with low incomes. In the United States, it is more common to hear references to welfare policy rather than to social policy. The net result is to think of welfare policy as a series of programs designed to assist poor and disadvantaged people, thus excluding social security and many other social programs from the welfare debate. However, this is shortsighted; when we use the term *social welfare policy* in this text we use it to describe all of the programs that the U.S. government provides to protect and advance citizens' standards of living.

There is a vast amount of literature devoted to discussing why governments need to provide social welfare for their citizens. One argument posits welfare provision as a relief program supplementing economic arrangements.[1] Governments provide services that absorb and control un-employment, disabilities, ill health, and aging. Social welfare policy is made necessary by the instability that is inherent in capitalist economies such as the United States. Another argument found in the welfare literature contends welfare policy regulates labor.[2] In short, provision of welfare is seen to be punitive and degrading, and instills in the majority of individuals the fear of being on government relief rolls; thus, many individuals would rather work than receive welfare relief. A further argument is that societies cannot afford to have large numbers of individuals who are suffering obvious inequalities without relief.[3] Welfare pacifies those individuals who without welfare relief would be forced to find resources through whatever means they could. Thus, it exists to help reintegrate disaffected groups back into the system.[4] In its broadest sense, welfare policy provides security to those in need. Such security can be temporary or permanent. A final argument found in the literature is that welfare policy fosters independence by encouraging citizens to be self-supporting.[5]

The U.S. government has always been much more reluctant than its European counterparts to intervene in the general area of social policy. Indeed, it was not until the 1930s that the federal government provided any sort of welfare and social security benefits for low-income and elderly people. Even then, the extent and level of coverage were extremely limited. This is in sharp contrast to many European governments that initiated social service programs beginning in the late nineteenth century (see Table 16.1).

The provision of social welfare in most industrialized nations falls under two general categories: policies that benefit low-income citizens and policies that help the general public. The first category includes general assistance programs that give money, food, or clothing directly to qualifying individuals; work assistance programs for people in need; and categorical assistance that targets aid for low-income individuals. Such programs can take many forms; for example, social insurance covering income losses due to illness, unemployment, and retirement. Another example would be social regulation programs protecting individuals from the problems of industrialized society (e.g., consumer protection and worker protection regulations). Box 16.1 summarizes the different approaches taken by industrialized nations in their attempts to deal with poverty. All industrialized nations have taken a specific approach to provide a variety of social welfare programs to citizens as a right of citizenship. The objective is to establish a safety net with the hopes that it will alleviate poverty among those who are chronically poor.

The provision of economic assistance by the government directly to individuals involves three basic questions: (1) how to determine who qualifies for social policy benefits, (2) how redistributive is the program, and (3) how assistance will be provided. When governments decide on

Table 16.1 Year of Introduction of Various Social Services in Selected Nations

Nation	Old-Age Pension	Unemployment Insurance	Sickness Pay	Medical Services
Germany	1889	1927	1889	1883
Britain	1908	1911	1911	1911
France	1930	1914	1930	1930
U.S.A.	1935	1935		1965

SOURCE: Adapted from 5.2. Theodoulou, *Policy and Politics in Six Nations, A Comparative Perspective* (Upper Saddle River, NJ: Prentice Hall), 128.

BOX 16.1   Antipoverty Approaches

APPROACH	OBJECTIVE	POLICY OPTION
Preventive approach	This approach attempts to ensure that individuals do not become poor.	Social security (old-age pensions); unemployment benefits
Alleviative approach	This deals with those individuals who are already poor and attempts to provide some kind of governmental assistance to alleviate their condition.	Temporary Assistance for Needy Families; food stamps
Punitive approach	This is based upon the assumption that if individuals are poor, it's because of their own moral and character defects. In other words, it is their own fault. Government should try to discourage them from being lazy by making it as difficult as possible to obtain public assistance in the form of governmental benefits. When government does have to provide assistance it should be minimally.	Workfare
Curative approach	Causes of poverty, such as lack of education and job training, should be cured. This approach emphasizes programs that attack the causes of poverty and is often used with a political strategy of giving low-income individuals some sort of control over the institutions that affect their communities. Community organization is encouraged.	Headstart; Meals on Wheels; literacy training; job training
Incomes approach	Individuals are encouraged to work while they receive government assistance. As their job-related income increases, their level of benefits decreases. The idea behind this is that an individual is better off working than not working.	Negative income tax; Earned Income Tax Credit; supplementary security income

---

eligibility for assistance, they can take one of two approaches: the public assistance or social assistance model or the social insurance model. In the public assistance approach eligibility for benefits are means tested. That is, in order to qualify for benefits recipients must demonstrate need. Proponents of such an approach argue that means testing allows governments to alleviate extreme poverty without spending government resources on individuals who are not truly needy. In the United States, social welfare policies are pre-dominantly means tested due mostly to its individualist heritage. Critics of public assistance say it is often the case that people who are truly in need struggle to prove their eligibility while others who are not in need qualify for benefits they should not receive by cheating the system through various fraudulent means. Means testing is also criticized because it often leads to stigmatizing. It is difficult to build public support for social policy because few people want to be labeled as poor.

Under a social insurance model of social welfare policy, all individuals in a given circumstance are eligible for assistance regardless of their degree of need. For example, all individuals who are unemployed are eligible for benefits. Citizens have entitlements because they pay taxes to support these programs and cannot be denied benefits. Citizens support social policy because they realize that they will get back some of their taxes in government benefits of some kind. The major criticism of the model is that it is hard to protect benefit levels without increasing taxes, because government revenues can be strained if the number of recipients increases. This is something that many taxpayers do not understand or support.

Governments employing the public assistance model are deciding that policy should be clearly redistributive with all taxpayers supporting the program, but with many of them never qualifying for benefits. The social insurance approach, on the other hand, allows for the possibility of all citizens benefiting in some way. Consequently, governments may limit the redistributive element in social insurance programs. In some nations this means programs are based on the principle of individual equity. Citizens receive benefits in accordance with their level of contributions. In other nations governments choose to base programs on basic needs. Benefit levels are set at a certain standard and citizens are paid a common benefit. This combines entitlements and a redistributive element. All citizens receive benefits of some kind, but the wealthy, through heavier tax contributions and less receipt of benefits, subsidize the benefits paid out to those in need. What type of benefits governments can choose to provide citizens is decided through their choice of policy instruments, which is discussed later in this chapter.

The provision of social welfare programs has aroused heated debate for several reasons. First, many critics claim that welfare encourages social dependency, with recipients choosing to become dependent on government support and remain unemployed. The second reason is they are concerned with the present and future costs of such provision. During the 1980s and 1990s, nation after nation has faced conflict over not only the type of social welfare provision but also the increasing drain inflicted upon national revenues. Governments face a true political dilemma: Should benefits provided by social welfare programs be decreased or eliminated to control costs, or should they protect those benefits by either cutting government programs in other policy sectors or by asking citizens to pay more taxes?

CONTEMPORARY SOCIAL WELFARE POLICY IN THE UNITED STATES

The United States was late in implementing social welfare policy mainly because of American political culture and its emphasis on self-reliance and rugged individualism. Such values encourage individuals to seek remedies from within themselves rather than from government or society. Consequently, there was a cold ideological climate for welfare policy provision. Poverty was seen as deriving from an individual's faults and not the system's faults. For most of the early decades of the twentieth century, social welfare policy was a local or private sector responsibility and a punitive approach to poverty was taken. As such, only a minority of individuals—"the worthy poor" as the literature of the day refers to them—received assistance.

Social welfare policy arrangements in the United States changed with President Franklin D. Roosevelt's New Deal program. This program established the tradition of federal government provision of social welfare. The Roosevelt administration was faced with changes brought about by the Great Depression, which began in 1929. Americans in the 1930s called upon their government to deal with poverty. From the 1930s on it became acceptable to many Americans and some policy makers that some individuals were poor through no fault of their own. This is an acceptance of the argument that there are systemic causes that go beyond some individuals' ability to manage. Under Roosevelt the Democratic party supported federal government intervention to address the problems caused by economic crisis.

The 1935 Social Security Act was the centerpiece of the New Deal and is the embodiment of a combination of the preventive and alleviative approaches to deal with poverty. The act established a system of social insurance, or income security, and is preventive in nature through the introduction of social security and unemployment compensation. Poverty was to be alleviated through transfer payments from the government to a specified population. The major program that fell under this category was Aid to Families with Dependent Children (AFDC).[6]

Social welfare was dropped from the institutional agenda with the advent of World War II and did not return to the agenda in the immediate postwar economic growth years. [7] Due to decreased poverty rolls, there was a general perception among both voters and policy makers that fewer people needed government help. It was during the 1960s that poverty and social welfare regained its place on the public agenda. The Kennedy administration formulated several programs that were later endorsed and passed as legislation. Most of these programs formed President Lyndon B. Johnson's Great Society and the War on Poverty programs. In reality, what these programs did was extend the New Deal social welfare programs.[8] Most of the established programs were either preventive or alleviative in their approach. However, a curative approach was also utilized by the administration.

For example, the 1964 Equal Opportunity Act was an attempt by the federal government to break the poverty cycle at an early age by providing a wide range of educational and job training programs, such as Head Start.

In the late 1960s and early 1970s, President Richard Nixon attempted to change the provision of social welfare by providing programs that could be identified with the Republican party and were inexpensive to fund. Nixon and critics of the Great Society program labeled much of the War on Poverty a failure. President Nixon, influenced by the work of the conservative economist Milton Friedman, pushed for a move away from the alleviative approach to an incomes model. Nixon and his supporters believed the alleviative approach created disincentives and encouraged welfare dependency through its promotion of welfarism.[9] In effect, what President Nixon did was change the focus of the social welfare debate away from the issue of poverty to a debate about how welfare should be provided by government. The 1970s were years of economic uncertainty, and Nixon and his supporters felt that welfare was a luxury the government and the middle-class could not afford. The Nixon administration championed the notion of "workfare." Simply, what Americans needed was work, not welfare. Workfare was a key component of New Deal social welfare policy making.

The election of a Democrat, Jimmy Carter, to the White House in 1976 did not alter the focus of the welfare debate. The 1970s saw a continuation of emphasis on the problems of welfare provision rather than a discussion of the underlying causes of poverty. By 1980 and the election of Ronald Reagan to the presidency, hostility to welfare among all sections of the population was high. Many conservatives advocated extensive government cutbacks. President Reagan and his supporters argued that social welfare policy was a failure, it cost too much, and it discouraged individuals from working. Critics argued that any rational individual would choose public assistance over a low-paying dead-end job with few benefits. To further their point, critics argued that the nation's economic ill health was due to being overloaded and burdened with the costs of welfare. Many conservatives argued it was the Great Society and War on Poverty programs that were directly responsible for much of the economic slowdown and the growth in the federal budget deficit. Basically, critics were returning to the philosophy that it's the individual's fault for being poor and not the system's fault.[10] Reagan and his supporters provided a vocal ideological resistance to active government. What Ronald Reagan did was to place welfare reform firmly on the institutional agenda. During the Reagan years and in his successor's administration, the United States undertook a prolonged period of policy formulation and debate around welfare policy. The 1980s and 1990s witnessed massive cutbacks in social policy that solidified opinion against the notion of welfare. Reagan and his successor George Bush took a punitive approach to welfare provision. The net result was retrenchment in welfare provision and an increase in poverty levels after 1980.

There was deep division for most of the 1980s and early 1990s over how welfare provision should be reformed. The Democrats were divided into three major factions: The first faction called for the expansion of current policy into new areas and new benefit levels, the second faction urged protection of the existing system with minor changes, and the third faction demanded wholesale reform of most programs. Republicans were also divided into two main camps: those calling for minor reform and those advocating sweeping changes.[11]

The debate over welfare reform from Reagan's election in 1980, to Bill Clinton's election to the White House in 1992, took place in the context of a divided govern-

ment. Republican presidents demanded welfare reform, whereas Democrat-controlled legislatures went from the expansion of benefits in some programs to contraction of benefits in others. Most program expansions were unfunded mandates that were passed only if they were to be paid for by state governments. During this period (1981 to 1993) implementation of funded and unfunded federal social programs took place largely at the state level. This spawned conflicting and spotty implementation across states which resulted in first, giving both sides of the reform issue fodder to exploit with the public, and, second, allowing for great program innovation at the state level. Many states were given permission by the federal government to explore many of the reforms that had been discussed at the federal level for many years previously. In certain states there was denial of benefits to certain categories of individuals, variations in means test and asset test levels, the introduction of work requirements for benefits, and time limits on benefit periods.

Although by 1992 poverty rates and other conditions of social ill health, such as the homeless, had grown, welfare was clearly perceived by many to be the root of America's problems. State after state had cut its welfare programs, and the public was united in its desire for federal welfare reform. Presidential candidates of both the major parties stressed their commitment to reform. The successful Democratic candidate Bill Clinton promised "an end to welfare as we know it." The electorate was rewarded some three years later with the reform they so badly wanted. Reform was made possible by the Republicans gaining control of Congress in January 1995 and the presence of a Democratic president who was committed to changing social policy arrangements.

Both houses of Congress passed resolutions in 1995 to roll back welfare and it was eventually signed into law in August 1996 by

President Clinton. At the time Robert Dole, the Republican Senate leader and a presidential candidate, argued, "Welfare reform is a story about an America where welfare is no longer a way of life and where people no longer will be able to receive endless federal cash benefits just because they choose not to work." The reform enacted was the 1996 Personal Responsibility and Work Opportunity Reconciliation Act. Some critics have argued this ended welfare as the United States had known it since the 1930s, and that it is the most comprehensive change in federal social policy since the 1960s.

Since the adoption and implementation of the 1996 reform, welfare provision has changed in the United States. The federal government now limits the number of people receiving welfare transfers and the time period of benefits. In the immediate years following the adoption of the reform, we saw a decrease in the number of people on the welfare rolls, due mainly to stricter eligibility

requirements. Essentially, social welfare policy demanded that recipients accept greater responsibility for their own support by requiring workfare. Workfare calls for welfare recipients to perform communal service and enroll in job training programs. (The main provisions of the 1996 legislation are displayed in Box 16.2.) Control over welfare policy shifted back to state governments from the federal government, giving state legislatures the flexibility to run their own welfare programs. The other important result of the reform was that welfare payments were severely limited. Thus, the reform can be classified as a punitive approach fused with an incomes approach. As President Clinton stated when he announced his decision to sign the legislation, "Today we have a historic decision to make welfare what it was meant to be—a second chance not a way of life."[12]

It is still too early to realize the legislation's full impact. However, some early observations can be made. First, the move to

---

BOX 16.2   Major Provisions of the 1996 Personal Responsibility and Work Opportunity Reconciliation Act

- AFDC was eliminated as a nationally funded federal–state contract that ensured cash payments to families and households supporting children.

- Created Temporary Assistance for Needy Families (TANF). This is a block grant that provides discretionary funding to individual states. States then provide for families in need with these funds. Thus, the 1996 act eliminates a national entitlement. Under TANF, cash support to families in need is limited. Recipients are limited to public assistance for a total of two years with lifetime benefits limited to five years.

- Teenage mothers can be denied benefits if they do not live in their parental home and do not attend school.

- The act also restricts childless adults, ages 18 to 50, to three months of food stamps during a three-year period.

- The policy also requires at least half of all single parents on welfare in any state to work or be in work-related activities by 2002 or the state will lose some of its federal block grants.

- The formula for food stamps was changed to reduce benefit levels almost 20 percent by the year 2002.

- The act denies to legal immigrants most welfare benefits until a five-year residency period has been fulfilled.

- In 1997, food stamps eligibility for noncitizens was eliminated as were disability payments.

federal block grants further decentralizes cash assistance to families in need. Second, the federally mandated work requirements and time limits present state governments with the problem of providing meaningful work opportunities for low-income individuals. Third, it is still unclear how successful implementation will be achieved. When deadlines are reached, how many state governments will refuse benefits to recipients once the ceiling on benefits is reached in 2002? The New York City Welfare Commissioner announced in July 2001 that an expected 46,000 recipients would reach the ceiling by the end of the year. Many advocates are uncertain how the city will meet the funding needs of such individuals.[13] A fourth observation is that the 1990s' booming economy and political compromises have led to almost all states receiving more funds than they did prior to reform, and yet the number living in poverty has not decreased significantly.[14] Many families are doing poorly and the number of children in extreme poverty (less than half the poverty rate) has increased.[15] Between 1995 and 1997, the mean income of the poorest 20 percent of female-headed households fell by an average of $580 per family; this was due mainly to loss of food stamps and other welfare benefits.[16]

Only time will tell whether the 1996 reform will endure or whether it will give rise to even more reform. It has already undergone some changes. In April 1999, exceptions to certain rules were enacted. For example, states may continue to provide benefits beyond five years to up to 20 percent of recipients based on hardship or domestic violence.

When George W. Bush spoke of compassionate conservatism in his campaign for the presidency, it is our opinion he was advocating a clearly developed political agenda. Compassionate conservatism undoubtedly represents for President Bush a rolling back of the state's frontiers; however, it is not a stereo-typical conservative commitment to wholesale cutting and withdrawal of government from the provision of social welfare. George W. Bush advocates civil society as an alternative to the bureaucratic welfare state: Society should take care of those in need without formal governmental intervention through regulation. In short, President Bush argues that governmental social programs cannot be scaled back without something in place to provide support to those individuals and communities that are falling behind. The alternative is to channel more support and resources to private charities, both secular and religious, to deal with poverty.

President Bush wants states to have the flexibility to fund private, public, or faith-based programs that successfully move people from the welfare rolls to employment. This follows closely his policy agenda as Texas governor. George W. Bush was the first governor to endorse the "Charitable Choice" provisions of the 1996 welfare reform legislation, permitting religious groups serving low-income people to be eligible for government antipoverty funds. This was the promotion of faith-based charities as providers of welfare services. One of Bush's first initiatives as president was to create an office in the White House devoted to supporting faith-based organizations. In July 2001, the House of Representatives approved the president's faith-based initiative. The measure boosts support for religious charities by making them eligible for more federal grants and by expanding tax deductions for charitable donations. Other additional changes in the tax code are being considered to enhance the replacement of the state in welfare provision by charities.

The other main area of President Bush's social welfare policy agenda is social security reform. In May of 2001, the president named a commission of sixteen (eight Republicans and eight Demo-crats) to make recommendations on social security reform.

The objective of the commission is to lay the groundwork for congressional support toward a social security system that allows for voluntary individual investment.

FORMULATION AND LEGITIMATION OF SOCIAL WELFARE POLICY

The 1996 Personal Responsibility and Work Opportunity Reconciliation Act will provide the case study for a discussion of the dynamics of formulation and legitimation. Four sets of actors clearly dominated the policy formulation process around social welfare policy reform in the 1990s: elected office holders, bureaucrats, interest groups, and experts.

Formulation of Welfare Reform

President Clinton originally submitted a proposal for welfare reform in 1994 that died in the 102nd Congress. After a new Republican majority was elected in early 1995, the party submitted the Contract with America legislation, which was their attempt at welfare reform. The proposal went quickly through the House, passing on a party-line vote. The proposal's passage through the Senate was more difficult. Senate Republicans were divided over the nature of the legislation. Conservative Republicans were in favor of legislation similar to what was passed in the House; however, moderate Republican senators wanted more flexible legislation allowing for more state flexibility and were willing to make compromises in order to get legislation that President Clinton would feel comfortable in signing. This is what prevailed; moderate Republican senators joined with Democratic senators, and on September 19, 1995, a modified version of the House bill

was passed. The president praised the legislation and indicated that he would sign it. However, liberal Democrats were not happy with either the House or Senate versions and argued that it ended welfare entitlement, whereas conservative Republicans argued the Senate bill was too liberal.

Areas of disagreement were resolved in the House–Senate conference committee with the decision by the committee to compile a bill that was closer to the House version. The Democrats refused to support the compromise legislation out of the conference committee. To further complicate matters, welfare reform was tied to budget reconciliation legislation with deficit reduction provisions that Clinton opposed. Thus, the president vetoed the budget measure in December 1995, which meant that he was also vetoing welfare reform as well. To force Clinton's hand, the Republicans separated welfare reform from budget reconciliation, and welfare was sent to the president as a stand-alone bill. Unhappy with many of the provisions within the welfare bill, Clinton vetoed it and was heavily criticized by his opponents for reneging on his campaign promise. Welfare reform had been vetoed twice and it seemed likely that change would not occur.

An opportunity to bring welfare reform to the legislative table once again was initiated by the National Governors Association (NGA) annual meeting in February 1996. The governors modified the House legislation and designed reform that was less restrictive and would result in around $44 billion in welfare spending over seven years. The House proposal had a target of $64 billion. The governors' proposal was more moderate than many conservative Republicans desired; however, it was closer to the Contract with America recommendations than to the Clinton 1994 welfare proposal. The governors' proposal gave state governments more flexibility and resources to spend on welfare. Many analysts viewed the governors' proposal as a compromise as it was supported by both Republican and Democrat governors. This led to the pressure for Congress and the president to come to agreement and pass legislation aimed at reforming welfare.

The significance of the role of the governors in the formulation process of welfare reform cannot be overlooked. As chief executives of the states, they would essentially be in charge of implementing any mandated change; thus, it was important to get their support for adopted legislation. What the governors did was to bring welfare back onto the agenda by creating a compromise that pressured congressional actors and the executive to act.

As far as interest groups are concerned, many liberal interest groups were shut out of the process because they could not work with the Republican majority. In essence, they could not agree that benefits and entitlements should be reduced. Conservative groups such as the Heritage Foundation were extremely influential and had the ear of the Republican congressional leadership.

Based upon the NGA proposal, congressional Republicans put forward new legislation in May of 1996. On cursory examination the new legislation looked as if it provided a strong basis for compromise. On deeper examination, however, it became apparent to many Democrats that Clinton would have no choice but to veto it, for the Republicans had tied welfare reform to Medicaid reform. Many governors and Republicans felt Medicaid reform would not only be a cost-cutting measure but also that it could provide state flexibility. Although President Clinton and many Democrats recognized the need to reform welfare entitlements, they were opposed to eliminating health coverage, even limited care, for low-income people. The proposed Medicaid revisions were seen as an attempt to end the federal government's responsibility for protecting the health of the nation's poorest individuals. Many Democrats felt this represented an obvious attempt to discredit both the party and the president on their desire to bring about welfare reform. The Republicans knew Clinton would veto the bill, and they knew he could be publicly criticized for reneging on campaign promises.

The White House continued to articulate Clinton's desire to compromise. Statements were made indicating that what the president wanted was a clean bill without Medicaid attachments promoting the notion of workfare, personal responsibility, and the protection of children living in poverty. By June the House and Senate committees began marking up the welfare–Medicaid legislation.

Legitimation of Welfare Reform

The first committee in June to see the new proposal was the House Ways and Means Human Resources subcommittee. The Democrats on the subcommittee proposed several amendments, ranging from restoring certain benefits to immigrants to vouchers for families so that parents could purchase certain items for their children. None of the amendments passed.

On June 12, 1996, the Ways and Means committee marked up the bill. The first amendment was a proposal backed by the president to replace the bill with an entirely new bill. This amendment failed and the bill passed in the committee by 23 to 14; one Democrat voting in favor.[17] The bill then went to the floor for consideration; however, as the legislation was being considered by other committees simultaneously it could not progress on the floor until all committees had reported back.[18] By June 19, all committees had reported back and the bill was sent to the Rules committee. It is usual practice for all legislation to be sent to the Rules committee before it goes to the House floor.

At the same time, the bill was being considered in the Senate. Only two Senate committees had jurisdiction over welfare reform: the Agricultural committee (food stamps) and the Senate Finance committee (dealt with all other aspects). It was obvious from Senate Finance committee deliberations that the bill was in trouble; in particular, the Medicaid proposal was problematic for many Republican and Democrat Senators. Republicans felt the proposal did not go far enough, whereas liberals felt it went too far. The Republican leadership faced a no-win situation. Additionally, many Republicans in Congress felt that they would suffer electorally if legislation was not signed quickly. Many were elected because they supported the Contract with America and would be judged if the contract did not deliver. To further complicate matters, Senator Robert Dole, the Republican presidential candidate, sent the Republican congressional leadership a public letter urging them to pass welfare reform legislation.[19]

Republican congressional leaders responded by announcing in July 1996 that Medicaid reform would be separated from welfare reform legislation. The policy window for passing welfare reform was now opening up. For most of July, President Clinton and the Republicans fenced each other over whether the bill would be signed into law. At times Clinton articulated that a turning point had been reached and compromise was possible. At other times he criticized the bill for being too stringent or he attacked certain provisions arguing that the proposal was penalizing legal immigrants and that it was making too many cuts in provision. With the Senate's detachment of Medicaid from the proposal, the House Rules committee prepared to move welfare reform to the floor of the House. On July 17, the Rules committee held a hearing on the bill under a "modified closed rule." This allowed for some amendments and the bill

was passed out of the Rules committee on July 18, and went straight to the House floor for consideration. The Democrats put forward a "replacement amendment" (replacing the entire bill with a new version), which was voted down, 258 to 170. Only 30 Democrats voted for the replacement. The vote demonstrated there was now bipartisan agreement on the proposal. The White House responded once again with mixed signals. There were statements indicating the president would sign because this bill was much better than any he had been presented with. However, there were also statements that criticized the bill for penalizing children, and a presidential veto was still a possibility.

The Senate received the House bill and passed the unanimous consent agreement, which allowed Senate floor consideration to take place on July 18, 1996. The first vote that passed in the Senate was approval of an amendment that replaced all language in the House bill with Senate language that had been approved in the two committees. Next, a voice vote approved an amendment by majority leader Trent Lott to detach the Medicaid provisions. On July 22, Bob Dole made a public statement urging Republicans to give Clinton a welfare reform bill that he could sign. On July 23, the Senate responded by approving the welfare bill by a 74 to 24 vote, 23 Democrats voting in favor, and 23 against. Of four amendments important to Clinton, two were passed. The president indicated he would sign the legislation, although he still hoped that changes he favored could be incorporated. The Senate and House passed different versions of the same bill so it was sent to Conference committee. At this point Clinton tried to get two provisions included: a voucher program for children and reinstatement of benefits to legal immigrants.

Both sides took to playing politics. The Republicans led by Newt Gingrich argued that Clinton had to sign whatever they wanted because they were in the driver's seat; Clinton talked about wanting to sign a bill but indicated a veto was still possible without saying why.[20] The Conference committee began negotiations on July 25, and the process was generally one of bipartisan cooperation. By July 29, agreement had been reached. The bill that emerged was closer to the Senate version than the House version. Clinton now had to decide whether to sign the bill.

A number of liberal interest groups mobilized to pressure the president to veto the legislation. Congressional Democrats lobbied Clinton for a sign of what he would do. The congressional vote would not take place until Clinton had announced whether he would sign or veto it. On August 1, 1996, Clinton met with his cabinet advisors and senior White House staff for a final discussion of the proposal. Opponents and proponents argued their positions to the president. Those in favor of a veto were led by Donna Shalala, Secretary of Health and Human Services; George Stephanopoulous, senior advisor to the president for policy and strategy; and Chief of Staff, Leon Panetta. This side argued that the bill was too stringent; it turned back sixty years of federal government responsibility for low-income individuals, and it put holes in the safety net.

Those in favor of Clinton signing were the vice president, Al Gore, domestic policy advisor, Bruce Reed, and political advisors Dick Morris and Rahm Emmanuel. They argued that the bill was a rationalization of resources, and encouraged work as a way out of the poverty trap in keeping with Clinton's campaign promise to place a time limit on welfare benefits. Underscoring the whole discussion was an acknowledgment of the political implications of not signing the bill and not delivering what Clinton had promised in 1992—an end to welfare as we know it. In short, in an election year could the president afford one more charge that he was incapable of keeping crucial campaign

promises? Others argued it could also be seen as another example of the administration's inability to control the legislative process. There was clearly a dilemma for the Clinton team. On one hand, many of them were ideologically opposed to welfare retrenchment; however, on the other hand, many of them were political realists who saw this issue as crucial to Clinton's electoral success.

After two and a half hours of discussion, Clinton left the meeting with Gore and Panetta. Within thirty minutes speech writers were told to write a "yes" speech. The president explained that afternoon to the public in a televised speech the reasoning for his decision. Bill Clinton basically told the public he did not really like the reform, but it was the best that could be expected from this Congress. He hoped to work on the bill and fine-tune it after the November election. Later that day, the bill passed 300 to 100 in the House. The Democrats were evenly divided. Twenty-four hours later, the Senate voted 78 to 21 in favor, 25 Democrats voting yes and 21 voting no. Of the Democratic Senators up for reelection, only one voted against the legislation.

On August 26, 1996, the president signed the welfare bill, arguing "Today we are taking a historic chance to make welfare what it is meant to be: a second chance, not a way of life." Many Democrats felt betrayed while Republicans such as Bob Dole criticized the president for selling out his party ideologically and playing politics. Without doubt, Bill Clinton transformed his position on welfare. Congressional Democrats also can be criticized, for they went against their ideological support of welfare and chose to support what they perceived the public wanted. Some analysts would contend that this is what representative democracy is truly about, that elected representatives were delegates of popular will rather than trustees of their constituents' desires.

THE POLICY PROCESS AND SOCIAL WELFARE POLICY

Social welfare policy formulation and decision making occurs in a variety of arenas and involves a large number of actors, all of whom are very active. It is an extremely complex, diffuse process because of the diversity of individuals directly affected, the wide range of available policy instruments that allow for input from a large number of actors, and the overlapping areas of jurisdiction. In short, the social welfare policy process resembles closely the dynamics of general policy making in the United States. Hence, like all policy making in the United States, social welfare policy making is highly decentralized.

The Department of Labor and the Department of Health and Human Services are responsible for most aspects of social welfare policy. State governments have a large say in federal welfare policies because of their ability to make many crucial decisions. Any major reform must gain executive approval and the approval of both houses of Congress. Within Congress, a number of committees and subcommittees in both chambers play an active role in policy formulation and decision making.[21] There is heavy interest group activity in social policy formation.[22]

In terms of the stages–heuristic it can be concluded that the delivery of social welfare since the 1930s involves all levels of government. The federal government is highly active in policy formulation. The federal government decides what types of programs and social issues will be addressed. Also, it is the responsibility of the federal government to establish minimum benefit levels when policy is adopted and to provide funding to states to support delivery of welfare services—for example, through grants in aid to support unemployment compensation.

The states are responsible primarily for implementation of social welfare. This responsibility includes drafting rules and regulations for eligibility. Individual state governments must supplement federal funding of welfare programs and additionally provide supplementary welfare assistance through their own general assistance programs. Such relief is available for individuals in need such as the elderly, persons with visual impairment or physical disabilities, or those who qualify under Temporary Assistance for Needy Families (TANF) who do not qualify for categorical assistance. People who need more than financial assistance are also taken care of in state-maintained institutions, such as facilities for those with mental illness or mental disabilities, orphanages, and senior citizen homes. Local government is also actively involved in the administration of various welfare programs. Local welfare officials decide if individuals are eligible to receive benefits and what amounts they should receive.

WELFARE POLICY INSTRUMENTS

Governments may have different policy goals in mind when they formulate and implement welfare policy solutions. Generally, welfare policy solutions can be categorized into three broad types: rights, rules, and inducements. Rights are basically the provision of services and programs that individuals are entitled to by nature of their citizenry and their very being, such as social security. Rules basically state who is eligible for what services and programs. Finally, inducements encourage or discourage individuals from receiving services and benefits.

Policy instruments chosen by American policy makers include government transfers providing cash payments or in-kind benefits, such as food stamps to individuals; government subsidies for certain basic needs, such as public transportation or housing available at below-market prices; and tax expenditures that reduce citizens' tax obligations when they spend their money for certain purposes; for example, lower sales taxes on food and income tax deductions for dependents and for owning a home. Additionally, the government provides a tax discount to low-income people known as an Earned Income Credit (EIC), which some people consider a welfare program. If calculated as an expenditure—although it is actually money the government does not collect—EIC is one of the more costly U.S. welfare programs.

SUMMARY

It is with the implementation of the 1935 Social Security Act that the federal government attempted to introduce a rational social welfare system. Unfortunately, public opinion polls from the 1960s on have indicated that many taxpayers, bureaucrats, recipients, and elected officials have never been happy with the system. Social welfare policy has remained a central issue that has been debated since its establishment. The debate climaxed in 1996 when congressional Democrats and Republicans compromised on legislation that changed the very nature of social welfare provision in the United States. Many critics argue that this particular reform represents an agreement by both political parties to cancel federal welfare policy as created by the New Deal. Critics also argue that the reform transferred control and responsibility out of the federal government's hands to individual states.

Welfare reform shows us certain lessons about formulation and legitimation. First, it is important to know where the locus of power is surrounding any policy issue; in the case of welfare reform it was Congress. Second, external forces are extremely important, as we saw when the National Governors As-

sociation played such a prominent role in 1996. Third, public opinion cannot be ignored if it is strongly articulated, and generally cuts across every social and political cleavage in society. In the case of welfare its unpopularity was so strong among so many groups and individuals that it stimulated the momentum for reform.

In the twenty-first century, the United States, like its European counterparts, will continue to look carefully at welfare policy expenditures. The United States clearly stands apart from many European nations in the severity of its cutbacks, in national government responsibility, in providing an economic security safety net, and an array of social services.

American social welfare policy is a continuing struggle over the issues posed by poverty, inequality, and other social problems. This continuing struggle is supported by public attitudes that are openly hostile to many welfare assistance policies. From the 1970s through the late 1980s, public opinion polls showed that less than 50 percent of respondents supported government intervention on behalf of low-income people.[23] General public support for the 1996 reform shows that there is less conflict over what the general public believes the role of government should be or what they think the taxpayers' burden should be. However, there is still deep-rooted political cleavage over the nature and cause of poverty and inequality in America.

What made such sweeping changes possible in the late 1990s was the widespread dismay with the welfare system that many characterized as symbolic of big government run amok—costing taxpayers money, demeaning beneficiaries, contributing to the breakdown of the American family by encouraging men and women to forget their marital responsibilities, and encouraging illegitimacy. In the early years of the twenty-first century, the United States no

longer guarantees that people in need and
their children are entitled to federal benefits
for as long as they need them. The safety net
has been removed for many of these Americans. It is clear that social policy reforms
since the 1980s are the result of several fundamental features of American politics: divided government; weak party discipline;
increasing for state government responsibility; high interest group mobilization; and
politics.

DISCUSSION QUESTIONS

1. What should be the goals of welfare
   reform?

2. Design a welfare policy for the United
   States that takes into account what you
   think citizens should be provided with.

3. Some people argue that welfare benefits
   are abused more often than not, thus
   they should be eliminated. Would this be
   an equitable policy choice?

SUGGESTED READINGS

Brueckner, J. K. "Welfare Reform and the Race
   to the Bottom." *Southern Economic Journal* 66,
   no. 3 (2000): 505–512.

Cavanna, H. *Challenges to the Welfare State.*
   Cheltenham, England: Edward Elgar, 1998.

Esping-Andersen G., ed. *Welfare States in
   Transition.* London: Sage, 1996.

Esping-Andersen, G. *The Three Worlds of Welfare
   Capitalism.* Cambridge, England: Policy Press,
   1990.

Freeman, R. B., R. Topel, and B. Swedenborg,
   eds. *The Welfare State in Transition.* Chicago:
   University of Chicago Press,1997.

Ginsburg, N. *Divisions of Welfare.* London: Sage,
   1992.

Miles, J., and J. Quadagno. "Envisioning a Third
   Way: The Welfare State in the Twenty-First
   Century." *Contemporary Sociology* 29, no. 1
   (January 2000) 156–170.

ENDNOTES

1. I. Gough, *The Political Economy of the Welfare
   State* (Basingstoke, England: Macmillan,
   1979).

2. R. Mishra, *The Welfare State in Capitalist
   Society* (Hemel Hempsted: Harvester
   Wheatsheaf, 1990).

3. C. Frankel, *The Democratic Prospect* (New
   York: Harper & Row, 1962).

4. F. Fox Piven and R. A. Cloward, *Regulating
   the Poor: The Functions of Public Welfare* (New
   York: Vintage Books, 1971).

5. D. A. Stone, *Policy Paradox and Political Reason*
   (Glenview, IL: Scott Foreman, 1988).

6. Originally called under the 1935 act titled
   Aid to Dependent Children.

7. Fox Piven and Cloward, *Regulating the Poor.*

8. For example, in 1965 Medicare was
   introduced as a program for health insurance
   for the elderly. In the same year, Medicaid, a
   program of health insurance for the poor, was
   also established. Other programs passed by
   the Johnson administration included housing
   subsidies, school food programs, and special
   programs for pregnant women.

9. Welfarism is the notion that the state takes
   responsibility for the financial security of
   those in society who are unable to manage
   their own resources.

10. Much of the conservative argument about the
    effects of welfare on individuals and the
    economy in general is based upon the work
    of the following authors: M. Anderson,
    *Welfare: The Political Economy of Welfare Reform
    in the United States* (Stanford, CA: Hoover
    Institution Press, 1978); G. Gildor, *Wealth and
    Poverty* (New York: Basic Books, 1981);
    T. R. Marmor, J. L. Mashaw, and
    P. L. Harvey, *America's Misunderstood Welfare
    State: Persistent Myths* (New York: Basic
    Books, 1990); and C. Murray, *Losing Ground:
    American Social Policy 1950–1980* (New York:
    Basic Books, 1984).

11. Democrats who wanted expansions
    recommended the reduction of means-test
    levels (or, occasionally, their elimination). The
    major reforms advocated were the addition of
    work requirements (dubbed workfare) and
    the creation of a sunset period for the
    provision of benefits.

12. As reported in the *New York Times,* August 1, 1996, sec. 1, 1.

13. As reported in the *New York Times,* July 6, 2001, sec. A, p. 19.

14. D. S. Nightingale and K. Brennan, *The Welfare-to-Work Grants Program: A New Link in the Welfare Reform Chain* (Washington, DC: Urban Institute, 1998).

15. A. Sherman, *Extreme Child Poverty Rises Sharply in 1997* (Washington, DC: Children's Defense Fund, 1999).

16. W. Primus, L. Rawlings, K. Larin, and K. Porter, *The Initial Impacts of Welfare Reform on the Incomes of Single-Mother Families* (Washington, DC: Center on Budget and Policy Priorities, 1999).

17. Gerald Kleczka of Wisconsin voted in favor of the bill.

18. The bill was also considered by the Agriculture committee, the Economic and Educational Opportunities committee, the Commerce committee, and the Budget committee.

19. J. Havemann, "GOP's New Welfare Strategy Has Democrats Reassessing," *Congressional Quarterly Weekly Report,* July 13, 1996, 1969.

20. J. L. Katz, "Welfare Showdown Looms as GOP Readies Plan," *Congressional Quarterly Weekly Report,* July 27, 1996, 2116.

21. In the House, the Ways and Means, Economic and Educational Opportunities, and Appropriations committees have been central. In the Senate, the Agriculture (because of the food stamp program), Finance, Appropriations, and Health, Education, Labor, and Pensions committees have been crucial.

22. By some estimates, nearly one-sixth of registered interest groups are active in health and social policy formation.

23. M. Schlesinger and T. Lee, "Is Health Care Different?" in J. Morone and G. Belkin, *The Politics of Health Care Reform* (Durham, NC: Duke University Press, 1994).

17

Immigration Policy

Implementing and Evaluating Policy Solutions

Immigration policy has been the subject of a contentious national debate for well over a century. With respect to the apparent failings of immigration policy to either effectively deter illegal entry or to manage efficiently the naturalization process, many critics suggest that the policies have been poorly designed by policy makers and poorly implemented by the bureaucracy—specifically the Immigration and Naturalization Service (INS).[1] The terrorist attacks on September 11, 2001, and the apparent ease with which nineteen terrorists entered the United States, have only further incited questions of why immigration policies, especially as they focus on illegal immigration, continue to be an almost classic example of policy failure.[2]

The positions on immigration policy fall roughly into two camps. The pro-immigration perspective emphasizes the historical and cultural value of immigration, as well as the short- and long-term economic benefits. Those supporters claim that immigration's ability to add to the economic and cultural strengths of the nation remains evident and as strong as ever, and that its failings and costs—both legal and illegal—are often exaggerated.

The anti-immigration perspective, in contrast, perceives a substantial socioeconomic problem, highlights the increasing social and budgetary costs and, since September 11, the substantial threat posed by immigration, legal and illegal, to national security. To adherents of this view, immigration is framed in terms of the costs, risks, and failures of policy. For those who adopt the anti-immigration position, current and future policies should emphasize all or some of the following: greater border enforcement, restrictions on social service benefits, increased restrictions on visas, greater workplace monitoring, and a reduction in legal immigration. Overall, it is the tensions between these two broad camps that have helped fuel the dynamic evolution in immigration policy. Immigration policies have, at varying times, been designed by policy makers to limit, control, aid, or punish the legal and illegal immigrant communities.

In general, the basis for immigration policy reflects a common desire among all nation–states to manage their population, control access to their borders, as well as to shape their national identities. Immigration policy represents the chosen set of rules, defined by legislation and administrative decree, "designed to govern [who can] legally reside and seek employment within its borders, as well as define those who are citizens and those who are not."[3] Thus, immigration policy is as much about defining what type of nation the state will be, as it is about who should be invited into the state.[4]

CONTEMPORARY IMMIGRATION POLICY IN THE UNITED STATES

Determining which foreign nationals, and how many, should be permitted to immigrate, as well as defining what is lawful immigrant status, is central to the debate over American immigration policy. How immigrants are formally defined by the federal government helps clarify the vulnerable position these individuals have in American society. For example, the INS defines an *illegal alien* as a "foreign born national who entered the U.S. without inspection or with fraudulent documentation; or a foreign national who entered legally, violated the terms of their visa status, and remained in

the U.S. without authority." In contrast, a *legal immigrant* is defined as "an alien admitted into the U.S. as a lawful permanent resident, accorded the privilege of living permanently in the United States."[5]

The overriding emphasis in national policy is to deter and punish the illegal entrant or resident within the United States. As a group, by INS definition they have broken immigration law designed to manage and control legal entrance into the United States. The operative focus of policy for legal immigration centers on the term "accorded the privilege of living permanently in the United States." Legal immigrants are granted a temporary residence that, depending on changing circumstances, can be revised or revoked. In fact, even naturalized citizens, if they are later found to have been deceptive or have broken the law during the naturalization process, can have their citizenship status revoked. Each of these definitions helps highlight what is the underlying, and often unstated, goal to almost all aspects of immigration policy–control.

The underlying goal of all immigration policy is to *control* access and entry, whether legal or illegal, into the United States. In terms of legal immigration, the goal of control entails regulating the method and number of individuals who may legally enter or reside within the United States. In contrast, policies focused on illegal immigration seek to control illegal entrance to the state, as well as limit access to government services and employment. Although control remains the central theme to all immigration policy, it is also possible, according to Michael Fix and Jeffrey Passel, to identify five more specific goals for American immigration policy:[6]

- Social
- Economic
- Moral
- Cultural
- National and economic security

Socially, immigration policies have been designed to aid and assist family reunification—especially among one's closest family members. Economically, critical workers, as well as certain qualified investors, are invited to immigrate in order to promote domestic economic growth and stability. Morally, current immigration policy provides asylum for certain refugees or persecuted populations. Culturally, aspects of immigration policy seek to further national diversity. The yearly green card lottery, for example, provides people from diverse national backgrounds the opportunity to immigrate to the United States. The goal of national and economic security represents the interest of the state to ensure territorial integrity and economic prosperity. Driven by such security-focused policies, immigration policies have been designed to regulate border access, detain and deport illegal aliens, identify threats to national security, monitor workplace employment, as well as enforce employer sanctions.

What is both implicitly and explicitly common to all the goals identified by Fix and Passel is a pervasive, often unstated assumption that the manner and method of immigration must and should be controlled for the betterment of the state. The assumption is that unfettered access to all who would choose to immigrate poses an unacceptable burden and risk to the state.[7] However, the debates over what are the costs or benefits from immigration, let alone what is considered *good* policy, persist because policy actors differ in the specific goals they desire from immigration policy.

In order to understand the failures and successes of past policies, it is beneficial to explore the historical evolution of immigration policy—both statically and in terms of policy. Further insight is gained from understanding the process by which immigration policies develop and are implemented. Additionally, an explanation of the policy instruments utilized to address illegal immigration

is discussed. In order to highlight the specific dilemmas intrinsic to implementing and evaluating immigration policy, one of the most significant pieces of recent legislation, the 1986 Immigration and Reform Control Act (IRCA), will also be discussed.

U.S. IMMIGRATION STATISTICS

What is clear is that immigration has played a central role in the growth of this nation's character, unlike any other in the world. As Table 17.1 shows, at the beginning of the twentieth century, as much as 14 percent of the population was foreign born. As of 1990, the percentage of foreign-born residents had declined to 7.9 percent, but increased between 1990 and 2000 to 11.1 percent. From 1940 to 2000, the number of foreign-born individuals averaged around 7.3 percent of the total population.

According to government statistics, the large influx of immigration that began at the beginning of the twentieth century has remained relatively stable over the last six decades—although a significant spike did occur in the last decade. Still, the current rate of immigration is lower than the highest rates of the early part of the nineteenth century. These numbers put into question claims that legal immigration has spiraled out of control. According to INS statistics, immigration to the United States between 1820 and 2000, was 66,089,431.[8] Between 1970 and 2000, legal immigration remained relatively steady, except for the spike following the amnesty program of 1986—totaling almost 21 million new immigrants (see Figure 17.1).

With respect to the region of origin, the character of immigration has changed with each decade (see Table. 17.2). In the early part of the twentieth century, the regional source of immigration was heavily skewed

Table 17.1 Total and Foreign-Born U.S. Population, 1900–2000

1900–2000	(in thousands)	Foreign Born	
Year	Total U.S. Population	Total	Percent
2000	281,421	31,100	11.1
1990	248,710	19,767	7.9
1980	226,546	14,080	6.2
1970	203,210	9,619	4.7
1960	179,326	9,738	5.4
1950	150,845	10,431	6.9
1940	132,165	11,657	8.8
1930	123,203	14,283	11.6
1920	106,022	14,020	13.2
1910	92,229	13,630	14.8
1900	76,212	10,445	13.7

SOURCE: U.S. Census Bureau, "2000 Foreign-Born Population in the United States," *Census 2000* (Washington, DC: Government Printing Office, January 2001).

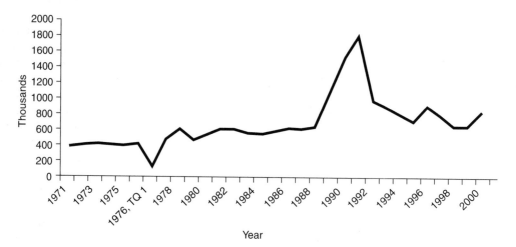

FIGURE 17.1 Immigration to the United States between 1970 and 2000

SOURCE: Based on data from the Immigration and Naturalization Service, *Fiscal Year 2000 Statistical Yearbook,* available at http://www.immigration.gov.

Note: The spike after 1986 is explained by the illegal alien amnesty program.

toward Europe, but is, as of 1990, now skewed toward Latin America and Asia.

According to the U.S. Census Bureau, as of 2000, an estimated 28.4 million foreign-born residents lived within the United States.[9] Among the foreign born, 51.0 per-cent were born in Latin America, 25.5 percent were born in Asia, 15.3 percent were born in Europe, and the remaining 8.1 percent were from other regions of the world.[10] Additionally, 58 percent of those foreign-born individuals entered the United States

Table 17.2 Regions of Birth for Foreign-Born Population

			Regions of Birth Reported				Latin	Northern	Region of Birth Not
Year	Total	Total	Europe	Asia	Africa	Oceania	America	America	Reported
1990	19,767,316	18,959,158	4,350,403	4,979,037	363,819	104,145	8,407,837	753,917	808,158
1980	14,079,906	13,192,563	5,149,572	2,539,777	199,723	77,577	4,372,487	853,427	887,343
1970	9,619,302	9,303,570	5,740,891	824,887	80,143	41,258	1,803,970	812,421	315,732
1960	9,738,091	9,678,201	7,256,311	490,996	35,355	34,730	908,309	952,500	59,890
1930	14,204,149	14,197,553	11,784,010	275,665	18,326	17,343	791,840	1,310,369	6,596
1920	13,920,692	13,911,767	11,916,048	237,950	16,126	14,626	588,843	1,138,174	8,925
1910	13,515,886	13,506,272	11,810,115	191,484	3,992	11,450	279,514	1,209,717	9,614
1900	10,341,276	10,330,534	8,881,548	120,248	2,538	8,820	137,458	1,179,922	10,742

SOURCE: Based on data from the Immigration and Naturalization Service, *Fiscal Year 2000 Statistical Yearbook*, available at http://www.immigration.gov.

Note: The term *foreign born* refers to individuals who were not U.S. citizens at birth.

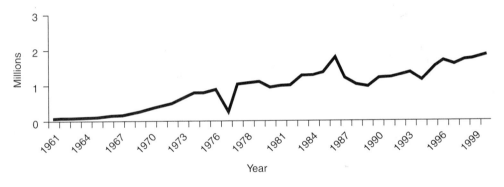

FIGURE 17.2 Deportable Aliens Located between 1960 and 2000

SOURCE: Based on data from the Immigration and Naturalization Service, *Fiscal Year 2000 Statistical Yearbook*, available at http://www.immigration.gov.

since 1980. Overall, the data suggest that immigration remains diverse in terms of region of national origin, but that the rate of immigration from specific regions fluctuated between 1900 and 2000.

In contrast, the number of illegal immigrants is extremely difficult to estimate. Determining the actual number of aliens poses a considerable analytical dilemma. Because no firm data exist, the number of possible illegal immigrants must be estimated using various statistical techniques. One rough measure of estimating illegal immigration is by considering the number of INS detainments and deportations. In 2000, according to INS statistics, 1,814,729 deportable aliens were located.[11] Since 1960, based on INS figures, the number of illegal aliens who have been "located" has increased, and averaged well over a million illegal aliens since 1983 (see Figure 17.2).[12] The government data, however, merely approximate the estimated number of illegal aliens who may actually reside within the United States.

Figure 17.2 charts the number of apprehended aliens deported by the INS, but not the number who may live within the United States. Attempting to estimate the number of illegal immigrants who live in the United States remains one of the most hotly debated issues within immigration policy. Clearly, estimating a large number of illegal immigrants serves as a powerful example of the failures of immigration policies, as well as providing political fodder for proponents of more punitive and drastic anti-illegal immigration policies. In contrast, if a small number of illegal immigrants is estimated, policies designed to limit entrance, residency, employment, and access to public services can be deemed to have been effective. At present, only rough estimates of varying accuracy exist as to the total number of illegal aliens who reside within the United States.

In 1996, the Cato Institute suggested that 3.4 million illegal aliens lived in the United States.[13] Other groups with less scientific measures, and a more anti-immigrant policy agenda, like the Federation for American Immigration Reform (FAIR), estimated that over 4 million illegal immigrants may reside in the United States as of 1996.[14] In 2001, FAIR suggested that the illegal immigrant population numbered between 8.5 and 11 million persons.[15] *Census 2000* approximated that upward of "at least 7 million and possibly as high as 8 million" illegal aliens reside within the United States.[16] Based on U.S. Census figures, "the total number of undocumented immigrants has at least doubled since 1990."[17] The INS, as of 2001, estimates the illegal immigrant population at between 6.5 and 7.5 million.

The statistics on immigration, both legal and illegal, seem to only reinforce the assumptions of both perspectives on immigration policy. Depending on which immigration numbers one may focus on, as well as how one chooses to interpret such statistical data, immigration policy can either be deemed a failure or a success. For instance, given the number of illegal aliens within the

United States, it is apparent that current and past policy has failed to hinder the absolute growth of illegal immigration. Anti-immigration actors have used such statistics as the mark of failure against certain immigration policies. Pro-immigration actors, in comparison, have pointed out that the number or rate of illegal immigration is difficult to assess, and that the extent of illegal immigration may be an indication that current policies have failed to encourage sufficient legal immigration. Similarly, the trends in the data on legal immigration can also be interpreted very differently.

From a proimmigration perspective, the number of foreign born, and the sheer diversity of nations, indicates that immigration is indeed critical to the diversity of the nation. Additionally, such advocates would also raise doubts over the perception that legal immigration has increased considerably, given that the data suggest a significant percentage decline when compared to the early part of the twentieth century. In contrast, critics of immigration policy would suggest that the influx of immigration since 1980 is too great, that the number of foreign born is too high, and that recent patterns of immigration favor one region—Latin America—over others. Unfortunately, it is all but inevitable that disagreements will emerge among policy actors over how to interpret immigration statistics.

Depending on one's perspective, statistics can be used to reinforce already held beliefs as to what types of immigration policy should be designed and implemented. However, an understanding of immigration policy must also be placed in the appropriate historical context. The history of American immigration policy raises many disconcerting questions. Although at times inviting and open, there are repeated periods where legislation and policies have been designed to severely regulate, control, and hinder the degree and scope of all immigration—legal and illegal.

EVOLUTION OF
IMMIGRATION POLICY

Immigration policy was a state-to-state responsibility until the Supreme Court declared, in 1875, the regulation of immigration a federal responsibility. The subsequent evolution of immigration policy is marked by a persistent institutional dominance by the federal government and a bureaucratic emphasis on federal agencies to implement immigration policies. In terms of the character and goals of policy, there are recurring periods of xenophobic-inspired restrictions and concerns for both economic and national security. One can identify a number of historical milestones in the development of immigration policy between 1882 and 2000 (see Box 17.1).

Roughly from 1882 to 1921, the primary goal of policy was to restrict immigration of certain groups through qualitative standards. The Chinese Exclusion Act of 1882 and the Alien Contract Labor Laws of 1885 and 1887 were adopted in response to the socioeconomic conditions and the belief among critical policy actors that Chinese and other foreign workers had contributed to the economic plight of the period. The goal of the federal government during this period was to prevent individuals of specific ethnic backgrounds, as well as certain classes of workers, from immigrating or remaining within the United States. National origin exclusions were expanded to include the Japanese in 1907 and all Asians in 1917.[18] The laws excluding Chinese immigration remained in place until 1942.[19] The Immigration Act of 1917 reinforced such qualitative restrictions on immigration by requiring literacy tests on all eligible immigrants.

Aside from ethnic and language-based restrictions, the Chinese Exclusion Act of 1882 and the Immigration Act of 1891 applied a head tax of 50 cents for each individual immigrant, as well as barring individuals of "questionable character" or those deemed likely to become public charges or dependent on public assistance.[20] Given the socioeconomic status of many incoming immigrants in the late nineteenth and early twentieth century, such policies represented a powerful obstacle to immigration. Additionally, under the 1891 act, the federal government established the first agency responsible for the implementation of immigration policy.

The Office of the Superintendent of Immigration (OSI), located first within the Treasury Department, assumed the responsibility for "inspecting, admitting, rejecting, and processing all immigrants seeking admission to the United States."[21] The initial mission of the OSI was to oversee and manage port-of-entry inspectors and to implement the mandates of current immigration policy that excluded certain groups on qualitative grounds. In 1895, the OSI was transformed into the Bureau of Immigration. Under the Immigration Act of 1900, responsibility to oversee the enforcement of the Alien Contract Labor Laws and Chinese Exclusion Act was assigned to the Bureau of Immigration.[22] By 1903, the bureau was transferred to the Department of Commerce and Labor.[23] With the passage of the Basic Naturalization Act of 1906, the functions of naturalization were transferred to the federal level, and assigned within the newly renamed Bureau of Immigration and Naturalization.

A refocus toward quantitative, rather than qualitative, restrictions highlights the character of immigration policy during the 1920s. The quantitative restrictions of a quota system were established under the Immigration Acts of 1921 and 1924. The goal of the quota system was to sustain a specific national, ethnic, and cultural makeup, based on the total number of that group within the United States. The 1921 act limited future immigration on a per-country cap of 3 percent, meaning that, depending on the size of the national group already within the United

Box 17.1   Legislative Milestones in Immigration Policy

Chinese Exclusion Act (1882)
- Suspended Chinese immigration for ten years
- Barred Chinese naturalization

Immigration Act of 1891
- Established federal authority over immigration policy
- Created the first bureaucratic office responsible for implementation of immigration policy

Immigration Acts of 1921 and 1924
- Established a quota-based system for immigration
- Based quota limits on national origins

Immigration and Nationality Act of 1965
- Repealed national origins quotas
- Established preference system that favored family unification and certain works skills
- Imposed first limits on immigration from Western Hemisphere

Refugee Act of 1980
- Established permanent procedures for admitting refugees
- No longer defined refugee status along ideological ground

Immigration Reform and Control Act of 1986
- Established sanctions for employers
- Provided an amnesty program for illegal aliens

Immigration Act of 1990
- Increased legal immigration ceilings
- Expanded employment-based immigration
- Provided expanded asylum for victims of war and natural disasters

Illegal Immigration Reform and Immigrant Responsibility Act of 1996
- Imposed restrictions on social benefits for illegal aliens
- Renewed emphasis on border enforcement

USA Patriot Act of 2001
- Broadened the scope of aliens deemed inadmissible
- Permitted detainment of legal and illegal aliens for up to six months if determined to pose a risk to national security
- Established a foreign student monitoring program

Homeland Security Act of 2002
- Abolished INS under the Department of Justice
- Placed INS functions under Department of Homeland Security
- Established two separate bureaus for immigration and naturalization

SOURCE: Adapted from Michael Fix and Jeffrey Passel, *Immigration and Immigrants: Setting the Record Straight* (Washington, DC: Urban Institute, 1994).

States, only 3 percent of that group would be permitted to immigrate to the United States every year. The 1924 act reduced the quota to 2 percent, further limiting immigration from eastern and southern Europe, and restricted immigration from Asian nations.[24] Additionally, in 1924, the U.S. Border Patrol was created to address the increasing number of illegal immigrants who began to appear in response to the more restrictive quantitative-based immigration policies.

During the 1940s, immigration policy was redefined within the context of the Second World War and the perceived threat posed by certain foreign nationals to U.S. national security. In response, policies were adopted that launched the Alien Registration Program that led to the recording and fingerprinting of every alien, as well as responsibility over internment camps and detention facilities. As this period would highlight, and as the events of September 11 would rekindle, an enduring tension exists between the ideal desire for a more liberal immigration policy and the priorities of national security.

Following the Second World War, the 1945 War Bridges Act, the 1948 Displaced Persons Act, and the Refugee Relief Act of 1953 assisted the immigration of returning spouses and families of American soldiers, and allowed the immigration of various refugees displaced because of the war. Additionally, a number of policies, such as the Hungarian Refugee Act of 1956, the Refugee-Escapee Act of 1957, and the Cuban Adjustment Program, served various U.S. cold war objectives to assist in the immigration of people from communist states. One of the most dramatic changes in policy, however, would follow the adoption of the Immigration and Nationality Act (INA) of 1965.

The 1965 INA repealed the national origins quota system that had been in place since the 1920s. Instead, a seven-category preference system was established to attract a variety of skilled workers and reunite immigrant families. However, INA placed quantitative restrictions on immigration from eastern and western Europe, and placed the first restrictions on immigration from nation-states of the Western Hemisphere. According to Fix and Passel, the impacts of the 1965 INA would be long lasting:

> The law replaced the national origins quota system with a uniform limit of 20,000 immigrants per country for all countries outside the Western Hemisphere. At the same time, though, the law placed a limit for the first time on immigration from the Western Hemisphere (most notably on Mexico). The law contained within it the seeds of the massive shift away from European immigration that would subsequently occur. It can also be seen as setting the stage for expanding illegal immigration from the Western Hemisphere into the United States.[25]

Evidently, in light of the increase of illegal immigration that followed the adoption of the INA in 1965, the issues of how best to deter illegal immigration garnered attention. In 1972, for instance, the House of Representatives "made its first attempt to penalize employers for hiring illegal aliens, imposing mild civil and criminal penalties for knowingly hiring undocumented workers."[26] The proposed legislation, however, died in the Senate. The growing debate surrounding the costs and benefits of legal and illegal immigration would continue well into the 1980s.

In 1980, the passage of the Refugee Act sought to redefine asylum status, which had previously been defined along ideological terms, to reflect more comprehensive standards. This period also resulted in the passage of a major piece of immigration reform, the Immigration Reform and Control Act (IRCA) of 1986. The IRCA established an amnesty program for illegal aliens and sought to deter future illegal immigration through the first mandated oversight of the workplace and sanctioning of employers. The

---

Box 17.2   Current Categories for Immigration under the Immigration Act of 1990

Family-Sponsored Preferences

First Preference
- Unmarried sons and daughters of U.S. citizens and their children

Second Preference
- Spouses and children of alien residents—unmarried sons and daughters of alien residents, twentyone years and older

Third Preference
- Married sons and daughters of U.S. citizens, their spouses and children

Fourth Preference
- Brothers and sisters of U.S. citizens, their spouses and children

Employment-Based Preferences

First Preference
- Priority workers (aliens with extraordinary ability, outstanding professors and re-searchers, multinational executives and managers) and their spouses and children

Second Preference
- Professionals, or those with exceptional ability, their spouses and children

Third Preference
- Skilled workers, professionals and other workers, their spouses and children

Fourth Preference
- Employees of the U.S. mission in Hong Kong, religious workers and their families, juvenile court dependents

Fifth Preference
- Employment creation

Diversity, Other Immigrant Categories
- Child born subsequent to issuance of a visa
- Widows or widowers of U.S. citizens
- Diversity immigrants, their spouses and children
- Spouses and children of legalized aliens
- Employees of certain U.S. businesses in Hong Kong, their spouses and children
- Diversity transition for natives of certain adversely affected foreign states
- Displaced Tibetans, their spouses and children

1990 Immigration Act continued this period of reform by revamping the selection and preference system for immigration. The 1990 act placed a greater focus on attracting particular work skills, adding to the cultural diversity, and providing temporary status to populations displaced because of war or natural disaster. The legislation also established the three main categories for immigration: family-sponsored, employment-based, and diversity immigrants (see Box 17.2).

Since 1990, tensions over the direction of immigration policy culminated in substantial restrictions on both legal and illegal immigrant populations. The Illegal Immigration Reform and Individual Responsibility Act (IIRIR) of 1996 represented one of the most dramatic changes in recent immi-

---

Box 17.3   Highlights of the Illegal Immigration Reform and Immigrant Responsibility Act of 1996

- Expanded Border Patrol funding, authorized the funding for the hiring of INS agents to investigate alien smuggling, provided $12 million for additional fences at points between the United States and Mexico, allowed cooperation of the INS with local and state law enforcement in pursing illegal immigrants
- Barred immigrants with illegal status of one year or more for ten years
- Developed three test-pilot workplace projects in five of the seven states with the highest illegal immigrant population
- Set minimum immigrant sponsor requirement at 125 percent of the poverty level
- Denied various social services, including social security, HUD housing aid, food stamps
- Denied visas for those immigrants wanting to attend a public or secondary school for over a year

SOURCE: Adapted from J. G. Gimpel and J. R. Edwards, *The Congressional Politics of Immigration Reform* (London: Allyn & Bacon, 1999), 290–295.

---

gration policy given its specific focus on limiting access to social services for the legal and illegal immigrant population. Some of the goals of the legislation are noted in Box 17.3.

More recently, the events of September 11 have once again fundamentally—and quite possibly permanently—reframed the debate on immigration policy toward the goal of national security. Ironically, before September 11, 2001, the Bush administration was considering significant, if not progressive, changes in immigration policy. Among the proposals being considered was a new temporary guest worker program, a possible second amnesty program for illegal aliens that would grant future permanent residency, the easing of restrictions on obtaining a green card, as well as additional immigration reforms between Mexico and the United States.[27] Even as late as September 7, 2001, President Vicente Fox of Mexico was confident that a deal on immigration and migration reform between Mexico and the United States could be reached within a short time frame.[28] The progress toward such progressive reforms was halted after September 11, 2001.

To critics, the terrorist attacks of September 11 represent the most dramatic example of the failings of U.S. immigration policy. For proponents of greater immigration, September 11 has reframed the issue of immigration into a context in which all immigrants are unfairly perceived as possible threats to national security. The realization that all of the terrorists were foreign nationals, that fifteen of the nineteen terrorists were Saudi nationals who obtained visas at the U.S. Embassy in Riyadh or at the consulate in Jidda, that some of the nineteen were able to train for the attack at American flight schools under student visas, that some had overstayed visas or fallen out of status while in the United States, and that some had been on terrorist watch lists unbeknownst to the INS, represents a powerful indictment as to the failing state of American immigration policy. The failings may be best exemplified by the fact that two of the terrorists received visa renewals from the INS six months after the terrorist attacks.[29] In short, the terrorist acts of September 11 provided a dramatic, if not the most tragic, indication of the consequences from failing to successfully implement and evaluate critical facets of immigration policy.

Since the fall of 2001, the federal government has adopted a series of aggressive policy actions, and is considering additional actions, to address the threat of terrorism and failings in immigration policy. These immigration changes will, in varying ways, profoundly affect the well over ten million visitors to the United States who require visas. Among the recent policy actions taken by the federal government include the passage of both the USA Patriot Act of 2001 and the Homeland Security Act of 2002.

Although not exclusively focused on immigration, the USA Patriot Act of 2001 redefined the scope of those ineligible for immigration, altered the basis by which a potential immigrant could be classified as a terrorist, expanded the federal government's apprehension powers over immigrants, and authorized surveillance of foreign students within the United States. In addition, influenced by the passage of the Patriot Act, the INS instituted sweeping changes in its federal regulations. These new "special regulations" have increased significantly the number and type of restrictions on all alien visitors and visa applications. The INS describes these special regulation changes as follows:

> Special Registration is a system that will let the government keep track of nonimmigrants that come to the U.S. every year. Some of the approximately 35 million nonimmigrants who enter the U.S.—and some nonimmigrants already in the U.S.—will be required to register with INS either at a port of entry or a designated INS office in accordance with the special registration procedures. These special procedures also require additional in-person interviews at an INS office and notifications to INS of changes of address, employment, or school. Nonimmigrants who must follow these special procedures will also have to use specially designated ports when they leave the country and report in person to an INS officer at the port on their departure date.[30]

These special regulations have changed the rules governing the entrance to the United States for all foreign visitors, students, and those traveling on business. The visa changes can restrict foreign travelers and those traveling on business to a term of thirty days. For foreign students, the new regulations prohibit a prospective student from starting school without first obtaining INS approval. In addition, the length of stay afforded by other classes of visas will be reduced from one year to six months. Most significant, male immigrants from eighteen Middle Eastern states, who are over the age of sixteen, will now be subject to fingerprinting, photographing, and questioning.[31] Overall, within the 107th Congress, and since September 11, 2001, a number of striking policy proposals, all with a similar goal of controlling immigration and ensuring national security, were being considered for adoption (see Box 17.4).

Aside from substantial changes in the character of immigration policy, the INS itself is the subject of fundamental revamping. The failures of the INS to successfully implement and evaluate its mandate, coupled with the increasing political anger over the

---

Box 17.4   Post-September 11 Proposals for Dramatic Changes in Immigration Policy

- Creating Student and Exchange Visitor Tracking Program (H.R. 3205 and S. 1618)
- Requiring background checks for incoming foreign students (H.R. 3239)
- Prohibiting student visas to students who are from a nation–state suspected of terrorism (S. 1627)
- Placing a moratorium on the issuance of all visas to all nonimmigrant foreign students (H.R. 322)
- Utilizing biometric technology in the issuance of visas (S. 1518)

depth of failures, resulted in some of the most dramatic bureaucratic changes within this agency and the entire federal government in over half a century.

The passage of the Homeland Security Act of 2002 has created an entirely new agency solely responsible for domestic security. Among its many security missions, the Department of Homeland Security will be responsible for all facets of immigration. The legislation formally removed the INS from the Justice Department, divided the agency into two separate bureaus responsible for naturalization and immigration, and placed a renewed emphasis on implementing the array of immigration policies that seek to deter and prevent the entrance of potential or suspected terrorists. The agency that will be responsible for enforcing immigration laws is the Bureau of Border Security. Immigrant naturalization will now be the responsibility of the Bureau of Citizenship and Immigration Services. In an attempt to reduce the backlog of naturalization and visa applicants, the new naturalization agency is also mandated to streamline procedures and establish the position of ombudsmen to monitor the effectiveness of the bureau.

Overall, the evolution of immigration policy, from one phase to the next, highlights how intimately interrelated the formulation of policy is to the socioeconomic and political period in which policy is made. At varying times, concerns over threats to the economy and national security, as well as outright paranoia and xenophobia, have characterized the changes in immigration policy. From the early racially motivated restrictions on certain ethnic groups and head taxes, to a quota-based system that sought to perpetuate a specific ethnic vision of America, early immigration policy remained fixated on controlling the very socioeconomic and demographic image of the nation. Until mid-1965, significant political tensions still existed as to what extent legal immigration was even

desired.[32] Since the 1980s, the perceived negative effects of illegal immigration, fueled in part by the recessions of the late 1980s and early 1990s, further targeted the illegal immigrant for what amounted to punitive actions, even as employer sanctions were poorly enforced and monitored. With the welfare reform policy initiatives by the mid-1990s, immigrants were once again the targets of new policies that restricted the access to social services even though a number of studies have found that illegal and legal immigrants have a positive economic effect on the country.[33] Since September 11 the anti-immigration perspective seems to have gathered wider political and institutional support. From the scope of policy actions already taken, to the initiatives still being proposed, immigration policy is again focused on greater national security—even at the expense of all other stated goals.

What policy actors must now consider, however, is why immigration policies failed in the past. Were such policy failures the result of poor implementation because of poor policy design, or because evaluation failed to grasp where the failings were? Inevitably, the success of future immigration policy will depend not only on how it is designed but also on whether the policies as designed are effectively implemented and evaluated.

IMPLEMENTING AND EVALUATING IMMIGRATION POLICY

As stated in Chapter 10, implementation is the action phase of the policy process. In immigration policy, as with any policy issue area, failure to implement a policy effectively results in a failure to redress the identified policy problem. Effective policy implementation depends on how well the policy was designed and whether any evaluation was conducted after implementation. Implementation and evaluation, however, do not occur within a political vacuum. To the contrary, as the historical evolution of immigration policy indicates, the design of such policy has developed within a political and socioeconomic environment in which the main target populations, the legal and illegal alien, were often negatively framed. The array of goals immigration policy was and is designed to achieve has only further complicated implementation. Hence, it may be argued that the very process by which immigration policies develop, a political policy process that does necessarily seek or result in the best policy, helps sow the seeds of future policy failure.

Bureaucratically, the primary agency responsible for implementation and evaluation, the INS, was and is an agency torn between two conflicting administrative realities—enforcement and service. Although the Homeland Security Act of 2002 intends to divide enforcement and service responsibilities, it is unclear what positive effect this will have on the implementation or evaluation of immigration policy. In terms of service, past demands on the agency to provide immigration and naturalizing services conflicted with the mission to prevent and deter any unwarranted or illegal immigration. Will such conflicts disappear under the new administrative arrangement? In the past, through funding and legislation, the overriding emphasis of the INS was visa inspection, border enforcement, and alien apprehension—even at the expense of naturalization. Will such goals lose prominence within the new department? In the end, it is unclear whether these service and enforcement geared agencies, now responsible for the implementation and evaluation of their respective set of immigration policies, will be any more or less effective than their predecessor.

Insight as to how to improve the effectiveness of these new immigration agencies

can be gained by looking at past policy. The following discussion focuses primarily on the issue of illegal immigration and the 1986 IRCA as an example of how poor design, poor implementation, and poor evaluation can all but ensure that the policy will be ineffective.

The 1986 Immigration Reform and Control Act—A Classic Policy Failure?

The Immigration Reform and Control Act of 1985 sought to address, in part, the problem of illegal immigration by recognizing that far too many illegal aliens were the result of both illegal entry over the border and what are called "nonimmigrant overstays":

> For aliens from most countries of the world, the typical way of joining the illegal population is to obtain visas for temporary visits and stay beyond the authorized period of admission. This segment of the population, referred to as "nonimmigrant overstays" constitutes roughly half of the illegal populations residing within the United States.[34]

The ability to overstay the temporary entrance visa suggests that these individuals have been able to work illegally irrespective of border enforcement. As a consequence, certain social costs accrue as a result of the failure of illegal immigration policies to deter entrance and employment.[35] For example, the GAO estimated in 1994 that "the state and local impact of illegal aliens [on education, Medicaid, and prisons in California] was $2.35 billion . . . while local revenues ranged from $500 million to $1.4 billion."[36] Educational costs for illegal children were estimated to run as high as $2 billion, and the cost for imprisoning over 18,000 illegal aliens was estimated at around $500 million annually.[37] Another study suggested that total expenditures to the state and taxpayer from illegal aliens is as much as

$1,690 per alien.[38] This persistent framing in which the illegal alien bears the primary responsibility for the negative social costs of illegal immigration helps to explain, in part, the failure of the IRCA to be implemented and evaluated effectively.

Whereas employer sanctions had been considered in the early 1970s, the overwhelming fixation with punitive regulation directed at the illegal alien continued until 1986. The IRCA was the first piece of legislation designed to address both the demand and supply aspects of illegal immigration. In other words, the IRCA sought to address the supply of labor provided from illegal immigration and the demand for cheap and unauthorized labor by employers.

Interestingly, prior to 1986, even though 138 relevant acts dealing with immigration and naturalization were passed between 1790 and 1993, the IRCA was the first to recognize and seek to regulate the role of employers in the illegal market, as well as the first to establish sanctions against employers.[39] The INS defined employer sanctions as follows:

> The employer sanctions provision of the Immigration Reform and Control Act of 1986 prohibits employers from hiring, recruiting, or referring for a fee aliens known to be unauthorized to work in the United States. Violators of the law are subject to a series of civil fines or criminal penalties when there is a pattern or practice of violations.[40]

As described, prior to the passage of the IRCA, the historical character of U.S. immigration policy targeted the illegal worker but overlooked the role of the employer in the illegal immigration equation. The IRCA attempted to rectify this legislative imbalance by empowering the INS to enforce employer sanctions and penalties. Still, the IRCA was not solely fixated on employer enforcement, but represented a far more sweeping and ambitious piece of legislation.

The IRCA included initiatives designed to protect the supply of legal foreign workers to perishable crop growers between fiscal years 1990 and 1993.[41] These programs were expected to improve employment opportunities for legal workers while addressing the problem of illegal immigration. In addition, the IRCA established an amnesty program that ensured the transitions of millions of illegal aliens to legal status. With respect to employer sanctions, the goal of the IRCA was to ensure greater economic security by deterring future illegal immigration vis-à-vis greater controls on employers who willingly hire illegal labor. Still, in evaluating the effects on illegal immigration, the data suggest that the IRCA had a limited impact.

An analysis of the number of aliens apprehended after the passing of the IRCA suggests that the three-year drop between 1986 and 1989 is best explained by the amnesty program's legalization of millions of illegal aliens. Moreover, based on the number of illegal aliens both apprehended and deported, as well as those estimated to reside in the United States, it is doubtful that the policy has had any success in deterring or preventing illegal immigration. As a 1991 Labor Department study concluded, "it is difficult for the analyst . . . to pinpoint which facet of the law led to specific changes in question."[42] In a study in 1990, the GAO is more direct and highlights the ease with which the IRCA and employment verification requirements were overcome by readily available fraudulent documents, indicating that the policy of employer sanction has not been implemented effectively.

Within the three years after the passage of the IRCA, the GAO evaluated and concluded that implementation of the employer sanction provision was less than successful.[43] Among the problems were confusion among employers as to what their responsibility was, that only 134,000 or 3 percent of all employers had received INS visits, and that between 1986 and 1989, only 3,532 businesses were fined with less than $5 million collected from them. Between 1989 and 1994, "fewer than half of the 12,700 U.S. employers that INS inspectors recommended be fined between 1989 and 1994 for employing illegal aliens . . . were in fact fined."[44] The average INS fine levied between 1989 and 1994 was only $1,612 and did not represent a significant punitive measure that would ensure widespread employer adherence.[45] The number of INS workplace inspectors actually dropped by half and led to a decline in workplace investigations, from 14,700 in 1989 to 6,000 in 1994.[46] In cities like Los Angeles, Chicago, San Antonio, Miami, and New York, the number of sanctions staff per 10,000 INS staff can range from a low of 0.9 of total agents to a high of 4.6 of total agents.[47]

As of 1996, only 700 workplace inspectors were part of the 19,000 employees of the INS.[48] In 1999, thirteen years after the adoption of the IRCA, another GAO study determined that since 1994 the INS had devoted only 2 percent of its resources for workplace enforcement, that only 3 percent of suspected employers were investigated, that the Department of Labor failed to provide information to the INS on potential employers who hire illegal aliens, and that the INS "infrequently imposed sanctions on employers."[49]

Since the IRCA, no significant pieces of immigration legislation have passed that deal with either positive or negative employer sanctions or any kind of improved employer-based enforcement.[50] In fact, the 1990 Immigration Act weakened many of the employer sanctions established four years previously.[51] In 1996, only three test-pilot programs were created to address workplace authorization and illegal immigration. The question remains why have employer sanctions not become a more attractive method for regulating illegal immigration? Was the IRCA and emphasis on

employer sanctions simply bad policy design, bad implementation, or the result of a lack of evaluation? The answers remain, to some extent, reflective of the difficulties of implementing immigration policy.

In 1991, a U.S. Department of Labor report stated that "removing one of the major incentives for illegal immigration—available employment—was expected to deliver handsome dividends of a tightening labor market (i.e., improved job opportunities, better working conditions and increased wages) to U.S. workers."[52] If this is the case, what policy logic explains the weakening of employer sanctions in the Immigration Act of 1990? Was this evidence or analysis simply not available to policy makers in 1990? Moreover, what can explain the failure to create and expand a national verification workplace program in the IIRIR Act of 1996? In terms of policy implementation and evaluation, it is evident, based on a number of GAO studies and recent policy actions, that the failures in implementation are because of the politics of the process that leads to bad policy design and poor implementation. In fact, the lack of institutional and budgetary resources committed to this segment of the IRCA, since 1986, raises real questions as to whether policy makers ever intended or desired to implement this part of the legislation.

A more thorough evaluation of employer sanctions remains elusive because of the overwhelming lack of implementation. How does one conclude the implementation of the employer sanctions program failed when the INS hardly ever enforced this aspect of the legislation? It is all but impossible, for instance, to determine what effect, if any, this legislation could have had on illegal immigration. Understanding these failures requires the realization that because the policy process does not operate in the absence of politics, the interests and agendas of the various policy actors will affect the effectiveness of implementation and the evaluation of immigration policy.

THE POLICY PROCESS AND IMMIGRATION POLICY

Politically, the lack of legislation dealing with employer sanctions is understandable. Elected representatives are susceptible to the political power of various interest groups, business lobby groups, their political parties, and their constituents. Because Congress and the president are the source for major changes to immigration policy, such as the IRCA, it is not surprising that a general political reluctance exists to develop policies that increase sanctions on American industries that hire and depend on illegal labor. From a political and policy perspective, the framing of illegal immigrants in a negative light only increases the political willingness of policy actors to focus punitive measures on the illegal alien and not the employer.

In terms of legal immigration, although substantial changes were proposed, and the growing political power of the Hispanic community had helped reframe the issue of immigration, the events of September 11 have all but squashed the political desire for easing restrictions or developing policies that better address the issue of immigration. Rather, because of the events of September 11, the legal and illegal immigrant population is once again the renewed focus of policies and regulations that appear to be extremely bent on control, and which are quite punitive in character. The design of such policies is more of a response to political and public concerns than a real desire to develop practical policies that address the problem and can be implemented effectively. Such reactions seem to consistently reflect the policy process and the making of immigration policy. When driven by certain political interests, policy makers develop dramatic policy actions that fail to consider how a misunderstanding of the policy problem, perceptions of certain groups, a failure to provide sufficient resources to critical agencies, a disregarding of past failures, and a poor understanding of implementation leads to poor policy design and execution.

From an administrative point of view, the INS is the agency responsible for policy execution. Historically, its many missions and the need to achieve many different goals have encumbered the agency. In terms of illegal immigration, the INS was and is clearly reluctant or politically constrained from pursuing a more aggressive employer sanctions program. In the past, the agency has all but failed to allocate sufficient institutional resources to this goal. Rather, the emphasis of the INS has been on border enforcement and deportation. No reduction in illegal immigration is possible if the INS is unwilling or unable to implement a critical policy, such as employer enforcement. To some extent, the economic value from illegal immigration is implicitly recognized by the failures of the INS to execute a more aggressive pursuit of employers who hire illegal labor. In other words, the failure to aggressively implement the employer sanctions program, to somewhat balance border with jobsite enforcement, clearly reflects the tendency by policy makers and the INS to favor implementation of policies that seek to control only the social costs from illegal immigration. In comparison, policies that may risk or jeopardize the economic benefits from illegal immigration—such as cheap labor—have been all but ignored or minimized over the last century.

Because of the political power and interests of certain actors, such as probusiness interests, additional federal legislation that targets employers is unlikely to develop. Given the political and economic costs involved with such a course of action, coupled with the political power of business interest groups, like the Chamber of Commerce, it is unlikely that Congress will be influenced or motivated to develop stronger legislation which could—if effectively implemented—have an impact on the rate of illegal immigration. In fact, if the current character of immigration policy is an indication, future policy will follow an even more punitive bent that targets the illegal and legal alien.

After a review of immigration policy, one confronts the realization that aspects of immigration policy are failing to have the intended impacts, not because it is necessarily poor policy but because no administrative or political will exists to design and implement more sensible policy. In comparison, because of skewed perceptions and persistent questions over the value of immigration, policy actions that are more punitive and more focused on the legal and illegal immigrant populations seem to garner, at specific periods, substantial support among policy makers.

IMMIGRATION POLICY INSTRUMENTS

Immigration policy, especially as it targets the illegal side of the policy area, includes a number of policy instruments. Specifically, the most common is the passage of legislation that creates new legal rules and sanctions that govern the nature of both legal and illegal immigration. Traditionally, the INS has been tasked to execute these new rules and sanctions as they apply to all facets of immigration. It is the responsibility of the INS to prepare and define proposed rules, interim rules, and final rules for the manner in which policy decisions will be implemented by the agency. These agency rules are used to control and define all aspects of the immigration and naturalization process. In addition, with the IRCA, fines and penalties can be used to alter the behavior of suspected employers. Moreover, in terms of legal immigration and naturalization, the INS is responsible for providing an array of services for temporary visitors, such as visa

extensions, as well as assisting the legal immigrant in his or her goal of residency and naturalization. Since September 11, 2001, the INS has placed renewed emphasis on enforcement, and the tracking and monitoring of all legal immigrants.

SUMMARY

The area of immigration policy represents a continuing struggle by the public and its decision makers to define the kind of nation America is and will be. For advocates of immigration, a more open immigration will add to the future strength of the United States. For opponents, immigration, both legal and illegal, represents a burden on state resources, represents a threat to domestic jobs, and, as of September 11, 2001, represents a potential national security threat. In part, the problems with immigration policy, as with any policy, reside within the stage of policy implementation.

It could be argued that the failures of immigration policy stem not from bad policy per se, but from ineffective implementation and limited evaluation of the implementation. Clearly, without effective implementation, every policy is all but doomed to fail. Yet, some of the failings of immigration policy, as discussed in the context of the IRCA, do not seem to exist because of a lack of awareness of the problems with the program or in the policy, or with weaknesses of the instruments, or even a fault in the design. Interestingly, the failures of implementation lie within the administrative and political unwillingness to implement or evaluate the policy solutions. Overall, one confronts a difficult "truth" that immigration policy may not be designed to effectively address the policy problem as it is identified publicly. Instead, as has been evident in the past, immigration policies may simply seek to achieve a set of political and administrative goals that center on control and achieving greater national and economic security. In light of September 11, it is fair to suggest that the future direction of immigration policy will continue to evolve in the direction of greater and greater control. What does remain unclear, however, is whether "good policy" will be developed, whether it will be implemented effectively, and whether evaluation studies can be used to improve future immigration policy when obvious failings emerge.

DISCUSSION QUESTIONS

1. What should be the primary goal of immigration policy? Discuss.

2. Do you agree or disagree with the assumption that employer sanctions could deter or prevent illegal immigration? Discuss.

3. Can immigration be fair to both the interests of the state and the immigrant? If so, what kind of immigration policy should the United States adopt in the post-September 11 world?

SUGGESTED READINGS

Capaldi, Nicholas. *Immigration: Debating the Issues.* Amherst, NY: Prometheus Books, 1997.

Fitzgerald, K. *The Face of the Nation: Immigration, the State, and the National Identity.* Stanford, CT: Stanford University Press, 1996.

Gimpel, J. G., and J. R. Edwards. *The Congressional Politics of Immigration Reform.* Boston: Allyn & Bacon, 1999.

Heer, David. *Immigration in America's Future.* Boulder, CO: Westview Press, 1996.

Hofstetter, Richard R., ed. *U.S. Immigration Policy.* Durham, NC: Duke University Press, 1984.

ENDNOTES

1. The extent of debate over the failures of immigration policy is best exemplified by the stark differences and opinions between various interest groups. Anti-immigration groups, such as FAIR, attempt to emphasize the costs from immigration. In contrast, proimmigration groups, such as the National Immigration Forum and the National Council of La Raza, stress the benefits from immigration. Additional information can be found at their respective Web sites: http://www.fairus.org, http://www.immigrationforum.org, and http://www.nclar.org.

2. The criticisms of the failures of immigration policy seem to run the spectrum, from policy actors that suggest enforcement policies are too weak on illegal immigration, to others that suggest the immigration and naturalization process is unfair and inefficient.

3. J. G. Gimpel and J. R. Edwards, *The Congressional Politics of Immigration Reform* (London: Allyn & Bacon, 1999), 5.

4. K. Fitzgerald, *The Face of the Nation: Immigration, the State, and the National Identity* (Stanford, CA: Stanford University Press, 1996), 17.

5. Immigration and Naturalization Service, Historical Reference Library, *An Immigrant Nation: United States Regulation of Immigration, 1798–1991* (Washington, DC: INS, 1991).

6. Michael Fix and Jeffrey Passel, *Immigration and Immigrants: Setting the Record Straight* (Washington, DC: Urban Institute, 1994), 11.

7. Examples of progressive immigration policy that seeks to redefine the goal of control are the establishment of free trade zones, such as North America Free Trade Agreement (NAFTA), and the creation of the European Union (EU). Under NAFTA, immigration restrictions were effectively reduced by the establishment of classes of workers that obtain work status without formal residency. However, NAFTA does not permit the free mobility of labor across borders, but continues to control the types of workers that can enter the United States. In contrast, the EU represents a bold example to remove state immigration barriers for all EU member states. However, the EU does not permit

open immigration and migration from non–EU states.

8. Based on data from the Immigration and Naturalization Service, *Fiscal Year 2000 Statistical Yearbook,* available at http://www.immigration.gov.

9. U.S. Census Bureau, "2000 Foreign-Born Population in the United States," *Census 2000* (Washington, DC: Government Printing Office, January 2001).

10. Ibid.

11. Ibid.

12. INS, *2000 Statistical Yearbook.*

13. Julian L. Simon, *Immigration: The Demographic and Economic Facts* (Washington, DC: Cato Institute and National Immigration Forum, 1996), 37.

14. John Miller and Stephen Moore, "A National ID System: Big Brother's Solution to Illegal Immigration," *Cato Policy Analysis No. 237,* September 7, 1995, 2.

15. FAIR, "How Many Illegal Aliens?," *FAIR Issue Brief* (January 2002). For more information, see the FAIR Web site at http://www.fairus.org.

16. D. Cohn, "Illegal Immigrant Total Is Raised," *Washington Post,* October 25, 2001, p. A24.

17. Ibid.

18. Fix and Passel, *Immigration and Immigrants,* 18.

19. Gimpel and Edwards, *Congressional Politics,* 95.

20. The Immigration Act of 1882 blocked or excluded the entry of "idiots, lunatics, convicts, and persons likely to become a public charge." The 1891 legislation barred polygamists, persons of crimes of moral turpitude, and those suffering from loathsome or contagious diseases. See INS, Historical Reference Library, *An Immigrant Nation.*

21. Ibid.

22. Ibid.

23. Ibid.

24. Gimpel and Edwards, *Congressional Politics,* 94–95.

25. Fix and Passel, *Immigration and Immigrants,* 18.

26. Ibid., 112.

27. J. F. Smith, "Bush to Weigh Residency for Illegal Mexican Immigrants," *Los Angeles Times,* September 7, 2001; J. Peterson,

"Immigration Emphasis on Guest Visas," *Los Angeles Times,* August 18, 2001.

28. Ibid., September 7, 2001.

29. Mark Potter, "Hijackers receive visa letters," CNN Web site, March 13, 2002.

30. See the INS Web site at http://www.ins.gov/graphics/lawenfor/specialreg/index.htm#special.

31. Thomas Ginsberg, "Visitors from 18 nations face scrutiny," *Philadelphia Daily News,* December 13, 2002.

32 Gimpel and Edwards, *Congressional Politics,* 3.

33. Studies by the National Research Council and the Cato Institute determined that immigrants may add as much as $10 billion to the economy each year, contribute to lower prices, pay more in taxes than they receive in public benefits, and have an overall positive effect on the national economy. However, other research studies suggest that the evidence is, at best, unclear as to what are the economic benefits or costs from immigration. For a review of studies on the effects of immigration, see Fix and Passel, *Immigration and Immigrants,* 86–94.

34. INS, *Statistical Yearbook* (Washington, DC: Department of Justice, 1995), 178.

35. For a good synopsis of various research efforts, see Simon, *Demographic and Economic Facts.*

36. United States General Accounting Office, "Illegal Aliens: Assessing Estimates of Financial Burden on California" (Washington, DC: Government Printing Office, 1994), 23.

37. Ibid.

38. Simon, *Demographic and Economic Facts,* 36.

39. INS, *Immigration and Naturalization Legislation 1790–1993,* available at the INS Web site http://immigration.gov.

40. See *INS Glossary* available at the INS Web site http://immigration.gov.

41. U.S. Department of Labor, *Employer Sanctions and U.S. Labor Markets: First Report,* (Washington, DC: U.S. Department of Labor, Bureau of International Labor Affairs, 1991), 3.

42. Ibid., 19.

43. GAO report to Congress, *Immigration Reform: Employer Sanctions and the Question of Discrimination.* (Washington, DC: GAO, March 1990), 30–90.

44. *Migration News* (December 2, 1996): 5–6, available at http://migration.ucdavis.edu.

45. Ibid.

46. Ibid.

47. INS, *Investigations Program: Full-Time Permanent Authorized Positions and Staffing Reports* (Washington, DC: INS, 1989).

48. *Migration News.*

49. GAO report to Congress, *Illegal Aliens: Significant Obstacles to Reducing Unauthorized Alien Employment Exist* (Washington, DC: GAO, April 4, 1999), no. GGD-99-33.

50. A review of immigration legislation between 1986 and 1993 suggests that even though eleven significant pieces of legislation were passed, none improved employer sanctions.

51. The Immigration Act of 1990 revised the enforcement activities that dealt with employer sanctions. See INS, "Immigration and Naturalization Legislation," *Fiscal Year 1995 Statistical Yearbook* (Washington, DC: INS, 1995), appen. 1–21.

52. U.S. Department of Labor, *Employer Sanctions,* xiii.

18

Defense Policy

Changing or Terminating

> We must account sufficiently for the interests of the large
> industrial nations to discourage them from challenging our
> leadership or seeking to overturn the established political or
> economic order . . . [and that] we must maintain the mechanisms
> for deterring potential competitors from even aspiring to a larger
> regional or global role.
>
> PENTAGON DEFENSE PLANNING GROUP

The end of the cold war in 1989 ushered in an era in which American national
security and defense policy would no longer be defined in the context of the
Soviet Union. At the beginning of the millennium, America stood as the only
global superpower. As the post-cold war era progresses into its second decade, defense policy must contend with a series of fundamental new challenges, risks, and
threats.

Among these risks are the emerging power of China, nuclear proliferation, regional instabilities, ethnic strife, religious extremism, and terrorism. The terrorist
events of September 11, in particular, emphasize the potent threat posed by international terrorism. Civil wars in parts of Africa, South America, and Asia threaten
to destabilize critical regions of the world. Religious extremism and conflicts continue to plague the Middle East, the Baltic region, Indonesia, and the relations between India and Pakistan. Concerns persist over the spread of weapons of mass

destruction among the so-called "evil axis" states of North Korea, Iraq, and Iran. Finally, the growing power of China suggests a coming era in which American superpower status will be directly challenged. In short, U.S. defense policy must be focused not only on traditional threats posed by states but also on an array of current and forthcoming security challenges.

Interestingly, whereas many other policy areas, such as education, health care, and the environment, contend with disputes over whether policy should be more public or private in character, no such debate exists in the context of defense policy. Moreover, with the terrorist attacks on New York City and Washington, DC in 2001, the continuing importance of defense policy is only further justified. Hence, the policy and political question is not whether there is a necessity for defense policy, but what kind of defense policy should the United States have. In order to answer this important policy question, the concepts of defense policy, national interest, and national threat will first be defined.

Defense policy represents the commitment by the national government to provide for and ensure a common defense for the nation. The role of the government in the defense policy area is well established. The logic that underscores the role for the central government is that in the absence of a common national defense, the state is vulnerable to attack, unable to defend or deter external threats, and is easily overcome by current or future threats. Essentially, the purpose of defense policy is to ensure the primary national interest of the state—national survival.

U.S. defense policy is not only a question of attaining a satisfactory level of power to defend the territory of the state but also serves greater interests. Defense policy reinforces America's global role as defined by policy makers. For the United States, because it is a superpower, global interests necessitate a defense policy that allows for global projection of military power. Successful power projection, however, requires that the United States possess a clear comparative military advantage—or dominance—against all enemy states, groups, and conceivable national threats.

In theory, dominance in military power provides the strategic position to successfully defend, deter, and respond to all threats. Such a strategic advantage in military power provides a basis with which to fulfill an array of national security missions, and also helps limit the human costs associated with the use of military force. When applying military force, a president can avoid the political consequences by limiting the number of casualties, both American and foreign. As is indicative of the evolution of defense policy, a growing technological advantage in military capabilities not only provides for more surgical attack but also helps reduce human casualties and the political consequences from such casualties. Still, determining the overall type of defense policy required by the state demands a clear definition of national interests.

National interest refers to the objectives and goals of the state.[1] Because national interest represents the primary directives of the state that ensure the health and survival of the state, it has implications for both domestic and international policy. A number of objectives comprise the national interest for any given state. Elements of the national interest include

- Military interests
- Economic interests
- Ideological interests
- Moral or legal interests
- Cultural interests

Military national interests involve two interrelated objectives. First, the preeminent national interest of the United States, and of any sovereign state, is national defense and territorial survival. Second, aside from national defense, the state may seek military dominance and influence that transcends its borders and extends throughout the international community. The United States, since 1945, has defined its national interest globally, not just territorially. For this reason, greater weight falls on the area of defense policy, because it is the extent to which the United States possesses the capabilities to project power globally that it maintains its military superiority.

Economic national interests refer to the basic goal of ensuring the economic growth, vitality, future, and prominence of the state. For the United States, given the international nature of trade and commerce, interests are no longer limited domestically, or to the region, but are global in scope and purpose. Moreover, economic interest also emphasizes the importance of promoting and ensuring global stability. Economic instability can pose a direct threat to the growth and stability of the state. Hence, defense policy ensures trade access to vital regions of the world, as well as promotes domestic or regional stability.

Ideological national interests entail the perpetuation of a specific national ethos and philosophy. In the case of America, such an ethos involves the promotion of liberty, freedom, and democracy. American defense policy can reinforce that ethos domestically by fostering national unity during conditions of crisis. Internationally, defense policy serves as a powerful symbol of America's ideology by protecting and ensuring freedom as American policy makers define it.

Taken to an extreme, an ideological national interest can promote nation building by forcing regime change on other states. As evidenced in Vietnam or Somalia, attempting to force a state to adopt a new political system and ideology is not easily accomplished. In the cases of Germany and Japan,

both actors were dramatically defeated to provide the domestic environment for the adoption of a new ideology. Still, the true importance of ideological national interests for the United States is open to some debate. A belief in liberty, freedom, and democracy has not prevented the United States from cooperating with regimes, such as Saudi Arabia and Pakistan, that are far from free and democratic. In reality, it is unclear to what extent ideology guides a definition of national security, or the application of military power.

Moral or legal national interests refer to the state goal to pursue a moral end, or adopt a legal framework, to guide one's actions. As with ideological national interests, what constitutes a moral or legal national interest is open to wide debate. Again, such national interests depend on how morality and legality are defined. Still, defense policy has served various humanitarian missions, such as the initial mission in Somalia to feed the hungry, attempts to curb the genocide in the former Yugoslavia, and when the U.S. delivers assistance in cases of natural disasters. Legal national interests, in comparison, can entail a preference by the state to abide by international law.

Cultural national interests represent the exchange of peoples, language, and cultures to foster greater affinity with other nation–states. The military, for example, will have exchanges with other defense departments from foreign governments, make port calls, attend international conferences, and conduct air shows to help improve the relationship between the United States and other states. In addition, such national interests, if successful, help promote a more positive image of the United States.

Overall, the primary national interests of the state are the pursuit of economic health and military security. Still, the sets of national interests, rather than being static, are dynamic and an evolving concept. As a 1997 National Security Council document indicates, the

---

Box 18.1 Scope of U.S. National Interests

1. Help foster a peaceful, undivided, democratic Europe
2. Support an expanded NATO (North Atlantic Treaty Organization), relationships with Russia and Ukraine, and a strengthened PFP (Partnerships for Peace) program
3. Reinforce ties with South Korea, Japan, Australia, and ASEAN (Association of Southeast Asian Nations) allies
4. Expand rapprochement with China
5. Promote open and stable global trade
6. Expand economic and political relations in Latin America and Caribbean
7. Further peace from the Middle East to Haiti, from Northern Ireland to Central Africa
8. Counter the security threats of NBC (Nuclear, Biological, Chemical) weapons proliferation, terrorism, international crime, drugs, arms trafficking, and environmental damage

---

United States must defend an expansive set of national interests (see Box 18.1).

In the future, a definition and redefinition of American national interests will occur as new political and policy realities emerge. These "new" realities are often highlighted by the emergence or an escalation in a national threat. What remains difficult to predict are what threats must U.S. defense policy prepare for.

The concept of national threats focuses both a state's national interests and defense policy. A national threat can be roughly graded from high to low depending on the level of risk. The highest national threat is that which directly threatens the survival of stability of the state, such as war with a major power, nuclear attack, terrorist nuclear attack, or chemical or biological attack. Other national threats of a fairly high risk are those that endanger vital regions or states, such as Europe or the Middle East. A regional war, for example, in such regional theaters would have substantial consequences for both of the parties involved and the United States.

Mid-level threats can include regimes that may be acquiring weapons of mass destruction that could threaten the region or the United States in the near future. The lowest national threat is posed by states or groups that differ with American national interests but that do not have the capability to execute their threats. However, in light of the terrorist attack on September 11, and the enormous economic, social, physical, and psychological costs resulting from an attack of only nineteen individuals using civilian airlines, the notion of what is a credible threat is no longer directly proportional to the tangible capabilities that the adversary possesses. Instead, even a small group of individuals, with certain means and determination, can pose grave national security threat to the United States. In the future, the nature and scope of threats that materialize will undoubtedly change, and will again compel a rethinking of America's defense policy.

CONTEMPORARY U.S. DEFENSE POLICY

Strategically, since 1945, the historical focus of U.S. defense policy has remained fixed on creating the geopolitical conditions that best serve America's national interests. At the end of World War II, the United States focused on creating an international system that ensured stability and mitigated threats to vital regions. The specific threat at the end of the war turned out to be the Soviet Union. The strategy to address the threat posed by the Soviet Union was described as "containment," and referred to a broad set of policies to isolate, cripple, and mitigate the economic, technological, social, and military power of another state.

In 1947, George Kennan was the first to articulate the need for a strategy to contain the Soviet Union. For Kennan, the policy of containment was designed "to confront the Russians with an unalterable counterforce at every point where they show the signs of encroaching upon the interests of a peaceful and stable world."[2] Underscoring the value and importance of the containment strategy was the National Security Conference Report 68 (NSC 68).

NSC 68 called for a dramatic shift in defense policy so that the United States would develop a *preponderance of military and economic power.*[3] As NSC 68 stated, national security would be determined only by a "rapid build up of political, economic, and military Strength."[4] Overall, both Kennan's strategy of containment and NSC 68 symbolize a consistent theme and goal within American defense policy—the goal of acquiring and maintaining a dominant level of military power against all threats. As some scholars have suggested, America's strategy from the beginning of the cold war was always a strategy of preponderance of power:

> The Cold War provided the impetus for the strategy of preponderance, which was directed against both the Soviet Union and the Western sphere. By integrating Germany and Japan into a network of U.S.-dominated security and economic arrangements, Germany and Japan were co-opted into the anti-Soviet coalition, and, just as important, these erstwhile enemies were themselves contained.[5]

The cold war was marked by an evolving defense policy. During the period of the 1950s, American defense policy focused on combating communist threats in Korea, maintaining stability in Europe, and expanding the nuclear deterrent. In the 1960s, the Cuban Missile Crisis, the emerging conflict in Vietnam, and enhancement of the nuclear deterrent were the focus of defense policy. The 1970s saw the withdrawal of the United States from Vietnam, conflicts in the Middle East, the oil crisis of the 1970s, the Iran hostage crisis, and the Russian invasion of Afghanistan. To some, in the late 1970s, the dawning of American power was near. The 1980s, however, saw a dramatic new era in defense policy and a rise in military expenditures.

In the 1980s, President Ronald Reagan initiated a substantial reformation in national defense and defense policy. Implementing one of the largest defense buildups in American history, Reagan was intent on changing the direction of American defense policy toward greater material strength. Aside from a substantial growth in defense spending, the dream of a national missile defense system became national defense policy. The "Star Wars" program was initially designed to thwart the Soviet Union's nuclear capability, and provide America with clear superiority in both conventional and nuclear power.

The consequence of Star Wars was to lead to dramatic attempts by the Soviet Union, under President Gorbachev, to reform and revitalize its economy to develop new technologies. However, reforms quickly led to structural and political weaknesses and the eventual collapse of the Soviet Union in 1989. By the end of the decade, the United States was the sole military and economic superpower.

The 1990s began as a period in which war in the Middle East threatened to envelop the region. The invasion of Kuwait and the threats against Saudi Arabia by Iraq represented a threat to America's economic and political interests in the region. The Persian Gulf War served as a powerful example of the success of America's defense policy. America's asymmetrical military advantage on the battlefield permitted the United States to defeat Iraq, the world's fourth largest army in 1991, in less than two months—with only 100 hours of combat on the ground. The remaining period of the 1990s, under then-President Clinton, ushered in a changing defense policy with reductions in defense spending and the use of military power to serve humanitarian goals in Haiti, Somalia, and in the former Yugoslavia. Criticisms of the Clinton administration, however, emphasized that global demands placed on a smaller military capability had needlessly taxed and overburdened the American military.

In the beginning of the twenty-first century, what seemed to be a period of relative peace was shattered on September 11, 2001, when the United States suffered its first direct attack since Pearl Harbor in 1941. The terrorist attacks of September 11 effectively shattered the perception that the United States was invulnerable to attack, or that the primary threats were only from major powers. In response to this unprecedented terrorist attack, the United States initiated a war against terrorism. This war on terrorism included direct use of American troops and military force against the now-defeated Taliban Regime, commitments to assist the Georgian government against insurgents, expansion of the antiterrorism programs against insurgent rebels in Columbia, assistance to the Philippine government against domestic terrorists, and, above all, the prosecution of a war against any and all remnants of Al Qaeda—the group headed by Osama Bin Laden and responsible for the September 11 attacks.

As of 2002, under the most recent national security review, the Bush administration refocused American defense policy on a strategy of preemption. Specifically, no longer will American defense policy be simply *focused on* deterrence and deterring threats of all kinds. Rather, the Bush administration has made it formal policy that the option of *preemption* is and will be considered a strategic option in dealing with all types of threats identified. The doctrine of preemption suggests that military force should and can be used to actively address any threat, even before it formally manifests:[6]

> The greater the threat, the greater is the risk of inaction—and the more compelling the case for taking anticipatory action to defend ourselves, even if uncertainty remains as to the time and place of the enemy's attack. To forestall or prevent such hostile acts by our adversaries, the United States will, if necessary, act preemptively.

President George W. Bush's revision of U.S. national security strategy was formulated in response to the array of explicit threats confronting the United States. In the post-September 11 world, defense policy must now address, more than ever before, the significant risk of biological, chemical, or nuclear threat against the United States by terrorist groups or rogue states.[7] The future of American defense policy will have to prepare for a wide scope of potential threats that include terrorism and more traditional international challenges. The scope and nature of these threats that risk American national interests, as defined by the 2000 Department of Defense *Quadrennial Defense Review (QDR)*, are as follows:[8]

- Cross-border aggression in vital regions
- Internal conflicts
- Transnational threats

- Humanitarian disasters
- Wildcard scenario
- Future global peer competitor

In terms of cross-border aggression, threats posed by nation–states, such as Iraq, North Korea, or other actors, risk stability in vital regions of economic or security interest. With Iraq, for example, the dependence on foreign oil has resulted in increasing concerns over the stability of the Middle East, and the threat posed by certain states to U.S. political and economic interests. Internal conflicts, such as insurgent groups or civil wars, represent the domestic threat posed to national economic, moral, and military interests because of potential instabilities within key allies or important states. Transnational threats are typified by the future fears of another terrorist attack. This threat may pose, for the near term, the greatest risk to American national security. Humanitarian disasters identify the risks of instability that arise within a state or region because of drought, famine, or natural disaster. With respect to the last two threats identified in the 2000 *QDR,* the wildcard scenario represents the all-encompassing unknown, whereas the future global peer competitor represents an implicit assumption that America's superpower status will be challenged in the future by a new great power. Although the DOD referenced both China and Russia, the evidence suggests that China may pose the greatest threat to the United States in this century.

China—The Next Global Peer Competitor

The rise of China as a new superpower may challenge both the definition of American national interests and the direction of its defense policy.[9] Based on economic projections, China will overtake the economic position of the United States by 2025.[10] By 2050, for instance, "this overtaking is expected to be complete as China's economic output is expected to be larger than the United States and the European Community combined."[11] More recent economic projections have concluded that consistent levels of growth over the next thirteen years will result in China's GNP surpassing America's in 2010.[12]

Relative to America's position, it is projected that if China achieves even "a percapita GNP just one-fourth that of the United States (about South Korea's ratio today), it would have a total GNP greater than the United States."[13] These estimations further suggest that the size of China's total middle class may surpass the entire population of the United States. With respect to military power, China's economic growth will undoubtedly help fuel the development of much more sophisticated military capability.

Although China's military expenditures are small, future defense investments could prove considerable within the next two decades—even surpassing the United States in total military expenditures by the end of 2020.[14] China has already begun to modernize its military by investing in a blue water navy capability, attack submarines, advanced satellite and reconnaissance technology, advanced bomber and fighters, and more modern nuclear arsenal.

For the United States, the emerging strategic environment poses a considerable challenge. Can U.S. defense policy ensure military superiority over all types of threats, which could include an even greater superpower? The answer, in light of growing Chinese power, suggests that American defense policy must adapt to the coming challenges. The importance of change in defense policy may be best grasped by the conclusions of a 1994 war game at the U.S. Naval War College modeled between the United States and a militarily resurgent China in the year 2020:

The U.S. was badly bloodied—despite the best efforts of the 80 participating military officers, intelligence analysts and [DOD] Officials. The key difference between the hypothetical adversaries was that China had a 21st Century military, bought off the shelf, while the U.S. fielded an updated version of its Gulf War force. Satellite-guided antiship missiles showered the U.S. fleet, which was naked to Chinese surveillance sensors high in space. As fast as the U.S. could blind the small, inexpensive satellites, the Chinese launched more, American aircraft carriers were forced to stay too far off China's coast to do much.[15]

THE POLICY PROCESS AND DEFENSE POLICY

Developing defense policy to address new threats is a policy process that occurs within a difficult political environment and involves a series of institutional and noninstitutional actors. These institutional actors include the president, the National Security staff, cabinet heads, intelligence officials, various political appointees, and members of Congress. Defense policy is also shaped by the active roles played by the joint chiefs of staff and senior members of the military services. Among noninstitutional actors, interest groups, the public, and the media represent three of the most important players shaping the direction and character of defense policy.

Defense policy is heavily influenced by each new president and significant changes can and do occur under each administration. As the commander in chief of the armed forces, and as head of the executive branch, the president has the policy power to effectively define the nation's priority in defense policy. The basic blueprint for the nation's defense policy is still formulated by the president, with assistance from the defense establishment and the national security staff. However, because budgetary appropriations are addressed by Congress, opportunities emerge that allow members of Congress, the committees, and various lobbyists or interest groups to directly shape the exact nature of defense policy. In addition, members of Congress have the power of oversight that permits investigations and analysis of any significant actions or changes in defense policy.

Because defense allocations that underpin and fund all defense policy initiatives are formally negotiated within Congress, each president must lobby for adoption of their proposed military budget and vision for defense policy. Even though much deference is given to a president's defense goals, divisions do emerge that affect many critical aspects of defense policy. For example, attempts by the Clinton administration to reduce unnecessary expenditures by closing military bases faced stiff resistance from members of Congress whose districts or states were affected. More recently, attempts by the George W. Bush administration to end the Crusader project, a project deemed needless by Defense Secretary Donald Rumsfeld, did not prevent affected members of Congress, lobbyists, associations, and corporations from lobbying and including monies for the Crusader project in the 2003 defense budget. Essentially, the formulation and adoption of defense policy is highlighted by many examples of needless defense expenditures, in some cases even unwanted by the president and the defense establishment.[16]

In terms of policy implementation, the DOD, which includes the armed services and various intelligence elements, is primarily responsible for executing defense policy. Although not part of the Defense department, other agencies such as the Central Intelligence Agency and the Department of Homeland Security do assist in the implementation of defense policy. In fact, since September 11, implementation of defense policy has increasingly depended on the cooperation and coordination among the intelligence services, the Department of Defense, and the Department of Homeland Security.

With respect to evaluation of defense policy, however, an array of actors are involved. Formal evaluations are conducted by executive and congressional agencies, such as the GAO, concerning the effectiveness and efficiency of various defense programs and missions. The GAO, for example, has conducted a variety of formal reviews of the defense policy that have evaluated the adequacy of defense spending and the value of certain defense capabilities in ensuring American national security.[17] In addition, through periodic reviews like the *QDR,* the DOD evaluates its threat environment and the need to develop or refine defense priorities.

Aside from formal reviews, defense policy is also the subject of intense political evaluations by a number of noninstitutional actors that have an important role in the policy process. Given the enormous budgetary allocations for defense, as well as the human costs associated with the application of military power, defense policy making is constantly open to scrutiny from interest groups, the media, and the public. Interest groups, such as those that represent defense industry interests, are especially active in attempting to influence changes in appropriations or general defense policy that favor their specific interests. As for the public and the media, the human costs associated with use of military power, as well as general attention given to matters of national security, provide these two actors with an ability to affect, in varying degrees, all aspects of defense policy making. Because of an understandable public and media sensitivity to casualties—both American and foreign— recent changes in defense policy, in terms of procuring military capabilities, have been influenced by a strategic desire to develop or

emphasize means that reduce the explicit human costs from war. For instance, the recent emphasis on air power during the Persian Gulf War of 1991, against Serbia during the Yugoslavian civil war, and against the Taliban in Afghanistan in 2000, reflect a desire to limit U.S. casualties that may be higher from more ground-focused military options. These changes in defense policy have been, to a great extent, influenced by the public and attention paid by the media. The media's role is especially significant in emotionalizing and fixating on the human costs of war, possibly at the expense of better analyzing whether the goals of the policy justify such a loss of life.

Since Vietnam, American defense policy making has been framed by a persistent concern over the level of casualties that are to be expected from an application of military power. For presidents, failures in defense policy, if costly in human terms, can and do prove politically damaging. In response, since the end of the Vietnam War, each president has pursued what some would argue is an almost irrational desire to minimize all costs from military action—even at the expense of more important policy goals.

In 1980, President Carter, after the first mission failed as it was being executed, did not attempt another rescue of the hostages in Iran. President Reagan withdrew American forces from Lebanon after the deaths of 241 marines in 1983. President George H. Bush ended the 1991 Persian Gulf War without dislodging Saddam Hussein over a concern of incurring greater casualties. In 1993, President Clinton withdrew American forces from Somalia weeks after the deaths of eighteen U.S. Army Rangers and U.S. Special Forces. President Clinton also remained reluctant to commit ground troops in the genocides of Rwanda and in the civil war within the former Yugoslavia. Finally, in 2001, President George W. Bush limited the use of massive ground troops, employed a limited number of Special Forces, and primarily utilized Afghanistan's opposition groups to overthrow the Taliban. Again, as with all previous presidents, Bush confronted numerous concerns over the number of military casualties that could have resulted in a broader war in Afghanistan.

The intrinsic dilemma within the making of defense policy is what changes must be made to deal with the array of threats confronted by the United States. The goal of dominance, and the need to maintain and possess a military advantage over all potential adversaries, further complicated defense policy making. In addition, as with all policy areas, defense policy cannot be divorced from the historical and political environment in which it develops. The concern over casualties, in particular, represents one of the most powerful factors affecting the need for the United States to remain dominant in military power. What remains unclear is what additional changes will have to occur in the near future in light of the threats confronted and these political concerns. In the end, the changes made or not made could well determine the future national security of the United States.

To Change or Not—Rethinking Defense Policy

Before the engagement, one who determines in the ancestral temple that he will be victorious has found that the majority of factors are in his favor. Before the engagement one who determines in the ancestral temple that he will not be victorious has found few factors are in his favor.

SUN TZU

U.S. defense policy is predicated on the pursuit of capabilities and strategies that perpetuate dominance in military power against any and all threats to national security. A consistent theme in recent defense and national security policy reviews is the strategic and tactical importance of maintaining this dominance in military power. Given the challenge posed by such a goal, it is not surprising that many of these defense reviews stress the importance of change, and the need to exploit new technologies, develop new military capabilities, new military thinking, and new approaches to warfare.

According to the 1993 *Bottom-Up Review (BUR)*, the 1997 *Quadrennial Defense Review*, the 1998 *National Defense Plan (NDP)*, and the 2000 *Quadrennial Defense Review*, American military power must remain predominant. This military force structure must be prepared to meet all threats on an array of battlefields with overwhelming capacity to defeat all threats and adversaries—an incredibly overwhelming challenge. American defense policy must be comprised of a force structure prepared to meet and respond to the "full spectrum of crises across the full range of military operations" across all geopolitical theaters.[18] As stated by *Joint Vision 2010*, a strategic plan developed by the Defense department, defense policy must be shaped to attain an unparalleled level of "full spectrum military dominance."[19] Hence, the driving goal for U.S. defense planners is to achieve and exploit, where and when possible, a new "revolution in military affairs (RMA)."

An RMA describes a significant and unparalleled transformation in the defense policy and the military factors critical to victory in warfare. Essentially, it represents a fundamental nonlinear change in the direction of defense policy away from previous military capabilities or strategies. Such RMAs are defined as a "major discontinuity in military affairs . . . which are brought about by changes in military relevant technologies, concepts of operations, methods of organization, and/or resources available."[20] Since the fifteenth century, the nature of warfare was transformed roughly eight times and four of these transformations occurred within the twentieth century (see Box 18.2).

The value of any one RMA is measured by its ability to fundamentally transform the strategic, operational, tactical, and political utility of war. RMA alters the nature of warfare—how it is fought and who will be the victor. However, no RMA develops in a political, administrative, or policy vacuum. Because by definition an RMA represents a dramatic change in the status quo, it can create opposition within the Department of Defense, the branches of the military, congressional members, think tanks, the cabinet, and the president. Nevertheless, developing, adopting, exploiting the dramatic changes from the next generation of RMAs is essential if the United States is to ensure its dominance in military power.

Can the United States deter or defeat a future peer competitor that could threaten America's national interests and its vision of the international status quo? The answer, in part, is found in changing defense policy to focus on exploiting the instruments of the next RMA—the revolutionary instruments of space, information technology, and unmanned weapons of war.

NEW DEFENSE POLICY INSTRUMENTS

The question of how future wars will be fought has sparked much speculation and debate. Defense policy demands one specific goal—an asymmetrical level of dominance in the future instruments of war. If attained, such asymmetry in power will allow the United States to deter, and possibly defeat, the next global peer competitor. In the nomenclature of defense policy, such asymmetry is referred to as "full-spectrum dominance." Full-spectrum dominance entails changing defense policy that will incorporate new operational concepts to maximize the lethality of American military power. These concepts are defined in Box 18.3.

As stated in the Defense department's *QDR,* the key to success for full-spectrum dominance is a "system of systems" that will integrate intelligence collection and assessment, command and control, weapons systems, and support elements.[21] The goal is to provide the interconnection between all elements of military force and provide a full range of information necessary for tactical and strategic success. Arguably, this proposed future force structure could be a smaller, more mobile, and more lethal force. Box 18.4 shows an outline of this proposed force structure.

Accomplishing future full-spectrum dominance will require changes in American defense policy that effectively exploit space, information technology, and un-

---

Box 18.3 Full-Spectrum Dominance Defense Policy

1. Dominant maneuver: Having a full picture of the battlefield, advanced mobility, and agile platforms to exploit weakness in the enemy

2. Precision engagement: Delivering precision force with the support of real-time information, common awareness of the battlespace, and flexible command and control to reengage with precision

3. Full-dimensional protection: Using passive and active defense to defend U.S. forces and assist force projection

4. Focused logistics: Fusing of information, logistics, and transportation technologies to deliver the right support at the right time

SOURCE: Department of Defense, *Quadrennial Defense Review* (Washington, DC: Department of Defense, 1997), vi.

Box 18.4 Proposed Defense Structure

Army—Four active corps with 10 active divisions (6 heavy, 2 light, 1 airborne, and 1 air assault); 2 active armored cavalry regiments; 15 National Guard enhanced separate brigades; other restructured National Guard divisions

Navy—twelve aircraft carriers, 11 air wings, 12 amphibious ready groups, 116 surface combatants, 50 attack submarines, and augmentation by Naval Reserve

Air Force—Fleet of 187 bombers, 12 active fighter wings, 8 reserve component fighter wing equivalents, and 4 National Guard dedicated continental air defense squadrons

Marines—Three Marine Expeditionary Forces, 1 reserve, and 3 air wings

Special Ops—Joint force of approximately 47,000 Army, Navy, Air Force, and reserve personnel

---

manned systems. As indicated in the conflicts in Yugoslavia, Iraq, and Afghanistan, the ability to exploit such technologies provides an enormous force multiplier. Also, such technologies can and will reap rewards by reducing the number of casualties on all sides, as well as focusing the power of the attack on the specified targets.

Space, and its role in providing and assisting American military power, will prove critical to the goals of U.S. defense policy. As the *QDR* boldly notes, the "United States must retain superiority in space . . . as intelligence, command and control, navigation, weather forecasting, and communication rely on space-based assets."[22] Already, for example, the Air Force is transitioning from an air force to a space and air force.[23]

In terms of the instruments of war, space capability proves essential because "the control of space is a critical enabler for the [military] force because it allows all U.S. forces freedom from attack and freedom to attack."[24] More important, a space capability will assist the potency, precision, tempo, and presence of all U.S. forces across a full spectrum of operations—whether against terrorists or a new state threat. The current space force involves four broad pillars of capability, as illustrated in Box 18.5.

Unmanned vehicles refers to the use of weapons of war that allow military personnel to be in remote control of the vehicle or instrument. The Air Force has utilized Unmanned Aerial Vehicles (UAVs) for the first time in a combat role in the war on terrorism in Afghanistan. Additionally, defense contractors are already testing a UCAV—an unmanned combat aerial vehicle—that would allow for increased maneuverability, range, lethality, and capability, as the aircraft would not need a pilot. In addition, future research will explore how unmanned land or naval vehicles, whether tanks, artillery, or missile destroyers, could provide an added advantage on the battlefield.

Box 18.5   Four Pillars of Space Force

1. Space support—Launch vehicles and satellite control
2. Force enhancement—Secure communication (e.g., MILSATCOM), navigation (GPS), TW/AA (e.g., nuclear detection), environmental monitoring, and ISR (classified assets)
3. Space control—Space surveillance and battle management/C4I, negation of other space assets, and protection of sovereign assets
4. Force application—BMD research with defensive intent; no offensive power projection from space

SOURCE: Department of Defense, *Space Program. An Overview for FY 1998–2003* (Washington, DC: Deputy Under Secretary of Defense [Space], Office of the Under Secretary of Defense, March 1997), 8.

Information technology, and the use of battlefield intelligence in real-time, will also prove essential to the effectiveness of future defense policy. As the 1997 and 2000 QDRs point out, the backbone of military innovation centers on improved information and command and control capabilities.[25] By utilizing information technology, all capabilities on the battlefield—from the individual soldier to artillery and aerial capabilities—can be integrated so as to maximize the force multiplier from American military power.

> In warfare, the information superiority that these capabilities will provide will significantly increase the speed of command, enabling forward deployed and early-entry forces to take the initiative away from numerically superior enemy forces and set the conditions for early, favorable termination of the conflict.[26]

The importance of information technology has already led the military branches to evaluate and change how they will fight future wars. For example, Force XXI, the Army's template for the future, is "focused on the interconnectivity of each echelon and between echelons."[27] Basically, the Army's Force XXI strategy is designed to organize a force around the creation and sharing of information so as to increase exponentially the force multiplier of every soldier. For the Army, the future military must possess a real-time situational awareness, constant intelligence gathering, an immediate deployment capability, and a greater flexibility in applying force on target. Overall, the shared service goals of the Navy, Air Force, and Army are to acquire information, disseminate it, and utilize it to interweave a truly joint force. This joint force will possess both greater lethality and a capability to respond to all threats whether through a clandestine special operation, a naval launched precision tomahawk, or a major power war. The challenge, of course, is whether such changes in defense can and will occur.

SUMMARY

For the United States, future national security and international stability depends to a great extent on the changes in defense policies that institutional actors will decide to adopt. The goal of American defense policy since 1945 has been unmitigated pursuit of dominance on the battlefield. This goal, however, is being challenged by both the changing epoch of war and threats that currently mark the post-2000 world. The question becomes whether the United States will execute changes in defense policy or it will be exploited by other actors that change their defense policies. Potentially, the current revolution in military affairs offers the promise to add a qualitative multiplier, to enhance the nonlinear effects of American military capabilities, and to further deter all kinds of threats—possibly even terrorism. Exploiting such changes, however, will likely require a fundamental change in the direction of defense policy.

The defense policy value of many traditional military systems, such as tanks, artillery pieces, heavy armored divisions, and aircraft carriers, will have to be reconsidered in the context of how much more efficient wars will and have to become. From a domestic political perspective, military power must be applied as efficiently and effectively as possible so that casualties are minimized. Globally, the scope of America's interests may have to be rethought in light of weapons systems that serve different roles in this emerging epoch of war and threat. For instance, in the near future, the aircraft carrier will remain a symbolic and potent deterrent. Clearly, a carrier's power projection will continue to exceed the capabilities of most nations. However, in the not-so-distant future, such a symbolic capability of American military power may prove a liability against an advanced military power. Against a global peer, for instance, who will likely possess space-based reconnaissance, attack submarines, and precision-strike capability, the carrier may represent nothing more than a perfect target no less antiquated than the battleships and cavalry of the past.

The very nature of American power may have to change to become far lighter, unmanned, and more lethal. Yet, the Army's goal in Force XXI remains the global deployment of one light division in twelve days and two heavy divisions in thirty days.[28] Although certain threats may necessitate such a response, such as another terrorist threat or a risk from lesser regional power, will the next major power war even last that long? Will two major powers, like the United States and China, be politically, technologically, and militarily capable of fighting a war for months? Again, changes in defense policy must consider that a level of

force must be possessed that is not only dominant in quality but that also minimizes the political and human consequences arising from a prolonged war. Achieving this balance in defense policy, in the future, may prove even more difficult.

In any event, we are left with an unsettling reality in defense policy. Given the scope of U.S. national interests, continued American military dominance is not an option but a strategic necessity. Achieving this goal will demand substantial policy change. It is unclear whether the policy and political process will encourage, support, and execute such revolutionary changes in defense policy. If not, then the national security of the United States could prove to be at much greater risk in the coming decades.

DISCUSSION QUESTIONS

1. What do you believe is the greatest national security threat faced by the United States? Discuss how the United States should respond in terms of changes in defense policy.

2. Can the United States address simultaneously all of the threats to its national interests identified by the QDR? If not, why?

3. Can U.S. defense policy change, prepare, and win the next major war—both politically and militarily—against a nation like China? Why or why not? Would the American public accept the costs of such a war? Discuss.

SUGGESTED READINGS

Cohen, W. *The 2000 Quadrennial Defense Review.* Washington, DC: The Department of Defense.

Hastedt, G. P. *American Foreign Policy.* Upper Saddle River, NJ: Prentice Hall, 1997.

Hilsman, R. *The Politics of Policymaking in Defense and Foreign Affairs.* Englewood Cliffs, NJ: Prentice Hall, 1990.

Hoge, James F., and Gideon Rose, eds., *The New Terrorism: Threat and Response.* New York: Council on Foreign Relations, 2001.

Hoge, James F., and Gideon Rose, eds., *U.S. Defense Policy.* New York: Council on Foreign Relations, 2001.

Kegley, C. W., Jr., and E. R. Wittkopf. *World Politics: Trends and Transformation.* New York: St. Martin's Press, 2001.

Kennedy, P. *The Rise and Fall of the Great Powers.* New York: Random House, 1987.

Organski, A. F. K. *World Politics.* New York: Alfred A. Knopf, 1958.

White, Jonathan R. *Terrorism: An Introduction.* Belmont, CA: Wadsworth, 2002.

ENDNOTES

1. G. P. Hastedt, *American Foreign Policy* (Upper Saddle River, NJ: Prentice Hall, 1997).

2. George F. Kennan, "The Sources of Soviet Conduct," *Foreign Affairs* 65, no. 4 (1947): 852–869.

3. NSC 68: U.S. Department of State, *Foreign Relations of the States,* 1 (1950).

4. Ibid., 2.

5. Christopher Layne, and Benjamin Schwartz, "American Hegemony—Without an Enemy," *Foreign Policy* (Fall 1992): 8.

6. See *The National Security of the United States,* September 2002, 19. For a copy of the report, go to http://www.whitehouse.gov.

7. For a discussion and analysis of proliferation, see Chris Kofinis, *Nuclear Diffusion: The Rethinking of Why Nation-States "Go Nuclear"* (master's thesis, University of Nevada, 1996).

8. W. Cohen, *Quadrennial Defense Review* (Washington, DC: Department of Defense, 2000), 1–10.

9. Mark Abdollahian, "In Search of Structure: The Nonlinear Dynamics of International Politics" (Ph.D. diss., Claremont Graduate School, 1996); Chris Kofinis, The Paths to War (Ph.D. diss., Claremont Graduate School, 2000).

10. Jacek Kugler, Ronald Tammen, and Siddarth Swaminathan, "Power Transition in Asia"

(paper presented at the ISA Conference, March 15–18, 2000).

11. Ibid., 7.

12. Michael Laris, "A Fast Drive to Riches," *Time* magazine, March 3, 1997, 32.

13. Richard K. Betts, "Wealth, Power, and Instability," *International Security* 18, no. 3 (Winter 1993/94).

14. This is a conclusion derived from research conducted in analyzing major power war. These projections do not take into account the post-September 11 increase. See Kofinis, *The Paths to War.*

15. Thomas E. Ricks, "How Wars Are Fought Will Radically Change, Pentagon Planner Says," *Wall Street Journal,* July 15, 1994, A1.

16. See R. Hilsman, *The Politics of Policymaking in Defense and Foreign Affairs* (Englewood Cliffs, NJ: Prentice Hall, 1990); Jacques S. Gansler, *Affording Defense* (Cambridge, MA: MIT Press, 1991).

17. For a review of GAO reports, go to http://www.gao.gov.

18. Department of Defense, *National Military Strategy* (Washington, DC: Department of Defense, 1997), 1.

19. Department of Defense, *Quadrennial Defense Review* (Washington, DC: Department of Defense, 1997) vi.

20. Michael J. Vickers, "The Revolution in Military Affairs and Military Capabilities," *War in the Information Age* (Washington, DC: Brassey's, 1997), 30.

21. Department of Defense, *QDR, 1997.*

22. Ibid., 17.

23. U.S. Air Force, *Global Engagement: A Vision for the 21st Century Air Force* (Washington, DC: National Defense University Press, 1997).

24. Ibid.

25. Department of Defense, *QDR, 1997,* 39.

26. Ibid., 40.

27. Theodore Galdi, *Revolution in Military Affairs?* (Washington, DC: International Security, Foreign Affairs and National Defense Division, December 11, 1995).

28. Institute for National Strategic Studies, *Strategic Assessment 1996: Instruments of U.S. Power* (Washington, DC: INSS, National Defense University Press, 1996), 173.

PART IV

The Art to the Game

19

Understanding Choices
and Decisions

The goal of this text is to provide a well-balanced and broad understanding of the field of public policy that also gives additional insight into the political dynamics that underscores policy making in America. As the title of the book suggests, one can look at the policy-making process as both an art and a game. Our purpose has been to provide a well-balanced discussion of the policy-making game—its language, the what, the who, the where, the stages of the process, and the many areas of policy important to American public policy and the nation. More ambitiously, we have endeavored to merge the practical and theoretical to assist how you will see and understand the complexity of the policy process. The "art to the game," if you will, is in understanding the policy process and applying frameworks, techniques, tools, and models to increase that understanding and change policy for the better.

Improving one's understanding leads to an interesting conclusion about the difficulty of creating optimal policy. Essentially, public policy and the policy-making process are not as hard as they seem. What makes policy-making difficult is the inescapable reality of politics throughout the policy process. In other words, what is "better" policy is not answered in the absence of politics, but within it. Such politics are sometimes institutionalized, exist within a variety of actors, but can and do change over time. Policy is not fixed, however, but is dynamic, and can change for the better and worse. The key challenge is becoming aware of how policy is made so that future decisions by the next generation of policy makers can be improved.

We believe that by realizing the implications of the broad scope of public policy, using the stages-heuristic approach as a conceptual framework, coupled with analysis of various areas of policy, both understanding and decisions will be enhanced. It is often the case that perfect decisions and perfect policy are an impossibility given the political and policy dynamics inherent within the policy-making process. Still, although we embrace the reality that perfect policies will prove elusive, we still strive to achieve that elusive goal of the perfect public policy—a well-identified problem; the issue set on the agenda with respective priority; a solution formulated and designed to solve the problem, implemented to achieve intended impacts, evaluated with a purpose to improve the policy, and changed or terminated when deemed necessary.

Of course, "perfect" policy, given the political realities of American policy making, may never be attained. Still, in continuously striving to improve how policy is made, as well as increasing our level of insights, we are confident that better decisions and better policy will result. Through the integration of the academic and applied approach, readers will develop both an understanding of policy making and the actual skills applicable within the policy arena. We have seen that policy making is a complex process with distinct overlapping stages. Different theories of the policy process have been formulated to explore the complexity of each stage of the policy process, from policy problem identification to policy termination. In addition, an invaluable array of applied consultative and policy tools have been introduced, such as policy analysis, agenda-setting methods, policy design, legislative and lobbying strategy, implementation analysis, and program evaluation models, that allow us to both learn and do as occurs within the government and real-world policy arenas. From such a real-world and theoretical perspective comes better understanding, the skills to make policy better, and the ability to make the "right" decisions at respective stages of the policy process.

From the discussion in previous chapters it is initially clear that policy can be created from within any part of the political system; that each policy arena is to some extent distinctive—although there are discernible process similarities within various stages; and that somehow all the actors come together and make decisions about which policy alternative best deals with a policy issue or problem. How all of these actors come together and understand the choices that are made can best be understood through a discussion of decision making.

Policy making requires that actors make choices among different remedies for dealing with problems. How this is achieved is best explained and understood through various decision-making models. None of the models were specifically developed to study public policy, but they do look at the decision-making process which is the heart of policy making. Thus, each of them offers a distinct way of answering the question how decisions and policy are made. What follows is a selection of the models most commonly used to understand the decision-making process. Each of these can offer a last degree of focus as one looks back at understanding the stages and dynamics of the policy process.

DECISION-MAKING MODELS

Rational Model

Governments make policies that promote maximum social gain. In short, the benefits of a policy should exceed the costs. A rational policy is one that produces the greatest benefit over cost in comparison to other alternative policies dealing with the same problem. One of the basic axioms of the rational choice model is that issues and problems are approached in a well-ordered sequence. Problems are identified and isolated; then the goals, values, and objectives of pertinent solutions to the problems are identified and ranked according to saliency. Next, various alternatives are formulated and weighted, and finally decision makers choose an alternative that will be the most appropriate means to secure described ends. The assumption is decision makers consider all possible courses of action, work out each of their consequences, and evaluate them before selecting the best choice, which is the one most likely to achieve stated goals.

In the rational model, even though each actor may pursue the preferred course of action, policy formulation is clearly a collective process. Hence, rational models help point out the realization that actors may be acting collectively, and the result is a suboptimal outcome.[1]

Incremental Model

Incrementalism as an approach is summarized in Lindblom's "The Science of Muddling Through."[2] Although "muddling through" is usually seen as a criticism of policy making, as a process it may have its own intrinsic merits. Lindblom outlines incrementalism as present oriented and frequently remedial in nature, focusing on making necessary changes and adaptations in existing practices. Therefore, incrementalism can be viewed as a fine-tuning of existing policy. It is decision making through what Lindblom refers to as small or incremental steps. The incremental model is seen as a simpler and more realistic way of making policy, because it is not a comprehensive and synoptic type of response. As policies

begin to fail or produce unsatisfactory or undesirable situations, small changes in policy are made by decision makers.

Group Model

In various formations, people also refer to this as the pluralist model. The tenet here is that public policy is the product of the struggle among competing groups.[3] The central arguments of both group theory and pluralism is that societies consist of large numbers of social, ethnic, or economic divisible groups who are more or less well organized. These groups, in political competition with each other, put pressure on government to produce policies favorable to them. The public interest tends to emerge out of the struggle of competing individual and group claims. Specific policies reflect the relative influence of the different interests on any given issue. Therefore, each policy area involves a distinctive set of problems and separate sets of political agents and forces. Public policy is the result of a unique process of interaction. The basic elements of pluralism and group theory are multiple centers of power and optimum policy developments through competing interests. One of the chief results of group competition is that often the policy solution, good or bad, that garners the most support is the one adopted.

Elite Model

This model holds that policies are made by a relatively small group of influential leaders who share common goals and outlooks.[4] Policy is not seen as the product of group conflict and demands, but rather as determined by the preferences of the power elite or ruling class. The preferences of the elite are adopted by policy makers; policies reflect their values and serve their interests. Thus, according to the elite model, public policy is determined not by the masses, but by a minority who have political and economic power.

Subgovernments Model

The subgovernments model argues that the government alone does not make policy choices but endorses decisions made by sections of the government in alliance with interest groups.[5] This partnership has been referred to as subgovernments or iron triangles.[6] All those involved in a subgovernment have similar interests. These structures develop around particular policy areas and involve coalitions of the relevant legislators, bureaucrats, and interest groups. Policy outcomes are determined by various subgovernments and revolve around their interests. Subgovernments, therefore, tend to develop around those specialized areas of policy that have a low level of public interest and awareness. This perspective has in recent years become outmoded among political scientists who argue that there are now larger numbers of interested actors than the three posited by the subgovernment model.[7] For example, Hugh Heclo argues that one should view the process as being dominated by issue networks, all of whom have substantial expertise in the policy area.[8] Such networks may also be referred to as policy communities.

Bureaucratic Corporatist Model

Government behavior and policy making is the outcome of bargaining or negotiation among individuals, such as interest groups, and governmental groups, such as the bureaucracy. Policy is not made by rational choice but through a push-pull system of politics.[9] Thus, policy emerges from bargains and compromises made by government ministers and bureaucrats representing different government departmental interests and priorities.

Decisions might not be in the best national interest, but in the bureaucrats' interest.

Institutional Model

Policy is seen as the product of institutional interaction. All policies have to be formulated, adopted, implemented, and enforced. It is the job of formal institutions such as executives, legislatures, judiciaries, and political parties to make policy.[10] Policy decisions are the output of large government organizations that function according to regular behavioral patterns.

Systems Model

The systems model views public policy as a political system's response to demands arising from the environment.[11] The political system is a mechanism through which popular demands and supports for the state are combined to produce policy outputs that best ensure the long-term stability of the system. Policy outputs may produce new demands that lead to further outputs and so on in a never-ending flow of public policy. The basic assumption is that political systems are analogous to mechanical operating systems with feedback and clear goals. The model stresses the interrelationship of the various actors and institutions in the policy process. The actors and institutions basically come together to turn inputs (demands and supports) into outputs (policy).

Which is the best model, in many ways, will be dictated by one's own ideological orientation. Each model provides a different answer and focus and sometimes combinations of the models can be used to explain particular policy-making situations. Box 19.1 outlines the advantages and disadvantages of each of the models. What is true at each stage of the policy process is decisions have to be made. The decisions that are arrived at determine

Box 19.1 Analytical Models—Pros and Cons

	RATIONAL	INSTITUTIONAL	INCREMENTAL	GROUP	ELITE	SYSTEMS	BUREAUCRATIC CORPORATIST	SUB-GOVERNMENTS
Advantages	1. Sharply defined focus 2. Can cover routine bureaucratic decision 3. Cost–benefit alternatives make it useful for reform, efficiency, etc.	1. Sharply defined focus by all decision makers 2. Easy to measure and gather data 3. Can approximate "lab" conditions via statistical analysis 4. Explanation and action "reformist" oriented	1. Sharp focus on bureaucracy and specific decisions 2. Predictive value high 3. Easy access to information makes statistical analysis easier	1. Broad focus on process and actual actors 2. Highlights the conflict nature of decision process	1. Sharp focus on power resources 2. Highlights the "rules-of-the-game" 3. Can be applied to both routine and nonroutine policy 4. Primarily explanatory	1. Broad focus on the entire process; its ongoing nature, action, and reaction of environment on policy and vice versa 2. Highly flexible 3. Easy to grasp heuristic 4. Good for both explanation and prediction	1. Same as "Game" and "Group" Models	1. Sharp focus on particular governmental institutions and relevant interest groups 2. Shows role of interest groups as active and not reactive

Box 19.1 Analytical Models—Pros and Cons (Continued)

	RATIONAL	INSTITUTIONAL	INCREMENTAL	GROUP	ELITE	SYSTEMS	BUREAUCRATIC CORPORATIST	SUB-GOVERNMENTS
Disadvantages	1. Is nearly impossible to fulfill 2. Narrow scope 3. Time constraints often make it hard to use	1. Narrow scope 2. "Re-formist" tendency may lead analyst astray	1. Narrow scope 2. Cannot cover innovations; rapid or massive change not well accounted for 3. Non-governmental actors or factors often ignored or missed	1. Tends to ignore "routinized" decisions 2. Ignores impact of unique person, event, or situation	1. Danger of "circularity" 2. Assumes power equals resources 3. Assumes power resources can be applied equally across issue areas 4. Data often difficult to get 5. Predictive value low	1. Focus is difficult to empirically apply and measure 2. Linkages often unclear 3. Tends to ignore routine bureaucratic decisions	1. Same as "Game" and "Group" models	1. Ignores size and number of interest groups 2. Ignores routinized decisions

SOURCE: Adapted from materials supplied by Professor Michael LeMay, California State University, San Bernardino.

not only what direction the policy will take but also what will be addressed on the agenda and what will be ignored.

SUMMARY

Public policy represents an especially challenging field of study. As much as "good" policy can resolve issues, improve quality of life, and utilize scarce public resources in the most efficient and effective manner, it is just as easy for "bad" policy to make the state of the society worse. It matters that we improve decisions and policy because it is only through better policies that substantial societal problems can be redressed and the polity can improve.

In the future, questions as to the role and responsibility of government, of the nature of public policy necessary, will continue. What may change, however, is the array and nature of issues that the society could have to contend with. From terrorism, poverty, environment, education, immigration, and health care, to other issues not discussed, the next generation of leaders and decision makers will face formidable challenges in developing the appropriate policy solutions in a future where limited public resources may require governments at all levels to make difficult decisions. As such, *The Art of the Game* has had an ideal goal: to improve society through better decisions and better policy. The challenge, of course, is appreciating the complexity of each stage of the policy process, and how better decisions and better policies are attainable through an improved understanding of American public policy.

DISCUSSION QUESTIONS

1. In your opinion which of the decision-making models best explains how public policy is made?

2. For successful policy making, do you think policy making is a game that must be played in a certain way?

SUGGESTED READINGS

Domhoff, G. W., *Who Rules America?* Englewood Cliffs, N.J.: Prentice Hall, 1967.

Golembiewski, R., "The Group Basis of Politics," *American Political Science Review,* 54 (December, 1960) 962–971.

Heisler, M. Corporate Pluralism Revisited, *Scandinavian Political Studies,* new series 2 (1979), 277–297.

Peterson, P. E. "The Rise and Fall of Special Interest Politics," *Political Science Quarterly,* 105 (Winter 1990/1991), 539–556.

Schattschneider, E. E. *The Semi-Sovereign People.* New York: Holt, Reinhart & Winston, 1969.

Schumpeter, J. *Capitalism, Socialism and Democracy.* London: Allen & Unwin, 1943.

ENDNOTES

1. P. R. Schulman, "Nonincremental Policy Making," *American Political Science Review* 69 (1975): 1354–1370.

2. C. E. Lindblom, "The Science of Muddling Through," *Public Administration Review* 19 (1959): 79–88.

3. R. Dahl, "Pluralism Revisited," *Comparative Politics* 10, no. 2 (January 1978): 191–204; D. B. Truman, *The Governmental Process,* 2nd ed. (New York: Knopf, 1971), 501–508.

4. R. Miliband, *The State in Capitalist Society* (New York: Basic Books, 1969), 131–137; C. Wright Mills, *The Power Elite* (Oxford, England: Oxford University Press, 1956), 3–15, 276–294.

5. Subgovernments are also referred to as iron triangles.

6. J. Leiper Freeman, *The Political Process: Executive, Bureau-Legislative Committee Relations* (New York: Norton, 1979); T. L. Gais et al., "Interest Groups, Iron Triangles and Representative Institutions in American National Government," *British*

Journal of Political Science 14 (April 1984): 161–186; A. G. Jordan, "Iron Triangles, Woolly Corporations and Elastic Nets: Images of the Policy Process," *Journal of Public Policy* 1 (February 1981): 95–123.

7. J. Walker, *Mobilizing Interest Groups in America* (Ann Arbor: University of Michigan Press, 1991).

8. H. Heclo, "Issue Networks and the Executive Establishment," in A. King, ed., *The New Political System* (Washington, DC: American Enterprise Institute, 1978), 87–124.

9. G. Lehmbruch and P. Schmitter, eds., *Patterns of Corporatist Policy Making* (Beverly Hills, CA: Sage, 1982).

10. J. Anderson, *Public Policy-Making: An Introduction* (Boston: Houghton Mifflin, 1990), 31.

11. D. Easton, *A Systems Analysis of Political Life* (New York: Wiley, 1965).

Appendix

Internet Resources

Assessing the Credibility of Online Sources

http://leo.stcloudstate.edu/research/credibility1.html
    This is a good guide on how to effectively and carefully assess the quality of Web pages.

SEARCH ENGINES: GENERAL INFORMATION

Journalist's Guide to Web Searches

http://www.newslink.org/web/
    The Journalist's Guide covers many of the issues mentioned in this appendix, such as Web site reliability and searching strategies. Because most journalists are sticklers for reliability, this site will help you find sound sources.

Search Engine Watch

http://www.searchenginewatch.com
    This is a site that covers the latest news and information about search engines. You can learn about the newest search engines, how to search them, and how to maximize the success of your searches. This site contains a great deal of interesting technical information as well.

THE MAJOR SEARCH ENGINES

http://www.altavista.com
  Best suited for searches on pop culture sites, such as celebrity photos, music, and the like

http://www.dogpile.com
  A "metacrawler" site that searches multiple search engines

http://www.excite.com
http://www.google.com
  As of this writing, the best search engine available

http://www.hotbot.com
http://www.lycos.com
http://www.northernlight.com
http://www.webcrawler.com
  A metacrawler that searches multiple search engines

http://www.yahoo.com
  Excellent for looking by topic heading, as in a telephone directory

LIBRARY RESEARCH

Information and links compiled by or about libraries are listed below.

Library of Congress

http://www.loc.gov
  catalog and links to other databases

Social Sciences

http://www.ksg.harvard.edu/library/
sosci_polisci.htm
  Political science and public policy from Harvard University libraries

OCLC WorldCat

http://firstsearch.oclc.org
  A database of books held by libraries throughout the United States and Canada.

This database will indicate the nearest library that holds this item (including yours). This is usually available through your library.

Also, do not forget to check your college or university Web page, or your local public library's page, which will likely have similar and often more current links to library sources.

JOURNALS, PERIODICALS, AND NEWSPAPERS

JSTOR

http://www.jstor.org
  Perhaps the best full-text source available, with access to journals in political science, economics, sociology, and several other disciplines. This site displays the text of journal articles in the same format as paper journals.

Project Muse

http://muse.jhu.edu
  Full-text access to journals published by the Johns Hopkins University Press. This tends to be oriented toward the humanities.

EBSCO Information Services

http://www.ebsco.com
  A subscription database service found primarily in academic libraries. This contains brief and full-text references.

OCLC Public Affairs Information Service

http://www.pais.org
  This is the online version of the printed PAIS index and its CD-ROM product—any version is remarkably useful for finding substantive policy information, including

books, reports, and government documents as well as journals.

GENERAL POLITICAL RESOURCES

Lists with links to governmental, media, and interest groups are included below.

Poly-Cy

http://pslab11.polsci.wvu.edu/PolyCy/
Internet resources for political science—an extensive set of links relating to politics and policy including links to educational institutions, interest groups, the media, think tanks, and the like

Project Vote Smart

http://www.vote-smart.org/

Yahoo Government and Politics

http://www.yahoo.com/Government/Politics/

National Political Index

http://www.politicalindex.com/
An extensive collection of links, many unusual or obscure, relating to politics and policy

PUBLIC POLICY RESOURCES

Lists with links to government, media, and interest groups with a specific reference to public policy are outlined below.

Public Policy Links at Poly-Cy

http://pslab11.polsci.wyu.edu/PolyCy/pspubpol.html
Also look for other subfields at the main Poly-Cy page for additional resources and ideas.

Policy.com

http://www.policy.com

Intellectualcapital.com

http://www.intellectualcapital.com
Both of these sites are general policy sites with links to interest groups, news articles, and other resources.

Public Agenda

http://www.publicagenda.org/
This nonpartisan organization seeks to improve policy makers' knowledge of public opinion on issues while improving citizens' knowledge of the issues.

GOVERNMENTAL RESOURCES

Links to federal, state, and local sources are listed below.

University of Michigan Documents Center

http://www.lib.umich.edu/libhome/Documents.center/
Links to local, state, national, foreign, and international resources, legislation, laws, regulations, proposed regulations: a stellar gateway to governmental information

Frequently Used Sites Related to U.S. Federal Government Information

http://www.library.vanderbilt.edu/central/staff/fdtf.html
From Vanderbilt University

U.S. Government Documents

http://www.cc.columbia.edu/cu/libraries/indiv/dsc/readyref.html
Links to invaluable information published by the federal government. This is a good

supplement to traditional sources of information available from your library.

GovBot Search Engine

http://www.nwbuildnet.com/nwbn/govbot.html
  A search engine for governmental Web pages and resources

Federal Government Search

http://regional.searchbeat.com/fed-usa.htm
  Another search engine of governmental and media resources

State and Local Government on the Net

http://www.piperinfo.com/state/index.cfm
  A state-by-state list of government information; primarily links to various resources

LEGAL RESEARCH

Sites that will help you find specific federal and state laws and regulations are as follows:

Lawguru.comlegalresearchpage

http://www.lawguru.com/search/lawsearch.html
  A commercial site, generally oriented toward lawyers but easily used by laypeople, that allows free access to federal and state laws and regulations. Navigation could be clearer, but it is an excellent resource.

Legal Information Institute at Cornell University Law School

http://www.law.cornell.edu
  This is an extremely useful site, providing legal research tools that were once affordable

only by big law firms. Search federal and state laws, constitutions, regulations, and other legal materials. This site is particularly good at summarizing and reporting the most recent U.S. Supreme Court decisions—if you read about it in the newspaper, you can read an authoritative summary here.

FedLaw from the General Services Administration

http://www.legal.gsa.gov
  A site developed for federal employees who need to do legal research, but available for public use. Some links are provided to important aspects of state law, but for serious research use the other resources.

Lexis-Nexis

http://www.lexis-nexis.com
  Consult your library to see if this resource is available to you. This and Westlaw are the best-known online legal research tools.

Westlaw

http://www.westlaw.com
  This subscription service may be available through your library, university, or county law library. Ask your librarian. The subscription fee is prohibitive for individual users, but you may know a lawyer or law student who could help you use this tool.

MEDIA AND INTEREST GROUPS

Links to news sites and information about interest groups are listed below.

Lexis-Nexis Academic Universe

http://web.lexis-nexis.com/universe/
  Article search and news database. This link may not work if you are connecting from

home, but may work if you are using a computer at your college or public library. Ask your librarian for details or for information as to where you can access this service.

Newslink

http://www.newslink.org
    Links to newspapers, magazines, radio/TV, and other resources by the American Journalism Review

PathFinder

http://www.pathfinder.com
    Time-Warner link to CNN, *Time, Fortune,* and other Time-Warner sites

CNN

http://www.cnn.com
    The Cable News Network site

MSNBC

http://www.msnbc.com
    The Microsoft and NBC Internet site

The New York Times

http://www.nytimes.com

Washington Post

http://www.washingtonpost.com

Los Angeles Times

http://www.latimes.com

Wall Street Journal

http://www.wsj.com
    Please note that this is a pay site.

Salon

http://www.salon.com
    An online magazine

Slate

http://www.slate.com
    An online magazine, owned by Microsoft but fairly independent of Bill Gates and Microsoft

http://dir.yahoo.com/News and Media/ Newspapers
    Yahoo's directory page for finding local newspapers in the United States

Associations on the Net

http://www.ipl.org/ref/AON/
    Extensive links to organizations, interest groups, and think tanks

PUBLIC OPINION

Public Agenda Online

http://www.publicagenda.org/
    Polls and discussion of current issues on the public agenda

University of North Carolina IRSS Poll Database

http://www.irss.unc.edu/data archive/ pollsearch.html
    Questionnaire search for opinion surveys

Gallup Poll

http://www.gallup.com
    Extensive online access to polls concerning elections and current events

General Social Survey

http://www.icpsr.umich.edu/GSS99/index.html
  Archive of survey results and online search
  for this national survey about attitudes,
  values, and behaviors

Roper Center for Public Opinion Research

http://www.ropercenter.uconn.edu/
  Index to polls

National Election Studies

http://www.umich.edu/~nes/nesguide/
nesguide.htm
  Guide to public opinion and electoral
  behavior from one of the most respected
  public opinion organizations in the nation

GOVERNMENTAL AND OTHER STATISTICS

  Sites with links to statistics compiled by
  governmental agencies and other
  organizations are included below.

Fedstats

http://www.fedstats.gov/index.html
  One-stop shopping for governmental
  statistics; links to sources of U.S.
  governmental statistics

Dismal Scientist

http://www.dismalscientist.com
  Current and historical economic
  information at the national and regional
  level

The Census Bureau

http://www.census.gov
  The Census Bureau Web site. Here you can
  find population and other demographic
  information from the national to the local
  level and learn how to buy CD-ROMs
  with extensive local-level data.

Economic Statistics Briefing Room

http://www.whitehouse.gov/fsbr/esbr.html
  Links to a wide range of current
  economic information

Economic Data

http://www.econdata.net/index.html
  Regional economic data links

International Statistical Agencies

http://www.census.gov/main/www/
stat_int.html
  U.S. Census Bureau links to statistical
  agencies of foreign governments

National Priorities Project

http://www.natprior.org/
  Analysis of federal budget spending
  priorities for states and cities